CW01020309

ONE AMONG MANY

45 Years Experience with Mackies of Belfast

Best Wishes

Stanley

Stanley Jebb

The photograph on the front cover was taken at a sales seminar held at the Mackie head office in the mid 1970's. All technical salesmen and overseas' agents were expected to attend the seminars which were held periodically, consequently there were over sixty present. (Photograph shows only a section). All these salesmen and agents played their part in securing contracts. The author was privileged to be a member of this great team – hence the title 'One Among Many'.

Back Cover Photograph - Scene from Mackies Iron Foundry

ISBN 978-0-9563717-0-6

All rights reserved. No part of this publication may be reproduced, stored in a retrieval system or transmitted in any form or by any means, electronic, mechanical, photocopying, scanning, recording or otherwise, without the prior written permission of the copyright owners and publisher of this book.

Published by Stanley Jebb
©2009 Stanley Jebb

Designed by April Sky Design
Colourpoint House
Jubilee Business Park
21 Jubilee Road
NEWTOWNARDS
County Down
Northern Ireland
BT23 4YH
Tel: 028 9182 7195
Fax: 028 9182 1900
E-mail: info@aprilsky.co.uk
Web site: www.aprilsky.co.uk

This book is dedicated to my wife, Helen, as a token of appreciation for her patience and understanding, also for her encouragement when I became frustrated and was tempted to give up writing.

INDEX

ACKNOWLEDGEMENTS

THE IDEA OF WRITING this book was first put in my head by Mrs. Tracy Hamilton, the older daughter of Mr. and Mrs. Paddy Mackie, several years ago at a Sunday luncheon party at her parents' home. Paddy and Julie also gave me much encouragement in the undertaking, as did Tara their younger daughter.

I did not keep a diary and despite having a good memory, I had to consult several of my business colleagues and friends for certain information. I'm particularly grateful to my contemporary, Desmond Morgan for reading the draft, giving useful advice, and writing the foreword. Desmond's advice was based on his wide experience in industry and commerce.

Initially my former secretary, Mrs. Marion Dornan undertook the typing but due to change in her circumstances she could not continue. Fortunately Mrs. Cathy King, also a former Mackie secretary, stepped into the breach. Words are inadequate to express my appreciation of the willingness and patience Cathy showed in typing and re-typing numerous drafts.

I was most fortunate on getting to know Mrs. Diana Kirkpatrick, a qualified librarian, who carefully read the numerous drafts and meticulously checked facts, grammar, punctuation etc. Diana is certainly a perfectionist!!

Time and space would not permit me to mention all my friends and colleagues who made contributions, but several merit acknowledgement.

A considerably younger Mackie staff member, Gilbert Watt, provided much useful information and relevant photographs. He also acted as courier between Mrs. Cathy King and myself. In addition having worked in many countries about which I have written, he has checked the accuracy of my accounts.

My closest friend and colleague is undoubtedly Joe McClelland. Joe could have written a much more interesting book than mine, but he preferred to let me write about his 'adventures'.

Several months ago I had the privilege of getting to know Professor Sir Bernard Crossland who has written numerous books. He very kindly volunteered to read the draft of mine. Having done so, he gave me very valuable advice based on his long experience in the academic and industrial world. Sir Bernard also offered sound advice on publishing and promoting the book.

My friend and colleague, Sammy McCoubrey was most helpful. I frequently consulted him about matters of mutual interest and he was always very positive in his advice. He also provided relevant photographs.

It was also most helpful to have the co-operation of Barry Pitman, graphic designer, with whom I had worked in Mackies on the preparation of illustrative brochures, advertising literature and exhibitions. Barry has advised on design, layout and appropriate photographs to be included.

Numerous other people made useful contributions and I solicit their forbearance that they have not been individually named.

FOREWORD

THIS BOOK IS AN interesting but true story of an individual and his career with one of the largest textile machinery manufacturers in the world – James Mackie and Sons Ltd., of Belfast.

For those not familiar with the textile industry, it is truly international and is an industry that has constantly evolved, adapting to new materials, new machinery and new methods of manufacture. It was in response to this continuous need for change that the success of Mackies can largely be attributed.

The Company was a privately owned family run business and was in existence for well over 100 years. At its peak it employed around 6,000 people (10,000 during the war years), and as such made a major contribution to the economy of Northern Ireland and that of West Belfast, where it was based.

It was a business that put the customer first, had a dedicated workforce and placed a great deal of emphasis on research and development, good design, and its ability to compete and service major projects worldwide.

The textile machinery that it produced included complete systems of machinery for processing all types of fibres, (with the exception of cotton) for a variety of end products.

A company of this magnitude required a strong, well organised sales and marketing team capable of operating worldwide. It is as a member of this team that my friend and colleague, Stanley Jebb, (the author) sets out his personal experiences with Mackies, which clearly reflect the international role of the Company and his numerous connections.

We are indebted to Stanley for putting this important part of Belfast's engineering history on record in such a humorous and interesting way.

Desmond Morgan
Technical Sales/Marketing Manager

MY FAMILY BACKGROUND

WHILE THE PURPOSE OF this book is to write about the very interesting experiences I had during forty-five years in the employment of James Mackie and Sons Ltd., Belfast, it seems fitting to launch my story with a brief résumé of my childhood and youth.

I was born on 10th July 1925 into a working class family, which lived off one of the main thoroughfares – Lisburn Road in south Belfast, Northern Ireland. I was the second child of an eventual family of four. My sister Winifred was two and a half years older, and I was followed by a brother, Reginald, then by a second sister, Edna. Either by calculation or coincidence, there was almost a similar period between each birth!!

My father was a builder and house repairer in a small way, and for a period moved with his work – consequently for the early years of my life we were an' itinerant' family. We eventually settled down in the Stranmillis district of south Belfast when Winifred reached the school age of six. Furthermore by then my brother had arrived, so with three children in the family my parents decided it was time to put our roots down. Winifred attended what was known then as a public elementary school, and on reaching six years of age, I joined her. This type of school catered for the total education of children and youth who had no prospect of going to college or university.

Unfortunately when I was eight years old my mother, a lovely lady, died of an illness which today is curable. For the following four years my siblings and I suffered at the hands of a variety of housekeepers, until my sister Winifred reached the school leaving age of fourteen and took on the role of mother. That was no easy task and was a huge sacrifice on Winifred's part. My formal education also terminated when I was fourteen years old, as my father secured a job for me in a store where he did his weekly shopping. This store was located in the renowned loyalist area of

Sandy Row, which before the advent of supermarkets was very popular with south Belfast shoppers. My job was to put fruit and vegetables on display each morning outside the shop on the sidewalk, then to assist two salesgirls during the day – come sunshine, rain, hail or snow! The duration of the working week was fifty hours. The shop opened at 8.30am Monday morning and closed 10.30pm Saturday night. As that was well before the days of prepacking all exposed food-stuffs had to be stored away or covered, consequently it was nearly midnight before one left for home. Wages were handed out on Saturday and at the end of the long week I was handed the princely sum of eight shillings, which under the metric system would be expressed as forty pence.

The Second World War commenced the year I started work, 1939, and subsequently radically enhanced my financial status. As the war intensified, Prime Minister Churchill demanded the production of more and more fighter planes and bombers. The company of Short and Harland Limited, which manufactured Stirling bombers and Sunderland flying boats at their Belfast factory, had to rapidly increase their production and to facilitate this, had to open several dispersal factories. One of the largest was at the show grounds of the Royal Ulster Agricultural Society, at Balmoral, on the outskirts of Belfast, quite near my home. On this complex there were several buildings, particularly the King's Hall, which admirably suited the manufacture of large aircraft. Through the offices of a good friend I secured a job at this factory in 1941 as an apprentice fitter. The pay was much better than in my previous job. When incentive bonus and overtime were added, my weekly wage rocketed to between £7 and £10 – depending on the jobs allocated to my journeyman. Despite the very attractive wages I was not entirely happy in my job. I wrongly concluded that the aircraft industry would not have a bright future after the war ended. At that time Mackies were also manufacturing aircraft, so I did not consider that company as it was my opinion that aircraft did not teach one proper fitting.

There was a small engineering concern in north Belfast, Stephen Cotton Company, which was still manufacturing textile machinery – their main product being hackling machines for the processing of flax. This was a large rather sophisticated machine and I considered the building thereof would teach me proper fitting. A neighbour of the family who was a foreman in Stephen Cottons arranged a job, but there was a hurdle to get over before I could accept his offer. Government regulations at the time stipulated that a person could be released from war work only if he or she had a very compelling reason. When I explained to my manager what I had in mind, he responded enthusiastically by saying he had severed his apprenticeship in Stephen Cottons and that I was making a wise decision. He immediately signed my release permit so I started my new job in

1943. I was not disappointed as I was given a good grounding in fitting under a very demanding journeyman, but the company left a lot to be desired. It was owned by two elderly brothers who had no heirs and its equipment was very antiquated and the company had no plans or capital for modernisation. However, I stuck it out until the war ended in 1945 and and thereafter the story of this book begins.

The recollections of Stanley Jebb – over 45 years: 1945 – 1990

James Mackie & Sons Ltd is referred to as 'Mackie' or 'Mackies' throughout this book.

THE EARLY DAYS

UK and Europe

AT THE END OF the Second World War, Mackies quickly reverted to the manufacture of their traditional equipment – textile machinery – mainly for the processing of flax and jute fibres. They were able to do so because obviously they had continued research and development, behind the scenes, during the war. In the case of jute machinery, Mackies had worked closely with Jute Industries Ltd, the leading manufacturers of jute goods in Dundee. The chairman of that Company was Sir William Walker, whose daughter, Margaret, later married John Mackie, the eldest son of Mr. Jack Mackie – known to the staff and workers of Mackies as "Big Jack".

In 1945 I was serving the final year of my apprenticeship in a small, antiquated company located in Tennent Street, North Belfast, named Stephen Cotton and Sons Ltd, then owned by two elderly Kennedy brothers, and their nephew, Henry. Their main product was Hackling Machines for the processing of flax, for which there was a sizeable market after the War. Although well educated, Henry had no business acumen whatsoever, and certainly hadn't a clue about industry, consequently, the company had little or no future, so I was looking for a job with better prospects.

The news soon got around that Mackies were looking for more fitters. When a colleague, who had slipped out the back gate of Cotton's Factory and gone down to Mackies, returned to say he had got a job and was starting in Mackies the following week – I decided to follow suit.

In those days a formal application was not essential. I simply emulated my friend by slipping out and cycling to Mackies. I reported to the Iron Foundry Gate House and asked to see the foreman of the Hackling Shop, who turned out to be a wee man called Billy Friers, wearing a brown coat and a "duncher". (A Belfast term for a cloth cap with a peak, worn by many workmen of that era). When he learned of my experience on

Hackling Machines he told me to report for work the following Monday.

As a matter of interest, I would mention that the colleague referred to earlier was Joe McClelland, who joined Mackies with me and like myself stayed until retirement, both retiring the same year. He became one of Mackies top installation engineers, while I ended up on the Sales Staff. Whenever possible I arranged for Joe to supervise projects for which I was responsible. We are still close friends sixty years on!!

I had been only a matter of weeks in Mackies, working in the Hackling Shop, when things began to move very rapidly. A personal friend, called Rowan Jennings, a draughtsman working on design and development, learned that I had joined the Company. It so happened that he was looking for a fitter to "mock-up" his ideas for trial in the Strand Spinning Co., managed by Mr Fraser Mackie and his son Michael. When the job was offered to me I readily accepted.

As I had no experience whatsoever in either flax or jute processing, Rowan Jennings arranged for me to join a team of eight outside erectors (installation engineers) who were being sent to Caldrum Works, Dundee, one of the mills in the Jute Industries Group which was being modernised with Mackie machinery. This was the start of an extensive modernisation programme of the Dundee Jute Industry, which was to extend for more than ten years from 1945.

Initially, it was intended that my stay in Dundee should be of two months duration at the most.

However, it was to last nine months, as when the installation at Caldrum Works was completed, my journeyman and I were transferred to Scott's of Hillbank Jute Mill. As I was still an apprentice, I was under the supervision of a "qualified" erector named Andy Baillie, who later went to India to join McNeill and Barry – a leading Jute Mill Company in Calcutta.

On my return to Belfast towards the end of 1946, I was presented with three alternatives and my choice would determine my future with the Company. Naturally, Rowan Jennings expected me to rejoin him in research and development. Furthermore, prior to leaving for Dundee, when not engaged by Rowan, I worked in what was known as the Mackhigh Drawing Shop where the foreman was an Albert Jemphrey – more commonly known as "the Cap" because he had a habit of adjusting his cap (duncher) frequently. He, of course, wanted me to rejoin his squad now that I was a fully-fledged fitter.

The third option was to remain on the Outside Erection, as the demand for "continental fitters" (erectors) was rapidly increasing, and orders from the Continent of Europe were starting to flow in. Consequently, the supervisors of the Outside Erection Department Bob Burton and Davey Rea, were anxious to enlist every suitable person. The choice was left to me and because of the opportunities to travel I opted for the Outside Erection.

During the following four years (1946 -1950) I was given various assignments in Belfast flax mills, and in flax and jute plants in Dundee. Indeed Dundee became like a second home, as there I made many friends with whom I'm still in touch nearly sixty years later.

Italy

In 1951 I was sent to Italy to supervise the installation of a small jute spinning plant in Jutificio de Ferne located near a village called Coazze (pronounced Co-at-zee) – about 30 Km N.E. of the city of Turin. This was a most enjoyable experience, apart from the evening of my arrival. In those days, travel was by ferry and train, as air travel was in its infancy. Having disembarked from the trans-continental express in the main Milan station, I set my two suitcases down, one on either side, close to each leg. Without moving I looked around for a snack bar to have some refreshments before boarding the connecting train to Turin. While my attention was diverted, one of my suitcases suddenly disappeared! I could hardly believe my eyes when I looked down!! I consulted the Thomas Cooks's Representative, who was nearby, and he told me that such an incident was not uncommon as the main railway stations in North Italy were frequented by "international thieves" who were experts at their job - so I could forget about retrieving my suitcase. Consequently I did not pursue the matter. Furthermore, the missing suitcase contained mainly tools that could be replaced.

The little jute mill nestled in an alpine valley with a sheer cliff of about 200 metres on one side and the ground on the other side rising more gently up to the village of Coazze, perched around 400 metres above the factory. Projecting from the main mill, on either side, were two long two-storied buildings with the main gate at the other end, thereby forming a rectangle, which in India would have been called a compound. On the ground floor of these buildings were stores etc., and on the first floor, living quarters for some of the workers. One was allocated to me. These quarters were very basic, being two whitewashed rooms with no modern facilities. A large enamel jug with a matching basin, on a marble washstand were the total washing facilities with fresh cold water being provided daily. The other engineer and I rigged up an improvised shower inside the factory by using electric conduit. The jet was provided by one person pressing his thumb over the end of the conduit and aiming the jet at the other person, which could be very painful if aimed at certain delicate parts of the body! Despite these primitive conditions, life was very relaxed and pleasant. Good food was provided, cooked by the wife of one of the workers, a delightful woman called Signora Theresa, who also did the clothes washing and cleaning.

Unfortunately, this dear lady had a premature death, resulting from cancer.

Only one person in the factory spoke English, a young man, named Giovanni, who had to cut short his university studies to support his divorced mother and younger brother – consequently it was necessary for me to pick up some of the language, which in that area, was not pure Italian but a dialect, Piedmontese, it being in the state of Piedmont. Apart from tuition from Giovanni, I also spent a lot of time with Giancarlo, the 12-year-old son of Signora Theresa, playing table games in the evenings and walking and climbing at weekends. Although Giancarlo did not speak English, and I only a smattering of Italian, we gradually devised our own language and were able to communicate remarkably well! On Sunday afternoons when my colleague and I did not go into the city of Turin, we climbed up to the village of Coazze to have coffee and other refreshments outside the little hotel. On most occasions we were joined by some staff and workers from the factory, also, by the Catholic priest and Waldensian pastor (a protestant sect existing long before the Reformation). Some had glasses of wine, while others enjoyed a selection of ice cream, (Gelato) and conversation flowed freely in a mixture of Italian and English.

It should be mentioned that Sven Mackie had been sent out ahead of me on a training course – he being at that time 18 years of age. His father, Mr Lavens told me not to be soft with him, and although generally speaking we got along well with each other, on a number of occasions it was necessary to clip his wings, and let him know that, although he inevitably would one day be my Director, I was then the boss!

Through Church connections, I met a Texan couple, missionaries who resided in Turin – Bob and Marianne McConnell. We became very good friends, and quite frequently I joined Bob on weekend trips, which he made to various places in the course of his Church work. Consequently, I was able to visit places of note in Rome, Pisa and Florence.

Visit with friend to leaning tower of Pisa.

At the end of six very pleasant months, I was instructed to travel directly to Belgium without returning to Belfast. As usual one had to make one's own travel arrangements. This taught me to use my initiative, which stood me in good stead in later life. My

Above left: *Bob McConnell and author outside St. Paul's Church, Rome.*

Above right: *Fellow installation engineer, Freddie Kavanagh at Trevi Fountain, which was the subject of the song 'Three coins in a fountain'.*

Below: *Freddie Kavanagh at St. Mark's Square, Venice.*

destination in Belgium was the city of Ghent rather than Brussels, as the majority of jute mills were located in Flanders. On my arrival at Ghent, Mackies agent in Belgium, a Mr. Mortier, met me. He naturally greeted me in English and I unconsciously responded to him in Italian which he surprisingly also spoke. This indicated that I was beginning to think in Italian and I now regret that I failed to pursue the study thereof to become a fluent speaker. This visit to Belgium was very brief, and there were no noteworthy experiences.

Germany

Most of my assignments in 1952 were in West Germany. The journey was made by ferry from Belfast to Liverpool, by train from Liverpool to Harwich (Essex) via London. A second ferry was taken from the Port of Harwich to the Hook of Holland, and then by the Rhine Express destined for Frankfurt. It was necessary to disembark at the town or city nearest to one's destination and get a local connection. I can well remember crossing the border from Holland, and being rather surprised by the ravages of War still in evidence. The re-building and restoration, which were well under way in some cities, had not made the same progress in the towns and villages.

My first job was in the town of Emsdetten, about 50 Km. from the Dutch border, in the state of Westfalen. The population of the town, at that time, was around 25,000, and the main industry was jute spinning and weaving, and all the mills were undergoing modernisation with Mackie machinery to a greater or lesser degree. Another Mackie erector and I were responsible for the installation of carding, preparing and spinning machinery in the Schulte Austum Spinneri and Webberi. During all my stays in Germany, only on one occasion did I encounter any unpleasantness from the German people and in that instance it was understandable. My colleague, Hugh Kirk, and I agreed, foolishly on my part, to meet up with four other erectors, working in the same area, to have Christmas lunch. The town of Burgsteinfurt (now Steinfurt) was chosen for the rendezvous. Christmas lunch for Mackie erectors would not have been complete without alcohol, although, I did not imbibe. At that time, the culture of having wine with meals had not become common among the British, so beer was the preferred drink. This flowed freely, so as the afternoon progressed tongues were loosened with rather unpleasant results as my colleagues threw caution to the wind by loudly expressing anti-German sentiments. This situation was not only embarrassing, but also frightening for me – I being stone cold sober! By some forceful persuasion in the late afternoon, I succeeded in getting the party out of the restaurant and on to transport for their respective destinations.

My own colleague, Hugh, a very quiet and reserved person when sober, became quite effusive when inebriated. I managed to manhandle him to the rear seat in the bus trailer - jam-packed with Germans in a somewhat similar state. Nothing I attempted could keep Hugh quiet, and he persisted in singing such songs as “Rule Britannia” and “There will always be an England”. When we reached Emsdetten and disembarked, we were followed by a group of irate Germans, to the little Hotel, The Westfalischer Hof, where we were staying. When Frau Schultze, the owner, realised the situation, she closed and barred the front doors. With the help of a German friend, we managed to restrain and calm “Hugo”, and get some solids into his tummy to absorb the alcohol. The locals outside were also persuaded to disperse. Needless to say, Hugh went to bed a very chastened person, and fortunately there were no further unpleasant repercussions. For me, being strictly teetotal at the time, it was not funny mixing with heavy drinkers. My colleague was “Hugo” to the German, while I was “Stanislaus”.

During the ensuing year (1952) I worked in various towns and cities in West Germany, including Bielefeld, a British Army Garrison town, and the city of Bremen. The latter was an interesting place. The city had been “carpet bombed” by the allies, and large areas still lay in ruins, even in 1952. To give some idea of the state of the city, I would explain that I stayed in a small hotel, Rehms Hotel, located in one of the main streets, Bahnhof Strasse. To reach the Jute Mill where I worked, a journey of around forty minutes by tramcar was involved, yet I could look out of my bedroom window on the second floor of the hotel and see the factory in the distance, the buildings in between still lying in ruins. However, the city authorities were

The scene of destruction in Bremen caused by allied bombing.

Left: *German friends, Gunter and Annie Nitsche and son, in Emsdetten – a town in Westfalen.*
Right: *Author with British military officer.*

then embarking on a unique scheme of rebuilding, which demonstrated German ingenuity. Instead of bulldozing and transporting the debris and dumping it outside the city, which would have been a mammoth task, there being hundreds of thousands of tons, the material was broken down on site, and the level of the city was raised. Suction pumps were placed at intervals along the banks of the River Weser, on which Bremen was built. These sucked the silt from the riverbed; the silt was then impelled along pipes to various areas of the city and poured on top of debris. When all the cracks and crevices were filled, the rubble was compacted and the site levelled for building. This system had a dual purpose – of dredging the River Weser, and providing in-fill for the building sites.

The German ingenuity was demonstrated in another respect. Wherever possible, buildings were rebuilt to their previous design and architecture. Thereby the former character of cities and towns was restored. Of course modern facilities were provided in the new buildings, particularly in hotels and offices.

During my final term in Bremen, I had a most interesting experience. My fellow erector, in this instance was Billy Walker, and we did not generally have our evening meal in the hotel, but dined in some nearby restaurant. One of our favourites was the "Helgolander Fisch-haus" – located a few hundred yards from the hotel on Bahnhof Strasse. The maitre d' in this restaurant was a dapper little man, always appropriately dressed in a dinner suit, white shirt, and bow tie, who spoke English fluently. Over the weeks, we became very friendly with this gentleman, and frequently had interesting conversations with him. Inevitably, from time to time, the subject of the War came up. One evening, he dropped what only could be described as a "bombshell"! He told us that he had been butler, and his wife, housekeeper, at Hitler's holiday resort, the ill-famed "Eagle's Nest" at Berchtesgaden, in Southern Germany. Naturally we treated this story with extreme scepticism, and our friend saw the look of disbelief on our faces. In response, the maitre d' offered to produce conclusive proof – provided my colleague and I promised to keep everything confidential, as he did not wish the facts to become common knowledge – this for personal and political reasons. To our surprise, the following evening when we were dining in a secluded corner of the restaurant, the maitre d' produced photographs, which were obviously authentic. One showed him serving coffee and other refreshments to "Der Fuhrer", who was sitting very relaxed at a table, with his head thrown back in laughter. The view over Austria in that photo was fantastic. It was evident from what was shown to my colleague and I, that the "wee man" was really who he claimed to be!

During my stay in Bremen I was also joined for a short spell by another erector, Jimmy Gilmore, who was a keep-fit enthusiast. At home he was a member of Clonard Swimming Club, and I was told that had he pursued that sport, he could have become an Olympic swimmer but for some reason of which I was not made aware, he decided to continue travelling for Mackies. By the way, to my knowledge, he was the only staff member in Mackies' long history, of hundreds if not thousands travelling, who was involved in a plane crash. My knowledge of the incident is at least second hand, so my record thereof may not be absolutely accurate in detail – but the story in general is true!

On one occasion Jimmy Gilmore was travelling by Air France, the flight for some reason transited at Hamburg, West Germany. On taking off, the plane crashed, and, on hitting the ground the fuselage broke in two. All the passengers, with the exception of Jimmy, who had been knocked unconscious, were evacuated. When Jimmy regained consciousness he attempted to rise from his seat in which he was still strapped, only to find that his legs would not function. It was later found that his back had been broken, but fortunately, his spinal cord had not been severed. Apparently, by using his arms, Jimmy levered himself out of the seat and fell into the aisle. He began to pull his body, slowly and painfully towards the light shining in through the fracture, at the same time, calling out. For what seemed to Jimmy to be an eternity, there was no response: Then he heard a voice shouting out in English "Anybody there"? – to which Jimmy loudly responded and was quickly removed from the wreckage. The rescuer turned out to be a British Airways staff member, who on arriving at the crash scene, decided on the spur of the moment to check if any passengers were missing. For Jimmy, recovery was painfully slow. Weeks suspended in a sling, in a German hospital, followed by a long spell of treatment and therapy in Belfast. Although Jimmy eventually became mobile again, his sports days were over, as were his days as an "Outside Erector". He ended up in what was known in the company as "The Erector's Graveyard" – officially the Scheduling Department!!

Most of my stay in West Germany, apart from the city of Bremen, was spent in relatively small towns and villages, in the state of Westfalen, where "Platt Deutsch" (Low German) is spoken. Most installations were in jute mills, except, in one instance, when flax processing machinery was installed in a linen mill in Bielefeld, a town about 50 Km. directly south of Bremen. That being a British Garrison town, the Mackie erectors were able to enjoy the facilities of The Red Shield Club, operated by the Salvation Army, also the NAAFI shop and restaurant. The German Frauleins manning these were always most willing to let us have BAF's (British Armed Forces Currency) in exchange for Deutsch Marks, as we gave them a good rate of exchange.

There was one short trip to Bavaria, South Germany, to the little town of Bamberg, located about 25 Km. north of Nurnberg, where the trial of the Nazi leaders was held. Apart from the fact that this was in the American zone, the scenery, the people, the culture, and even the language were all different from the north. Naturally, the language was German, but of an entirely different dialect and pronunciation. I was sorry that it was not practical to stay longer, as I found the attitude of the people more relaxed and friendlier than in the north.

Belgium

Early in 1953, I was instructed to go from Bremen directly to Belgium where the first job was at a company called Janssen Freres, which operated a small jute Mill in the village of Berlare, located about 25 Km. northwest of Brussels. The other erector, Jimmy Kennedy, and I stayed above a little café-cum-bar, called Zaal Kets. In this instance, the accommodation was also very basic. We had to share, not only a small room, but also a bed. There was no bathroom: a jug of water and a basin were provided in the bedroom for daily toilet. A zinc bath in an outhouse was used for the periodic wash down. The facilities were completed with a dry lavatory in the back yard. The entertainment amounted to an evening visit to some other café in the village, and a movie in the local cinema on Saturday evening. The sound track of all the movies shown was in English. The couple who owned the Zaal Kets had a young son and teenage daughter who lent Jimmy and I their cycles to get around and to go to the small lake resort, The Donk, about 3 Km. from the village.

One evening, shortly after arriving in Berlare, Jimmy and I wandered up the village street and called into another café/bar. Like me, Jimmy was not a drinker, so we both usually drank coca cola. Having just come over from Germany, and not having picked up any Flemish which was the local language, the village being in Flanders, I proceeded to order "Zwei coca cola". The madame behind the bar looked at me in disgust and said: "You speak English, don't you? On this occasion I will forgive you, you are very welcome in my bar, but never, never speak German while here"!! It turned out that Madame Bertha, as we came to call her, although Belgian had spent her childhood in Yorkshire, England. More interestingly, during the war she had been a "white shirt", that is a member of the underground movement against the Nazis. In contrast, those who collaborated with the Germans were called "black shirts". Such was Madame Bertha's support for the allies that she became a "staging post" for British soldiers who escaped from German prison camps.

In this she was fully supported by her husband, who had not been to England and did not speak English, so he was under less suspicion. He kept a cow in the nearby woods ostensibly to provide milk. When he went into the woods each day to milk the cow, Madame Bertha sent food and messages with him, which he hid in a hollow tree where the escaped British prisoners knew to look, having been informed by other "white shirts" along the way. On at least one occasion, there were German soldiers billeted in Madame Bertha's house, while three escaped British soldiers were hiding in a nearby shed. These British soldiers had given Madame Bertha their addresses in the U.K. so that she could eventually contact their families to ascertain if they made it home or otherwise. Naturally, Madame Bertha had hidden the piece of paper very carefully to prevent the Germans from finding it. She did this so successfully, that she herself could not find it. She was so perturbed about this that she asked my advice as to how she could find out if the Boys had made it home. I suggested that, if she could recall some details, no matter how vague, we together could compose a letter to the War Office. While we were contemplating this move, she made an interesting discovery! Several evenings after discussing the matter with Madame, my colleague and I went along to her café, as we were in the habit of doing a couple of times a week. On this occasion, Madame Bertha was noticeably happy, she gleefully produced a piece of a newspaper, brown with age, on which details relative to the British servicemen were written. It being that time of year, Madame had decided to do a bit of

Top and bottom: *Friends of the author who he met when working in Berlare, Belgium*

spring-cleaning. She being a Roman Catholic had a crucifix on the wall of her bedroom. This was made of light beaten metal, and was hollow with a clip-on back like a photo frame. She lifted the crucifix down to dust and as she ran the duster down the back her fingers touched something slightly projecting, and her memory clicked! When the back of the crucifix was removed - there was the folded piece of newspaper! I understand that

Madame Bertha wrote to the addresses given, and was pleased to learn that all three servicemen had reached home safely.

From Berlare I moved to Tamise (Temse), a town a further 15 Km. north of Brussels, to install one Jute Finisher Card in Orlay's Jute Mill. This factory was on the outskirts of the town, so en-route I called in to report my arrival before looking for living accommodation. As I entered the factory, a woman emerged from the gatehouse and asked me in an English accent if I were the Mackie monteur. It transpired that, like Madame Bertha, she too had grown up in England, in her case, in Lancashire. She told me that her husband was the Director's chauffeur, hence the reason why they resided at the factory. She also told me that, if I so desired I could have a room in her house as her daughter was in hospital with a long-term illness - an offer that I readily accepted. The family set-up in that house was unique. The mother, two sons and a daughter, although Belgian, conversed in English, read English magazines, and played English records. The father spoke only Flemish, but understood English and somehow did not feel left out. This Madame had also been a "white shirt" during the war, and the weapons - mainly rifles, she and her colleagues had used, were stacked on top of the wardrobe in my bedroom. Needless to say, my stay with that family was very pleasant.

After completing the job in Tamise I was instructed to go to the town of Eekloo, about 45 Km. further west in Belgium, near the Dutch border, to supervise the installation of additional machines in a Jute Processing plant which had been supplied a short time previously. Interestingly, the Company was called India Jute Mills. I now wonder if that was a coincidence or if it was an omen for the future! The son of the proprietor, who was a very bad asthmatic, could not spend long periods in the dusty atmosphere nevertheless he managed the Mill. A very good working relationship developed with this young man and I was treated extremely well by his Company.

While in Eekloo, I stayed in a small hotel in the town square called Hotel Cambrinus. This was owned by an elderly lady and managed by her daughter. Artisans of various nationalities were staying in the hotel at the time, and sometimes in the evening we sat together in the bar-cum-restaurant, chatting. On occasions the daughter and her husband joined us. It was amazing to listen to her switching from Flemish to English, or French or German, without hesitation. I found many Belgians to be outstanding linguists, which perhaps is not surprising – the country of Belgium being squeezed in between France, Germany, Holland and Luxembourg. After being in Germany, I also found the Belgians to have a very relaxed attitude to life. The Germans were inclined to talk about the last War and the next War with some apprehension, while the Belgians said we've survived two long wars – so another one will not get us down!

There followed a short spell back in West Germany. Firstly in the town of Emsdetten where I had worked previously, and then for a few weeks in the nearby village of Mesum. In both jobs I was given the responsibility of familiarising another erection engineer, a Gerry Farnin, with the pros and cons of installing and commissioning a Jute Finisher Card. That was in the month of December 1953. That year, the Mackie erectors in Germany decided to meet and celebrate Christmas in Bremen, but having learned from my previous experience, I had no intention of joining them! My colleague, Gerry Farnin was of the same mind, as he felt he had been drinking to excess and would be in trouble with his wife when he returned to Northern Ireland, for not having saved more cash. We, therefore, mutually decided to spend the festive season in Amsterdam, which was easily reached by train.

As it was our intention to have a quiet time, we took the minimum of clothing with us, which later proved to be a mistake. On Christmas Day, we took a boat trip on the Zuider Zee – a vast gulf penetrating far into Northern Netherlands. This gulf has been divided since then, by a dam into the Ijsselmeer and The Wadden Zee. The boat stopped at Marken Island, where we visited a typical Dutch House and watched the famous Edam cheese being made. It was interesting to see how the family members all slept in one room, using bunks against the walls of the room. The small house being also the Cheese Factory!

Scene in Amsterdam.

An Amsterdam tourist boat.

During the boat trip, Gerry and I got into conversation with two young ladies from the U.S. Air force, who had "hitchhiked" on an American Military plane from West Germany. It transpired that these girls had no plans for that evening, so the two Irish lads gallantly invited them to make a foursome for Christmas dinner – an invitation which was readily accepted. The uniform the girls were wearing during the day gave no indication as to their rank, but when they named the hotel in which they were staying, we realised they were certainly not in the lower echelons. With some trepidation, Gerry and I returned to our little side-street hotel to spit and polish – and to try and smarten up our rather shabby suits!! With even more apprehension, we arrived at the girl's hotel at the arranged time, and asked the reception to let our guests know we were waiting. As we waited in the foyer, our eyes nearly popped out when we saw two attractive gold-braided female Air-force Officers coming towards us! This presented a challenge, as neither Gerry nor I was familiar with Amsterdam and certainly did not know of a reputable restaurant. Quick action was needed, so I told Gerry to keep the girls chatting while I consulted one of the hotel receptionists. This gentleman was most helpful. He not only recommended a very good restaurant, but also phoned a friend who worked there and booked a table. An excellent meal was enjoyed, followed by a boat trip along the canals to see Amsterdam by night. Such an event would not faze me now, but looking back, I'm amazed that everything went so smoothly. I also wonder that Gerry and I had sufficient cash to "do ourselves proud" – as that was long before credit cards were in vogue.

That spell in West Germany proved to be the swansong of my working career in the Continent of Europe, as I was instructed to return to Belfast. According to the stamp in my passport, that was at the end of January 1954. On reporting to Outside Erection Department in Belfast, I was told that one of the Sales Directors, Mr. Peter Paisley, (known as "p" squared), desired to see me. There were two non-Mackie Sales Directors at that time, Peter Paisley and John T. Gailey.

When I went into Mr. Paisley's office, his greeting was: "Where have you been, Jebb, I've been waiting for months to see you"!! My reply was "that is understandable due to the fact that we both travel extensively, so obviously when one was in Belfast the other was away". Without further ado "p" squared said, "How would you like to join the Sales Staff"? In response I said that I would be very interested, provided it involved travelling, as I would not like to be stuck in an office in Belfast. When I was assured that the new job would involve travelling, I readily accepted the offer.

Those who are old enough to remember "p" squared will recall that he was very curt and gruff, so he simply said, "Come in tomorrow morning in your good suit and report to Austin O'Donnell". I thanked him and said I wouldn't let him down. His retort was –"Don't worry about me – I'm a b. old man, don't let yourself down"! That was probably around April 1954.

The following couple of months, during which I shared an office with Austin O'Donnell, an "outside erector" who had been promoted to the Sales Staff sometime previously – were most boring. He was a rather staid character and certainly not a good conversationalist. The only excitement during that period was when Austin "nicked" a cigarette ash into a wicker waste paper basket – causing it to go on fire! In an attempt to put out the fire, Austin stamped on the basket with the result that his foot got stuck in the burning basket. I was of no help, as I couldn't contain myself at the sight of the usually sober Austin dancing around with the burning basket stuck fast on the end of his upraised leg. Very cruel of me!! However, the incident caused no serious damage, not even to Austin's foot!!

THE REPUBLIC OF INDIA

The largest democracy in the world

Preface – Republic of India is born

On 27 January 1950, the Indian constitution takes effect, making the Republic of India the most populous democracy in the world. Mohandas Gandhi struggled through decades of passive resistance before Britain finally accepted Indian independence. Self-rule had been promised during World War II, but after the war triangular negotiations between Gandhi, the British and the Muslim League stalled over whether to partition India along religious lines. Eventually, Lord Mountbatten, the viceroy of India, forced through a compromise plan. On 15 August 1947, the former Mogul Empire was divided into the independent nations of India and Pakistan. Gandhi called the agreement the 'noblest act of the British nation', but religious strife between Hindus and Muslims soon marred his exhilaration. Hundreds of thousands died including Gandhi, who was assassinated by a Hindu fanatic in January 1948 during a prayer vigil to an area of Muslim-Hindu violence.

Of Gandhi's death, Indian Prime Minister, Jawaharlal Nehru said, 'The light has gone out of our lives, and there is darkness everywhere.' However, Nehru, a leader of the Indian struggle for independence and Gandhi's protégé, persisted in his efforts to stabilize India, and by 1949 the religious violence began to subside. In late 1949, an Indian constitution was adopted, and on 26 January 1950, the Republic of India was born.

With universal adult franchise, Nehru hoped to overcome India's 'caste-ridden' society and promote greater gender equality. Elections were to be held at least every five years, and India's government was modelled after the British parliamentary system. A president would hold the largely ceremonial post of head of state but would be given greater powers in times of emergency. The first president was Rajendra Prasad.

Nehru, who won his first of three subsequent elections in 1952, was faced with staggering challenges. A massively underdeveloped economy and overpopulation contributed to widespread poverty. Nehru also had to force the integration of the former princely states into the Indian union and suppress movements for greater autonomy in states like Punjab. In his years of struggle against Britain, he always advocated non-violence but as prime minister sometimes had to stray from his policy. He sent troops into the Portuguese enclaves of Goa and Daman and fought with China over Kashmir and Nepal. He died in 1964 and was succeeded by Lal Bahadur Shastri. Later, Nehru's only child, Indira Gandhi, served four terms as a controversial prime minister of India.

India's National Flag

There are a variety of opinions about the symbolism of the National Flag of India. Right from the outset it caused controversy between Mahatma Gandhi and Jawaharlal Nehru.

On 15 August 1947 the dominions of India and Pakistan were established. India adopted the familiar horizontal tricolour of orange, white and green with a blue Ashoka Chakra at the centre. The tricolour had been used, unofficially, since the early 1920's as the flag of the Indian National Congress, with the colours representing Hinduism (orange), Islam (green), and a hoped-for unity and peace (white). More unofficially, the flag was patterned on the other example of struggle against British imperialism, Ireland. Most often, a blue spinning wheel was shown in the centre derived from Gandhi's call for economic self-sufficiency through hand-spinning.

The spoked Ashoka Chakra ("the wheel of the law" of the 3rd century BC Mauryan Emperor Ashoka) replaced the Gandhian spinning wheel to add historical "depth" and separate the national flag from the INC party flag (and Indian political party flags are another tale).

—∞—

In June 1954, Pat Gailey, the son of the Sales Director mentioned earlier, came home on leave from Calcutta, India. Pat had been a young lieutenant in the Royal Navy, but decided not to make the Navy his career. On leaving the Navy he had joined the Company, I think in the early 1950's. Shortly after joining, he had been sent to India to replace Bob McCauley, who had been Mackie's representative in Calcutta since India opened up after the Second World War. Bob wished to return to the U.K. on a permanent basis.

At that time Mackies rented office accommodation from their Indian agents, Robert McClean and Co. Ltd. That company in turn, rented a suite of offices from Duncan Brothers – a large British company in Calcutta. In 1953, the India Jute Industry, comprising 112 Jute Mills, began to modernise on a large scale, so a young man in his early 20's named Bryan Hall, was sent out to join Pat Gailey.

Shortly after returning to Belfast, Pat Gailey came into my office and asked if I was Stanley Jebb. When I replied in the affirmative, Pat said he had come to forewarn me of a forthcoming interview with Mr. Lavens Mackie. He went on to explain that he and Bryan Hall had limited practical experience on Jute Machinery and that I had been proposed as a suitable candidate to fill the obvious vacancy in the Mackie team in India.

As expected, in a couple of days, Mr. Lavens called for me. He put the proposition to me and told me to think it over. In response I told Mr. Lavens that it was unnecessary to delay the decision, as I was keen to take on the challenge. The only request being that I would be permitted to have my summer holidays – then, two weeks in July, Mr. Lavens acquiesced and told me to make the necessary arrangements to travel to Calcutta as soon as possible thereafter. Once again, one was left to use one's own initiative.

With the help of the Travel Department, at that time - one girl, and the doctor in the First Aid, I had the requisite inoculations and booking to fly out of London by BOAC (now BA) on Friday 13th August 1954. Some folk said that I hadn't chosen a very auspicious day or date – but it proved to be very fortunate for me!

The flight, which was by a Super Constellation Aircraft, took off at around 10am on Friday and headed for Frankfurt, the first port of call. The plane was a prop. job, having what we in India would call "four punka's" (propellers). Although then it was considered to be modern, the aircraft was not equipped to fly above storms, much to my discomfort!! We were no sooner over the English Channel, than she began to bump and bounce and my tummy became decidedly queasy!! When I could stick it no longer, I headed for the toilet and got rid of any food that there was in my tummy. On returning to my seat, I found the stewardess waiting to mildly "tell me off". She made it clear that I should remain in my seat and use the "sick bag" in the pocket of the seat in front, and said she had a plentiful supply. The seat beside me was occupied by a very cultured well-dressed lady who told me not to be embarrassed. Indeed, to lessen my embarrassment, she volunteered to move to another seat temporarily. She went down the aisle, but returned a few minutes later to say that numerous other passengers were feeling unwell – so there was no point in moving!

As the flight approached Frankfurt, the stewardess returned to say that lunch would be served in the Airport restaurant and that I should endeavour to eat something. When I expressed doubts about being able to do so, she asked my lady companion to ensure that I took the advice given. With her lady-like manner and gentle persuasion, my friend succeeded in getting me to take the soup and dessert. She was like a mother to this inexperienced air traveller!!

As soon as we were airborne again, the stewardess brought a cup of tea and a small tablet – the latter did the trick, as very shortly I was as right as rain. At that time, being a stewardess was a much sought-after job, so applicants had to be well educated and capable - unlike today when "cabin attendants" as they are now called, are in many instances just glorified waitresses.

The next port of call was Beirut, where the flight arrived on Friday evening. There, the passengers and crew members were bussed to The Bristol Hotel, where we spent the night. Around twenty passengers were allocated to each stewardess, whose responsibility was to ensure that they were comfortably accommodated and had dinner. The next morning after breakfast, at the reasonable hour of 10am, the captain announced that we should be on our way to the Airport for the next stage of our journey. Like the stewardesses – the captain's role was somewhat different from today. At some stage during the flight he would walk through the passenger cabin in full uniform, including his gold braided cap – certainly not in shirtsleeves – with gloves in his hand. On his way through, the captain would stop and have a word with each passenger, particularly those in the first class cabin. Travelling by air then was so much more pleasant than today, there being no over-crowded airports, nor large jam-packed aircraft.

The remainder of the flight, after Beirut, is quite vague in my memory, apart from the fact that we stopped at Karachi, which was then the capital of Pakistan, being well before Islamabad was built. At Karachi, accommodation was provided at "Speedbird House" – operated by the airline. It was there that experienced travellers changed into their tropical gear, but I had yet to learn the "tricks of the trade"!!

Eventually, the flight reached Calcutta, and touched down at Dum Dum Airport. That name came from the nearby Munitions Factory, where "dum dum" bullets were produced. The nose of that type of bullet flattened on impact, which made it more deadly than the ordinary bullet. Some years ago the Calcutta Airport was renamed "Netaji Subhas Chunda Bose Airport" – after the Bengali freedom fighter. It was around 6.00am on Monday 16th August when we landed. I was welcomed to Calcutta by Bryan Hall, then a good-looking man in his early twenties. Those who knew Bryan will recall that he always liked to create an impression – so he had two "chauffeur" driven cars waiting – one for my luggage, and the other for he and I to travel in. My luggage would easily have fitted into the boot of one car – nevertheless, I felt important!! As it was the monsoon season when I arrived, even at 6.00 am, it was very humid, although not particularly hot. I can't recall having taken in much of the surrounding scenes along the over-crowded road into the city, probably due to jet lag. However, there was plenty of time for observation during the following years as I was to traverse that road frequently, at all times of the day and night, to meet Mackie Erection Engineers and other visitors.

For a few days, I stayed with Bryan Hall, who was then living in the Gailey's apartment in Rajah Santosh Road, Alipore – one of the select residential areas of Calcutta. That was basically a one-bedroom flat with an attached box room – so it was not practical for both to continue to reside there. Consequently, a small flat comprising a bed/sitting room with bathroom was rented in one of Jenny Christensen's establishments. This Scandinavian lady had a thriving business going, purchasing large houses from "ex-pats" leaving India, and turning them into apartments. Each house, or group of houses, had a central kitchen from which the food was collected by one's bearer (Indian servant). The first bearer I employed was the old type who wore a white turban, and had been given the name – David. He stayed with me for around eight years, but as he grew older, he was joined by his nephew Swami, who eventually took over and became more of a butler than a bearer to me and remained with me until I left India in 1972. My current residence "Swami Kuthi" is named after him. "Kuthi" being Hindi for "house".

Swami, my bearer. The word 'bearer' projects the wrong image. He was more a butler who managed my household for 14 years.

The next step was to get fitted out with "tropical" gear. The Mackie boys all went to Sales the Tailors, in Free School Street, near Isaiah's Bar, generally known as "The Prophet's Bar" and largely frequented by merchant seamen - for obvious reasons!! Before the advent of lightweight terylene suit fabric, the popular form of office dress for businessmen, particularly European sahibs was white trousers and a jacket with a white background, but with fine coloured stripes. I chose blue. Always a shirt and tie, no matter how high the temperature.

The only concession for going to a Factory or Jute Mill, was an open-necked short-sleeved shirt!!

At the beginning, my main responsibility in India was to supervise the Mackie Erectors installing machinery in the India Jute Mills – mainly in and around Calcutta, and later on in the new mills being set up in East Pakistan (eventually to become Bangladesh). As mentioned already, in 1954/55 there were 112 Jute Mills in Calcutta, located along the banks of the River Hooghly (Hugli) – this being a tributary of the Holy Ganges (Ganga) – stretching from 50 Km. upstream to 40Km. seaward: Calcutta itself being over 90Km. from the mouth of the River.

The majority of those Jute Mills were then still owned by British Companies such as Duncan Brothers, Thomas Duff, James Finlay, and Andrew Yule and Co. Ltd. However, the "Marwari's" were moving in and the Mill Managements were gradually being Indianised. The Marwaris were a merchant class, originally from the town of Marwar in the State of Rajasthan, located about 100Km. south of Jodhpur. They were taking over, not only from the British, but also from the Indian Jews and Armenians. The leading Marwari families were the Bajorias, Birlas, Goenkas and Singiuhias. A good relationship was being established with these people by the Mackie staff. There were several exceptions to the Marwaris – the most notable being the Jains who took over the New Central Jute Mills from Andrew Yule. These people have a religion distinct from Hinduism. Appropriately, Jainism, whose ideal is the realisation of the highest perfection of the nature of man, which it holds, was in its original purity free from all pain and the bondage of life and death. The term "Jain" is derived from the Sanskrit word "Jina" which means "Victor" or "Conqueror", and implies conquest over the bondage, which is imposed by the phenomenal world. The actual historical founder of Jainism was Vardhamana, called Mahavira (Great Hero), who was born in the Republic of Vaishali, now the State of Bihar, north of the city of Patna – the state capital.

There was also the very reputable family – the Mafatlals from Bombay (now Mombhai), who purchased Gagalbhai Jute Mills. They were very good friends of Mr. Lavens and were at one time interested in having a shareholding in The Lagan Company. Indeed they offered Rs700/- for a Rs100/- share, but Jim Rogers, for a reason known only to himself, wanted the unreasonable price of Rs1000/- per share!!

To get back to the Indian Jute Industry. On my arrival, Mackie machinery was being installed in six Jute Mills, requiring ten erectors, as for larger installations, two erectors were provided. To assist these erectors, we employed local fitters (mistrys), and the Mill Companies provided others. Generally, the modernisation was confined to Carding, Preparing and Spinning Departments.

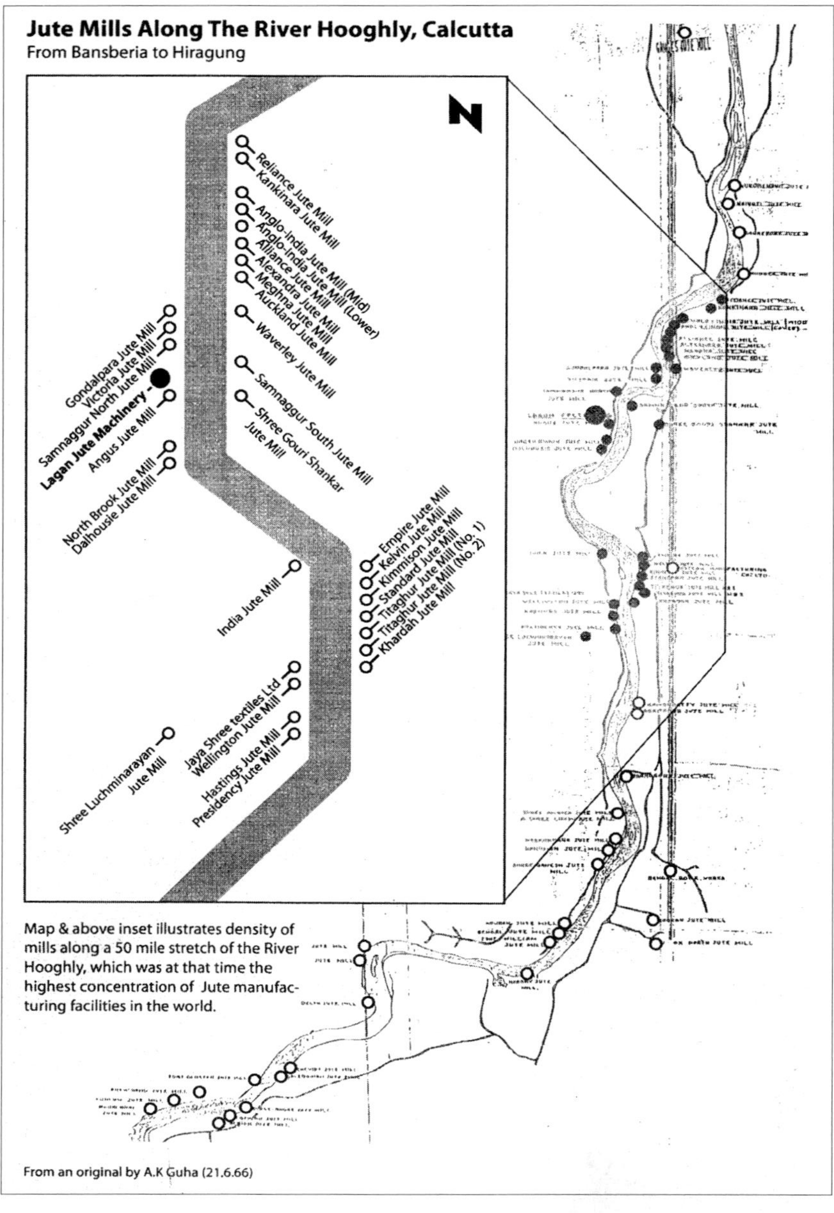

Map & above inset illustrates density of mills along a 50 mile stretch of the River Hooghly, which was at that time the highest concentration of Jute manufacturing facilities in the world.

From an original by A.K Guha (21.6.66)

The Company policy was to visit each new installation at least twice a month, so my daily routine was somewhat as follows – I was wakened by my bearer at 5.30am with a cup of tea and a banana – an old Indian custom for European sahibs. A quick shower was taken, often cold, to waken one up! It was advisable to be on the road by 6.00am to avoid the "real" congestion on the suburban roads. I had been allocated a Standard Vanguard station wagon and a Muslim driver, who had been given the name of Micky, a quiet reliable and capable driver. Even at that early hour he had to negotiate heavily laden trucks, bullock carts, hundreds of cycles, and cycle and hand-pulled rickshaws. The most unpleasant obstacles were the "honey carts" with women queuing up with dry toilet buckets on their heads – to have them emptied. It was beneficial to have a handkerchief soaked in eau-de-cologne at the ready!

A journey of 40 Km. (25 miles) could take anywhere between 2 to 2.5 hours. It was desirable to reach the first Jute Mill on one's itinerary before 8.00am as the manager, having started his day at 6.00am normally returned to his residence at 9.00am for breakfast. In all Jute Mill compounds there were living quarters for the staff, and in many also recreational facilities such as a social club, a swimming pool, and tennis courts. Indeed, Angus Jute Mill of Thos. Duff, and Budge Budge Mill of Andrew Yules had golf courses attached. Annual "tamashas" (competitions) were held between the staff of different companies, consequently, the staff members came into Calcutta only on special occasions, and of course, the ladies for shopping. Arriving early enabled me to meet the manager, visit the Mill with him to check on the progress of new machinery installation, and to have a chat with the Mackie erectors. The Mill manager, probably a Scotsman at that time, would often ask me to join him and his wife for breakfast. This provided a good opportunity to establish and later cement a good relationship with him. If breakfast was provided at the first Mill visited, it was then practical to visit one or two other Mills in the same area before returning to Calcutta for lunch. If the visit to the first Jute Mill was prolonged, one would return to Calcutta and have breakfast at the Calcutta Swimming Club and then put in a couple of hours at the office before lunch. In any event, it was always good to get home at lunchtime, and have a nice hot shower and wash the dirt from one's hair and body. Once upon a time I had hair!!

Author's chauffeur, Tamang.

The early part of the afternoon was spent in the office, dealing with incoming mail and preparing reports, and then it was off to the head offices of the Jute Mills visited that morning, to report to the "Burra Sahibs" of those companies. The working day was rounded off by a further spell in the office, which took the time until around 7pm. In the first year or so, it was not my responsibility to attend cocktail parties or business dinners, so after the evening meal I could retire to bed.

Air-conditioned bedrooms were then a luxury not available to the ordinary "five-eights"! Nevertheless, I slept soundly under a punka (fan).

In the early years, the office secretaries were female, mainly Eurasian, as young ladies from Indian families were still very restricted, and there were not many young Indian males with secretarial skills. By the way, the term Anglo-Indian has come to be used for those of mixed English and Indian descent, but strictly speaking that term applies to a person born of English (British) parents in India. However, of the two secretaries in the Mackie office, initially one was a "pure" English lady married to an Armenian, named Lynn Glover. She was Pat Gailey's secretary and was quite a lady! She could do three things at one time – smoke, swear and type! The other was a shy little girl named Cynthia Alcantra, probably of Portuguese-Indian descent, who was allocated to work for me – so a third secretary had to be employed in preparation for Pat Gailey's return. This was quite an amusing experience! To access Bryan Hall's office, it was necessary to pass through my office. It was mutually agreed that as the candidate passed me I would assess the lady's physical attributes, then Bryan would test her secretarial abilities. We could see each other through a glass dividing door, the understanding being that the one who got the "thumbs up" from both of us would be employed. When a tall girl with a very good figure came in, I gave her the thumbs up without hesitation, and as she proved to be very proficient, Bryan did likewise – so Vera Chapman was employed. She proved to be an excellent choice and remained with the company until her partner, an Englishman, was recalled to the UK.

The author with Miss Vera Chapman, office secretary (Bryan Hall's)

The Lagan Story

In early 1955, many more Indian Jute Mills decided to modernise, so orders began to flow into Mackies in ever increasing quantities. One example being 110 Sliver Spinning Frames for the Thomas Duff Mills – consequently there was increased pressure from the Indian Government on Mackies to implement its policy of partial indigenous manufacture. This had been anticipated, so Pat Gailey discussed the matter with the Mackie board when home on leave in the latter part of 1954. As a result, a decision had been taken

Dinner party for office staff – L to R. Colin Metcalff, Cynthia Alcantra (worked for Colin and author), Miss Vera Chapman, Vera's partner, Lynn Glover (Pat Gailey's secretary) Mr. Glover.

to commence with Silver Spinning Frames. The plan was to continue to import the High Precision components and to have all the cast iron parts manufactured locally. Prior to that, only the very basic heavy parts were obtained from local foundries to reduce freight costs.

On the return of Pat Gailey in the latter part of 1954, implementation of the proposed plan commenced and things moved very rapidly. There was an influx of visitors from Belfast, spear-headed by Mr. Lavens and Jim Rodgers, the latter's responsibility being to draft the articles of association for the new company. The first necessity was to decide on a name, and if possible, to incorporate something that would link Belfast with India. On the way to the office one day, Pat Gailey noticed that a Hindi movie entitled "Lagan" was being shown in a leading Calcutta cinema. This was quite a coincidence, as Pat, having Connswater Jute Mill, Belfast in mind, had been thinking – why not name the new company after a Northern Ireland river? Enquiries were made to ascertain the meaning of the word "Lagan". It was found that "Lagan" corresponds to a word of similar sound in Bengali, which has a wide variety of meanings, but generally signifies a close attachment to or association with things or people. The most common use of the word is relative to an Indian Wedding, which as is well-known can last several days. Guests will often ask when does the "Lagan" take place. That is the actual ceremony of religiously uniting the couple in matrimony. This seemed to be a most appropriate word to use, Lagan being the name of the river on which Belfast is built and in a sense the new company would link Belfast to Calcutta. It was, therefore, decided to call the company The Lagan Jute Machinery Co (Private) Ltd. In the remainder of the article, the company will be referred to as "Lagan". Suitable premises were rented from Thomas Duff and Company at their Angus Jute Mill premises, located about 40 Km. from Calcutta on the Grand Trunk Road – a road with a great history – as will be seen from the following write-up.

The Grand Trunk Road (abbreviated to GT Road in common usage) is the Indian Subcontinent's first, largest and oldest major road, linking Calcutta on the Bay of Bengal coast with Kabul in Afghanistan via the Khyber Pass. The Grand Trunk Road spans a distance of over 2,500 Km. and connects up the important cities of Benaras, (now Varanasi), Kanpur, Delhi, Amritsar and Lahore.

The Grand Trunk Road was built in the 16th century by Sher Shah Suri, the then Emperor of India, with the intention of linking together the remote provinces of his vast empire for administrative and military reasons. Originally known as the Sadak-e-Azam (The road of the Emperor), the Grand Trunk Road was the traditional route for invasions of the subcontinent by Afghan and Persian invaders, as well as one of the most important trade routes in the region. Later renamed and improved by the British rulers of colonial India, the Grand Trunk Road was sometimes referred to as the "Long Walk".

Offices and part of the Lagan factory

Today the Grand Trunk Road continues to be one of the major arteries of India and Pakistan, and the Indian section is part of the ambitious Golden Quadrilateral Project. For over 400 years from before Rudyard Kipling's time to the present day, the Grand Trunk Road has remained "a river of life such as exists nowhere else in the world".

It was decided to initially have a Machine

Shop and an Assembly Bay at the Lagan factory. To assist in planning these two departments, Sam Annesley, the engineering and production director, and Syd Thompson, the Foundry director, visited Calcutta. All requisite machine tools, jigs, fixtures etc. were shipped from Belfast, and transporting the large machine parts, such as the planing machine bed, along the Grand Trunk Road, through the numerous towns and villages, was quite an undertaking, but very experienced and competent clearing and handling agents were appointed, consequently all the machinery and other equipment arrived at the Lagan Factory without mishap.

As I had contact with several local engineering companies in the course of ordering basic cast iron parts, which were already being made in India, I was asked if I could recommend someone who would be a suitable manager for Lagan. In response I suggested a Mr. Maurice O'Shea, then the manager of Britannia Engineering Co. Ltd., who I found very helpful and efficient in executing the orders placed with his company. He was interviewed, if I recall correctly, by Pat Gailey and Sam Annesley. They were obviously impressed by him, so he was employed and installed as manager. To assist Maurice O'Shea, a well qualified and experienced Mackie draughtsman – Billy Luney was selected to join the Lagan management. He arrived in Calcutta in February 1955 and immediately set about the preparation of the floor and foundations to accommodate the machine tools as they arrived. As the production for the spinning frames got under way, Billy Luney was joined by John Scott who had been an outside erection engineer for ten years.

Unfortunately, despite being an experienced engineer, it soon became evident that Maurice O'Shea had his own agenda: as a result of which his relationship with the two Belfast men became very strained. In an attempt to impose his own will, he adopted some rather dubious methods and in 1956, after returning from a familiarisation visit to Belfast, he took a decision without consulting the Lagan directors, so Pat Gailey, then had no alternative to sacking him. As was logical, Billy Luney, who had proved himself very capable, was promoted to the position of manager, ably assisted by John Scott.

The plan was that Lagan would manufacture ten spinning frames per month, but right from the outset that production figure was exceeded – indeed around the mid 60's over forty machines per month were turned out. Eventually, to meet the demand for machinery from the Jute industry the following steps were taken in a phased manner.

a) The management personnel were increased until there were seven "ex-pats" at the factory.
b) The indigenous manufacture of several types of Jute drawing frames was introduced.

The team from Mackies responsible for setting up the Lagan Company.
Top: *L to R. Jim Rodgers, Sam Annesley, Babs Gailey and author.*
Bottom: *L to R. Bryan Hall, Pat Gailey, Sid Thompson and Mr. Lavens Mackie.*

c) A second building was rented from Thomas Duff, thereby almost doubling the floor-space available.
d) A larger iron foundry was set up on a separate site, at a place Adisaptagram, 16 Km. further up the Grand Trunk Road. There having been previously a small foundry set up by Pat Gailey in the Anglo India Jute Mills Compound on the other side of the river Hooghly.

Lagan proved to be a very profitable company as following figures will show. In India, not only then but still, they use unique terms for stating quantities of money, and other commodities. A lakh is one hundred thousand, but is written 1,00,000, while a crore is written 10,00,000. The registered capital of Lagan was 50 lakhs. The called up capital was initially 12 lakhs with later call up of a further 12 lakhs. In one particular year the profit exceeded one crore. When Lagan was set up the rate of exchange was Rupees (RS) 13/- to £1.00 Sterling. Several years later the Rupee depreciated so the rate became RS 18/- to £1.00. It remained at this level for a considerable number of years. It now hovers around RS 60/- to £1.00. It was an unwritten law of the Indian Government that the workers should share in the profits in the form of a "puja bonus" annually in the month of October when the main Hindu Pujas (religious festivals) are celebrated. On the year in question Lagan paid the equivalent of 26 weeks wages on top of the regular salary.

While all these developments were taking place at the factory, there were parallel changes at the Mackie/Lagan office in Calcutta. The space available at Robert McLean was totally inadequate, so a larger office was rented. As the trend was for companies relocating to move away from the congested area of Clive Street, Pat Gailey chose accommodation on another main road in Calcutta, Chittaranjan Avenue. The new office was large enough to facilitate the requisite office staff for a small company including the directors and senior staff. On the setting up of The Lagan Company, Pat Gailey had been appointed chairman and joint managing director, Bryan Hall the other managing director and I, the junior director. A very capable Indian accountant was employed as company secretary. He was a Bengali gentleman named Bikash Chunda Ray, who became known to his colleagues as "B.C.". All three Belfast men continued in a dual capacity as technical consultants for the parent company.

The business for Mackies increased to the extent that there were over thirty Mackie erection engineers in Calcutta, assisted by a squad of Indian mistrys (fitters) working in at least fifteen Jute Mills, all requiring frequent visits. It was consequently essential for me to have some assistance, so for this purpose, Colin Pringle Metcalfe was sent out from Belfast. That was in 1956, probably towards the middle of the year. For several months, Colin and I shared a one-bedroom apartment, also transport, an imported jeep, and got on very well together, except on the odd occasion when Colin had too much booze!! It didn't take Colin long to get into the swing of things. Being a rugby player he quickly joined the Calcutta Football Club, which, despite its name was actually a rugby club. In fact, it was that club which donated The Calcutta Cup for which England and Scotland compete annually. In those days there was a rugby team, made up mainly of British in most major Indian cities, and such outposts as the Tea Gardens, who played in the All India Rugby Union League. As soon as there was a room available, Colin moved to reside at The Light Horse Club, more commonly known as the "Tight" Horse Club for obvious reasons!!

When the rugger boys went out on the town, they really "went to town"!! On occasions when the normal "watering places" closed around midnight, they would retire to the Golden Slipper Night Club, more commonly known as the "Brass Boot", which stayed open until 4am. Afterwards they would go across the road to "Nizams" an open food stall specialising in kebabs. Sometimes they would also purchase a couple of dozen raw eggs for an "egg fight", resulting in their clothes needing dry-cleaned!! In mentioning these things, I've no desire to cast aspersions on Colin – far from it!! My intention is to show the exuberant side of his character. Colin and I were not only business colleagues, but also very good friends. Indeed this friendship lasted for over forty years until his death. I will revert to Colin later in this article when writing about East Pakistan – now Bangladesh.

During the latter part of the 1950's, in addition to regularly visiting the Mackie erectors in the Mills in which they were working, I chaired monthly meetings with them in the Calcutta office. At that time they worked five and a half days a week, so the meeting was held on a Saturday morning. Those meetings were invaluable as they enabled me to prepare a comprehensive report for Belfast, on all installations, and highlight faults found on the machinery. On reaching Belfast, the report was handled by "Big Jack", who investigated all problems mentioned and replied promptly outlining the corrective steps that were being taken in Belfast or that should be taken at our end in India.

When Bryan Hall returned from home leave in 1956, he rented an apartment in another of Jenny Christensen's establishments. This was a spacious flat above The Swiss Club, which had a large veranda overlooking the tennis courts, and was very suitable for entertaining. Bryan and I decided to use the facilities to host a party for managers of the Jute Mills under modernisation – then still all Scotsmen. We divided the veranda, which had two doors leading from the lounge - the half managed by Bryan was stocked with alcoholic and soft drinks and was called "Snake-Hips Hall's D.T.Bar" while the other half, for which I was responsible provided "eats", coffee and tea, and was named "Spendy Jebb's T.T.Bar". The nickname – Spendy was given to me by a fellow apprentice in Stephen Cotton's, who lived on the Grosvenor Road near the Spendlove C. Jebb Company. We invited the secretary, Vera Chapman, mentioned earlier, to act as hostess, as she had an attractive personality and was a good singer. During the course of the evening, Vera sang several songs and concluded with "When Irish Eyes are Smiling". A typical dour Scot, Bob Gracey, the manager of Union North Jute Mill, made the following comment – "A bra Irish singer, but the sun must have been purdy hot in Dublin"!! Vera reacted by laughing heartily as she had no complex about her colour or mixed blood. She proved to be a great hostess!! That manager was quite a character! As mentioned earlier, air-conditioning then was quite rare, even in bedrooms. In an effort to provide some cool air at night, thick coconut matting was suspended like a blind in the open bedroom window and soaked with a hose. This cooled the air being blown in. However, Bob Gracey had his own idea. During the hot season he exchanged his pyjamas for a "nightie" – which he put in the fridge an hour or so before going to bed. I don't know how his wife reacted to that!!

There were two events in 1956, which stand out in my memory – not that they were in any way connected. The more important of the two was the visit of the Queen and Duke of Edinburgh to the sub-continent, a tour that included Calcutta. The route in from the airport to the Raj Bhavan, formerly the Viceroys Palace, now the State Governor's residence, passed the six storey building in which our office was located. In fact, it turned right, just below the office, so there was an excellent view from the office roof. The British residents were rather concerned, as some months previously, the bi-partite leaders of Russia, Bulganin and Khrushchev (I called them Snowball and Baldy) had travelled the same route and the crowd in their excitement mobbed the open limousine in which they were travelling, so the two leaders had to be transferred to a police van. Our worries proved to be unfounded as the royal visitors were treated with great decorum. It was amazing how the streets of Calcutta were cleaned up, buildings repainted, and unsightly things covered with brightly coloured muslin. Even minutes before the Queen's motorcade arrived, jamedars (sweepers) were busy with dustpans and hand brushes, sweeping up little bits of paper! In the back of the first open limousine stood the Queen and beside her the Indian Prime Minister, Jawaharlal Nehru. The Duke of Edinburgh travelled in the second car with Mrs. Indira Gandhi, Nehru's daughter. There were over one million people lining the route from the airport – a distance of about 25 Km. but amazingly there was no restiveness whatsoever, simply warm applause and a ripple of voices calling "the Rani, the Rani" (the Queen, the Queen). Many of the Indian people were disappointed that she was not wearing her crown. However, they were delighted when later, for official receptions, she wore a tiara.

The U.K. Citizens Association held a reception for the Royal couple, at the Calcutta Race course when the Queen and the Duke mingled with the guests. The Mackie/Lagan folk kept together in a group and the Duke stopped to enquire what we were doing in India, no doubt recognizing our accents. When he was told we were involved in modernising the Jute Industry, he immediately asked if our company had supplied the machinery to Adamjee Jute Mills in Dacca, (now Dhaka) that being the largest Jute Mill complex in the world. We proudly answered in the affirmative. The Sirocco folk were standing next to us, and when they informed the Duke that their company supplied the bulk of Tea Machinery used in India, he amusingly retorted – I didn't realise tea was manufactured! As the Royal couple prepared to leave the reception, I was nearly involved in an embarrassing incident. As they got into their open limousine, the Queen standing on the right of the Duke, the guests very rudely surged towards the vehicle, and I found myself being pushed ever closer to the side where the Queen was standing. On the spur of the moment I stretched out my arms and managed to jam my hands on the side of the car, probably about eighteen inches from Her Majesty, and thereby pushed back the people, which enabled the driver to move off. Had my hands slipped the headlines the following day could have read – "British expat. businessman knocks over Queen"!! I would thereby have had a special mention in the Mackie Annals!! The following day I went out on the Maidan (the Central Park) often referred to as "Calcutta's Lung", with the object of shooting some 8mm movie film. There is a wide road running the length of the Maidan from the Victoria and Albert Memorial to the Governor's House, where the Queen and the Duke were staying. I knew the time at which the Royals were scheduled to return from an official function, so I headed for that road only to find that it was lined by Indian families, four or five deep. When the Indian folk saw a European "Sahib" with a movie camera, they immediately made a passageway and invited me to go to the front of the crowd to get a good picture, typical of the friendliness of the Indian people in general. In thanking them I must have made a remark about "my Queen" – they immediately responded –"She is also our Rani!".

The second event in 1956, which stands out in my memory, was the visit of the well known evangelist Dr. Billy Graham. It is quite a coincidence that I am writing about him at the moment as I've just heard on the News that Billy Graham preached last Saturday, to a large congregation in New York, which he claimed was his last sermon as he is suffering from Parkinson's and Prostate Cancer. A rather tragic climax to a career spanning over four decades, during which Billy preached in at least 200 countries to over 200 million people.

To get back to Calcutta in 1956. During a brief visit to the city, Billy Graham was invited to address leading European businessmen, mainly British, at a luncheon in the Saturday Club (nicknamed – "The Slap and Tickle). As Pat and Babs Gailey were members of that Club, they kindly obtained tickets for Bryan, Colin and me. Needless to say many businessmen, including Bryan, were very cynical about the event. Initially quite a number went no further than the bar where they stood, having their "Pink Gins" or "G and T's". However, when Billy went to the rostrum and began speaking, one by one they left their drinks sitting on the bar and took the chairs provided. The audience was held spellbound for over half an hour. Even Bryan admitted that Billy was an outstanding public speaker. The luncheon was a buffet, so I had the opportunity to have a nice chat with Dr. Graham and found him to be a very affable and interesting person.

For some reason, relationships between Mr. Lavens and the Gaileys were never entirely relaxed. In addition, Bryan seemed to have some antipathy towards Pat, in my opinion totally unjustified. Up until recently I thought this state of things caused Pat in 1959 to decide to resign from the Company. However, I recently learned from Pat himself with whom I still keep in touch, the real reason for his decision. I can do no better than quote Pat's own words. "As to my leaving, I left for two reasons which have nothing to do with Lavens or Bryan. By 1959 Mackies dominated the Jute machinery scene through the Indian sub-continent and South East Asia. When McLeod's and Birla committed to Mackie modernisation there were no more mountains to conquer. I was not a salesman anymore, only an 'order taker' and I was getting bored. The second reason was as I looked around the Company I counted about twenty young Mackie offspring working in the place and said to myself 'what chance have I got of ever running the Company?' So I left to find new challenges and opportunities". While I now appreciate the validity of Pat Gailey's reason for leaving the Mackie/Lagan set-up, at the time, I greatly regretted his departure, and that I would no longer have him as my boss. During the five years that I had worked under him I found him very considerate and he had given me a lot of wise counsel and guidance. Obviously Pat had been contemplating this move for some time as he almost immediately joined the management of The Ludlow Jute Company, Calcutta, in a senior capacity. That Company was then owned by the Stone family of USA. This event took place when I was home in Belfast, if I recall correctly due to the death of my father, also during the annual visit of Mr. Lavens to Calcutta.

On his return to Belfast, Mr. Lavens informed me that I had been appointed joint Managing Director of Lagan, and added that Bryan was not entirely pleased with the arrangement as he felt he should be sole

M.D. but he, Mr. Lavens, insisted that his decision was final. I assured Mr. Lavens that there would be no unpleasantness on my part, as I would always recognise Bryan to be the senior of the two. This I also conveyed to Bryan on my return to Calcutta, and of course demonstrated it during subsequent years together. To maintain the Lagan Board of three resident Directors, Mr. B.C. Ray (Bikash) our accountant had been promoted to the position of Financial Director, as well as Company Secretary.

In parallel with the increase of business in India, there was a rapidly developing market in East Pakistan (now Bangladesh). This to a large degree was due to a rather inexplicable decision of the British Government when partitioning the Sub-Continent at the time of Independence. One wonders at the logic of splitting the State of Bengal and giving the eastern part to Pakistan and retaining the western section in India, which meant that East Pakistan was 1000 miles (1600 Km). from the major part of the country, West Pakistan, and the then state capital Karachi. The situation was made more untenable, indeed ridiculous, by the fact that the two parts were divided by India, not a particularly friendly neighbour!! It did not make sense geographically, politically or economically. The last-mentioned particularly applicable to the Jute Industry, in that all the Jute Mills i.e. The Processing Plants were located in India West Bengal, while the Jute Fibre was grown almost totally in Pakistan East Bengal. This inevitably had political overtures for both countries. India felt it could not depend on Pakistan for the supply of raw jute, while Pakistan was unsure about the supply of Jute Finished goods from India. The outcome was that India embarked on an ambitious programme of Jute cultivation, while Pakistan decided to invest heavily in new Jute Mills. The latter caused India to decide to modernise its Jute Plants in order to be competitive. Of course these developments worked out hugely to Mackie's benefit.

Initially, business in East Pakistan was handled from the Calcutta office, staff members taking it in turns to visit that territory, but towards the end of the 1960's, Colin Metcalfe had become largely responsible for that area. As business increased, the workload naturally grew.

One Saturday in 1959, Colin and I decided to have lunch together in the Saturday Club, Bryan being otherwise engaged, as Mr. Lavens was in Calcutta on his annual visit. During lunch, Colin and I discussed the situation in East Pakistan and both were of the opinion that it was time to set up an Office in Dacca (now Dhaka). In fact, Colin stated that he was prepared to spearhead the move, assisted by a suitable person. By coincidence, we both thought of Leslie Vize, an Outside Erector who was a candidate for the Staff. By mutual assent we put the proposition to Bryan, the following Monday morning suggesting that he should discuss the idea with Mr. Lavens on his arrival at the office later in the morning. Both Colin and I were rather taken aback by Bryan's reaction. He told us that the idea was impractical, indeed quite stupid, and that he most certainly would not support it. That was mild to what we were later subjected to when called to meet Mr. Lavens. I was the main target for the harangue as it was obviously assumed that I was the instigator of the proposal. However, Colin and I mutually decided to let the matter drop.

Ironically, one year later, in 1960, the idea was implemented, precisely as Colin and I had proposed, in that Colin was sent to Dacca to set up an Office, and Leslie Vize was chosen as his assistant. Unfortunately, the latter proved to be a bad choice as Leslie and Colin were never compatible. Despite that fact, the Office in Dacca was a major asset to the Company's business as numerous large jute mills were duly established with predominately Mackie machinery being utilised. This in no small measure was due to Colin's hard work and dedication, plus that of his associates, Bill Surgenour and Desmond Morgan, who were posted to Dacca after Leslie Vise was transferred to Bangkok.

In 1960, around the same time as Colin, a young lady called Joan Aiken arrived in Dacca. She was of Scottish extraction, but born and reared in Bermuda. Joan was attached to UNTAB, a section of the U.N. which provided technical assistance in a variety of fields, her responsibility being advisor to The Women's Programme. Inevitably ex-patriates from different parts of the world, living in Dacca, met one another, if not professionally, then on social occasions. To mark some auspicious date, possibly the birth of Robbie Burns the Scottish Poet, a formal ball was held in a Dacca Hotel

Joan and Colin Metcalfe and friends in Dhaka, Bangladesh

and Colin and Joan attended this independently. By the time they were introduced by Colin's Scottish host, Colin was pretty well oiled and the conversation that ensued was not at all friendly. Apparently, Colin told Joan that he had little time for United Nations personnel, as he considered they were paid exorbitant salaries for doing little or nothing! Joan was not easily cowed so was more than a match for Colin and heated words were exchanged. Some time later they met in the Narayanganj Club and despite the previous altercation they got into conversation. When Joan told Colin about what had happened at the earlier event he, being sober on this occasion, was horrified. They kept in touch and over a relatively short period of time a friendship developed. As often happens, dislike turned to love, and Colin and Joan were married in 1962. A marriage which was hugely successful and very happy due to the two persons being very compatible. Indeed they were only parted by Colin's untimely death in August 1997.

In the late 1960's business for both Mackies and Lagan continued to increase. Correspondingly it was necessary to build up the expatriate staff in Calcutta and to move to a larger office to accommodate the extra personnel. Many Companies were moving away from the previous business centre to a less congested area of Calcutta, off the main Calcutta artery, Chowringhee Road. A very suitable office for the Lagan Company was found in Park Street, which previously had been a residential area with some shops and cafes. I was given the responsibility of planning the layout of the new office, and deciding on the furnishings. I opted for a modern design of desks and other accessories some of which did not entirely please Mr. Lavens during his subsequent visit, indeed it led to a mild confrontation between Mr. Lavens and me, which had a rather amusing outcome.

In addition to the main office, separate rooms were provided for the Senior Executives. The largest room was designed for a dual purpose to serve as Bryan's office and a boardroom. My office was considerably smaller, but was tastefully furnished with a desk for my secretary, and a small settee and coffee table. On seeing it, Mr. Lavens first comment was that I needed to add only a tiger skin on the floor and a blonde to make it like a whore's boudoir. Quite by coincidence a few days later, a secretary of one of our good clients, a Eurasian with quite pale skin and bleached hair, came to deliver a tiger skin which her boss had acquired for Mr. John, who was also on a visit to Calcutta with his wife, M2. I immediately unwrapped the tiger skin, spread it out on the floor and asked the young lady to take a seat. I then went to Bryan's office and told Mr. Lavens that I had completed the furnishing of my office as suggested by him. Needless to say I was nearly thrown out on my ear!!

There then arose a question of living accommodation for the additional European staff. A very satisfactory solution was found. The Company doctor's niece and her husband, Arabindu and Nilima Dutta, had become very good friends to Bryan and me. This couple had acquired a building site in a good residential area of Calcutta, Tollygunje, with the intention of building a house for their retirement. We came to an arrangement, primarily with Nilima, who was a very competent person, to advance money to the Duttas to enable them to build two houses, each containing two apartments on their site. Those were built in 1960/61, and provided living quarters for four families. The residence was named Lagan Dutta Hall. The four apartments were built to a very attractive design, chosen by Nilima, each having servants' quarters and a garage with a very nice common garden.

From 1960 till 1965 the Calcutta Office and the Lagan Company continued to run smoothly and profitably, so Bryan Hall felt free to travel more extensively and to visit Belfast more frequently. In 1966 this routine suddenly changed, when Mr. Lavens Mackie died, and Bryan was appointed to succeed Mr. Lavens as Sales Director, which made it necessary for him to reside in Belfast on a more permanent basis. Consequently, B.C. Ray and I became Joint Managing Directors, with Billy Luney as Production Director. Bryan was given a good send off from Calcutta.

During the subsequent six years, I continued in the dual capacity of M.D. of the Lagan Company and Senior Technical Consultant for

Lagan Company directors. L to R. Billy Luney, B.C.Ray, Bryan Hall and author

Mackies in S.E.Asia. I later learned that in 1972, the Mackie Board of Directors radically changed its policy on the Lagan Company, under the direction of Mr. Jim Rogers, who had become Chairman of the Belfast Company. It was apparently decided to dispose of the Lagan Company to a suitable buyer, preferably the Government of India. For certain reasons it was decided that the necessary negotiations should be carried out by an Indian staff member, Mr. R.P.Marik, so I was instructed to return to Belfast in April 1972.

Labour Trouble

From the inception of the Lagan Company in 1955 until 1970 relations between the management and the workers were excellent, despite the fact that the majority of the latter, if not all, were members of a communist trade union. This was largely due to the union secretary Guruji Mukherji by name who was a very capable and honest man, in fact he was also well educated and could have been a university professor, had he chosen an academic career. In preference he had decided on a humble life and in all sincerity to devote his time and talents to the welfare of workers. The factory managers, firstly Billy Luney and then John Scott, had a good rapport with this man and were able to settle all issues amicably to the benefit of both employer and workers. As already mentioned the Union secretary was very honest and never asked for a bribe nor was he ever offered one. The company as a token of appreciation periodically made a contribution to a charity of his choice.

Regrettably during 1969 a bad element infiltrated the work force and caused considerable unrest. This festered for some time and came to a head in 1970. There was an altercation during which the labour officer, who would now be called the human resources executive, was manhandled, although not seriously. When this was reported to me I decided to take immediate and stringent action. I firstly told John Scott, who was then manager to sack the miscreants, who numbered thirteen, a step which if I recall correctly, was taken on a Friday. Realising there would be serious reaction from the workforce I further instructed John to start early the following Sunday morning and evacuate each member of the management and his family at intervals of an hour from the residential compound to Calcutta where accommodation had been arranged. He and the labour officer should be the last to leave after ensuring that all equipment had been shut down and the factory gates securely locked. The final action to be taken was to have a notice printed and fastened to the main gate, stating that from 12 noon that day the Lagan factory had ceased to operate. This I was able to do legally under the Indian constitution.

I maintained this stand for six weeks despite pressure from the Bengal State Communist Government. It was inevitable that the workers would lose patience and take action to force my hand by some form of intimidation. The most common "weapon" used by workers in India was the "Gerhao". This involved surrounding the "Burra Sahib's" office and keeping him imprisoned until he relented. The expected happened about five weeks after the closure of the factory. One day as lunchtime approached I was informed that the workers had gathered in the car park in front of the building in which our office was located on the third floor. I immediately phoned my apartment to inform Swami my bearer, and a friend who was staying there that I might not be home for lunch.

After careful thought and some consultation I sent a message to the leaders of the demonstration stating that I was prepared to meet a delegation of not more than eight workers and got a ready response. When the members of the delegation were escorted into my office they showed no aggression or ill-feeling. They stood respectfully on the other side of my desk. Although they understood English I took the precaution of having an Indian staff member present to act as translator so that there would be no misunderstanding. I then put three questions to the group, but insisted that each of the eight would answer individually. The questions were:-

1. How long have you worked for the Company?
2. Has the management ever treated you unfairly?
3. Was the dismissal of the troublemaker justified?

All had worked a considerable number of years for Lagan and their answers to the other two questions were favourable, so I told them to go down and tell their fellow workers to come to their senses and to arrange through our labour office to meet me again so that we could come to an agreement to reopen the factory, but that under no circumstances would the dismissed workers be reinstated. The outcome was that a document drawn up by the management stipulating twenty six conditions was signed by the workers' representative without question and the factory was reopened a week later.

The saga did not end there. The first time I visited the factory after the reopening, the news got out and the sacked workers were waiting for me as I exited the main gate of the factory complex, and surrounded my car, shouting and waving their fists. Fortunately my driver, Tamang a very reliable Napali, had taken the precaution of locking the car. Of course several of the men stood in front of the car forcing it to stop. Once again Tamang showed great foresight by keeping the engine running and revving it quietly ready for a quick take-off. When the attention of the men blocking the way was distracted, Tamang "stepped on the gas" and shot across a paddy field to the main road. We headed to a nearby Jute Mill as I was very friendly with the manager there. This person phoned a local police officer known to him.

It was rather amusing to see a truck full of armed police arriving to escort me to the police station nearest to the factory. When I arrived the attackers had already been arrested. In many police stations in small towns in India the cells are simply small cubicles with bars at the front open to the road, as was the case in Chandnaggar (Chandnagore) to which I was taken. As I got out of the car the "boys" shouted and shook their fists through the bars at me!! The police officer who recorded my statement tried to persuade me to file a charge of attempted murder, but I told him that under no circumstances would I consider such action, as in my opinion the loss of a job was sufficient punishment. My only request was that the police would prevent the guilty men from intimidating the management and the workers at the Lagan factory.

From then until I left in 1972 there were no further problems with the workers, in fact the action I had taken seemed to increase their respect for me. This was singularly demonstrated when I took Bertie Hunt to visit Lagan factory in 1984, when it had become a Government of India concern. When we drove through the main gateway I found all the workers assembled in the courtyard with a banner across the main building with the words in large letters "WELCOME BACK MR JEBB, GO AWAY MR PANI"; the latter then being the Indian M.D. There was an amazing spread of fruit, Indian sweet meats and other goodies laid out in the main office. All very embarrassing for me in the presence of Mr Pani.

The second unpleasant experience was entirely my own fault. From time to time there were "hartals" in Calcutta. These were general strikes during which life came to a standstill and it was foolhardy for anyone to venture out in a car as there were workers demonstrating in every area of the city. They normally were one day stoppages but on occasions would last for several days. On one occasion during a lengthy 'hartal' the staff living at Lagan Dutta Hall became rather bored, and as the Tollygunje Club was quite close, some of the "Boys" were tempted to take the risk of going there for a few holes of golf. Initially Sammy McCoubrey and Billy "Babu" Hamilton were the first to venture out. Billy was given the name "Babu" and is still known to many as "Billy Babu" because of his fondness for Indian curries! As Eric Totten was unwell Kaye, his wife was particularly 'fed-up' so I, not setting a good example as the "Burra Sahib" suggested we should follow the "Boys", make a foursome and come back together, so we set out in another car.

All was deathly quiet on the roads and at the club and therefore we became very apprehensive. After a few holes of golf we decided to head for home, and all travel in one car, leaving the other at the club. Nothing untoward happened until we were near our residence, when we ran into a procession of demonstrators, some of whom blocked the roadway, surrounded the car, and starting shouting and gesticulating!! Sammy and Billy bravely got out of the car and tried to reason with the mob, but with very little success. The sticks and stones began to fly, and the tyres of the car were deflated. I was particularly concerned about Kaye and told her to get down on the floor. Being at the wheel I decided to make a dash for it despite the flat tyres, and dived down a side avenue, leaving Sammy and Billy to fend for themselves. They apparently walked calmly after the car, and had there been further violence they could have taken refuge in one of the residential gardens which they passed. Needless-to-say, we were all glad to be back in the security of our own compound with the Durwam (guard) on the gate, a chastened but wiser foursome!!!

Some years previously, when the Indian Government was putting pressure on Mackies to Indianise at least 40% of the Lagan Shareholding, B.C. Ray and I found a very reputable Indian Company willing to pay Rs700 for each Lagan share registered at Rs100. Had Mr. Lavens been living it is possible that this offer would have been readily accepted, as he was very friendly with the family that owned the Indian Company in question, and was aware of their excellent reputation. However, for reasons which later became clear, the very attractive offer was unacceptable to the then Mackie Directors, particularly the Chairman!! Ironically all the Lagan shares were subsequently sold to the Indian Government at a give-away price. There was obviously method in that apparent madness!! As I later learned the Mackie Directors did not wish The Lagan Company to fall into the hands of an Indian organisation which would run it efficiently and thereby present competition to Belfast. The assumed advantage was not only short-sighted, but also short-lived, as other manufacturers of Jute Machinery were springing up in India and China, and were about to enter the market. However, other plans for the Belfast Company were afoot.

In addition to Mr. and Mrs. Lavens, other members of the Mackie fraternity visited Calcutta during the 1960's. Among these, as mentioned already were, Mr. and Mrs. John. The latter was designated "M2" to distinguish her from Mrs. Lavens who was referred to as "M1" – as it was felt inappropriate to call her Mrs. B. before she was able to marry Mr. Lavens.

Initially, Mr. John and his wife stayed in The Oberoi Grand Hotel, but eventually decided to move into my flat at Tollygunge, as not only was it more homely, but it was also convenient to their friends from The Inchcape Group, who resided in Tollygunge.

On the one occasion that Mr. Denis visited India, he also stayed with me. Unfortunately, his stay was rather spoiled when he contracted dengue fever and was confined to bed for several days. That was in November 1963 – the year in which President Kennedy was assassinated, as I well remember wakening Mr. Denis early one morning after reading the headlines in The Statesman newspaper.

Mr. Leslie also came out to have a look at the Lagan Factory, but nothing of note happened during his visit. That reminds me that his mother, Dorothy, also visited India, with three of her golfing friends. She, of course, was not interested in our business, but rather in sightseeing and trying out the three golf courses in Calcutta. In that respect Irene Luney was a great help being a keen golfer, as were Billy and their daughter, Ann.

Looking back, I think I most enjoyed the visits of Mr. Paddy and his wife, Julie, despite the fact that the latter and I had our moments – due to the fact that I was rather assertive, perhaps I still am (!), and liked to air my knowledge of India!! I recall one incident with some embarrassment. Paddy had gone to Dacca to visit the Jute Mills in that area and to discuss relevant business (with Colin) while Julie remained in Calcutta. By this time Colin Metcalfe's younger brother Desmond had joined the Calcutta staff, and having been friendly with Julie for years invited her to join him for dinner. I told Julie that I thought it was inappropriate, and that I felt responsible for her in the absence of her husband, which was very high-handed on my part, but fortunately both Desmond and Julie were very charitable and did not tell me where to go, although such a response would have been totally justified!! No doubt there was a little jealousy as Julie

Arrival of Mr. Leslie Mackie on visit to Calcutta. L to R. John Peacock (first Indian sales director BOAC/BA), author, Mr. Leslie, and Mr. C.M.Mukerjee (Lagan Travel executive).

was a very attractive young lady. Looking back we both laugh about the incident. Indeed recently Julie showed her sense of humour. It had been Desmond's intention to entertain Julie at a popular Calcutta restaurant called the "Blue Fox". When I celebrated my 80th birthday last year Julie presented me with a lovely ornament of a fox with a blue ribbon tied around its neck. Not many of the other guests knew the significance of the gift. During one of their visits David Chamberlain was also on a trip to the Far East, so we went as a group to Rangoon (now Yangon), and then on to Bangkok, and if I recall correctly, David proceeded to Japan where he had spent some time after joining the Company.

Much more could be written about business life in the sub-continent during my 18 years residence, but sufficient has been said to convey the very important part played by the Mackie Company and its staff in that area of the world for over 30 years after Independence was granted to that part of the British Empire. However, it was not all work and no play for the Mackie personnel. I would therefore like to write briefly about other aspects of what, for me, was a very pleasant life in India, a country that I came to love.

Social, Church and Charitable Activities

Entertainment of clients and overseas visitors was an important part of the job. Two cocktail parties were held annually during the visit of Mr. Lavens and M1. The first was a rather sedate affair for the "burra sahibs"

Dinner at Firpos – renowned Calcutta restaurant. L to R. Author, Julie Mackie, Paddy Mackie and Desmond Metcalfe.

and their wives – all of whom left at a respectable hour. The second for the Mill Managers and their spouses – was much less inhibited and normally a little diplomatic pressure was needed to get rid of the hard core! Indeed it was necessary in some instances to "pour" certain managers into their cars, with assistance of their drivers.

The number of guests at each cocktail party was considerable. In the second instance well over one hundred, as naturally the managers' wives were invited, also senior members of the office staff. It was consequently quite an undertaking to recall the names, so Bryan and I had a clever arrangement. The parties were held on the lawn of Queen's Park, which was Bryan's residence after the Gailey's left. From the entrance gate to the lawn was a walk of fifty to sixty yards so I met the guests at the gateway, made sure I had their names correctly, then escorted them along the pathway to where Mr Lavens, M1 and Bryan were standing under a floral arch at the edge of the lawn.

On approaching Bryan I would say clearly: "you know Mr. & Mrs. so-and so of such-and-such a company". Bryan would then respond; "of course I do" and he then introduced them to the visitors,

Mr Lavens used to express amazement at Bryan's retentive memory!! Occasionally I mischievously hesitated with my announcement and Bryan would give me an appealing look. However, generally speaking the teamwork went smoothly.

One year I had to leave Calcutta unexpectedly, while making preparations for the cocktail parties, as something urgent had arisen further east so Bryan assumed the responsibility for sending the invitations. He and Adrian Gubbay, who will be identified later, colluded to play a prank on me. There was a receptionist in the showroom of the General Electric Company (GEC of the UK). This young lady was a Eurasian named Loren Fredericks with rather startling figure and a cat-like walk, as a result of which she was known as "snake-hips". I had purchased some light fittings from her for the apartments at Lagan Dutta Hall and had become quite friendly, although I considered her "too hot to handle". When I returned from my business trip in time for the annual cocktail parties I received a phone call from Adrian Gubbay who said he wanted to tell me something in confidence. He went on to say; "that fellow Hall, in your absence has invited "snake hips" to one of the cocktail parties". I immediately sensed something fishy, but Bryan's secretary confirmed that he had written the invitation card. What he didn't know was that Bryan had retrieved it from the mail and had thrown it in the wastepaper basket.

I was quite perturbed as Mr. John and M2 were also on a visit to Calcutta, and I thought the latter would not be impressed if Loren Fredericks turned up in a micro-mini skirt. With this in mind I phoned

Loren to confirm the invitation and suggested that she should "cut-a-dash" by wearing one of her many attractive saris. The joke back-fired on Bryan and Adrian as Loren turned up looking "A Million Dollars" so much so that Mr. John and, to a lesser degree, Mr Lavens neglected the other lady guests. Indeed the men in general gathered around Miss Fredericks like bees round honey. I was also excused from joining other staff members for the traditional scrambled eggs at the end of the cocktail party , so that I could escort the said Lady for dinner.

Smaller functions were held in one's apartment or in one of the local restaurants, the most popular being the famous Italian owned restaurant – Firpos – which was very up-market. Alternatively there was Princes in The Oberoi Grand Hotel, or one of the numerous clubs. Club membership played an important part in the life of the expatriates, and indeed subsequently in that of Indian businessmen. There was a wide range of clubs catering for a variety of social activities. For many years in several clubs only British nationals were granted full membership. Those of other European nationality and even U.S. citizens were admitted only as "Associate members" – a policy which continued for some years after Independence was granted to India. The one exception was The Calcutta Club, which admitted reputable people irrespective of their nationality or colour of skin. The Chairmanship of that Club alternated annually between a European, mainly British, and an Indian. Its popularity and success continues to this day.

The most prestigious was The Bengal Club, which, for many years, catered for only top flight executives. Next in status was The Tollygunge Club, which could best be described as a Country Club – having a racecourse, a golf course, a swimming pool and a good restaurant. Of course racing enthusiasts preferred The Royal Calcutta Turf Club, while keen golfers chose The

Author with friend Loren Fredericks.

Royal Calcutta Golf Club. I never graduated beyond the "B" course in that Club! The Calcutta Swimming Club was the most popular for young folk when out on holiday from college and school. The Company paid the membership fee of one club for each staff member and family for the club of his or her choice.

During my years in Calcutta, I was a member of a small non-conformist Church, although as a lay preacher, I took part in services of a variety of other Churches – including St. Paul's Cathedral, Calcutta. The other members of the little Church were predominantly Malayalas from the State of Kerala, which lies mainly along the south-western coast of the Peninsula of India. It absorbed the former princely states of Travancore and Cochin. About 25% of the state population claim to be Christian. Those of the Syrian Orthodox Church claim continuity from the reputed Indian Apostolate of St. Thomas. There is reasonable evidence that the Apostle Thomas went to India in the first century. Ironically, Kerala was the first state in India to democratically elect a Communist Government, followed some years later by West Bengal. The Malayalas, in general, are a well-educated and capable people, as Kerala leads India in literacy. Many Malayalas are senior business executives in India, the Gulf States, USA and other parts of the world. Most of my colleagues in the little Church held responsible positions in International Companies – such as Swissair, Cathay Pacific, Union Carbide, and Indian Oxygen.

Around 1960 Mr. Lavens accompanied by M1 and I visited the port city of Cochin in Kerala, where coir fibre is hand- processed for matting, ropes and other basic commodities. Our visit was part of a tour of South India arranged by R.N. Goenka, the owner of National Jute Mills in Calcutta, also the proprietor of one of India's leading dailies – The Indian Express. During the visit to Cochin, Mr. Lavens and I took the opportunity of looking into the feasibility of producing machinery to process coir, but this proved to be totally impracticable.

I was a founding member of Gideons International – one of the first branches, or as the Americans call them "Camps", being set up in Calcutta. People who travel widely are aware of this Organisation, which among its activities provides bedside Bibles for reputable hotels. I was Chairman of the Calcutta Branch for the allotted time of three years. When Mr. Lavens heard of this interest of mine, he complimented me and said that I should feel free to use the Company's facilities, if necessary, to further the work of Gideons, as he admired the organisation. Consequently, the monthly Committee meetings were held in the Lagan Office, the Bibles were stored in the Spare Parts godown, and transport provided, when required. My membership of the "Gideons" opened many useful doors. I gained entrance into large reputable hotels, educational establishments, and

Visit to South India –arrival at Madras (now Chenai) Airport.
L to R. Mr. Lavens Mackie, M. One, and author.

government departments and was introduced to lots of important people. With a couple of my fellow Gideons, one of them being Billy Luney, I was invited to the Raj Bhavan to present a VIP Bible to The Governor of West Bengal, to Fortwilliam Military Encampment to make a similar presentation to General Manekshah, G.O.C. Eastern Command – who later became Chief of Staff and the First Field Marshal in the Indian Army. I also came to know leading politicians. Such contacts were inevitably beneficial to business.

The East India Charitable Trust (E.I.C.T.) was established in 1949. It was set up to bring a number of charitable organisations under one umbrella and was financed mainly by British Companies located in Calcutta, to help those in the Eurasian (Anglo-Indian) Community, with special needs. During the days of the British Raj, the Eurasian had enjoyed considerable privileges. The males were given fairly responsible jobs in the railways, the police and in commercial establishments. Most secretarial posts in companies and other organisations were filled by the ladies. However, after Independence, certain prejudices began to surface. The Trust covered a wide range of activities. An orphanage was set up for needy babies, and a school-cum-college previously established by a Scottish Missionary, Dr. Graham, was brought into association with the Trust and supported financially. More details on this amazing educational establishment will be given later. Three residential homes for older and retired Eurasians were also built. The Mary Cooper Home catered for those who could afford to pay towards their keep, and was considered by the residents to be select. The Tollygunge Homes catered mainly for the poor and destitute Eurasians, while St. Mary's Homes provided care for the sick and disabled of that community. Each establishment was supervised by a committee of honorary members, and a representative from each, mostly the chairperson, formed the central committee of the E.I.C.T.

I personally became involved in the Tollygunge Homes after moving to reside in that district, as the Home was within walking distance of Lagan Dutta Hall. Initially I acted as honorary treasurer and eventually as chairperson, and in the latter capacity became a member of the central committee of the E.I.C.T. One of the rules of the East India Charitable Trust was that senior members of the various committees must be British and Christian. However, I in collusion with a Scottish lady, both of us about to leave India on a permanent basis in 1972 – broke that mould. By putting pressure on the central committee we were successful in persuading them to appoint Mrs. Nilima Dutta as chairperson of the Tollygunge Home. She has held that office ever since, that is for well over thirty years, and has carried out its responsibilities most effectively and to the satisfaction of all concerned.

Due to the decrease in the number of expatriates in Calcutta, the task of raising funds and maintaining the Home to the desired standards has become more and more onerous in recent years. However, Mrs. Dutta has travelled widely and has been very successful in raising funds from abroad – indeed "Help the Aged" has become interested. She has also been very attentive to the happiness of the residents, particularly at festive seasons such as Christmas, and is no doubt one of the longest serving members in the history of the E.I.C.T.

The history of the Tollygunge Home goes back over 150 years. They started off as an Alms House to provide food and shelter for the needy and maintained by what was known as the District Charitable Society. It was then located in North Calcutta in a very poor part of the city. After a few years the premises used were no longer available. The West Bengal Government expressed its willingness to donate a suitable site in South Calcutta in the district of Tollygunge on the condition that it be used

Tollygunge Homes, with chairperson Mrs. Nilima Dutta.

exclusively for charitable purposes. The Society decided to accept the offer so the Tollygunge were set up. When the East India Charitable Trust came into being in 1949 it took over the running of the Homes.

For the first 30 years they served almost exclusively the Eurasian community but as the numbers of that ethnic group declined the doors were opened to all communities but unfortunately there is a reluctance on the part of strict Hindus to live at the Homes because of the dietary habits of the other residents.

There are six buildings in the complex, which is quite extensive in area. The two largest buildings are dormitories, one for men and the other for women, each capable of accommodating up to 30 persons. Attached to these is a large dining room, which also serves as an Assembly Hall, in which church services are held twice a month and in which other forms of entertainment take place. The other buildings provide accommodation for married couples, staff quarters, an infirmary and T.V. room.

Up until around 1970 there was no Cheshire Home in Calcutta. Sometime earlier I had been approached by a Colonel Lahira, a retired officer from the Indian Army, and Mrs. Bunty Aurora, whose husband was General Aurora Singh, G.O.C. Eastern Command, to join a committee to raise funds for the establishment of a Cheshire Home in the city. By that time, Group Squadron Leader Cheshire had reached a stage in life when he was unable to travel as extensively as he had done in previous years. As this was a noble cause, I responded positively to the invitation.

The initial step was to find a suitable site for the Home. As I was by then chairperson of The Tollygunge Homes, I was asked about the possibility of a piece of the extensive site at Tollygunge being donated to the Cheshire Home's Trust, as the use of the land for that purpose would fall within the State Government's regulation. Logically I had to seek the approval of the central committee of the E.I.C.T. When I did so, the reaction of that body, particularly of the chairperson, Bob Wright, was very favourable, so a plot of suitable size was set aside.

In addition to appealing to companies and individuals for donations, I suggested that a major event should be organised to raise funds. The idea appealed to the other committee members and inevitably I was given the task of spearheading the arrangements. Due to the extensive travelling of the Mackie and Lagan staff members, and I in particular, excellent relationships had been established with all the major airlines flying to and through Calcutta. I therefore decided to solicit their co-operation and they responded very positively.

It was unanimously decided by the committee to have a dinner dance, which was held in the very renowned Firpos Restaurant. As we were receiving the support of International Airlines, I hit on the idea of calling the event "A Night in the Air". Lagan suppliers provided publicity materials such as posters, while the airlines supplied table decorations and uniforms for the band members and the singer. They also arranged for air stewardesses to act as hostesses.

As the wife of the G.O.C. Eastern Command was a leading supporter, NCO's from the Indian army were admitted to the "Lido Bar" off the main restaurant for a concessionary entrance fee. The whole evening was a huge success, and the funds raised as a result, amounted to over £7,000 – no mean sum at that time!

As the Group Captain was unable to come to India the New Cheshire Home was officially opened by General Aurora Singh, who by then had become a well-known and popular figure, having commanded the Indian Army in the "Liberation" of East Pakistan.

On some occasions the work of The Gideons and the E.I.C.T overlapped.

General Singh Aurora GOC Eastern Command, officially opening Cheshire Home.

Cheshire Homes India
FOUNDATION LAID BY
LT. GEN. JAGJIT SINGH AURORA, P.V.S.M.
G.O.C-IN-C, EASTERN COMMAND
ON FRIDAY 21ST JANUARY, 1972
FUNDS DONATED BY
CITIZENS OF CALCUTTA

In one instance the "peon" in the Lagan office brought a message from the reception indicating that an R.C. priest with an Irish-sounding name wished to see me regarding Bibles. When he was shown into my office, the priest stated with a pronounced Irish brogue that he came from East Belfast

Author with Indian General.

to work in India. He then informed me that he was currently conducting a seminar at Lavinia House – a residential home for teenage and older Eurasian girls whose families did not live in Calcutta. That home had been originally associated with the E.I.C.T., but when it became increasingly difficult to find staff to supervise the girls, the responsibility of running the Home was assumed by the R.C. Church. The priest then went on to say "I would like your good-self to come and present Bibles to the girls". I most willingly visited the Lavinia House the following day, accompanied by two fellow-Gideons, as it was a rule of the organisation that a presentation should not be made by a single member. After an introductory talk, "Youth New Testaments" were formally presented to the girls and complete Bibles to the nuns who staffed the Home.

A more notable occasion was a visit to Dr. Graham's Homes, Kalimpong. The town of Kalimpong is a Himalayan hill station in the Darjeeling District of West Bengal, situated about 3933ft. (1200m) above sea level on the saddle from Deolo Hill to Durbin Danda Hill. The town was for many years the terminus of the mule-trade route from Tibet. In the 18th and early 19th century, the Scottish Mission was very active in that area, and left a noteworthy legacy. Initially the Mission established three important institutions in Kalimpong, namely The Scottish Universities Mission College, St. Andrews Colonial Homes for destitute children, primarily Eurasians, and Dr. Graham's Industrial Homes. After Dr. Graham's death, the last two were amalgamated and were named simply Dr. Graham's Homes. (See attachment).

A Scottish businessman, with whom I was friendly, Bill Burt, was chairperson of the Homes committee in the early 1970's. He invited me to accompany him on a visit to Kalimpong to preside at the induction of the school prefects, to speak to all the students at the Sunday morning Church Service, then in the afternoon to visit the cottages and present Gideon youth New Testaments to all the boarders. This trip involved flying by Indian Airlines on Saturday to Bagdogra, 480 Km from Calcutta, then travelling the remaining 70 Km by jeep through the mountain passes; the latter was a delightful journey. On the Sunday, in addition to speaking at the Church Service, I gave a brief talk to each of the foster families, and at the clinic. Consequently I gave well over twenty mini sermons that day. The foster parents in the cottages were known to the boys and girls as "uncles and aunties". Interestingly, there was a lady from Bangor, Co. Down, there – Auntie Flannigan!

As is obvious, I came to love India, and apart from business associates, I made many really good Indian friends, perhaps the closest being the Ghosh family and its connections. Dr. Ghosh was appointed the company doctor, and his pharmacy, Alex. Ross's of Park Street was the source of all required medication. As he was small of stature and pretty rotund – he became endearingly known as the "wee Doc"! The Ghosh family was unique in several ways. In the immediate family there were two sons and two daughters.

Dr M M Ghosh, Lagan Company Director.

The doctor's older brother had a similar family, but unfortunately he and his wife died when their children were young, so Dr. Ghosh and his wife "adopted" their two nephews and two nieces. The adopted family naturally referred to the doctor and his wife as "auntie" and "uncle", so as their own children later came along they also used these terms rather than mum and dad. Indeed, in India, children in general use these terms out of respect for older friends, even when the latter are not related. As we became friendly with the Ghosh family, Bryan Hall and I also got into the habit of using these terms. In keeping with this custom I became "uncle" to many younger Indian friends.

Two months before I left India on a permanent basis I had an interesting, but sad, experience which for me was also very emotional. On the 2nd February 1972 Dr Ghosh died, as a result of cancer. As all the surviving male members of the family lived abroad his niece Nilima had to assume the responsibility for arranging the funeral and all other aspects of his cremation, although, one son and a nephew returned to India for the actual ceremony. I also considered it an honour to attend.

Hindus do not put the body of the deceased in a coffin but lay it out on a charpoy, (bier), like a small bed, with a bamboo frame and coconut roping. The last act before the body is burned is to have an imprint of the deceased's feet. They put a red dye called "Sindur" on the feet and push a sheet of paper against the feet and rub to get an imprint.

Naturally, Hindu Priests were present to conduct what might be called "last rites" as the Doctor was a devout Hindu. He was also Doctor to the Armenian community so the Priests of that religion also participated. Nilima then requested me to conduct a Christian service and although taken a little by surprise I managed to say something relevant and discreet.

There was then a rather amusing incident and in describing it I have no desire to be offensive or disrespectful. The Doctor and his family lived on the fourth floor of an apartment building which had no elevator so the body on the charpoy had to be brought down stairs, which was quite a precarious exercise, however, Nilima, although small, can be at times a real "sergeant major" and she barked orders to the coolies carrying the charpoy as they manoeuvred the stairs and the deceased's body rolled around on the charpoy, however, the stairs were negotiated successfully and the body arrived safely for the funeral cortege. When we reached the crematorium the eldest son and the eldest nephew performed the necessary ceremony before the body was cremated.

My friendship with the surviving members of the Ghosh family continues to this day, particularly with the niece, Nilima, who I have mentioned several times previously, indeed, she and her family continue to be very close friends. As will be evident from my previous comments,

Nilima is a unique lady, although small in stature she is big in heart and mind. Having received an important part of her education in England, Nilima in some ways is very westernised, yet maintains her Indian culture and dress, diets and deportment. Nilima's was a love marriage to a very delightful man, an Indian born in Burma (now Myanmar) called Arabindu. He was a cultured, kind hearted and friendly person: sadly Arabindu died in 2004 after suffering several health problems, leaving Nilima a very lonely person after a long and happy marriage. The situation is somewhat ameliorated by visits to and from her two daughters, Nima and Amita, their husbands and families, who live in London.

Nilima has many connections in Ireland, not only through Bryan and myself and staying at our respective homes, she also became very friendly with Paddy and Julie Mackie and has spent periods at Mahee Island.

In addition, her eldest daughter had her primary education at Loreto College in Calcutta and completed her studies at Loreto College Coleraine. Also, one of Nilima's brothers married an Irish girl and is living in Cork while her cousin who was affectionately known as "Baby", being the youngest in the family also married an Irish girl and is living in Benburb. Both are doctors who have retired.

I have also just learned that for her work at Tollygunge Homes and her connection with the old and poor Nilima has been honoured by "Help the Aged" for her many efforts. If it were not for the fact that the rules of the East India Charitable Trust which have not changed since the last century, one stipulating that the Chairperson has to be Christian, Nilima would have undoubtedly been President of that organisation.

I can recall also many other interesting people with whom Bryan and I became friendly. Indeed I could write a separate book on the subject but I will restrict myself to a few of the most interesting persons.

There was a company in Calcutta owned by a Jewish family, B.N. Elias. The three main units in the group were Agarpara Jute Mills, National Tabacco and Oriental Engineering. The sons of the founder did not reside in India but left the running of the Calcutta companies to a relative called Adrian Gubbay, who was a suave, good-looking, capable businessman, but was a "high-flier". His loves were not as the saying goes; "Wine and Women" but as the song puts it "Cigarettes, Whisky and Wild, Wild, Women". His motto was "a short life but a merry one". Normally Adrian ate only one good meal each day, that being lunch. He did not have breakfast and seldom an evening meal, and did not drink alcohol during the day but made up for it in the evening. Adrian was well-known and popular in the Calcutta business community, and in the local restaurants and clubs. When he was invited to a dinner party Adrian would order "scotch broth" as a joke and the bearer would know what he meant, so would bring an empty soup dish into which Adrian would pour his whisky and soda. Don't get me wrong Adrian was never rude or embarrassing in company. Indeed he was very gentlemanly.

Adrian's first marriage to a Jewish girl broke up but not before they had two sons, and neither Bryan nor I got to know his first wife. Being single again Adrian played the field but "specialised" in overseas cabaret girls when their act came to Calcutta, which eventually resulted in Adrian's second and very successful marriage. In the early 1960's a cabaret act called "The Benny Trio" came to Calcutta. As the name suggests there were three members, Benny, his sister Norma and his cousin Nirma, all Cubans, whose family had moved to the USA. It was Norma who caught Adrian's eye as she was a very attractive sloe-eyed girl. She became known to me and others as the "Cuban Cutee", after she had fallen under Adrian's charm. This, unlike previous fraternisations which were short-term, and when the girl left Calcutta it was a case of "out of sight, out of mind", was to have a future.

After several months "The Trio" left for Hong Kong, and to put it mildly Adrian was forlorn. At the time Bryan, who was more of a drinking companion to Adrian than I, was on home leave, so Adrian turned to me for solace, consequently I found myself joining Adrian almost every evening as a "shoulder on which to cry". A couple of visits to Hong Kong to see Norma did not dampen Adrian's ardour. Eventually Adrian "took the bull by the horns" brought Norma back to Calcutta and married her. She proved to be a gem, not only having a good effect on Adrian, but also forming a good relationship with his mother, his first wife, also being loved by his two sons. As will be seen from the photo opposite, Norma was quite an exotic dresser, not only as far as frocks but also when it came to hairstyles and wigs. On one occasion when a British Airways flight was delayed at Calcutta two stewardesses phoned me, my name having been given to them by a colleague who knew me, to see if I could suggest how they should spend the evening. I responded by asking if they would like to see a little of the social life in Calcutta. I had in mind a party that was being hosted by Adrian and Norma at their apartment. There were around thirty guests of whom half were ladies, the wives and friends of the men present. Most of the ladies if not all were wearing wigs provided by Norma. I also gave the girls the low down on all present and they were quite fascinated. When Norma commenced playing golf, every time she went out on the golf course in her shorts and tight fitting tops, the men's golf went haywire!!

Around 1960 Bryan Hall became very friendly with a very beautiful Indian girl, Reeta Roy. She was a Bengali, although born in Assam, and was probably then in her early twenties. Shortly thereafter she became

Guests at cocktail party. Extreme left – good client and friend Adrian Gubbay and extreme right his Cuban wife, Norma Maria.

an air-stewardess with British Airways, and her friendship with Bryan deepened. If I had been asked my advice then to Bryan would have been "Marry the Girl" but at that time there was a taboo on mixed marriages in the British community. Eventually "crunch time" came and Reeta and Bryan decided to part company. On the Saturday when that decision was made I joined Bryan at Nilima Dutta's home where he really drowned his sorrows. That outcome did not affect my friendship with Reeta, in fact she periodically phoned me to discuss personal problems and sometimes we met for a meal. The only thing I asked for from Tara Lodge after Bryan's death was a portrait of Reeta which I have hanging in a corridor in my bungalow. Unfortunately, Reeta eventually made a bad marriage and is now a rather unhappy person.

Through Reeta, and as a result of our extensive travelling, Bryan and I became friendly with quite a number of BA Flight Crews, one being a rather unique young lady, Vera Chindy, who was a Parsee from Bombay (now Mumbhai). Perhaps before writing anymore about Vera I should give a brief explanation about the Parsee (or Parsi) community. The Parsees are descendants of the ancient Persians who emigrated to India on the conquest of their country by the Arabs in the eighth century. They first landed in

Reeta Roy, a close friend of Bryan Hall's and BOAC/BA stewardess, having dinner with author.

India in A.D. 766 but the exact date of their settlement at Bombay which is the principal centre of their community is unknown.

The Parsee women are described by one writer in the following manner "They have small hands and feet, fair complexions, beautiful black eyes, finely arched eyebrows and long black hair. They appear freely in public". The Parsee calendar is divided into 12 months each of 30 days. The other 5 days being added for Holy Days are not counted. On Feast Days a division of five watches is made under the protection of five different divinities (1) The deity who created the trees, shrubs and flowers. (2) The deity presiding over the mountains and mines, (3) The deity directing the course of the sun, (4) The deity who stands for truth and friendship and (5) The deity who presides over departed souls.

The Parsees neither bury nor cremate their dead. The corpses are placed in the "Tower of Silence" where the flesh is consumed by birds of prey and the bones drop into quick lime. I used to say to Vera that the thought of her lovely body being subjected to such treatment horrified me!! On their New Year's Day the religious Parsees go to the Fire Temples to worship the sacred fire, which is perpetually burning on the altar. Unless they duly perform this ceremony, they believe, their souls will not be allowed to pass the bridge of Chinvad, leading to heaven.

Although in terms of the population of India the Parsees are a very minor community, the figure given to me some time ago was around 120,000 in total, they have made a considerable impact on the economy of the country and in some cases on other aspects of Indian life. They are by and large well educated and highly cultured, also very renowned companies are owned and controlled by Parsees, the prime example being the Tata Group which owns a large steel company, a plant for the manufacture of Mercedes trucks and cars, also controls a large chain of hotels, the very reputable Taj Mahal Group.

Vera Chinoy. A typical Parsee young lady, who became supervisor of all BOAC/BA Asian cabin staff.

It was impossible to ignore Vera Chindy due to her good looks and attractive personality. She was also a very confident and capable young lady, so it is no surprise that she came to the attention of the Senior Executives of British Airways not only in Bombay but also in London and Hong Kong. As the airline continued to recruit more Asian girls, Vera was promoted and eventually was appointed a Senior Stewardess, being responsible not only for the Indian stewardesses but for those recruited from all S.E. Asian countries.

Unfortunately both Bryan and I lost contact with Vera after we left India, which is a great pity as she was a lovely and sincere friend. One can only hope that she found a good husband and is still living and happy. Parsees normally marry within their own community but I think in that respect Vera was quite broadminded.

One could continue to write at some length about India, but I hope sufficient has been said to give more than a flavour of my experiences in that fascinating country.

Over thirty years later I still keep in touch with former Indian colleagues who are also personal friends. I will confine my reference to three people.

Sisar Das Gupta, the last Mackie trained managing director of The Lagan Jute Machinery Co. (P) Ltd. who endeavours to visit Belfast once a year to attend the Mackie Old Boys Club annual dinner.

Dilip Mallick who has established his own company – Shimna Engineering (P) Ltd. to manufacture jute processing machinery. During a visit to Calcutta in 2000, I had the privilege of laying the foundation stone for his new factory and Helen, my wife, planted a tree.

Amin and Dr. Rozana Huq, who have resided in Belfast for over thirty years. Their son Shakeel is married to a Belfast girl and they have a little son called Jordan. Their daughter, Natasha is a very attractive, highly qualified young lady.

Top: *The author in discussion with Sisar Das Gupta, Indian sales consultant who became the last M.D. of the Lagan Company.*

Right: *The author laying the foundation stone of a new factory for Shimna Engineering Private Ltd. This company was established by Colin Metcalfe and a former Mackie staff member, Dilip Mallick.*

Helen, the author's wife, planting a sapling on the same occasion.

Friends of Dilip Mallick and author - Amin and Rozana Huq.
For several years Amin was part of the Mackie Technical Team

Mackie/Lagan staff members at Bryan Hall's farewell.
Back row – L to R. Eric Totten, Maurice McBride, Chris.Bradley, Derek Mackie, John Kirk, Jim Smith and Billy Hamilton.
Front row – L to R. Mrs. Bradley, the author, Kay Totten, Sadie McCoubrey, Sammy McCoubrey, Bryan Hall, Jean Hamilton, Kathy Smith and Pat McBride.

NEPAL

The land of the Gurkhas and Sherpas

IT WAS NECESSARY TO visit Nepal periodically as there were two Jute Mills in that country requiring modernisation. Furthermore from time to time Nepali and Indian entrepreneurs expressed interest in setting up new plants. The two existing Jute Mills were located in a town called Biratnagar, just over the North Eastern border of West Bengal. However, it was necessary to fly to the capital Katmandu, then on an internal flight by Royal Nepal Airlines to Biratnagar. The latter could be quite hair-raising as in that area there were no proper airfields, so the aircraft, then a Dakota, had to land in a flat field. Indeed at that time the Katmandu airport was also very basic. When a plane appeared over the mountains surrounding the city, a hooter would be sounded and young boys with lathis (bamboo sticks) would run and chase the cows, goats, dogs and other stray animals off the airstrip. Furthermore, flights from Calcutta were operated by only two airlines, Royal Nepal and Indian Airlines, both not of a particularly high standard.

The former employed a number of foreign pilots such as Australians, some of whom were past their "Fly By" date!! Consequently, some of the Mackie personnel had rather scary experiences. For example, one evening a staff member Noel Lavelle, having finished his business was sitting in the bar having a drink with several of the other hotel residents. When it reached a fairly late hour he asked to be excused and mentioned that he had to catch an early flight to Calcutta the next morning. One of the other men at the bar asked him which flight? When Noel specified the airline and flight number, the person who had asked, responded; "Relax my friend, I'm your pilot" and continued to quaff his beer.

On another occasion I flew by Indian Airlines on the Calcutta/ Katmandu sector. The cabin steward noticed that I had a movie camera and warned me not to take photographs. I told him that I was well aware of the restriction on aerial photography having come to India when he was a wee boy. The following day on the internal flight by Royal Nepal Airlines the plane made a stop en route to Biratnagar. It landed in a field where there was no terminal building. It being a hot day the passengers and crew, including the Captain, stood under the shadow of the wings. The Captain, in this instance a Sikh also noticed my movie camera. He asked me if I had taken a shot of the mountains, the Himalayas. I told him I was aware of the restriction on aerial photography. He retorted "absolute nonsense, come up to the cockpit when we take off". When I took up his offer and went to the flight deck, he handed over to his co-pilot, vacated his seat, and opened a small window on the side towards the mountains. He then told me to take his seat and hold the camera firmly out of the window. Before I could do so he looked out the window, turned and said to his co-pilot, "we are too far away, bring her in a bit closer". The co-pilot responded immediately, the plane banked towards the mountains and when it was close enough to please the captain flew along the complete range, thereby I was able to shoot an excellent view of all the peaks including Mount Everest.

As those who take an interest in politics are aware, the political situation in Nepal for the past sixty years or more has been very volatile. By the end of World War II the Rana family had been ruling in Nepal for more than 100 years and the time for change had come. Nepalis studying in India had come in contact with democratic ideas and in 1946 the Nepali congress party was formed by the brothers Koirala. Not only were the people standing against the autocratic rule of the Ranas but King Tribhuban (Tribhuvan) who had received a liberal education from tutors, determined to take his place as a constitutional monarch, but in November 1950 he felt threatened so left his palace to take refuge in the Indian Embassy in Katmandu, from where he was allowed to proceed to India.

A revolution then broke out headed by the Nepali congress and early in 1951 terms were agreed between Maharaja Mohan and the congress leaders by which a ten man cabinet composed half of Ranas and half of the Nepali congress assumed the Government. King Tribhuban returned to Katmandu on 13 February as a constitutional monarch. So a form of democracy had come to Nepal. During the following decade there was a succession of more or less ineffective governments. In 1955 King Tribhuban died and was succeeded by his eldest son Crown Prince Mahendra. In December 1960 King Mahendra dissolved parliament, suspended part of the constitution, and took over the administration himself so monarchy returned to Nepal. The King appointed a council of ministers to assist him in governing the country. A form of Government which has prevailed until quite recently.

When King Tribhuban sought refuge in India he apparently spent some time in Calcutta and stayed at the "500 Club", an establishment which was no longer in existence when I arrived. The manager of that club was a white Russian known by the name of Boris who looked after the King extremely well, for which the latter was most grateful. After returning to Nepal King Tribhuban obviously heard of the demise of the "500 Club" and that as a result Boris was out of a job. As a gesture of appreciation he proposed that Boris should come to Katmandu and open a Hotel. What was even more surprising, he offered Boris a former palace which was no longer used by the Royal Family. The offer was readily taken up by Boris and the new establishment when opened was named "Hotel Royal".

At that time there were no modern Hotels in Katmandu so when on a visit to that city I stayed at the "Royal". It was evident that Boris had spent very little money on altering or modernising the building. The furnishings were basic and the plumbing antiquated, but there was an air of enchantment and former grandeur about the place. The domestic side of the business was supervised by Boris's wife, a very attractive Scandinavian lady. A unique feature of the hotel was the bar called the "Yak and Yeti". In the centre of the room was a large circular elevated fireplace with a copper canopy. In the cold season a log fire was kept burning brightly. There were seats around the fire, and a broad slate ledge for the drinks, and there was a lot of camaraderie among the guests on dark evenings.

Boris had other business interests in Nepal including farming. His wife being Scandinavian apparently had some acquaintance with Ingrid Bergman, the well-known movie actress, as she and her husband were partners in the farming company. During their periodic visits to Nepal Ingrid and her husband stayed in the "Hotel Royal". Unfortunately, they were not there during any of my visits.

Noel Lavelle – technical sales consultant.

Other staff members took turns in visiting Nepal, mainly Noel Lavelle. He particularly enjoyed these trips as he had a British Officer friend who was stationed at the Gurkha recruitment camp where Noel was permitted to stay. Britain and India both have an agreement with the Nepalese Government whereby they can still recruit Gurkhas for their respective armies. The payment which the British Government makes in Sterling contributes to some extent to Nepal's foreign exchange balances. Regrettably despite all the effort the only business that came out of Nepal was partial modernisation of the two existing Jute Mills.

As I write this, news has come through that the situation in Nepal, particularly in Katmandu, is anarchic. There has been a general uprising of the people which doubtless has to some extent been inspired by the Mauists. The present King Gyanendra (whose name means Wisdom from God), which he will really need in the present circumstances, dissolved the elected parliament in February 2006 and replaced multi-party democracy with the previous system of absolute monarchy.

An email has just been received from a friend working in Nepal who describes the current situation as follows: "The people's movement is continuing and gathering momentum. There are daily protests and demonstrations right across the country, which are sometimes put down quite brutally by the security forces. A wide variety of professional groups and others came out in support of the movement and in protest against the violence of the military personnel. It is now more a peoples movement than one led by political parties. In an attempt to calm the unrest the King agreed to hand over power to the people and ask the party alliance to nominate a new Prime Minister, which did not satisfy the masses. He then reluctantly gave way and more recently requested the elected politicians to form a new government. This resulted for the time being in a cessation to the rioting and demonstrations but it remains to be seen whether it will satisfy the extreme left elements who seem determined in forcing the King out of office and the setting up of a Republic. If the situation were to deteriorate further it could have more serious repercussions as it could

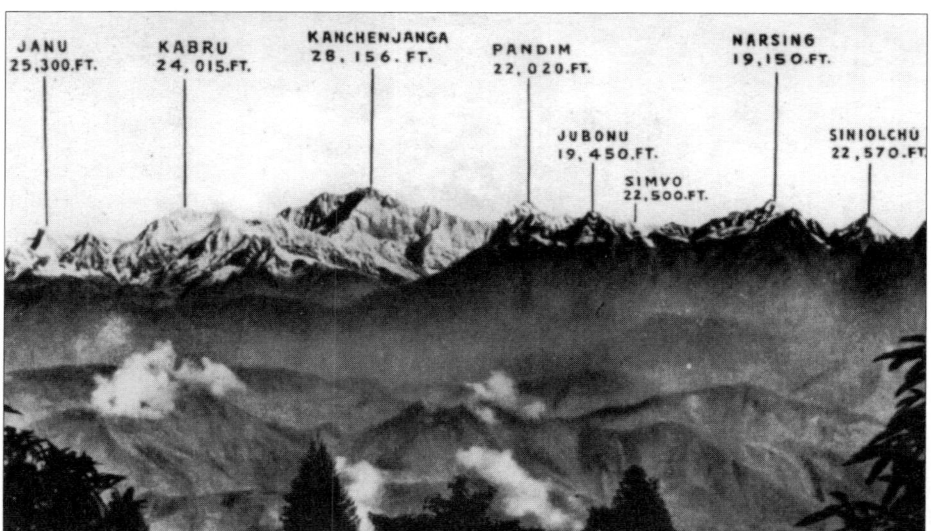

Peaks of the Himalaya range

put India and China on a collision course". The fact remains that Nepal seriously needs a more democratic and elected government.

Kathmandu surrounded by Himalayas

Fragile burden – go carefully

BURMA (MYANMAR)

The long struggle of Aung San Suu Kyi

When I arrived in Calcutta in 1954 negotiations were well underway with the Industrial Development Corporation, a Burmese Government Organisation, for the setting up of a 500 loom Jute Mill to produce sacks for agricultural products, mainly rice. The negotiations were supervised by Pat Gaily and came to fruition in 1955 when a contract was signed. After the signing of the contract, if I recall correctly, six young Burmese men were sent to Belfast for training. The names of only two come to mind, U Mye Bu and U Than. These two eventually became senior members of the management and stalwart friends of Mackies. In fact I understand that the former is still alive in 2006.

The machinery and other equipment was shipped in 1956 and installation took place in the latter part of that year and in 1957. I can recall these facts because I was home on my first leave from India in 1956 and shared a large office with Jack Bunting, Austin O'Donnell, Bob McAuley and David Chamberlain. The last mentioned was then preparing to go to Japan. I was then assisting Jack Bunting in organising the shipment of all the equipment and I can recall an incident when "Big Jack" came into the office and asked Jack Bunting if the reinforced steel for the factory floor had been shipped. It was quite an altercation as Jack, in his inimitable way, tried to explain to Mr Jack the situation and the latter demanded a straight answer then telling Bunting to let him know the position of the shipment. Without further delay he stormed out of the office. When Mr Jack had left the office Jack Bunting turned to the rest of us and said in his very polite manner "a very rude man". Eventually Jack discovered that the shipment of the steel rods had been overlooked and they were still in the steel rack, so enquired how he could go about signing on at the unemployment bureau, or as they say in Belfast the "Buru" but Mr Lavens was more understanding and told Jack to get the steel despatched as quickly as possible.

Perhaps one should refer to the political situation in Burma at the time. In 1942 as the Japanese prepared to invade Burma they recruited Burmese living in Thailand, and particularly in Bangkok and formed what they called the Burma Independence Army under the command of a group known as the "Thirty Heroes" who were members of a Burmese Political Party whose aim was to oust the British. However, it turned out to be a "Ragbag" army and was soon disbanded by the Japanese after their arrival in Burma.

In 1943 the Japanese declared Burma to be an Independent State and set up a civil administration under a collaborator called BA Maw. In his cabinet was one of the "Thirty Heroes" Aung San who was put in charge of defence also U Nu, who was supposed to look after Foreign Affairs, in the puppet government. A small Burma National Army (The BNA) was organised under Ne Win. My reason for mentioning these facts and names will become obvious later.

As the British Army regained control of Burma in 1945 the BNA led by Aung San, switched sides and harried the retreating Japanese. Aung San then became national leader and his creation, the Anti-Fascist People's Liberation League (The A.F.P.F.L.) had overwhelming support throughout the country. This party demanded complete independence, at the Governor's council in October 1945, and the then British Labour Cabinet agreed to accept the outcome of a national plebiscite. The A.F.P.F.L. won an outright victory in the elections for a constituent assembly. The only section of the population which did not want to join a union of Burma was the Karen, a Hill tribe.

On the 19th July 1947 it looked as if disaster had struck when Aung San and several of his closest associates were assassinated at a cabinet meeting. However, under his successor U Nu Burma's progress toward independence went ahead. On 17th October 1947 a Treaty was signed with Britain under the terms of which the Independent Republic of the Union of Burma came into existence at 4:30 am (the hour chosen by astrologers) on the 4th January 1948. The First Prime Minister of the New State was U Nu. The Burmese in general are obsessed by the predictions of astrologers and fortune tellers.

U Nu's government was socialist with a program of nationalisation, but it had to fight for survival against almost universal disorder complicated by a communist rebellion, a Karen rising and other political events. However, it gradually gained the upper hand and was able to establish a good measure of stability. The economy was then based on the export of rice. From June 1953 onward world rice prices gradually weakened, therefore, Burma had to seek new markets, and in the process to develop economic relations with China, Japan and USSR. Although in foreign policy U Nu espoused Jawaharalal Nehru's neutralism.

Of course, The export of rice necessitated a reliable supply of Jute sacks. There was also the need to conserve foreign exchange hence the importance of setting up a Jute Mill for the indigenous manufacture of jute sacks.

The U Nu Government was still in power when the Jute Mill was set up and commissioned. In fact in a general election in 1956 U Nu's party was re-elected, but shortly thereafter things began to fall apart for U Nu and his party as a result of in-fighting in the latter. In addition there was considerable unrest throughout the country. The situation became so serious in October 1958 that U Nu resigned and handed over to General Ne Win, who by then was Army Chief of Staff, who pledged himself to restore internal peace and then hand back to a democratic Government. However, the General obviously got a taste for power as apart from two years, from April 1960 to March 1962, General Ne Win headed a military Government as both President and Prime Minister up till 1988 when he had to relinquish power because of his age. His daughter Sandra Ne Win tried unsuccessfully to don her Father's mantle. A Military Government remains in power until today. Backed by the army Ne Win arrested U Nu in 1962 and since then the latter has not appeared on the political scene.

My first trip outside the Indian sub-continent to other parts of Asia was to Burma. That was after my return from home leave in 1956. There was only one reasonable hotel in Rangoon (now Yangon), the Strand Hotel. Indeed hotel accommodation was at a premium so guests had frequently to share rooms. Having booked in and unpacked, I for some reason went down to the lobby and overheard an Englishman arguing with the receptionist and stating that he was quite unwilling to share a room with a stranger. During the course of the argument the number of the room in question was mentioned and I recognised it as the one in which I was staying, I then approached the gentleman in question and introduced myself as the other occupant of the room. There must have been nothing suspicious in my appearance as he immediately dropped his objections and signed the hotel register, as far as I can recall we hit it off quite well. The other thing I can remember is that I wakened up the first morning with a splitting headache, which did not result from imbibing too much alcohol. As mentioned previously in the early days in India air conditioning was rare and one slept under a punka (a fan) so this was my first experience of air conditioning. It did not take me long to become accustomed to the colder environment. Air conditioning eventually became a necessary luxury in the Far East.

The Mackie representative at that time was a rather suave Burmese businessman called U Kyaw Thaung, He was not only suave but also shrewd in business and an opportunist in the political sphere. He handled business for Mackies through one of his several companies, New Burma

Trading, which also represented De Haviland the Aircraft Manufacturers who produced the First Jet Passenger Plane the "Comet". When the Democratic Government was in power U Kyaw Thaung dressed in Saville Row suits and drove a Mercedes Benz car. When the military took over he switched to the traditional dress, which is a cylindrical skirt called a "Longyi or Lungi" worn folded over at the front and tied in a special way at the waist. It reaches down to the ankles and is worn by both sexes. Coupled with the Lungi the men wear a single-breasted short jacket called an Eingyi or Aingyi. The womens' garment is similar but double-breasted, often short-sleeved.

U Kyaw Thaung also considered it judicious to downgrade from the Mercedes to a rather battered Volkswagon Beetle, as the military authorities obviously did not approve of anything too ostentatious. Furthermore, it was not wise to display any trappings of wealth. There was also a general feeling of "Big Brother is Watching You", consequently, confidential discussions did not take place, as previously in the office or indeed in the home. After we had dinner together U Kyaw Thaung did not drive me back directly to the Hotel but took a lengthy detour during which business matters were discussed. Evidently, he was confident that the "Beetle" was not bugged!!

Our agent was very hospitable and frequently invited one to his home. When such an invitation was extended some discretion had to be exercised and the question posed; "are we going to Number One wife's house or to Number Two wife's house"? The "Number One" was a business lady, in fact a film producer, while "Number Two" was more of a family person, somewhat younger, attractive, with a lovely personality, her name was Barbara, and I and the other Mackie boys definitely preferred her. I'm pleased to say that "Number One" gradually faded into the background and eventually disappeared from the scene, resulting in Barbara becoming in all senses the "Number One". She also produced U Kyaw Thaung's son and heir Moe Kyaw Thaung who inherited his father's business and indeed his acumen in both the business and political spheres. Eventually there was another son and three daughters in the family.

When Barbara was in good health she visited Northern Ireland on a couple of occasions and stayed at Tara Lodge. Unfortunately, in later life Parkinson's disease developed and she now is quite severely handicapped, however, her son Moe has arranged for her to live in his luxury penthouse in Singapore and is very good to her.

When I look back on my visits to Burma I think of another interesting experience I had at Rangoon Airport Migladon. Having finished business, I was returning to Calcutta. I was taken to the airport by U Kyaw Thaung and in those days security was very lax so our agent joined me in the terminal building. When I handed my ticket to the person behind the check-in desk of Cathay Pacific I noticed that he went into the office behind the desk and didn't reappear for quite some time. I pushed my way into the office and found that the counterfoil had been removed from my ticket and was sitting on his desk. I immediately grabbed this and asked him what was the problem, he said that the flight had been overbooked and that I was being offloaded. By this time, being an experienced traveller, I told him that in no way would this happen and I pointed to the 'ok' on my ticket and told him that the if the aircraft took off without me there would be legal action, then said that I would be waiting with U Kyaw Thaung for the call to board. After some time had elapsed and the plane landed, he came out very sheepishly and offered to escort me to the plane in advance of the other passengers and apologised for the inconvenience. He was quite taken aback when I boarded the plane and was greeted by the senior stewardess "hello Stanley, nice to see you". When I explained to her the problem that had arisen she said that if necessary I could sit in the jump seat at the back of the cabin with the captain's permission, in any event I could have my choice of seats. It pays to know the ropes when travelling with some international airlines. The stewardess was the said Loren Fredericks or "Snake Hips" from Calcutta who had left G.E.C. and joined Cathay Pacific Airlines.

As business continued to develop in Burma and Thailand Leslie Vize was transferred to Bangkok in 1965 initially working from the office of our Agent there, Yip In Tsoi Company. He later assumed responsibility for Burma in 1967. In that capacity he was successful in obtaining contracts for two more Jute Mills. By that time the Jute Industry came under the umbrella of the Ministry of Industry (Textiles).

In all the work involved in negotiations for the two new mills Leslie Vize was ably assisted by Alfredo Portig who prepared the proposals and technical data in Belfast and personally carried them to Burma. I can well remember having to work all day Saturday with Alfredo, our respective secretaries and other staff members to complete a large proposal to enable Alfredo to fly out late that afternoon. When it came to around 2 p.m. the documents still had to be put in folders and then packed with brochures etc in cartons suitable for transportation. It was, nevertheless, necessary for Alfredo to leave the rest of us and dash back to Mahee Island to change and complete his packing. It reached a stage when the unpacked documents and cartons had to be dumped loosely on the back seat of my car and a dash made for the airport. I was accompanied by Barry Pitman, the Advertising, Art and Design man in Mackies. The assembling and packing of the documents was carried out under the stairs in the old departure lounge of the airport. When all the cartons plus Alfredo's luggage were all safely checked in, we each relieved the tension with stiff G&T's!!

As a result of his periodic visits to Burma, Alfredo came to love Burma, and I know he has many happy memories of times spent there. By that time there was another 'first-class' hotel in Rangoon, the Inya Lake, as the name suggests located on the shores of an inland lake. It had been built by either the Cubans or the Russians, I can't clearly recall which, but in any case neither the building nor the fittings were of particularly high quality.

Alfredo Portig

Another former Mackie staff member, Gilbert Watt, is also very familiar with Burma. He spent several long periods in that country and after leaving Mackies he worked for Moe Kyaw Thaung, whose business is now based in Singapore, for political and other reasons. I'm indebted to Gilbert for a lot of the information on the political situation in Burma over the years.

People interested in Burma will be very familiar with the name Aung San Suu Kyi. In some correspondence the name will be prefaced by "DAW" which is the title given in Burma to a respected married lady. This lady has had an incredible life. She is the daughter of Independence hero Aung San, and was only two years old when her father was assassinated. Her name is also fascinating. In Burma, as in other S.E. Asian Countries, a child doesn't necessarily take the name of his or her parents, but in honour of her father she took the name of "Aung San" and also included the second name of her mother who is known as Khin Kyi (pronounced "Chee"). Suu Kyi spent her first 15 years in Rangoon, that was up till 1960. She then accompanied her mother to Dehli when the latter was appointed Burmese Ambassador to India. While there Suu Kyi studied politics at Dehli University, before moving on to Oxford where she studied politics, philosophy and economics at St Hugh's College. She was obviously a young lady with high principles as fellow students remember her being teetotal and only willing to sleep hugging a pillow, despite the free-spirited wind of the sixties blowing through the University!! How unlike the present day female students who recently were reprimanded for coming down to breakfast in short nightdresses and negligees!!

In 1972 a British academic, Michael Aris, replaced the pillow, when

Aung San Suu Kyi

he married Suu Kyi. They had two children, Alexander in 1973 and Kim in 1977. In the mid eighties Suu Kyi spent considerable time in Japan and India working as an academic.

In 1988 Suu Kyi returned to Burma to nurse her dying mother, Khin Kyi. That was when the student protests against the regime of General Ne Win were gathering pace. Due to her background Suu Kyi empathised with the students and on the 24th August 1988 she addressed an estimated 500,000 people at a rally in front of the famous Shwedagon Pagoda in Rangoon during which she made one of her first calls for a democratic government. The then dictator, Ne Win, had stepped down the previous month and his successor, Senior General Than Shwe ignored the calls for change and replied with brutal force, killing thousands of pro-democracy demonstrators on the streets of Rangoon.

Shortly thereafter Suu Kyi formed the National League for Democracy (NLD). She led that party to a landslide victory in 1990, genuinely winning 82% of the vote in a general election. She received three times as many votes as Nelson Mandela did in his first election. Despite that overwhelming victory the military Junta refused to hand over power and instead placed Suu Kyi under house arrest. The prime mover against the democracy party and Suu Kyi in particular, was Senior General Than Shwe who took over as Head of State and Prime Minister in 1990. The Head of the military Junta in Burma normally acts in this dual capacity. In 1991 Aung San Suu Kyi was awarded the Nobel Peace Prize.

The 27 May 2006 should have been a day of celebration for Suu Kyi and her National League for Democracy, as it was the sixteenth anniversary of their crushing victory, but the leader was still under house arrest. The restrictions on Suu Kyi have been in force for over sixteen years. Admittedly, she was released from house arrest in 1995, due to international pressure and suspension of aid from Japan, but her movements were restricted to Rangoon. In August 2000 Suu Kyi attempted to leave the capital to meet supporters of the NLD but was stopped by the police on the outskirts of the city. She and more than a dozen of her colleagues set up camp in their

Top: *Shwedagon Pagoda.*

Left: *Arthur Larkin - Commissioned the first jute mill in Burma, then moved to Africa and ultimately became Senior Consultant for France and the Benelux countries.*

cars at the spot and defied a request to return home. The confrontation lasted for several days. The aim of the stand-off on the part of Suu Kyi was to let everyone know that the opposition had the basic democratic right to travel freely in its own country, but unfortunately it resulted in a second period of house arrest which lasted till 2002.

When her husband Michael Aris died in 1999 the Military Authorities would probably have permitted Suu Kyi to come to the UK, but her dedication to her people and nation caused her to skip the funeral, out of fear that she would not be permitted to return to her homeland. This decision also meant that she has not seen her children and their families for years. The hard liner Lt. General Soe Win was appointed Secretary-2 of the Military Council in February 2003 and six months later promoted to Secretary-1. It is quite probable that he was the main instigator of Suu Kyi's re-arrest in May 2003.

Detention in a two-storey villa overlooking a lush tropical garden and Inya Lake in central Rangoon may sound not too unbearable; however, a more accurate description of Suu Kyi's circumstances would be home solitary confinement, as visitors are banned and she sees regularly only her housekeeper, the housekeeper's daughter and a gardener-cum-errand-boy. Even her doctor's visits have been curtailed to once every couple of months. Surprisingly a U.N. special envoy who was permitted to visit her said "that although her conditions were deplorable he found her uncowed and feisty – she is the Suu Kyi I've always known".

The current term of house arrest ended on 27 May 2006 and supposedly was reviewed by the Military Junta, who decided to extend it by a further year. This is hardly surprising when it is considered that the ruling council is currently headed by three hard line Generals. The attitude of International Leaders, especially those of the A.S.E.A.N. Alliance (Association of South East Asian Nations) is inexplicable, indeed inexcusable in light of other interventions in recent years, nevertheless there appears to be some nervousness in the Military Junta which is demonstrated by their decision to move the seat of Government from Rangoon to a site near the town of Pyinmana about 160 Km. (100 miles) north of the current capital. Many analysts are at a loss to explain the reason for the move, as the proposed site is in a remote mountainous region. The Burma Information Minister told reporters that the new capital would be in a more strategic location and would have quick access to all parts of the country. Analysts are sceptical. They think it is possible that the country hard line rulers are worried about foreign invasion, or want more control over ethnic minorities in the border areas, or may even be following the advice of fortune tellers!!

According to Aung Kin, a Burmese historian based in London, the country's Army is much stronger than its Navy, so it would be more comfortable to defend a land perimeter such as Pyinmana than the coastal city of Rangoon. The isolated site will also provide the authorities with increased secrecy. In any event Burma will be accepted back into the international community only when democracy is restored.

Even if Mackies still existed there would be little or no business from Burma as the three Jute Mills are running very badly and the few spare parts and other equipment required are sourced from India or China, so ends the "Mackie Era" in yet another country.

I have just learned that Arabindu Dutta, the husband of Nilima Dutta, who was mentioned in the Indian chapters, was a contemporary in politics with Aung San. In fact Arabindu had been put in solitary confinement by the British but was released at the time of independence and was able to get out of Burma to India before the assassination of Aung San and his other colleagues.

—∞—

As this footnote is being written, this courageous lady has again been detained in prison, simply because an unnamed American male swam across the Inya Lake and intruded her premises uninvited. The episode looks suspicious as there is an election pending and the ruling junta knows that if she were to stand – she would win overwhelmingly.

Mackie installation engineers
L to r. John McCready, Roy Gilchrist and Raymond Purdy.

Burmese delegation visit to Belfast 1977.
Mackie staff – extreme left, Leslie Vize -Technical consultant for Burma, second from left Desmond Morgan – head of wool and semi-worsted dept., fourth from right John McConnell – assistant sales director.

British War Memorial, Rangoon.

CAMBODIA

The land of "The Killing Fields"

In the early 1960's enquiries came from various sources in this country regarding the viability of setting up a Jute Mill. In the year 1960 Prince Norodom Sihanouk became head of State on the death of his Father King Norodom Suramarit. His government also expressed interest in such a project, as the cultivation of Kenaf had already commenced. The relation of kenaf fibre to true jute is explained in the section under Thailand.

Initially Mackies were put in touch with a supposed influential businessman called Kim Chantarit who claimed to have contacts in the right quarters. I was given the responsibility of meeting and having discussions with this man. On one visit to Phnom Penh I was accompanied by Gordon Mackie, and we both found him quite suave and impressive. Although Kim Chantarit did introduce us to various people there seemed to be no one with any commercial or political clout, nevertheless we soldiered on for several years with him, even when David Chamberlain was contacted by a businessman from Hong Kong, a Mr Maurice Green, I persuaded him to give Kim Chantarit another chance. However, the problem was solved when Kim committed some political blunder and was declared 'persona non grata' by Prince Norodom Sihanouk and had to flee the country. Arrangements were then made for me to fly to Phnom Penh to meet Mr Maurice Green, who had a Trading company in Hong Kong called Arnold and Company Ltd.

On arrival at Phnom Penh I was met by Mr. Green who took me directly to the office of the president of the company interested in setting up the Jute Mill. It turned out that he was also the Minister for Tourism, his name being An Kim Kom. An hour was spent in this gentleman's office discussing the project and as a result I came to a very definite conclusion. I should say at this stage that our competitors Fairbank Lawson Textile Machinery Company of Leeds were also involved in negotiations. On leaving the office and getting into the car I told Mr. Green of my conclusion

HRH Prince Sihanouk (now King) and his daughter HRH Princess Buppha Dhevi

and said that it was quite obvious that the Minister in question was already in the pocket of FLTM. Needless to say, Mr. Green was quite taken aback and began to dispute my conclusion. I then told Mr. Green that I was the factory representative and if he wished to become our agent I would call the tune and he should dance to it. It was not my intention to be rude but simply to set the ground rules.

It was then pointed out by Mr. Green that our competitors had an agent locally whose staff naturally spoke fluent French, whereas neither Mackies nor he had any similar facility in Phnom Penh. I told him I accepted that and said that we should go to the British Embassy. He then retorted there was no point in doing so as two British companies were involved and the Embassy staff would not take sides.

I told Mr. Green again that I knew what I was doing and instructed the driver to take us to the British Embassy. When we got there I didn't ask to speak to a British person but asked for a Madame Somaly, with whom I had become acquainted during previous visits. This Cambodian lady made me very welcome and invited us into her office. When I explained the situation she agreed to come and translate and type for us each afternoon after the Embassy closed at 2.00 pm. This lady's husband had also to flee the country and I knew that she needed extra finance to educate her daughter, a girl of around 10, called Samarine, so I agreed to pay her well for her work. I would also mention that Mrs. Green, although born in Singapore, was of Swiss extraction and consequently had a basic knowledge of French, so was able to assist Madam Somaly in translation work and typing.

Our competitor's representative stayed in the same hotel as the Green's and I and possibly had made some useful contacts in the hotel so a lot of "cloak and dagger" work took place. For example, we referred to the president of the proposed Jute Mill company as AKK and as we had opted for the support of the Minister of Industry he was referred to as MI. When we first met the latter he confirmed our suspicions and he advised us not to leave any of our papers lying around our bedrooms as the hotel staff could be bribed to provide copies (in our absence) to our competitors.

Mr. Green had also solicited the assistance of 2 local men, one a Cambodian a Mr Hassavy and the other Chinese, a Mr Hueng. These gentlemen acted as couriers but could be better described as moles as they had contacts in all the Government departments including the Palace and kept us fully informed of every twist and turn in the saga. The pendulum swung to and fro as one week we would be informed that the contract would be awarded to Mackies, then a few days later we learned that the decision had gone in favour of our competitors.

After many months of negotiations the Greens and I were invited again to visit Phnom Penh in early 1965 for the final decision. We were told to be at the office of AKK at 5.00 on a Thursday afternoon. We arrived on time and were informed that the board of directors was having a meeting and would definitely come to a final decision that evening. Several hours passed during which Mr Green became more and more agitated. I should mention that he had spent 3 years in a Japanese internment camp and consequently had a pronounced shake in his hands which became more pronounced the more nervous he became. Perhaps it was cruelly said that he didn't drink much but spilled more!!

The Minister of Industry had not put in an appearance that evening and about 8 pm the secretary of the company came downstairs to inform us that the directors could not agree and therefore they had sent for the Minister of Industry to act as referee. Eventually around 9 pm the MI came through the door and gave us the thumbs up. A couple of hours later by which time Maurice Green was a nervous wreck we were called to join the meeting at which the MI acted as spokesman. He told Mr. Green and

I that not being a member of the company board he had to remain neutral but after considering all details and asking for his advice the board had decided in favour of Mackies. The look on AKK's face indicated that he was not one of the directors in favour. However, he had to go along.

The MI then said that there were several points in the contract which required clarification and he would go through these one by one and asked for my response. By the way all those negotiations took place through an interpreter as the MI and the directors all spoke in French. As each point was raised the MI would nod his head almost imperceptibly in the affirmative or negative. As each point was clarified the MI instructed the company secretary to note the alteration in the margin of each page of the Draft Contract. When all points had been dealt with the president of the company AKK said that as the next day was a holiday the revised contract would be retyped and signed on the following Saturday. The MI responded to say that this was totally unnecessary as the alterations written in pen could be initialled and the existing contract signed which would be quite legal. Very reluctantly AKK and his fellow directors agreed and so the signing took place around midnight. AKK then very reluctantly made a speech congratulating us as representatives of Mackies and I responded appropriately.

In the meantime the MI had instructed the secretary of the company to phone the restaurant "Café de Paris" and asked them to remain open so that we could have a celebratory dinner. As we were leaving the office, Mr Maurice Green and I were about to go to our car when the MI, who during all the months of negotiations had spoken only French, took me by the arm and said in fluent English "Mr Jebb, you and I shall walk to the restaurant as I have a lot to tell you". During the course of that 10 minute walk he informed me of the manoeuvrings that had gone on behind the scenes and that he had always been in favour of Mackies. There was of course a very valid reason for that which I will not elucidate.

Another incident makes me wonder why the MI did not disclose initially that he was fluent in English. For various reasons our proposal had been submitted in French but after some alterations had been carried out locally in English the MI asked if he could have it translated into French and if this could be done within a matter of days. Due to the time limit it was not practical to request Belfast to send out a French translation so Mr Green and I flew to Hong Kong taking a copy of our competitor's offer which was already in French. As the technical terms of both offers were basically similar I used FLTM's proposal to translate our quotation by using similar technical terms and had it typed by Mr. Green's secretary. We then flew back to Phnom Penh. When the Minister looked at the proposal and saw the imperfect French he smiled but stated that at least he understood the technical terms more clearly. Once again it was necessary for me to improvise and use my own initiative.

The site chosen for the new factory was on the outskirts of a town called Battambang, about 200 Km. north west of Phnom Penh. The installations of the Mackie machinery commenced around May 1966, the building having been supplied by a French company. There was a team of four erection engineers sent by Mackie, one from Calcutta and three from Belfast. As I checked their names before writing this I discovered an interesting fact. Dick Wilkinson being in his sixtieth year was the oldest erector in the Far East, if not of the total erection staff, while Gilbert Watt, who was in his twenty-first year was no doubt the youngest. In fact, he celebrated his twentieth birthday in Thailand before his arrival in Cambodia.

The British Ambassador to Cambodia at that time was a very personable and competent man, Hal Brown, with an equally attractive and capable

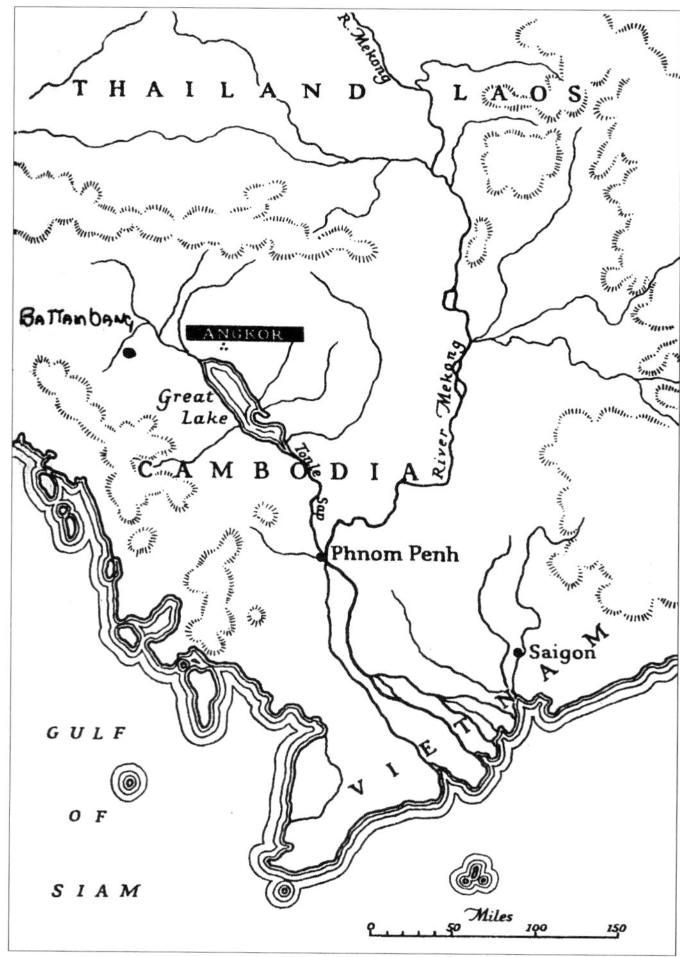

Map showing location of Jute Mill 240km (150 miles) northwest of Phnom Penh

wife, Molly. They were Scottish and exhibited the best traits of the Scots. They treated the Mackie staff extremely well and entertained them on special occasions. At Christmas 1966, while they restricted the lunch to their family, the Mackie erectors were invited to dinner that evening, prior to the cocktail party later for all the British residents in Cambodia.

While the installation of the machinery was in progress I decided to invite Hal and Molly Brown to visit the factory. This involved a journey of 200 Km. by a rather poor road. I suggested that they should travel in the official limousine with the Union flag flying as that would create the right impression in the countryside and at the factory, a proposal which met with the Ambassador's approval. There was also the question of accommodation for the Ambassador and his wife at Battambang. The main hotel in the town was very basic and in international status would not have merited even one star. Furthermore the living quarters at the mill had not been completed. The visit could have been accomplished in one day as Hal and Molly could have left Phnom Penh early in the morning and returned late in the evening of the same day, and they were quite willing to do so, but the mill management and workers wished to have a reception for the visitors in the evening so some improvisation was necessary.

Mackie packing cases which were made of reasonably good timber have been used for many purposes, some quite unique, for example, near the Delignon Mill in Saigon what might be termed a "Public Convenience" was created. Long packing cases in which lengthy sections of steel rollers had been packed, were taken with the lids removed and large holes bored in the bottom about three feet apart. These were then mounted on stilts at the edge of the river and served as latrines. However, Mackie packing cases were used for a more noble purpose at Battambang, Cambodia.

The best of timber from empty packing cases was selected and used to prefabricate a small "chalet" more accurately a hut. This was furnished with an air conditioner and other necessities and made as comfortable as possible. Hal and Molly being down-to-earth people had no complaints. The mill management and workers spared no effort in organising what could best be described as a barbecue, in the factory compound. There was entertainment by traditional Cambodian dancers and local musicians, the weather at that time of the year was ideal in the evening for an open air event. I had also scoured the town of Battambang for bottles of reasonable quality French wine, which was not readily available in that area of Cambodia. The whole event went remarkably well and once again demonstrated what a little initiative and improvisation can accomplish.

It was necessary for me to visit the site several times before the installation of the machinery commenced to ensure that the laying of the floor and other necessary preparations were completed in time to receive the machinery. One such visit took place in July 1965 to coincide with similar arrangements by the company president An Kim Kom and a couple of his co-directors. The company had been registered as Societe Khmere du Jute, generally referred to as "Sokjute" for short. I travelled to Battambang from Phnom Penh by car on Friday 9th July accompanied by Mr Hassavy and Mr Hueng the local "Reps" engaged by Maurice Green.

It was my intention to return directly to Phnom Penh the following day, Saturday, to catch a flight to Bangkok around 10 a.m. on Sunday morning, but events were to dictate otherwise. We were entertained to dinner by A.K.K. on the Friday evening in his local office. The food was excellent having been cooked by one of the Royal chefs in the nearby Government house. During the meal someone let slip that the following day was my fortieth birthday. On learning this A.K.K. insisted that I should join him in Siem Reap, a town near the ancient capital Angkor, the following evening to celebrate the auspicious occasion. I told him, that while I greatly appreciated his kind invitation it would not be practical to accept, as it was essential for me to connect with the Sunday morning flight at Phnom Penh and it would not be possible to make the journey by car from Siem Reap in time. On hearing this, the President, who as mentioned already was also the Minister for Tourism, excused himself and was away from the table for about ten minutes. He then returned to tell me that he had arranged for a Cambodian Air-force plane to be available at the Siem Reap airport on Sunday to take me back to Phnom Penh where all formalities would be waived, consequently I was without excuse. Before telling about my birthday celebrations it might be appropriate to say something about Angkor the ancient Cambodian capital.

The empire of the Khmers grew from earlier Kingdoms in the region: firstly the state called Funan, then the realm of Chenla, and finally Kambuja, when the Khmers attained their glory. Each in turn succeeded its forerunner by a process of dynastic usurpation or conquest, yet all are stages in coherent, unbroken evolutionary political and cultural development leading to that final climax at Angkor.

There was only a short night between the clouded sunset of the Chenla Kingdom and the brilliant sunrise of the Khmer Empire. Around the end of the eighth century a young man of about twenty acceded to the throne in Chelna. He was to reign for sixty years and to firmly establish the Khmer Empire with a constitution and religion which was to last for the next six centuries, during which the word "Kambuja" began to be employed to describe the country over which he ruled. He was known as King Jayavarman. The suffix "Varman" became common to all the Kings of Chenla and later Kambuja derived from an Indian title, which can be translated as "protector".

In the first decade of his reign Jayavarman was greatly concerned about the site of his capital so he was determined to find a location where he could develop a strong administration free from foreign interference and could be fortified against the rivalry of feudal Kings in areas surrounding his Kingdom. So diligent was he in this quest that he changed the location four times. On the second occasion he left the valley of the great Mekong river, migrated up its tributary Tonle Sap and chose a region to the North East of the Great Lake, where Angkor now stands. So began Angkor's extraordinary career. King Jayavarman died in 1001.

Over the following 180 years there was a series of Kings, some of whom reigned for only a few years and there was frequent political unrest. In 1181 Jayavarman VII came to the throne, when he was more than fifty years old. He was a zealous mystic, a vigorous warrior and a tireless builder. In all these directions his creative urge seemed to be limitless. Under his masterful influence the Kambujan empire became wider and mightier than at any time before or since. Jayavarman's greatest undertaking was the recreation of the main capital, now famous as Angkor Thom, its central temple is the Bayon, the most celebrated Khmer monument after Angkor Vat.

There were a dozen Kings over the two centuries following Jayavarman VII, but their names need not be recorded as they made no recognisable impact on history. Furthermore, the initiative in S.E. Asia moved elsewhere. In 1350 the Thais moved their capital from Sukhothai to Ayuthia (Ayudhya) much nearer to Angkor. From there the Thais could raid Kambuja more

Angkor Wat, seen through main entrance

easily and from 1350 to 1430 wars between the Thais and the Khmers were almost incessant. The country of Kambuja was never conquered by the Thais but they did raid Angkor and carried off its removable treasures. It was never re-established as Kambuja's capital because as demonstrated by the raids it was too near the Thai border and very vulnerable. The then King in 1434 moved the Capital further west to the site of Phnom Penh on the banks of the Mekong river where it continues to this day.

One student has written; "The Khmers left the world no systems of administration, education, nor ethics like those of China; no literatures, religions nor systems of philosophy, like those of India; but here oriental architecture and decoration reached its culminating point". That came to an end when Angkor fell, and that is why the ruins of Angkor are amongst humanity's most precious heritages. During my visits French Archaeologists were engaged with the assistance of labourers and suitable tradesmen in rescuing the temples, courtyards and buildings from the clutches of the forest and restore the architecture. This work was rudely interrupted by Pol Pot and his lackeys but I learned recently on the news that the first phase of the renewed restoration program has been completed. This has been a long parenthesis, but I thought it would be of interest.

Now to get back to my 40th birthday celebrations. As arranged with the Minister AKK I arrived in Siem Reap late Saturday afternoon and he came along in the evening to entertain my colleagues and I to dinner. As we sat in the hotel lounge one of the hotel staff, a very attractive young lady passed, and I happened to comment on her good looks. The Minister immediately clapped his hands and gave orders that the young lady should join us. A very scrumptious dinner was provided by the hotel after which we retired to Prince Sihanouk's local palace where we were entertained by the "Royal Corps de Ballet". When this programme finished we were escorted to waiting cars which took us out along the road by the Mekong river. I can remember the evening well as the heavens opened and the rain was very heavy. When the cars stopped we had to negotiate a plank walk-way to a chalet built on stilts on the edge of the river. One side of the floor of the chalet was raised and carpeted and all the men were provided with lungi's which we were expected to wear to recline on the carpets, having removed our trousers, but thankfully not our underpants!! Some waiters from the hotel arrived with crates of beer and other alcoholic drinks. Obviously the Minister and his colleagues were taking advantage of the occasion to enjoy Royal hospitality. The Minister then clapped his hands and instantly there appeared a retinue of Cambodian girls all dressed in the National costume which was similar to that worn by the Burmese ladies except the blouses were more colourful and sequined. Being the guest of honour I was told to pick the young lady of my choice. I immediately explained to the Minister that if I did so it would only be to discuss through translation by my colleague Mr Hassavy the customs and other aspects of the country as even if I had been interested in going further, which I certainly was not, I would not have risked my own reputation and that of the company by indulging in front of Ministers of the Cambodian government. I don't think there was anything subtle about the arrangement as would have been the case in some other countries, however, when the young lady joined us, through Mr Hassavy's translation, we had a very interesting conversation regarding her background, customs and family.

The events concluded well after midnight and I was glad to return to my hotel to prepare for the early flight by air-force plane the following morning to Phnom Penh. To say the least this was an interesting experience. The aircraft although not modern was adequate and competently flown by the air-force pilot so I connected with the international flight to Bangkok as planned.

Unfortunately, several years later the Khmer Rouge Cambodian Communists under Pol Pot and supported by the Vietnamese took over and the "Killing Fields" commenced, consequently, the Jute Mill was not properly maintained and lay dormant for a number of years, although I understand that recently an attempt was made to restore it. Indeed, after the communists were overthrown and Norodom Sihanouk was restored this time as King, Joe McClelland and his wife paid a couple of visits to Cambodia. Some spare parts had been financed by Oxfam. This was quite an experience for Joe and his wife Iris as they had to fly from Singapore by a plane belonging to the International Organisation World Vision and they had to sign a document indemnifying the organisation from any responsibility. When travelling outside the Jute Mill in Cambodia they also had to do so under an armed guard. They also had the unique experience of visiting a memorial to the killing fields, which really comprises of hundreds of thousands of bones and skulls, not a pleasant sight.

As is well-known, during the "killing fields" era Pol Pot and his cohorts had a policy of eliminating the educated class. Even although that was not anticipated during my visits Madame Somaly expressed the desire to get out of Cambodia and go to Hong Kong for the sake of her daughter. I deeply regret that Maurice Green and I did not in some way assist her to fulfil her dream as she would inevitably be considered one of the privileged class. Obviously I don't know what happened to Somaly and her daughter. There is a faint glimmer of hope in that her grandmother and the Queen Mother were good friends, so there is a slight possibility that the latter would influence her son, Prince Norodom Sihanouk, to protect her friends. There is little or no possibility of finding out. In recent years Cambodia, particularly Angkor, has opened up to tourism so I would love, with my wife Helen to revisit that country, even briefly, as I still find news and TV programs about it fascinating. My keenness is increased by the reports of friends who have recently visited Cambodia.

Top and bottom: *Skulls and bones from 'Killing Fields'*

Right: *Village street*

Below: *Centre of Battambang*

Right: *Small roadside temple*

Top: *Joe and Iris McClelland with Cambodian children.*
Bottom:*Joe McClelland and work team.*

LAOS

A sleepy little country

As far as I am aware there was never any serious enquiry from this country regarding a Jute Processing Plant nor any other type of Mackie machinery, and certainly no business ever emanated from there. However, Laos featured in my business life in connection with frequent visits to North Vietnam due to the convenience of airline connections between the Laotian Capital Vientiane and Bangkok on the one hand and Hanoi on the other. It was also practical to use the British Embassy in Vientiane for various purposes and on some occasions to obtain visas for Vietnam.

Modern day Laos, or as it is now officially called the Lao People's Democratic Republic (abbreviated Laos PDR) has its roots in the ancient Lao Kingdom of Lan Xang, established in the 14th century under King Fa Ngum. In the late 19th century it became part of French Indochina. It was granted independence from France on the 19th July 1949. When I and other members of the Mackie staff visited Laos in the 1960's the monarchy was still ostensibly in power, but the communist forces, the Pathet Lao, controlled large areas of the country. In 1975 they took control of the Government thereby ending the six-century-old monarchy.

There were several interesting experiences in Vientiane for me and other Mackie staff members. On one occasion when I visited the British Embassy, for some reason which necessitated handing in my passport, the person who took the passport looked at the document and said "that's an interesting name". It turned out that he was a Jebb but we were unable to determine if we were related.

Our Agent for Vietnam from 1974 was a Mr Henry Guy, of City Merchants, London, about whom I will give more information when I write about that country. In his previous transit visits through Laos he had discovered a small bar in Vientiane where the owner was prepared to give a very good rate of exchange for "green backs". I can't recall the then official rate between the Kip and the US Dollar (the kip is the national currency of Laos). However, I do remember clearly that the Madame was willing to give us ten times the official rate. She undoubtedly made a profit on her transactions as there were many locals accumulating dollars in the hope of getting out of Laos and going to the USA before the Pathet Lao took over completely. This arrangement stood us in good stead when purchasing incidentals in Vientiane as the following story will illustrate. Of course the hotel bill had to be paid in hard currency.

On the return journey in June 1976 from Vietnam the delegation stayed overnight in Vientiane. Prior to the dinner Bryan Hall and Leslie Vize decided to have a few drinks in the hotel bar and I was acting as the Chancellor of the Exchequer. The pre-dinner drinks that evening would have cost around £90 at the official rate, whereas they actually amounted to only £9. There was a sequel to this story, as after dinner, while the rest of us retired to bed the two "Boys" BDH and LVV asked me for some cash as they wished to have a look around the town!! The next morning we learned that they didn't get to bed too early, as apparently in one of the bars they got into conversation with several young Laotian men who subsequently invited them to a club in some obscure area. It transpired that it was a club frequented by the Pathet Lao. I don't know if the two "Boys" were taking a risk, but in any event nothing untoward happened.

A year or so later I again proved the advantage of having a few extra US Dollars. It was necessary for me to accompany a Mr Peter Heroys from Grindlay's Bank to Hanoi, as there were some points to clarify relative to the financial agreement between Grindlays and the Vietnamese Government. When business was completed I was able with a little "incentive" to the Government Travel Rep to secure two seats on Air Vietnam from Hanoi to Vientiane, but was told that all flights by Thai Airways from Vientiane to Bangkok were fully booked for a week ahead. On hearing this Peter Heroys stated emphatically that he was not going to spend a week inVientiane and would prefer to wait in Hanoi until he had a confirmed onward flight. I told him equally as emphatically that I was taking the flight booked, but had no intention of sitting around in Vientiane. I think his unexpressed reaction was "Big Head" thinks he can walk on water. He eventually reluctantly accompanied me.

On disembarking at Vientiane and going through the customs I was approached by quite a presentable young Laotian, asking if he could be of any help. I told him to see me beyond immigration. On getting through I slipped him a Ten Dollar Bill and told him that I wanted two seats on the Thai Airways flight to Bangkok that afternoon, and added that there would be more "green backs" if he were successful. He responded by saying that I had given him an extremely difficult if not an impossible task. However,

I had learned that he and his brother were qualified doctors anxious to get to the USA.

I then said to Peter Heroys that we would hedge our bets by going to the Thai Airways office. On getting there we were told by the booking clerk that the British Embassy had been trying for a week to book two seats for us but there was no chance for several days. On hearing this Peter turned and said "I told you so" and no doubt felt like adding "Smart Ass"!!

He then asked me "what are you going to do now?". I said "calm down we will return to the airport and enjoy a leisurely lunch". Probably Peter forced himself to eat but I relished the French cuisine with a glass of wine. As the afternoon wore on the embarkation lounge became jam packed with passengers, predominantly staff from the various embassies with diplomatic bags handcuffed to their wrists. This explained the non-availability of seats as each diplomat booked two, one for him or herself and one for the "dip bag".

The plane arrived from Bangkok, it being an Avro 748. The formalities of offloading incoming passengers and preparing for the return flight to Bangkok took over an hour during which Peter became more and more tense. Then my Laotian friend pushed his way through the crowd and surreptitiously signalled to follow him. We were taken to the check-in desk, relieved of our luggage and escorted to the place in advance of the other passengers, but not before my Doctor friend was adequately rewarded.

There were two very annoyed diplomats on board who had to nurse their "Dip Bags" while Peter Heroys sat in stunned amazement. I felt guilty and embarrassed, I don't think!! Business in the Far East makes one a bit shrewd, if not subtle. It is essential to know the tricks of the trade and indeed of the travel business!! Unfortunately, my cleverness did not enable me to obtain any business for Mackies in Laos. There will be some other interesting experiences in Vientiane when I write about North Vietnam as on most occasions we travelled to Hanoi via Laos.

THAILAND (SIAM)

The King and the Orchid

IN THE 7 CENTURY A.D. what is now Thailand was populated by the Mon and Khmer civilisations who were heavily influenced by Indian culture. At this time the Thai tribes from Yukunan province in China moved to the area of present day Thailand largely to avoid the warring Mongols and in particular Kublai Khan. These people (Aboriginal forest dwellers) were called "Syumas" by the Khmers. From this term came the words "Siam and Siamese" being the old Khmer for the country and its people. The new settlers brought with them very pronounced Chinese influence and it is generally accepted that this was the start of Thai history. Over the next few hundred years tribes from other places also settled in the same area which to some extent could account for the variety of facial features found in present day Thailand.

The old official name of the country was "S-jam" which translates into English as Siam. In June 1939 it was decided to change the name to "Praethet Thai" or Thailand in English, which means "Land of the Free". I will consequently from here on use the name Thailand.

The Chakri dynasty ruled Thailand for 150 years, having been founded in 1782. During that period the Siamese Kings ruled as absolute Monarchs and were supreme. They were assisted by the Royal Princes who were heads of the various government ministries. On 24th June 1932 this was all to change as there was a Coup d'Etat led by army officers most of whom had been educated in Germany. As a result the absolute monarchy was abolished and Siam became a constitutional monarchy. There was no bloodshed as the revolution took place quite peacefully. The Thais are a peace loving people and in that sense the country is unique as since 1932 frequent coups have taken place all with little or no blood letting.

As I write this chapter at the end of June 2006 five days of celebrations have taken place in Bangkok and throughout Thailand to mark the 60th anniversary of the current King's ascension to the throne. King Bhumibol

Asulyadej (Rama IX), who is 78 years of age ascended the throne in 1946 following the death of his older brother. He has reigned, holding few powers, through 17 military coups, 20 different Prime Ministers and 15 constitutions. Indeed he is the world's longest serving monarch.

King Bhumibol gained the respect and admiration of his subjects in the early years of his reign by travelling relentlessly throughout the country and taking a personal interest in rural development. However, it has been his timely intervention at times of crisis that has earned him the gratitude of many Thais. Most recently in April 2006 his wise intervention ended a stand-off over a disputed election which could have become extremely serious. During the recent celebrations the open displays of affection by the general public for the King were genuine. Few Thais have anything but praise for the man whom they describe as the very soul of their nation. During the celebrations when the King addressed the nation from the balcony of the palace, it is estimated that almost one million people gathered at the peak of the Royal audience.

After ascending the throne at the age of eighteen King Bhumibol went to Switzerland to continue his education. The coronation ceremonies were postponed to enable the King to do so. During his stay in Switzerland the young King occasionally visited Paris and on one of such visits he met a young Thai lady in her late teens, the daughter of his Highness Prince Chandaburi Suranath, a member of the diplomatic corp and the Thai Minister to France. This gentleman ultimately became the Thai Ambassador to the Court of St. James. The young lady's name was Mom Rajawongsi Sirikit, generally known as Sirikit. The chance meeting in Paris ripened into friendship and understanding.

Some time after the friendship had become really firm King Bhumibol was involved in a serious car accident in Geneva, resulting in a fairly lengthy stay in hospital in Lausanne. The young lady Sirikit, accompanied by her mother, frequently travelled to Lausanne to visit the King, during his long road to recovery and convalescence. As a result the friendship blossomed into a serious Royal love affair. When his majesty was well enough to leave hospital he arranged for Sirikit to continue her studies at Riante Rive, a boarding school in Lausanne. They were eventually married on 28th April 1950, which was considered an auspicious day. There will be further rejoicing and widespread celebration in Thailand on 12th August 2006 to mark Queen Sirikit's 74th birthday.

My first visit to Thailand was in October 1955 which was very brief and according to the stamp in my passport was in transit to Singapore. I did not become seriously involved in Thailand until around 1960 and thereafter my visits to Bangkok took place very frequently. Indeed when I visited the city in September 1986, Paul Lamszies, regarding whom I'm about to write in detail, told me that it was my sixty ninth visit. Of course on many occasions, particularly latterly, they were in transit to Laos and Vietnam.

In the 1950's/60's Bangkok was known as the Venice of the East. It was a relatively small city with many narrow tree-lined roads, with Klongs (canals) running alongside. In the business centre I had the choice of three hotels, the Trocadero, Pacific and the Oriental, the last being the best. Single-deck tramcars ran down New Road, the main street in that area. The name was rather a misnomer, as it was a narrow potholed roadway, with untidy sidewalks and small shops and bars on either side. What massive changes have taken place to the city over the thirty years I visited there, and I understand even more so over the last fifteen years. The Klongs (canals) were filled in and narrow roads turned into dual carriageways, incorporating flyovers. Multi-storey blocks and hotels have multiplied, indeed Bangkok could aptly be described as a "concrete jungle"

The life of Paul Lamszies is in itself a fascinating story, indeed some years before his death he wrote a book about himself entitled "A Merchant in Asia". However, I will restrict my comments largely to his involvement with Mackies. He could rightly be called "The Father of the Thai Jute Industry". Paul hailed from East Prussia where his father had a farm near the then capital Koenigsberg, but he decided that agriculture was not for him, as he desired a more adventurous and exciting life, and in pursuit of such chose the Far East.

The country of Thailand had a particular attraction for young German men with ambition, as relations between the two countries were favourable, whereas that was not the case between Thailand, France and Britain, the two colonial powers in most of the other S.E. Asian countries. Paul arrived in Bangkok in 1926 and initially stayed in the famous Oriental Hotel situated on the Eastern Bank of the Chao Phraya River. This hotel still exists but of course has been enlarged and modernised and is considered among the best in the world. It has an interesting history as many famous people have stayed in it such as Somerset Maughan and Joseph Conrad, not forgetting Jimmy Rogers, Mackie Chairman, Bryan Hall, Sales Director, and yours truly!!

In 1930 Paul set up his own Trading Company called Hamburg-Siam Co. Things became very difficult for his company and even more so for Paul personally during World War II. Thailand swung away from its traditional friendship with Great Britain, and in December 1941 permitted Japanese troops to pass through the country to invade British Malaya. This was followed by Japanese occupation of the country. That was quite a new experience for the Siamese/Thais as their country had never been colonized. Surprisingly in January 1942 Thailand declared war on Great Britain and the United States although the allies did not retaliate.

When the Japanese were defeated, Paul with other German nationals was put under house arrest, but according to his book it was not very onerous and was relatively brief.

However, in Europe events were much more tragic for Paul in that he lost all his remaining family members. One brother was killed in action, while his mother, surviving brothers and sisters all committed suicide by taking poison, thus Paul was left alone in the world. The rest of his life in many respects was rather lonely. In 1952 he proposed to an attractive young Swiss lady, Jacqui, but she told him he was too old. Despite this they remained very good friends and Paul treated Jacqui's eventual family like his own.

Now to get back to Mackies and the Thai Jute Industry. In 1937 Paul Lamszies in the course of his business pursuits met the then Thai Minister of Economic Affairs Phra Boribhand, who was looking for ways and means of conserving foreign exchange. Rice was one of Thailand's major exports. This necessitated the import from India of large quantities of Jute sacks for packaging of the rice, which obviously involved the expenditure of foreign exchange, indeed hundreds of millions of Baht. The Baht being the Thai currency. The possibility of using a locally grown fibre, known as "China Grass" was discussed at the meeting. There were two issues to be resolved, namely, could the local fibre be processed effectively and economically and if so would the quality of the sacks produced meet international standards?

Paul Lamszies – originally from East Prussia, spent most of his life in the Far East and became M.D. of Yip in Tsoi Ltd., Mackie's agent in Thailand.

The fibre grown in Thailand became known initially as Siamese Jute (or For-Kaeo) and eventually as Kenaf (botanically Hibiscus Cannabinus). It was akin to Roselle grown in Indonesia. It was coarser and somewhat dirtier than even low qualities of true jute and up until then had not been processed in any appreciable quantity. As Paul knew nothing about Jute sack production he contacted a friend Mr Classels in Bremen, the latter in turn consulted one of the leading Jute Mill companies in that city, Jute Spinnerei and Weberei, in whose Mill I personally installed machinery as mentioned in my recollections of Germany. That company whole-heartedly recommended James Mackie and Sons Ltd, Belfast.

When Mackies were contacted arrangements were made for Bob Elliott, who was then on a visit to Japan, to stop off at Bangkok, on his return journey. As a result of his meeting with Paul Lamszies, he suggested that several tons of Kenaf fibre should be sent to Belfast for experimentation. Subsequent tests carried out on the Mackie experimental plant indicated that 60% Kenaf blended with 40% true Jute could be satisfactorily processed. Just as this information was received by Paul, World War II started so all his dreams seemed to be shattered.

After the war Paul's business life also dramatically changed. Firstly, he found it necessary to liquidate his Hamburg Siam (Hamburg-Thai) Company. However, prior to this in 1944 Paul had met Mr Yip the major shareholder in Yip in Tsoi and Co. Ltd a relatively large trading company based in Bangkok. One of the other main shareholders was Mr Chu a brother-in-law of Mr Yip. Evidently Paul Lamszies made a good impression on Mr Yip at the meetings, as he was asked by the latter if he would be prepared to work with his company. Initially Paul worked as an "Associate" but within a relatively short time he was appointed an Executive Director. A very good relationship developed between the three businessmen, two Thai/Chinese and the third a German, with the result that in October 1948 Paul was offered and accepted a shareholding in Yip in Tsoi.

Despite all the changes in his life Paul had not forgotten his dream, indeed as he himself put it, he had become obsessed by the idea of establishing a Jute Industry in Thailand. He still had the support of the Minister he had met in1937, Phra Boribhand, who by this time had become a director in the Thai Rice Company, consequently he had a second reason for promoting the idea. The two worked together tirelessly and eventually were successful in convincing the Ministry of Industry about the soundness of the scheme. Consequently the first order was placed with Mackies in 1949, twelve years after the idea was conceived. When this plant went into production it was proved that 100% Thai Kenaf could be used for the production of sacks, as a result of which an entirely new market opened up for Mackie Jute processing machinery.

To assist Paul Lamszies in his day to day work two young men were employed by Yip in Tsoi, both of Chinese extraction, but having Thai citizenship. One Herbert Chang by name could possibly be called a merchant, used to wheedling and dealing and the other Bill Hwa a qualified engineer, specialising in the air conditioning field. During my frequent visits to Thailand I worked closely with both, but to a greater extent with the former. We became good friends and formed an effective trio. Herbert and Bill are both still living, and of course retired, but we continue to keep in touch. During his first visit to Thailand Gordon Mackie became very friendly with Bill Hwa as I felt that Gordon, having been with me all day

Bill Hwaphongchai – mostly called Bill Hwa – originally from China, but spent most of his life in Thailand. He with his friend Herbert worked with me on early contracts for jute mills.

in the office and on visits to clients, would not want to be hanging around with me in the evenings.

During the period of my responsibility for Thailand, which was up until 1965, when Leslie Vize was transferred to Bangkok, a further seven Jute Mills were set-up with Mackie machinery. However, I will refer in detail to only a couple relative to which I had some interesting experience. After Leslie Vize's (or as he was sometimes called L.V.V.) transfer I was still involved in Thailand, but to a lesser degree.

Around 1961 during one of my visits to Bangkok Herbert Chang and I discovered that our competitors Fairbairn Lawson Textile Machinery Co., of Leeds (FLTM) were engaged in serious discussions with some party regarding setting up a new Jute Mill near Bangkok. Surprisingly not even Paul Lamszies, who always kept his ear to the ground had previously got wind of these negotiations. It was consequently necessary for Herbert and I to engage in some "espionage" work. Our clandestine enquiries soon revealed that the project in question was being supported by the Ministry of Finance, also that the person spearheading the negotiations was a Mr Pongswasdi Suriyotai, a personal friend of the then Prime Minister Field Marshal Sarit Thanarat (1958-1963). The latter was a very powerful man in Thailand at that time. We lost no time in contacting Mr Pongswasdi and so negotiations began.

The person representing FLTM was a Mr John Page, a very competent and likeable gentleman, who I had met previously in Calcutta. Unlike in Cambodia there were no cloak and dagger activities on this occasion. John Page and I came to an understanding not to clash with one another in arranging meetings for discussions and entertainment. The negotiations were quite protracted as, despite the Prime Minister and the Ministry of Finance being involved, no single bank would provide the requisite guarantee. As a result of perseverance we eventually found four reputable banks in Thailand each willing to cover twenty-five percent of the contract value, so Mackies secured the business.

The site for the new Plant was on the highway from the city to Don Maung, Bangkok's main airport. A unique feature of that airport was the army golf course between the runways. The buildings for the Jute Mill were supplied by Taylor Woodrow Exports Ltd, a company with which Mackie had worked on numerous projects. Keeping in mind the Prime Minister's interest in the Jute Mill everything had to be to the highest standards, so the whole compound was attractively laid out with gardens and staff and workers' quarters. The eventual manager was a Mr Punlop Rajavejjabbhisal, who was trained in Belfast and married a girl from Northern Ireland. Writing these tongue twisting names reminds me of the delight I used to take in introducing Thai visitors to the Mackie Directors at lunchtime in the Dining Room. For example one such visitor was General Thepsedin Naj Ayudhya. Of course it would have been quite in order to use the first name but I liked to be a little wicked, and have a Director asking, "What did you say"?

The new plant near the airport was appropriately named the Bangkok Jute Mill Co Ltd. It was officially opened by the Prime Minister in early 1962 which was a most interesting experience. Despite the fact that the field marshal's residence was quite near to the factory he did not deign to

Official opening of Bangkok Jute Mill. Second from left – Field Marshal Sarit Thanarat, Prime Minister, The lady to the author's right is the Prime Minister's 'official' wife.

travel by road but arrived in style in his double-bladed helicopter. Two lamp posts had to be removed from a roadway in the factory compound to provide a helipad. When the aircraft touched down and the ramp was lowered, the crew, comprised of pilot, co-pilot and two very attractive stewardesses, all dressed in uniforms, descended and stood to attention while the VIP's disembarked. The Prime Minister was accompanied by his "official" wife. A large air-conditioned limousine drew up alongside the helicopter steps so that the couple were not exposed to the sun for too long and had not to walk any distance. They were thereby conveyed to the main entrance of the factory where the welcoming party was waiting, which included Mr Pongswasdi, Paul Lamszies and yours truly! The Prime Minister was escorted by his friend and Paul, while I had the honour of accompanying Madame. It was useful to have friends in high places, as I proved shortly after this event.

I was on a flight from Phnom Penh to Bangkok when I suddenly realised that I had forgotten to obtain even a transit visa for Thailand. When the immigration officer at Don Maung Airport checked my passport he told me to book an onward flight leaving within 48 hours and that my passport would be impounded in the meantime. He looked at me incredulously when I told him that my passport would be released with a valid visa the following day, on the instructions of the Prime Minister, with whom I had some business to transact. Needless to say things happened exactly as I predicted!!

When referring above to the Prime Minister's wife I purposely used the term "official" as it was reputed that he had one hundred "wives". While this probably was more than a slight exaggeration he certainly had a multiplicity of female partners. When he died in 1963 Madame Number One proceeded to confiscate the property of all the other "ladies". When the Thai Government learned of this they intervened and instructed her ladyship to return all that she had impounded, including houses and cars to the other "wives", who they said were the rightful heirs. Furthermore, they put her under house arrest until she had done so!! When the "Profumo Affair" in Britain hit the headlines in the Bangkok newspapers the Thai politicians and indeed their wives were quite amused, as their attitude was if a man hasn't a few girlfriends he is not fit to be a minister!!

There was another project in Thailand for which I could personally take credit. The Adamjee family had repeated misfortunes in business. In the days of the British they had a flourishing business in Burma but were forced to leave all when the Burmese Government decided to dust everyone of Indian extraction. The Adamjee family then invested heavily in East Pakistan, including setting up the World's largest Jute Mill, only to lose everything again when Bangladesh was established in 1971 and

West Pakistanis were no longer welcome in the new country, so they were somewhat reluctant to invest to a large degree in Pakistan.

One of the most industrious of the Adamjee sons was Hanif, with whom I cultivated a good relationship. Around 1964 Hanif visited Bangkok with the object of discussing the viability of setting up a Jute Mill in Thailand. Needless to say Paul Lamszies and I encouraged him to do so. Of course he had no intention of investing in a large Plant similar to the Adamjee Jute Mill near Dacca. The smallest economical and balanced plant recommended by me was one comprising 76 Sacking "Onemack" Weaving Machines to give an annual production of 5 million sacks which appealed to Hanif.

It was decided to locate the factory at the town of Khon Kaen about 400 Km. (250 miles) north of Bangkok. Two of Yip in Tsoi Directors were appointed to the Board of Khon Kaen Jute Mills Ltd., in fact Mr Chu Chutrakul became chairman. On my recommendation a Belfast man was appointed Mill Manager, Larry McVea, whose first experience in Jute Mill Management was with Bird & Co. India, in their North-Brook Mill. Then I recommended him to the Directors of the French Company which owned "Sovijute" Mill in Saigon. As a result he was appointed Manager of that Plant. When the political situation changed in South Vietnam, Larry with other Westerners had to leave the country so I referred him to Hanif Adamjee who engaged him as Manager, firstly for Khon Kaen, and then for his Malaysian Jute Mill.

Towards the end of 1964, negotiations commenced for a new Jute Mill to be established up country at a place called Sikew, about 220 Km. (135 miles) north of Bangkok. This was most interesting as one potential investor was Mr. Pongswasdi who had severed his connection with Bangkok Jute Mill after the death of the Prime Minister, Field Marshal Sarit Thanarat. Possibly it would be more correct to say that he had been forced out when a new Board of Directors was appointed, as his son in law, Mr. Somnam Nandhabiuat, also left Bangkok Jute and was involved in the new project.

After the establishment of Bangkok Jute there was also another related development, which involved Yip in Tsoi. The cultivation and processing of Thai fibre, mainly kenaf, had been so successful that Paul Lamszies decided the company should go into export. In organising the necessary set-up, Paul involved the young man mentioned above, who I will subsequently refer to as Somnam for simplicity. The Thai fibre was exported under the brand name of "YIT", and seemed to be a success from the outset.

The contract for the new Jute Mill Plant was signed early in 1965 and for obvious reasons was called Sikew Jute Mills Co., Ltd. Mr. Pongswasdi was appointed Chairman and his son in law, Somnam, Managing Director. For some reason, of which I'm not aware, Yip in Tsoi decided to invest in the new Jute Mill Company, so two of their Directors, a Mr. Chu and Mr. Khoon, were appointed to the Board of Sikew. On reflection, this was not a wise move for Yip in Tsoi, they being Mackie's Agent. Over the subsequent four to five years, there were rumblings in the Jute Industry, as the other members of the Thai Jute Mills Association did not at all like the idea of Mackie's Agent having a share holding, albeit a small one, in any Jute Mill in the country. They thought, rightly or wrongly, that Sikew could be given preferential treatment, or at least there could be a clash of interest.

While all this was going on, changes had taken place in staff at Yip in Tsoi handling the Mackie business as the two young men brought in by Paul Lamszies for that purpose resigned. Bill Hwa, joined an American trading company, and Herbert Chang, set-up his own company, which he named Thai Textile Engineering Ltd. Of course, as already mentioned, Leslie Vize, a Mackie salesman, had been transferred to Bangkok and was based at Yip in Tsoi.

In 1971, Mackies came to the conclusion that the Agency Agreement was not in their best interest. Although reluctant to break their long association with Paul Lamszies, they felt it imperative to terminate their Agency Agreement with his company. It seemed most appropriate to transfer the Agency to Herbert Chang's company, due to his wide experience with Mackie machinery. I understand by this time his company's name had been changed to Thaitex Far East Co. Ltd. When the new appointment was made it was obviously appropriate that Leslie should transfer to Herbert Chang's company together with his very competent secretary, Mrs. Pongsai Sunthornramgsri, affectionately known as Pongsai.

Despite this fact I kept in touch with Paul Lamszies. Indeed I still have the last letter he wrote to me in September 1986, in rather shaky handwriting. He died in December 1989. Towards the end of his life Paul became unsteady on his feet, so his secretary accompanied him wherever he went during the day, as did his old driver. Strangely despite being German, Paul preferred British cars to German or American. His favourite was an Armstrong Siddeley Sapphire. I recall sitting in the rear seat which was quite high and feeling like waving out to the passers-by like the Queen.

I don't know if Paul adopted Buddhism but he apparently stipulated that there should be a Buddhist ceremony at the time of his death, a wish with which his secretary complied. She was very loyal up to the end. It was obvious that Paul had treated her well.

Business for Mackies in S.E. Asia gradually declined, until in 1985 it no longer justified keeping staff members in Bangkok, so it was decided to recall Leslie Vize to Belfast. However, having lived in Thailand at that time for twenty years, Leslie felt he could not settle in Belfast, so he resigned from

L to R: Peter Atkinson (Mackies) Herbert Chang (Thai Textiles) person unknown, Leslie Vize (Mackies) and client.

Mackies. Naturally, during his years in Bangkok, Leslie had established many good contacts and was well aware of the potential for business. He had also the requisite Thai partners in Pongsai and her husband, Manoti. Although Thai nationals, they were of Chinese extraction and had the business acumen of that race. They made an excellent partnership and together set-up a company called Comtek International, which continues to trade to this day. Of course, Pongsai and her husband have taken advantage of the opening up of China and frequently visit that country.

There was always a lively nightlife in Bangkok but this increased dramatically during the Vietnamese war when the American G.I's came over for rest and recreation. The Thai police endeavoured to restrict the nightclubs that sprang up to cater for this influx, to one area of the city. Other visitors and tourists were inclined to avoid that area as there were literally dozens of bars and nightclubs in and around the tourist hotels. Those who have visited Bangkok will probably have heard of or possibly have been to "Patpong"!! That is a short street, much less than a quarter of a mile long, with bars down each side and in the alleyways off it. It is said that if one started early in the evening and had a drink in each bar one would not have visited all by the next morning!!

There were of course more "respectable" bars and nightclubs particularly those in or attached to good hotels. There was one in particular near the President Hotel, called the Sani Chateau which Paddy and Julie Mackie visited when they were in Bangkok. There were of course "Hostesses" but nothing ever took place that would embarrass lady visitors and a man could sit at the bar unmolested.

I could write much more about Thailand, but I hope sufficient has been said to give the reader a flavour of my experiences in that fascinating country over the thirty years during which I visited it. I would place it as my second most favourite country after India.

Floating market on Chao Phraya River, Bangkok.

Classical band which accompanies traditional dancers

Sunee, a typical Thai lady and friend of Mackie staff

Li Vize and Pongsai

SOUTH VIETNAM

A divided country

THIS IS THE NAME commonly used for the country that existed from 1954 to 1976 in the portion of Vietnam that lay south of the 17th Parallel. The division of Vietnam occurred during the Geneva Conference in 1954 after the Viet Minh fought to end almost 100 years of French rule in Indochina. Unlike the other French possessions in Indochina, which were nominally protectorates, the southern part of Vietnam was the colony of Cochin-China, which had its capital at Saigon. As a colony it occupied a unique legal position in that it had been annexed to France in 1862, and even elected a deputy to the French National Assembly in Paris. French colonial interests were consequently stronger in Cochin-China than in other parts of French Indochina.

The state of Vietnam, which later became the Republic of Vietnam was created through co-operation between the anti-communist Vietnamese and the French Government on 14 June 1949 during the first Indochina war. The former emperor Bao Dai was appointed Chief of State, and the agreement was known as the "Bao Dai Solution". This was an attempt by the French to grant partial independence to Vietnam, while still retaining substantial control over the country and keeping it from communist rule. This formulation was rejected by the communist Viet Minh led by Ho Chi Minh who were fighting for full independence.

The Geneva Conference, mentioned already, determined that the State of Vietnam would rule the South of the country pending unification on the basis of supervised elections in 1956. The planned elections and unification did not take place as Chief of State Bao Dai was deposed by a strongman Ngo Dinh Diem, who proclaimed the Republic of Vietnam on 22nd October 1955 and became a virtual dictator. The failure to unify the country and Diem's autocratic rule led in 1959 to the formation of the Viet Cong which initiated an organised and widespread guerrilla movement against Diem's government. Although initially cautious, Hanoi backed the insurgency which grew in intensity and support.

When I first visited Saigon in September 1959 President Ngo Dinh Diem was still very much in power. On the front of the Presidential Palace there was a huge picture of him and when his name was mentioned the ordinary citizens spoke in subdued tones, if not in whispers, as most people felt; "Big Brother is watching you"!! I recall one evening one of the Jute Mill management, George Marbeouf, at my invitation joined me for dinner. I had chosen a good restaurant in an area where some of the night-clubs were located, so George insisted on parking his car in a road some distance from the area, even though it meant quite a walk to the restaurant. He explained that it would not be "good for his health" if the President got the impression that he was out "living it up". This amazed me as George's car was a Citroen deux-chevaux of which there were literally hundreds in Saigon, all the same slate grey colour and similar in design. It was therefore evident that the security police checked the registration numbers of all cars parked in certain streets.

The purpose of my visit in September was to survey an existing Jute Mill and discuss plans for modernisation and expansion. I recently learned from Pat Gailey about the origin of this Jute Mill. In 1955 Pat had to interrupt his home leave to go to Rangoon to finalise the contract for the first Burmese Jute Mill. After completing this assignment Pat went on to meet a Mr Gerard the President of a French company Etab Delignon which had substantial interests in Vietnam, including seven rubber plantations. Apparently, this company had a small Jute weaving plant of sixteen French circular (Fayolle) looms, in Hanoi, North Vietnam. The jute yarn for these looms was imported from France. The Delignon company saw the inevitability of a communist takeover in the North, so decided to move the weaving unit down to Saigon and at the same time to install a plant to produce their own jute yarn, and with this in mind contacted Mackie. On arriving in Saigon Pat Gailey was pleasantly surprised by Mr Gerard's approach. The latter simply said; "lets have a quotation for the machinery required to set up a viable sacking plant". Consequently Pat was able to sell Delignon preparing machinery from the batching to the winding and beaming. They also accepted his recommendation to expand and balance the weaving section by purchasing eighteen Mackswell looms ex the weaving department in Belfast. The new Jute Mill Company in Saigon was named Societe Vietnamienne du Jute, Sovijute for short.

The company did not always seek Mackie's advice, as representatives from other manufacturers persuaded them to try out their weaving machines, namely Fairbairns, Sagem and Mecatiss, consequently, their weaving department became a real hotchpotch!! In my proposals for expansion I'm afraid I added to the mixture by convincing them to install a unit of SA 30 Onemacks, however, with the expertise of Larry McVea, the Belfast man who I recommended for the position of Mill Manager, we succeeded in getting the plant operating very efficiently.

When I visited Saigon in 1959 Mr Gerard was still the President of Delignon and I formed a good relationship with him, also later with his successor Mr Jacques Polton and his second in command Philippe Piechaud. I've lost track of Mr Gerard but still keep in touch with the last two. In fact I met Mr Polton and his wife during a visit to Paris a couple of years ago, when he invited my wife Helen and I to a very select club located next to the British Embassy in Paris. During the evening I reminded Mr Polton of his one and only visit to Belfast forty years previously. At that time Mackie had very little choice in hotels and so booked their most important visitors into the Grand Central Hotel in Royal Avenue, which those of us who are older recall was anything but grand by today's standards. On checking in the Poltons were horrified to find that there were no ensuite rooms so their first errand was to one of the nearby shops to buy dressing gowns in order to be decently dressed when going to the toilet or bathroom. Mr Polton was quite surprised that I remembered the incident.

During the 1960's I made periodic visits to Saigon as there was steady business for Mackie. The Viet Cong were then very active in the countryside and in 1961 President John F Kennedy decided to increase the level of US involvement in the form of US military advisers to assist the South Vietnamese army in countering the insurgents. By the time of President Kennedy's assassination in 1963 there were 16,000 US military advisers in Vietnam. Despite this action the situation continued to deteriorate and travelling outside Saigon was fraught with danger, nevertheless, senior executives from Delignon had to take the risk of regularly visiting their rubber plantations up country. The Viet Cong operated out of the jungle which covered vast areas of the country, so the trees and brushwood on both sides of the main roads were cut back for a distance of 100 metres (328 feet) to make ambushing by the Guerillas more difficult.

On one occasion Mr. Gerard asked me if I would like to accompany him on a visit to a couple of the rubber plantations. I don't think Belfast would have approved but I decided to take the risk. Despite being French Mr. Gerard had a high-powered American car, which he himself drove as, unlike the expatriate businessmen in India, the French in Indochina did not generally employ local drivers. If I recall correctly the journey in either direction took over two hours and Mr. Gerard dropped below 140 K.P.H. (85 MPH) only when passing through towns and villages. It was most interesting going around the plantations with him and his managers and although I can't remember seeing any security guards there were probably some in the background and South Vietnamese soldiers weren't far away. The plantation managers and their assistants were also French, so in keeping with their culture, they had a pretty substantial lunch accompanied by aperitifs and wine and I can well recall that as they sat in easy chairs having coffee and discussing business in French, I had the greatest difficulty in staying awake. I was certainly glad to get back to the Majestic Hotel that evening, wash the red dust away in the shower and tumble into bed!!

That was not my only experience of war conditions. Civil flights landing at or taking off from Than Nhut Airport, Saigon had to give precedence to military aircraft. On one occasion an Air France flight on which I was a passenger sat on the apron for well over an hour while fighter planes and bombers took off and landed. I normally used Air France flights into and out of Saigon as they took the responsibility of obtaining entry and exit visas, however, on one occasion they let me down. I arrived at Than Nhut Airport thinking that Air France had done their usual efficient job. I checked in, my baggage was labelled and a boarding pass handed to me. The ground stewardess then checked my passport and began to look rather disconcerted. She asked me to return my boarding card. A less experienced traveller may have complied immediately, but I certainly did not. In response I asked why I should do so and was informed that I could not leave on the flight as my passport didn't contain an exit visa. I told the young lady firmly, but I hope not arrogantly, that the omission was the fault of her airline, Air France, as they undertook to obtain the necessary visa, indeed they legally should not confirm a booking in the absence of an exit visa and that they had marked my ticket "OK". Furthermore, if the flight took off without me I could take legal action as it was essential for me to reach Bangkok that day.

The Sovijute Director Philippe Piechaud had accompanied me to the airport, so I told the stewardess that I would be having a coffee and discussing business with my friend while awaiting the call to board the aircraft. I seemed to be the only one of those involved who was calm about the situation! I observed a lot of activity around the Air France desk, the stewardess in conversation with the immigration police, and phone calls being made. Eventually the Air France local manager appeared in his bedroom slippers. After more than an hour's delay the flight was called and I was told I could board. I obviously wasn't the most popular passenger on that particular flight.

During thirty six years on the Mackie sales staff I lost only one contract and I don't think there was much one could have done to prevent that happening. The USA were then giving aid to South Vietnam which was being channelled through United States Overseas Mission (USOM). The head of that organisation in Saigon was a Mr Greenfield. Somehow or other Gardella, the Italian manufacturer had gained that gentleman's (I did not feel like calling him that at the time) confidence. Gardella's so called representative was a "soldier of fortune", I think he was an Armenian who was out to have a "killing" and then get out of the country. I discovered this at our only private meeting. Having made an appointment with him, I asked Philippe Piechaud to accompany me, ostensibly to act as interpreter. Being totally unaware of who Mr Piechaud was the Gardella Rep proceeded to tell him how badly the Mackie machinery was working in the Sovijute Mill. Philippe found it difficult to contain himself, but managed to keep a straight face during the meeting.

I decided to test the water by asking the Armenian if he was committed to Gardella. In his response he told me that he would be prepared to switch if Mackie made him a more attractive offer. When I told him that Mackie normally restricted commission to five percent, and only in extenuating circumstances would go higher, but no way would go beyond ten percent, he almost laughed in my face. When I endeavoured to give Mr Greenfield of USOM statistics on the Mackie plants compared to those equipped with Gardella machinery he told me that I was being a negative salesman. Although the outcome was a foregone conclusion I attended the meeting for the awarding of the contract. After Mr Greenfield made a flowery speech the inevitable happened and the contract went to Gardella. Naturally, I was very upset and I can recall that in my fax to David Chamberlain informing him of the decision I quoted the words of Adlai Stevenson when he lost the US Presidential Election; "I'm too big to cry, but it hurts to laugh!!

At the conclusion of the meeting I congratulated Mr Greenfield and said to him that in around eighteen months at least two things would embarrass him. Firstly, he would be uncomfortable meeting me and secondly he would appeal to someone not associated with Gardella for help. In response he made some scathing remark to the effect that I was a bad loser. Both my predictions proved to be correct. During a visit after the Dofitex Mill, as it was called, went into production, one evening Mr Greenfield and some friends were dining in the restaurant of the Caravelle Hotel in Saigon, when a friend and I chose the same rendezvous. We were escorted to a table quite near to Mr Greenfield's and he totally ignored me and I wisely did not embarrass him in front of his friends. Prior to my visit Mr Greenfield had approached my friend Larry McVea, the Manager of Sovijute, for advice and suggested that he should visit the Dovitex Mill. Larry asked me to accompany him, which naturally I was delighted to do. When we got to the Mill we found the situation shambolic. As a result of our visit Larry told Mr Greenfield that the Carding and Weaving could be made to work reasonably well but that the Drawing and Spinning frames would have to be replaced. There was a report later, the truth of which I can't prove, that Mr Greenfield lost his job over the decision.

To return to the political situation which continued to deteriorate. In 1965 US President Lyndon Johnson decided to send in combat troops and the conflict steadily escalated to become what is commonly known as the Vietnam War, but to the communists as "The Anti-American Resistance War for National Salvation". In 1968 the National Liberation Front ceased to be an effective force after the Tet Offensive and the war was taken over by regular army units of North Vietnam. Despite their superior armaments and logistics, in my opinion the US soldiers had really no chance of defeating the "Little Green Men" as the North Vietnamese soldiers were called because they were small, wiry and wore green uniforms which blended in with the jungle in which they operated. They dug a network of tunnels under the jungle like rabbit warrens. As the GI's armed to the teeth patrolled through the jungle little heads and shoulders would suddenly pop up firing bullets or throwing a hand grenade, then disappear as quickly as they appeared. If a GI attempted to follow them he would get stuck in the entrance to the tunnel and be blown to pieces. The jungle was also riddled with booby traps of a wide variety.

As the number of deaths of US soldiers mounted and more young men were drafted into the armed forces for Vietnam, the Johnson administration began to encounter widespread anti-war sentiments. Initially protests erupted on college campuses and in major cities but by 1968 the unrest had spread to every corner of the country. This resulted in Lyndon Johnson announcing in late March 1968 that he would not stand for re-election and the final outcome was the election of Republican Richard Nixon who claimed to have a secret plan to end the war. It transpired that his plans were basically similar to those of his predecessor, namely to continue the covert discussion with the North Vietnam Government which had been initiated in Paris in 1968 and to try to extract American forces by a process called "Vietnamisation".

All Nixon's efforts were an abysmal failure and as a last resort he ordered intensification of the air offensive which unleashed a series of deadly bombing raids on North Vietnam's major cities Hanoi and Haiphong. These resulted in not only intense protests all across the USA but also in international condemnation. The expanded air war also did not deter the communists and the DRV army continued incursions further into the South. The end finally came when the DRV tanks rolled south along national "Highway One" and invaded the capital Saigon which fell on 30th April 1975.

As the North Vietnamese took over, the remaining Americans had to beat a hasty and ignominious retreat. They brought their naval ships in alongside the jetties on the Saigon river but they were soon besieged by locals trying to escape, predominantly the wives and girlfriends of the GI's. This resulted in tragic scenes as the marines beat back the flood of refugees with the butts of their rifles and other blunt instruments, as they tried to clamber up the sides of the ships. The situation became so chaotic that the naval ships had to withdraw into the river. The evacuation continued as those who the Americans considered eligible were permitted into the compound of the US Embassy to be ferried by helicopter from the roof of the building to the ships on the river. The scene outside the embassy gates rapidly became as shambolic and pitiful as it had been earlier at the jetties.

By that time I was based in Belfast and Leslie Vize was responsible for that area but no more business was forthcoming from either Sovijute or the other Jute Mill. Apparently Philippe Piechaud the former director of Sovijute visited Saigon in the late 1990's and attempted to visit the factory but was refused permission by the communist authorities to go inside. Out of sentiment he did go to the area and heard the hum of the machinery and the click clack of the looms so the plant was obviously operating after a fashion, probably maintained by spare parts from China.

INDONESIA

The land of the "Garuda"

EACH COUNTRY I DID business in had its own unique features, many of which amazed me and Indonesia was no exception. This country is part of the Malay Archipelago which is the largest group of Islands in the world. In Indonesia itself there are more than 3,000 islands, the principal ones being Sumatra also, Java, Borneo (Kalimantan) and Celebes (Sulawesi) which extend from East-West for more than 4,600 Km. (3000 miles) across the equator in the Indian and Pacific Oceans.

The majority of the Indonesians are Muslims of the Shafi's sect. There is however a sizeable minority of Christians and Hindus. The Chinese in Indonesia may be characterized as being of the Buddhist-Confucianist belief. The colonial history of the country has been somewhat chequered. The Portuguese arrived in the Spice Islands (Moluccas) in 1510, followed by the Spaniards and almost a century later by the Dutch (1596) then by the British. However, the Dutch eventually became dominant and the territory became part of the Netherlands (Dutch) East Indies and remained so until it became independent on 27 December 1949, except for a short period of administration by the British.

In 1602 the Dutch East India Company was incorporated by the Netherland State-General, initially for the purpose of trading, but it eventually acquired territorial possessions in parts of Java and Sumatra, in addition to the Moluccas. Through mal-administration and corruption the company became bankrupt and in 1798 the Netherlands state nullified its charter and took over the company's affairs and property. Before any reforms could be put into effect, Napoleon occupied the Netherlands and the British took over the Dutch East Indies for around five years (1811-16). The British Lieutenant Governor, Sir Thomas Stamford Raffles, introduced some reforms aiming at free production by the Indonesians for export. When the Dutch again took over the administration of the territory they continued this system.

After Japan's wartime occupation ended, independence was proclaimed by Sukarno, the independence movement's leader. The Dutch formally transferred sovereignty in 1949 after an armed struggle, Sukarno remaining in power until 1967, when he was succeeded by General Mohammed Suharto who came to power after an abortive coup. During the Sukarno regime corruption was widespread and government departments were most inefficient. The new President imposed authoritarian rule while allowing technocrats to run the economy. They did so with considerable success, as there was a period of unprecedented economic growth and Indonesia emerged as a regional power.

When I first visited Indonesia in the early 1960's Sukarno was still in power, but was losing his grip on things and had married a Japanese girl by the name of Dewi. Many Indonesians were beginning to look on him as a playboy rather than a politician. Under Sukarno the economy to a large degree had stagnated and tourism was on a very small scale. Indeed there was only one first class hotel in the capital Jakarta, the Hotel Indonesia, a member of the Intercontinental Group, so accommodation was at a premium. I cannot recall why but at that time there was anti-British feeling in the country to the extent that a mob attacked and burned down the British Embassy which was across the road from the Hotel. This sticks in my memory as a member of the security staff who was known as the "Mad Major" paraded round the burning building playing the bagpipes. I think a more appropriate name for him would have been the "Crazy Scotsman"!!

At the time of my first visit the Mackie Agent was Calico Printers Ltd., whose head office was in Manchester UK. Their man in Indonesia was a young man named Jim Champion, the son of Sir Harry Champion, a well-known figure in the Manchester Cotton Trade. His wife Molly was from South Africa. The purpose of my visit was to survey the Mackie machinery in a government jute mill, P.K. Goni Rosella which had been extensively damaged by fire. As mentioned earlier rosella was the name given in Indonesia to the fibre known as kenaf in Thailand and mesta in India. The Rosella factory was located in the town of Surabaya in East Java. That was a centre for the textile industry so Jim Champion and his wife lived there. They very kindly invited me to stay with them, an offer which I most gratefully accepted as the hotels in Surabaya were very basic.

I well remember the flight from Jakarta to Surabaya by the National Airline Garuda. The aircraft was a pretty ancient DC4 and entry to the passenger cabin was through the galley just at the rear of the flight deck. The partition between the galley and the cabin had a door, unlike modern aircraft which have curtains or screens. As is customary when the plane was airborne the cabin attendants came through to check on the passengers.

For some reason the partition door stuck and could not be opened from the cabin side and despite loud banging on the door by the stewardess the flight deck crew did not hear so there were no refreshments during the ninety minute flight. Fortunately, there were also no emergencies!!

The name of the National Airline, Garuda, is most interesting. The Garuda, a mythical bird, is also the official emblem of the Indonesian State and has embedded in its body the Coat of Arms containing the five principles of the Nation. Garuda's origins in Indonesia go back to the first century A.D. when sailors and traders from Southern India came to the shores of the fertile islands looking for rice and riches. They brought not only goods and techniques but also their literature. In this literature, there were stories of the origins, or Puranas, with the story of the mighty Garuda Bird among them. The history of the Garuda since then would constitute a book in itself so I will confine my comments to the part it plays in modern Indonesia.

As a national symbol, the modern Garuda is designed to demonstrate past history with the modern nation, therefore the current emblem differs considerably from the traditional Garuda. It is obviously an eagle rather than the mythical bird, in fact it is rather like the German eagle. The old Javanese traditionally claimed that the Garuda carried the elixir of immortality. Its modern representation carries a motto in its claws which reads "Bhinneka Tunggal Ika" the official translation of which is "Unity and Diversity".

There is a coat or arms embedded in the Bird's body. It consists of five related emblems which represent five principles. These are called the "Pancasila Principles" (Sanskrit) and are the foundation of the Indonesian Nation and are supposed to guide the decisions and actions of the government and the citizens.

The five emblems are:-

The Central Star – The Oneness of God
The Chain – Humanitarianism
The Banyan Tree – National Unity
The Bull's Head – The People's representation and Consensus
The Twigs of Rice and Cotton – Social Justice

The Garuda has flown very far. He has carried the God Visnu, he has been the Sultan's vehicle and now carries the state philosophy of Pancasila and the state's motto of Bhineka Tunggal Ika (Unity in diversity). He also carries passengers under the secure wings of Garuda Indonesia, the National Airline!!

Now to get back to Mackie business. To assist Jim Champion a local by the name of K.M. Tedokoesoemo was employed by Calico Printers. He resided in Jakarta and for simplicity was known as "Ted" or Tedjo". As his name suggests he was a pure Indonesian, but like many of his compatriots spoke English fluently. While Tedjo had the right contacts in government circles and was an extremely nice person, he had not the necessary business acumen so Jim Champion also engaged the services of a Chinese businessman who was a very shrewd operator. His Chinese name was Dr Oey Jam Oey, known to me and the Mackie boys as Oey. However, when speaking to government officials we had to be careful to use his Indonesian name of Dr U Wijandana, as the Indonesian Government officials were very fastidious about nationals adhering to their foreign names.

When I first visited Indonesia there were three Government owned jute mills all equipped with Mackie machinery, the one I have already referred to in East Java and the other two in Central Java. During the period of my involvement contracts were negotiated for three privately owned factories, the proprietor of one being a Mr Probo Sutedjo the brother of President Suharto. Most of the negotiations for his project took place in his residence.

It is regrettable that the British government was never fully aware of the valuable contacts that Mackie established in many overseas countries, furthermore, they did not appreciate the very considerable amount of foreign exchange earned by the company. However, one must remember that the members of the Mackie family were not keen on publicity, indeed I understand that Mr Jim declined when nominated for a knighthood, nevertheless, I get very angry when reminded of Harold Wilson's remarks about the people of Northern Ireland being "spongers".

Good relationships were cultivated with the senior executives in the government department responsible for the Jute industry for which I used the abbreviated name P.N.P. XVII particularly with the President Director Mr Sutedjo also the Production Director Ir (Engineer) Soedarsono. I recall on one occasion negotiating a contract with these two gentlemen. Bargaining commenced about 9 am and after some friendly "toing and froing" we reached an agreement around 11 am. I was then somewhat taken aback when Mr Sutedjo said, "now Mr Jebb go away and have the contract typed and return to my office at 2.30 pm this afternoon. We will then sign the contract and you can entertain my colleagues and I to a celebratory dinner this evening".

This presented a problem as Calico Printer's office was in Surabaya so we had no typing facilities in Jakarta. "Tedjo" decided to phone a friend to see if she would be available and fortunately she agreed to do the work. She was instructed to take a taxi directly to Hotel Indonesia, which should have taken about fifteen to twenty minutes, but we did not take into account the traffic gridlocks as lunchtime approached. Mid-day came, then 12.30 and 1.00 pm. Meantime "Tedjo" and I bit our nails, walked to and fro in the room, and frequently looked out the window!! Why we did so I don't know as all taxis looked the same and even if it had distinguishing marks it would have been impossible to pick it out in the traffic jam outside the hotel. The lady arrived about ninety minutes before the deadline and typed like a demon, enabling Tedjo and I to get to the Government office only about five minutes late. The contract was signed without further ado and a good dinner enjoyed by all concerned that evening.

When Calico Printers curtailed their activities in Indonesia the Mackie Agency was transferred to Dr Oey's company P.T. Winiharto which continued to handle the business when Leslie Vize took over. The Oey or Wijandana family was quite unique. Oey himself was an extremely sharp businessman being able to "run with the hare and hunt with the hounds". His wife Tiang, also Chinese, was a very competent lawyer and eventually became a High Court Judge in Darwin, Australia. When Oey decided to take up residence in Singapore, it was his daughter rather than his son who assumed responsibility for P.T. Winiharto. She seemed to have inherited the brains of her mother and the acumen of her father. I don't know if the company is still in existence.

SOCIALIST REPUBLIC OF VIETNAM

A united country

As mentioned in the section on South Vietnam, the war in that country ended in April 1975 and totally unexpectedly less than a year later, in fact towards the end of March 1976, Mackies were contacted by a businessman called Henry Guy, from the City of London, whose company, City Merchants, had already been engaged in trade with Vietnam by handling the export of timber from that country. The purpose of Henry Guy's phone call was to inform Mackies that the Government in Hanoi was interested in setting up a factory for the manufacture of jute carpets for export to Russia. They obviously were fully aware of the performance of the existing Jute Mills in Saigon then renamed Ho Chi Minh city and had specified our company in particular.

It was arranged that I should accompany Mr Guy on a visit to Vietnam to pursue the matter. Plans were quickly drawn up for the trip, so on a date mutually decided I met Henry at Heathrow Airport. I cannot recall how we decided to identify one another but in any event there were no hitches in the arrangement. Henry turned out to be a very affable person with a permanent smiling face, so we hit it off from the moment we met and became firm friends. The idea was that we would fly firstly to Bangkok, where visas would be obtained for Laos and Vietnam. At that time direct flights from Bangkok to Hanoi were very infrequent so it was more practical to travel via Vientiane, Laos.

In accordance with the policy of Henry's Company we travelled economy class but chose Singapore Airlines because of the excellent service in both classes. Having arrived early at Heathrow Airport we were able to choose good seats right at the front of the economy section. I had my preference of an aisle seat, while Henry was quite happy with a centre seat, a lady passenger being at the window. I mention these details to relate an amusing incident during the flight. Before boarding the flight Henry mentioned that he found it difficult to sleep on board an aircraft, and in response I told him that I "could sleep on the edge of a razor blade"!! and perhaps I could suggest a "palliative" to him.

Shortly after we boarded in the afternoon when the stewardess came along and enquired if we would like an aperitif before dinner I suggested to Henry that he should join me in a dry martini, gin based. When he agreed I quietly told the stewardess to make it a double, "straight up". Henry obviously enjoyed the drink, and despite my advice to sip it and savour the taste, he consumed it like a long drink and decided to have a second. The result was that when Henry was only halfway through dinner he started nodding off, also tended to lean over towards the lady on his left, who after several attempts to push him back was not at all amused. Eventually the stewardess removed Henry's tray and got him propped up, so he slept soundly for a good part of the flight. I can't remember if I then discovered that Henry snored quite loudly when he slept, but I certainly did later when I shared a room with him. Indeed he not only snored, there was a cacophony as he also grunted and whistled!

After a couple of days in Bangkok Henry and I flew by Thai Airways AVRO 748 to Vientiane, where we also spent several days, appraising the commercial attaché at the British Embassy of our movements. We also had dinner with the Ambassador and his wife. I had an interesting experience whilst there. For some reason when we produced our passports to one of the Embassy staff, he took one look at mine and then said "that's a good surname, I also am a Jebb". We were not able to determine if we were related.

I well remember our arrival at the Hanoi Airport which then was very antiquated having no landing lights nor modern navigational equipment. Any aircraft arriving after sunset was guided in by an old fashioned searchlight mounted on a truck, similar to those used during World War Two to spot enemy aircraft. The terminal building was also very basic. On disembarking we were handed two forms to complete. The immigration form was fairly routine but the customs questionnaire was something else!! There were two A4 size pages on which we had to list virtually every item in our luggage almost down to paper clips and safety pins!! Strangely enough they did not seem to be interested in bottles of duty free scotch and brandy we had brought in. Furthermore, it seemed evident that most of the customs officers did not understand the details entered on the forms as they gave them a casual glance and promptly cleared the suitcases. Probably the main purpose of the form was to put on record the traveller's cheques and foreign exchange brought in by the passenger, thereby trying to prevent the expansion of the black market in currency.

During our first visit to Hanoi Henry and I were met at the airport and looked after by a government official from one of the State Trading

Organisations who was responsible for hotel accommodation and transport, as at that stage there was no unallocated hotel space and no taxi service. The functions of foreign embassies was also little understood, so we were not put in touch with the British Embassy during that visit and we considered it unwise to short circuit our hosts and go independently to the Embassy. We later established a good relationship with the Ambassador and his staff.

Our hosts, the Ministry of Textiles, booked Henry and I into a local hotel which had previously been a Monastery. It was very basic but spotlessly clean. Our "rooms" were cubicles which had been created by partitioning a large hall. Each cubicle was furnished with a bed, a wardrobe and a wash-hand basin in the corner. If I recall correctly there were no doors on the cubicles, but simply curtains. However, we weren't worried as strict honesty then prevailed in Vietnam. My most vivid memory of our stay there was when each evening, as we relaxed before dinner I took a whisky soda into Henry. After the first sip he would gaze towards the ceiling with a look of pleasure on his face and exclaim "Nectar from the Gods"!!

Our discussions took place with a committee of six people from the Ministry of Textiles and were very straightforward despite being through translation, although several of the committee spoke English quite fluently. They simply told Henry and I that they wished to have a proposal for a complete factory, including buildings and other accessories to manufacture Jute yarn to supply existing carpet looms which were located in small units in the surrounding towns and villages as a "Cottage Industry". The cheap carpets produced were for export mainly to Russia. The technicalities were discussed and a ballpark figure of the cost was given. The committee members expressed satisfaction with the discussions and provided me with a "Letter of Intent" to Mackies pending the submission of a detailed quotation. The whole procedure took less than a week, consequently, when I returned to Belfast David Chamberlain and Bryan Hall expressed surprise that things had gone so smoothly. Of course one had to keep in mind that "Letters of Intent" don't always result in a contract!!

It took around two months to prepare the quotations as prices had to be obtained from other suppliers for equipment not manufactured by Mackies, in particular for the buildings from Taylor Woodrow Exports Limited. When all the details had been assembled in an attractive package, arrangements were made for Henry Guy and I to revisit Hanoi and Bryan Hall proposed that Leslie Vize should join us from Bangkok as he had got to know the British Ambassador in Vietnam, apart from that it was logical that Leslie should accompany us, Vietnam being in his area. Of course by this stage the Vietnamese Embassy in London was fully aware of what was going on so visas were issued expeditiously.

Furthermore the Ministry of Textiles must have enhanced our status as on this second visit we were booked into the only "modern" hotel in Hanoi, the "Tang Loi" or Victory Hotel. I use the term modern relatively, as it had been built by the Cubans, indeed was probably a gift from the Castro government and merited a one star grading. However, the bedrooms were air-conditioned and were ensuite. It was also in a very pleasant location on the edge of a lake. Of course as previously, transport and a "guide" were provided by our hosts.

We checked into the hotel in the late afternoon and decided to unpack and have a shower before dinner. I had just showered and dressed when there was a knock on my bedroom door. I opened it to find a tall grey-haired European gentleman standing with something wrapped in a sweater under his arm. There was immediately a look of recognition on his face and he said "Jebb of Bangkok Jute Mill;" how surprising!! He, Bob Tesh, had been the Commercial Attaché in the British Embassy in Bangkok when we negotiated the contract for the Prime Minister's Jute Mill and helped me to get approval from London for the relevant bank guarantees. He was now British Ambassador to Vietnam and had come to the hotel to welcome us to Hanoi, the parcel under his arm being a bottle of scotch from the Embassy supply. He was fully aware of the purpose of our visit and asked us to keep in touch with him, which naturally we agreed to do.

The negotiations on this occasion were prolonged. The two parties discussed the proposal which I submitted primarily the technical aspects thereof. Drawings of the proposed site and other necessary data were provided. The site chosen for the new factory was a place called Thai Binh, which was located about 100 Km. (60 miles) South East of Hanoi. When all technical details were agreed it was suggested by the Vietnamese officials that we, Henry Guy and I, should return to the UK and prepare a final scheme, then return to Hanoi to negotiate a contract. That was in May/June 1976 which was quite amazing as the Vietnamese war had ended only a little over a year previously.

The preparation of a final proposal was quite an undertaking. It entailed getting together representatives of all parties involved, mainly the building contractors Taylor Woodrow Exports Ltd. and the Bankers Grindlays, so that the respective quotations would be properly co-ordinated. The task took around three months consequently all the documents were not ready until the end of September 1976. At the same time a team of qualified people had to be organised, namely technicians, legal and financial experts, also a secretarial person. In addition, as none of the companies involved had an office nor agent in Vietnam, all requisite office equipment and materials from a typewriter down to paperclips had to be taken by the team.

There were no worries whatsoever relative to the secretarial arrangements as there was in Mackies office in Belfast a highly qualified and experienced secretary Margot Wills, who at the time was the Company's Public Relations Executive. Margot had wide experience in the secretarial field having been P.A. to our Sales Director Mr Lavens Mackie, and after his death being responsible for entertainment arrangements for important visitors also for similar facilities at trade exhibitions. A competent team of six was assembled, five men and one lady. A huge amount of luggage was also assembled; Margot and I recall about twenty-eight pieces.

The team set off from Heathrow on 24 October and arrived the following day in Bangkok, where we spent a couple of days obtaining visas for Laos and liaising with Leslie Vize, and then proceeded to Vientiane. There with the assistance of the British Embassy staff travel arrangements for the last leg to Hanoi were finalised. On the 29th October in Vientiane we celebrated Margot's birthday the delicacy on the occasion being boiled eggs!! It was decided that an advance party comprising Henry Guy, Margot and myself should fly to Hanoi to prepare the way for the others. We flew on an executive jet and arrived in Hanoi around 8 p.m. so the plane was guided in with an old fashioned searchlight as already described. I cannot recall how the special flight was arranged or why it was permitted to land

Members of Mackie delegation l to r. Campbell Scotland (Taylor Woodrow), Peter Jakes (Taylor Woodrow), Jim Mawhinney (Contracts), Margot Wills (Secretarial), Henry Guy (City Merchants) and author.

after the airport had shut down. Later events also indicated that neither the British Ambassador in Hanoi nor the Vietnamese officials were aware of these 'special' arrangements.

When we disembarked, or I understand, the modern term, primarily in U.S.A. is deplaned, we found the terminal building in darkness, and that everything had closed down. We were certainly not worried that there would be no immigration or customs checks, but Henry and I were somewhat concerned that there was no government official nor transport waiting for us. Of course for Margot it was all part of a new experience. Henry and I being experienced travellers didn't panic. He headed for the control tower which was still manned and where he assumed the air traffic controller would understand English. I found a public telephone on an outside wall of the terminal building. In any event we both got through to the British Ambassador's residence and Jean Tesh, his wife, answered. When she was informed of the situation she told us to stay put and a couple of cars would be sent to the airport to bring us to the residence where a meal and accommodation would be waiting. From that time the support and the hospitality we received from Bob Tesh and his wife Jean were outstanding.

During the day the time taken to travel by car from Hanoi City to the airport was unpredictable, as there was only one bridge crossing the Red River at that point. This was a massive steel structure providing a road and rail link to the capital. It was in a bad state of disrepair, although as far as I could ascertain it had not been severely damaged by US bombing, nevertheless it seemed to be held together by bits of wire and when a train passed over, the occupants of a car could feel it bouncing! That particular evening the traffic must have been quite light as the embassy cars reached the airport in around forty five minutes. When we arrived at the Ambassador's residence we were warmly welcomed and a hot meal was ready after which Henry and I retired to the guest bedroom, while Margot was accommodated in the library which doubled as a bedroom.

The following day which was a Saturday was spent liaising with the Ministry of Textiles to arrange transport for the other four team members who were due to arrive that evening with most of the luggage. We were assured that a suitable bus had been laid on and rooms booked at a hotel in the port city of Haiphong, which is about 100 Km. (60 miles) East of Hanoi. Henry and I felt that the Tang Loi Hotel in Hanoi would have been preferable, but were simply told that the chosen location was more suitable for meetings between the two parties. On the Ambassador's advice we accepted our hosts' decision. However, our apprehension grew when we saw the old fashioned bus that rolled up to the Embassy that evening. The others arrived in the late afternoon and were certainly not impressed when they saw the mode of transport, but we all had to make the best of the situation. The luggage was piled on the rear seats of the bus and the team accompanied by six or seven government officials occupied the remaining seats. The journey to Haiphong which took about two hours was uneventful, as it was dark so we couldn't see anything, but a couple of us had to stand at the back of the bus and attempt to keep the suitcases from sliding all over the place, as the bus bumped along the pot-holed road. The worst was yet to come!!

The first shock came when we entered the hotel. The main door led into a large central hall badly lit and very shabby. There were lots of Vietnamese about, some at tables having meals and others just milling around. Most of the team were allocated rooms on the ground floor, while Henry and I were given a double-room on the second floor. When I escorted Margot to her room I don't know who was the more shocked, her or me. The room had been painted a dark green many years previously and inevitably the paint was rapidly peeling off. The toilet facilities were a partition about four feet high in the corner of the room with a pipe somewhat higher and bent over like a walking stick, fitted with a tap to turn on the water, obviously cold! There were three single beds with very thin mattresses and rather "grey" sheets. All this was bad enough but to add to the horror there were large cockroaches crawling and jumping all over the place. By that time our hosts had gone to another "Hotel" so we were stuck there over the weekend, and it was necessary to improvise.

The Taylor Woodrow "boys" Peter Jakes and Campbell Scotland had been given a room across the passageway, and as I've said already there were three single beds in Margot's room, so I suggested that they could get ready for bed in their separate rooms, then Peter and Campbell could come and sleep in Margot's. This was mutually agreed as it was the best that could be done under the circumstances. Henry and I then headed to our room on the second floor. The upstairs rooms were built in a "U" shape around three sides of the central hall, with a balcony running round outside instead of a corridor, so the central hall was open right up to the top ceiling. I give these details, so that the reader will understand that any rumpus on the balconies resounded around the huge open space. When Henry and I reached our room we found a group of East Germans sitting round a table right outside the door quaffing beer. They were already pretty well "oiled" and were riotously singing German "Drinking Songs"!! One in particular I remember from my days in Germany "Wer Soll Das Bizahlen!? (Who will pay for us?)". This went on till 2 a.m. but I can't recall how badly or otherwise Henry and I slept. However, we all survived until Sunday morning!!

After a rather unappetizing breakfast we were sitting around a table in the central hall discussing our next course of action, when three visitors arrived. The British Ambassador, Bob Tesh, his wife Jean had driven down to ascertain how things were panning out, and to bring us some "liquid refreshments" They were accompanied by an official from the U.K. Foreign Office who was on a visit to S.R.V. They all agreed that the accommodation was totally unacceptable and that we should make that clear to our Vietnamese hosts on Monday morning. The Ambassador did not say if he intended to take action in his capacity but later events indicated that he probably did intervene.

On the following Monday morning we lost no time in making our feelings known to the Vietnamese officials when they arrived at our hotel. The outcome was that in the afternoon we were on the move again to a place called Dong Chou located on the coast about 100 Km. (60 miles) south of Haiphong. On this occasion additional Vietnamese from various government departments joined the party, consequently there was insufficient room on the bus for all our luggage so it was decided by the Mackie team members to take only sufficient clothing and toilet requisites for one or at the most two nights. The idea was that Jim Mawhinney and Peter Heroys would return to Haiphong the following day to collect the remaining suitcases, which duly happened.

Although Dong Chou was only 100km. (60 miles) from Haiphong the journey took 3.5 to 4 hours, this due to the fact that the Red River had to be crossed by ferry near its estuary. The crossing was a fascinating experience as the ferry was a pontoon type raft towed by a large motorboat, the latter being fastened to the ferry with a wire hawser. The ferry was firstly loaded with buses, trucks, carts and a variety of other modes of transport, and people, and then crushed into the spaces in between. I found myself staring at the wire hawser less then two feet away. Of course when the motorboat moved the hawser became taut and there was considerable strain on it. During the crossing I prayed silently that it would not break and decapitate me!! The way in which the crew navigated the craft across the tidal river and manipulated it to the landing stage on the opposite side was truly amazing!!

The journey which was by daylight enabled us to see something of the countryside, which was quite pleasant with its fields of paddy and other agricultural crops. We were also very pleased to see large areas allocated to the cultivation of kenaf. The landscape was made more picturesque by the background of mountains covered with lush, verdant vegetation. That part of Vietnam has heavy rainfall during the wet season.

The accommodation at Dong Chou was a rest-house for government employees and was what we would call a small motel. It was as expected quite basic, but was very clean and situated in very pleasant surroundings. It certainly provided a more congenial atmosphere for business discussions than the hotel in Haiphong. Furthermore, the building containing the

Members of negotiating team from Vietnamese Ministry of Industry and Textiles with Jim Mawhinney, colleagues and author.

bedrooms and dining hall was elevated on "stilts" so to some extent was protected from "creepy crawlies" and other types of vermin. The food was also quite palatable and cleanly prepared and presented. It was luxury compared to the previous hotel, nevertheless, some improvisation was necessary as the toilet facilities were in a separate building from the bedrooms, so Margot did her morning face washing etc by using the hot water from a large flask provided for drinking purposes. At night Margot got into bed with her handbag and her other personal nick-nacks, also a torch light which I had taken out with me. She then lowered and tucked-in the mosquito net and felt reasonably secure. In the evening the other team members played roulette on a small wheel, which I think Peter Heroys, the banker, had brought with him while I generally read.

There were two weeks of very detailed technical discussions, sometimes tough, but always friendly. All aspects of the processing machinery were discussed with me, the buildings with Peter Jakes, and the electrics with Campbell Scotland and so on. The plan was that the financial arrangements would be taken up later with Jim Mawhinney and Peter Heroys. Of course Margot was at each meeting taking notes. She was fully occupied at other times retyping the sections that had to be revised. All in all Margot fitted in very well and was a useful member of the team. She did not feel dominated by men as there were ladies on the Vietnamese side! Indeed the protocol was signed by the Vice Chairperson of the Thai Binh province Madame Nguyen-Thi-Dinh.

The event was celebrated by a dinner hosted by Madame Nguyen, who during the course of the evening carried on an animated conversation with Margot despite the fact that neither spoke the other's language. After the dinner, which by Vietnamese standards was sumptuous, there was a programme of Vietnamese music and dancing. When we enquired about the theme of the songs which a very attractive young lady sang we were told they were all about their beloved leader Ho Chi Minh. Three examples are "when you are planting rice, think of Ho Chi Minh; when you are fishing, think of Ho Chi Minh; when you are chopping wood, think of Ho Chi Minh", not very profound but understandable in that culture!! As usual, even in socialist countries, the meal was accompanied with plenty of "liquid". In addition to rice wine there was a selection of other "wines" of local vintage. They would not have appealed to the connoisseur but our boys decided to relax after a fortnight of hard work and one of the team decided to enter into the "spirit" of the evening so he participated in the programme by his rendering of the party song "Why was he born so beautiful"! There were also other light moments.

During our stay at Dong Chou when Henry had his first shower, which was above a bath, he as normal left his slippers at the side of the bath. During the shower he looked to see his slippers floating away as the bath was not fitted with a stopper or drain pipe. In the cubicle just behind the lavatory there was an aperture in the wall about ten inches square which was unglazed, for what purpose I don't know. On one occasion when Margot was using the lavatory she glanced back and saw she had an audience, as there was a group of Vietnamese standing on the embankment behind the building gaping down. Margot, being Margot was totally unfazed and decided to give the audience a good view!!

Speaking of the lavatory, Jim Mawhinney has just reminded me of another incident. The lavatory was not fitted with a flush system and there were no toilet rolls provided. Margot in her usual thoroughness had included these in our luggage. When a person went to use the toilet he or she took a bucket of water and a toilet roll. On one occasion when Peter Heroys, who was a typical banker rather precise, was on his way to perform with a bucket of water in one hand and a toilet roll in the other Jim caught him on camera, Peter being totally unaware. The first he knew of it was when he saw the photograph published in the bankers' journal on his return to London.

The last incident I will cite involved Henry Guy. One evening when we had all changed into our night attire there was a power cut. I suggested to Henry that he should cross the compound to the staff quarters and attempt to locate an electrician. Henry being a gentle person and always ready to help went off like a lamb into the inky darkness. I think I gave him the torchlight. Of course he was already wearing his pyjamas, dressing

Grindlay's Bank executive, Peter Heroys with toilet facilities.

gown and bedroom slippers. After a few minutes we heard a commotion and peered into the darkness only to see Henry beating a hasty retreat with a couple of dogs snapping, not at his heels, but at his posterior!!! All in all as a team we had great fun and got along famously.

There is a difference of opinion between the three Belfast members of the team as to when the proposed site for the new factory was visited. In any event it is logical that it took place during our trip south, as the town of Thai Binh where the site was located is about halfway between Haiphong and Dong Chou, around 50 Km. (30 miles) from each. According to Margot we stayed overnight in a military barracks. The visit to the site was essential as I needed to assess its suitability, while Peter Jakes required soil samples. It was also necessary for Campbell Scotland to ascertain the nearest source of electricity for power and lighting. All three objectives were achieved during the visit.

When all technical details were agreed and the protocol signed we were informed by the Vietnamese officials that subsequent negotiations on financial and legal matters would take place in Haiphong consequently we would be moving camp once again. As is often the case in communist countries no explanation for a sudden change of plans is given, and from my previous experience in China I had learned not to ask questions, so the "caravan" set out once again! Fortunately on this occasion our host chose a somewhat better hotel in Haiphong, as usual very basic but smaller and cleaner. The food could be described only as adequate.

The ensuing discussions were held in a nearby government building. The financial terms obviously had to be agreed before the legal section could be drawn up. Inevitably the question of discount, as far as the Vietnamese were concerned topped the list. This was anticipated so Jim Mawhinney and I had discussed what our approach should be. Unfortunately, in this respect I made a major miscalculation by adapting a piecemeal approach. Although we were in a position to offer a sizeable reduction I decided to start him with a minimal discount of 1.5% and gradually increase the percentage during what I expected to be protracted negotiations. This had worked for me on numerous previous occasions, but in this instance I was in for a shock. When I mentioned the figure of 1.5% there were murmurings among the Vietnamese delegates, who then got up from their chairs, exited the room and thereby brought the meeting to an abrupt conclusion. We the Mackie team members were left shocked and nonplussed!! We hoped, admittedly without much optimism, that negotiations would be resumed the following morning, but our "friends" made no contact whatsoever and did not appear as hoped. Somehow we found out that they had already left for Hanoi. If the Vietnamese had planned shock tactics they had been very successful. On the advice of the British Ambassador, we, the Mackie delegation, also returned to Hanoi to regroup. Once again Bob Tesh and his wife gallantly came to our assistance in providing accommodation.

The Vietnamese, who are normally very polite people, had left us "high and dry" in Haiphong without any communication as to the "state of play"! They had also made no arrangements whatsoever for future meetings. Furthermore had it not been for the British Ambassador and his wife we could have found ourselves "homeless". Perhaps this was a further attempt by the Vietnamese to teach us a lesson but it was a rather thoughtless and indeed a very rude way of treating guests in their country. Probably they assumed quite rightly that the Ambassador would not leave us in the lurch. Henry Guy and I were given the guest bedroom at the Ambassador's residence while Jim Mawhinney slept in the library. Other members of the team were given the use of an apartment at the Embassy, there being a couple from the Embassy Staff on home leave.

I cannot recall precisely how negotiations between the two parties were resumed, but I don't think I would be far wrong if I said the Ambassador, Bob Tesh, played some part. In view of the delicate situation I decided not to "carry the can" alone. From the outset it had been planned that Bryan Hall would join the team for final negotiations and for the signing of the contract, so I and my Mackie associates felt that stage had been reached. Indeed if I recall correctly Bryan was already in Bangkok, anticipating a call. Consequently he, accompanied by Leslie Vize, responded very promptly to a telex from me. On Bryan's arrival in Hanoi I appraised him fully about what happened and advised him against any "horse dealing"; rather that he should take only "two bites of the cherry". Keeping in mind that we could afford to go to ten percent I suggested that he should firstly offer 7.5% which in all probability would not be accepted. In that event he should call the bluff of the Vietnamese committee by going up to 10% and by saying if this figure were not accepted, we as a team would pack our bags and leave as he could not afford to go beyond that figure. That approach was adopted by Bryan and had the desired effect. After the 10% offer was made there was silence on our part and muted discussion amongst the Vietnamese. There followed some tense moments, then the Chairman of the committee got up, stretched across the table and shook hands with Bryan. There were then handshakes all round!

It was then all stations go, as the Vietnamese expressed the wish to sign a contract without undue delay. The dining room in the apartment above the Embassy was turned into an office.

I made the necessary revisions to the machinery section of the contract in long hand, which was checked by Henry Guy. Margot and Peter the banker both typed the revised pages. We must have borrowed the second typewriter from the Embassy. The new pages were inserted in the correct order in the folders by Jim and Henry. Peter and Campbell dealt with the building and electrical sections. Leslie Vize plied us with toast, scrambled eggs and coffee to sustain us as the work carried on well into the night. Bryan and the Ambassador were enjoying liquid refreshments, the Ambassador's favourite tipple being pernod and soda.

The technical section of the contract was completed mid-afternoon a couple of days later and turned out to be quite a sizeable document. It was immediately submitted to the Vietnamese committee for vetting. The financial section followed several hours later having been revised by Jim Mawhinney in consultation with Peter Heroys. The Vietnamese went through both documents with a fine toothcomb raising multifarious and sometimes inconsequential points, for example insisting that the word "provide" be changed to the word "supply"; the argument in their opinion being that the word "provide" was not sufficiently conclusive!! It was a torturous process, as the committee members, some of whom were not fluent in English kept a dictionary at the ready and frequently referred to it. At the time of reference an exchange between the Vietnamese in their language would take place!! We on our side had to exercise extreme patience, because as we had already learned the slightest negative move could upset the whole applecart!!

Late in the evening of the second day the Vietnamese expressed their satisfaction. The requisite copies of the two documents were set out neatly on a table and Bryan Hall and the Ambassador were summoned, one to sign and the other to witness, and despite the lateness of the hour the clients insisted on an immediate celebration. This did not surprise me, having had a similar experience in Cambodia. All who had been involved in the negotiations including the British Ambassador retired to a nearby restaurant where a meal had been arranged by our hosts, during which there were numerous "toasts". To facilitate these each guest was provided with a small glass, similar to the type we would use in the UK for taking medicine. These for each "toast" were filled with rice wine which had a real "kick". Each of the Vietnamese from the Chairman down called for a toast and of course the "Mackie" Boys had to respond. On each occasion it was a question of "bottoms up"!! This had to be for real as the polite gesture was to hold the small glass between the index finger of each hand and turn it towards the proposer to show that it had been emptied.

At the outset Bryan Hall indicated that he would prefer "scotch" to rice wine. This was readily provided but was poured neat into Bryan's little glass. When he downed the first drink it hit the back of his throat like a detonator, causing him to cough and splutter into his "hankie". He looked across the table in amazement as I appeared to be knocking back the rice wine like a veteran. He was unaware that I, having learned a lesson in China three years earlier, had a bottle of soda water under the table from which I surreptitiously replenished my little glass on each occasion. I cannot recall clearly how Bryan resolved his problem. He probably asked for a bottle of soda water and used a larger glass to mix the whisky and soda to refill his small glass. In any event the party passed pleasantly and concluded well after midnight.

During Bryan's visit of several days there were some rather amusing incidents. The Australian Ambassador had kindly agreed that Bryan and Leslie could stay at his residence. They slept and had breakfast there but joined the team for the rest of the day. One evening when most of us were busy at the Embassy, Bryan and Leslie remained with the British Ambassador at his residence and inevitably indulged in their favourite tipples. When we called it a day at nearly midnight, Henry and I decided that on our return to the residence we would attempt to reach our bedroom without being inveigled into the drinking party. I should explain that the Teshs lived on the first floor, and the rooms were located around an octagonal landing. Each room had what we in India called bat-wing doors, with small square windows in the upper half. The lower panes of glass were generally painted to provide privacy in the bedrooms. Henry and I managed to reach our bedroom undetected and quietly unfolded and closed the doors.

The room where the trio were drinking was directly across the landing, so Henry and I decided to have a peep to see the "goings-on". Over the years wee peepholes had been scratched in the paint so we got down on our knees and each looked through one of these, and the sight that met our eyes was quite amusing. A rather animated discussion was in progress across the table, although each participant was depending very much on the table to keep himself upright! Perhaps, "his Excellency" was the worst of the wear!! It was probably around 1 a.m. when they finally "gave in", and what followed was a bit of a pantomime. The three staggered down the stairs and apparently the Ambassador insisted that he should drive

Bryan and Leslie to the Australian Embassy. Bob Tesh just about made it to his car, at which point Jim Mawhinney came out of his room and intervened. He managed to dissuade the Ambassador from attempting to drive his car and suggested that Bryan and Leslie should walk to their "digs". Apparently when the two "Boys" were left to their own devices an argument ensued. One said they should go left while the other maintained the correct way was to the right. I don't know to this day how or at what time they made it to the Australian Embassy. However, they turned up next day safe but I would not say "well"!!

On a day off, it may have been a Sunday, or possibly a national holiday, our guests proposed that we could either visit a place of historical note, or go to the National Mausoleum to see their late President Ho Chi Minh lying in state. His embalmed body lay on an elevated platform behind thick glass for viewing. It was lowered each evening into an air-conditioned crypt. We decided in favour of a visit to the Mausoleum. When we arrived there was a queue four deep and several hundred yards long, kept in order by smartly dressed military guards. Despite being government guests we had to take our place at the back of the queue. At that time Bryan still smoked and as the queue moved slowly forward he lit a cigarette and put his other hand in his trouser pocket, indeed all of us moved in a relaxed manner. However, when we reached the bottom of the steps leading to the Mausoleum one of the guards brusquely told Bryan to extinguish the cigarette and take his other hand out of his pocket, he also ordered everybody to keep their hands by their side.

On entering the Mausoleum the queue became single file under the instructions of yet another guard. The visitors then proceeded down the left-hand side of the catafalque, around the end and returned on the right-hand side. They were not allowed to stop or turn towards the catafalque. It was simply eyes right like a military salute, a rather regimented but interesting experience.

When everything had been signed, sealed and settled it was quite an undertaking to get the team, which had increased to eight, back to Bangkok, where they split up and went different ways. In the section on Laos I mentioned the experiences some members of the team had on a stopover in Vientiane which I won't repeat. On the way back to the UK Margot and Jim had the opportunity to stop off for a few days in Calcutta to see the Mackie/Lagan set-up there and to meet some Indian friends particularly Mrs. Nilima Dutta and her wider family circle. It was my responsibility to carry the contractual documents to Belfast and there was a rather serious incident before they and I landed back safely in the Mackie office. I reached Belfast late one evening, so did not hurry into the office the following morning. It was around 11 a.m. when I was approaching

Members of Mackie delegtion on visit to Ho Chi Minh Mausoleum.

Mackies by a side street, to avoid the traffic on the main Springfield Road. I was less than a quarter of a mile from the factory when two men stepped out in front of the car. When I lowered the window I was informed by one of the men that they were taking over my car in the name of the I.R.A. In response I told him that I was expected at Mackies in a matter of minutes, also that on the rear seat were very valuable documents. My remonstrations were of no avail, and I dared not take the risk of making a dash for it, not knowing if the men were armed.

It is not appropriate to go into all the details of what followed, as I mention the incident only to show the risk to which the contractual documents were exposed. It is sufficient to say that I was held in a nearby house while my car was used to transport a bomb to blow up the Queen's University bookshop. Before being released I was informed where to find my car, and that it was undamaged, furthermore, that the important papers were stacked neatly in the luggage boot. I followed the instructions given to me very precisely, having been warned by the I.R.A. not to deviate. It turned out to be a considerable walk as the car had been parked at some distance from the scene of the hijacking. However, I found the car undamaged, the keys in the glove compartment and the copies of the contract in the boot, consequently, the documents had quite a circuitous and eventful journey from Hanoi to Belfast!

The next stage was to specify and order the machinery and other equipment, for which I was very fortunate to have the advice and assistance of my long time colleague and close friend Joe McClelland who had many years of experience in that field. When the time came Joe was the obvious choice to supervise the erection of the buildings and installation of the equipment.

Of course while the equipment was being manufactured other events directly connected with Vietnam were taking place. While on home leave early in 1977 Robert and Jean Tesh were invited to Belfast. They arrived on the 25th January for a two day stay and were royally entertained under the supervision of Margot. They stayed in the guest house at Bryan Hall's residence, but were wined and dined in several of Belfast and district best hotels. The Ambassador had a tour of the Mackie factory while Margot took his wife shopping. His visit culminated with an interview for BBC Northern Ireland.

The next event was a visit to Belfast by a Vietnamese Government Delegation under the auspices of Henry Guy, our agent who accompanied them from London. That visit took place at the end of April 1977 and lasted four days. Margot and I welcomed the visitors at the Belfast International Airport, and I vividly recall the special arrangements we considered necessary, not only because of the importance of the visitors

H.E. British Ambassador Robert Tesh and his wife, Jean, on visit to Mackies in Belfast. l to r. Jim Mawhinney, author, Jean Tesh, Margot Wills, Robert Tesh and Bryan Hall, Mackie sales director.

but also having in mind the prevailing political situation in Northern Ireland. It must have been a fairly large delegation as the Company's two Rolls Royces and the one Bentley were utilised rather than some of the smaller cars in the fleet. As indicated by my experience hijackings were not uncommon at that time and it was realised that three large limousines in procession were bound to attract attention so as a precaution we took a rather circuitous route from the airport to the factory. Furthermore by radio contact the cars were kept well apart.

Meetings with the delegation were held not only at the works, but discussions also took place during evening meals in restaurants. Peter Jakes the representative of the building contractors, Taylor Woodrow, came over from London for some of these meetings. The members of the delegation also visited the Belfast City Hall to meet the Lord Mayor and were presented with gifts, including a plaque bearing the City Coat of Arms. The visitors left for London in the late afternoon of the 28th April after a successful visit.

There was a sequel to this visit which did not go so well. Henry Guy's company, City Merchants, felt that they too should show hospitality to the Vietnamese visitors while they were in London. They arranged a reception for 5 p.m. one afternoon in their city office and invited me as a guest. When I arrived in good time I found that City Merchants had really "gone to town". A well stocked bar and a very delicious looking buffet had been set up in their office and all company directors were present and waiting. Five o'clock came and went and the special guests did not arrive. In certain

Vietnamese government delegation on visit to Mackie in Belfast.

Vietnamese delegation meeting Belfast Lord Mayor, Sir Myles Humphreys.

countries in the Far East particularly China it is polite to arrive a little late in case the host is not fully prepared, but never beyond ten minutes.

The Vietnamese invitees eventually put in an appearance at around 5.30 p.m. without any apologies for their lateness. To make matters worse they sipped at soft drinks and refused to touch the excellent food that had been specially prepared. After little more then half an hour they made some feeble excuse and left. Poor Henry naturally was very embarrassed in front of his directors and other visitors. Probably I was the only one who fully understood the situation having already experienced Vietnamese rudeness. It is to be hoped that the Vietnamese now being engaged more widely in international trade will have learned something about business ethics and protocol.

It was normal procedure for Mackies to offer training facilities at their Belfast factory for an appropriate number of students from a country which ordered an appreciable quantity of machinery and equipment. An offer was made to and accepted by the Vietnamese authorities responsible for the Jute Mill Project. The six students chosen arrived in Belfast in October 1977 for a two months course and were placed under the care of Mr. Harry McConnell – the Students' counsellor, who himself had been an Outside Erector (installation engineer) for many years. The Vietnamese students were unique in several respects. Firstly they had made the long journey from Hanoi to a French port by train, then by ferry and train to Belfast, a trip of several weeks duration. Obviously their government had decided that they could not afford the cost of air travel. While in Belfast Mackies paid for accommodation and food and gave the students a small allowance, as pocket money.

The Vietnamese knew how to economise so they were able to save sufficient to purchase what to them were luxuries such as cameras and radios. Strangely, although bicycles are common in Vietnam some purchased modern western cycles. Getting them back to Vietnam by ferry and train would have been difficult if not impossible, so Harry McConnell had the extra task of arranging for the cycles and larger items purchased to be packed and shipped with the machinery. How the students dealt with the customs and excise at the other end I don't know!!

Despite the fact that their 'digs' were at least four miles walk from the Mackie factory the students chose to walk rather than use public transport. When driving home one used to see them sauntering along, not in a group, or even in pairs, but strung out in a single file, with some distance between each, an eastern habit! On one occasion I called into an off-licence near where the students stayed and found each buying a can of beer. To the consternation of the manageress they split open the cans inside the shop and began to drink. The manageress began to panic, fearing that if a policeman or inspector were to walk in she would lose her

Vietnamese students who came to Mackies in Belfast for training. Mackie staff members in group. Second from right back row – Harry McConnell (Student counsellor). Extreme right – Jim Mawhinney (Contracts manager).

licence. As she talked excitedly and waved her arms, the Vietnamese stood nonchalantly enjoying their beer. I came to the rescue by ushering them out of the shop.

For Harry McConnell the students' supervisor there was many amusing, but also harrowing incidents. Harry's placid nature and sense of humour saw him through so the course finished and the students were sent on their way without any major mishaps!!

In August 1977 Henry Guy and I again made a trip to Vietnam to ascertain how the erection and installation were going. This obviously involved a visit to the factory site at Thai Binh. As already indicated Joe McClelland had been put in overall charge of the project, and was accompanied by his wife Iris, as after their two sons had grown up and got married she had decided to go with Joe whenever practical. Mackies considered this as a wise decision and fully supported the couple financially and otherwise. Together Joe and Iris had some amazing, indeed hair-raising experiences. For example they had been in Nigeria during the civil war and had worked in Cambodia after "The Killing Fields" struggle. On the latter occasion they had an armed escort when travelling!! As a result of her many experiences Iris had become a master, or should I say a "Mistress of improvisation".

At Thai Binh the McClelland's had been provided with a small "suite" in a typical Vietnamese hotel. The word "suite" is a misnomer as the accommodation comprised a bedroom, bathroom, and a small sitting area all very basically furnished. There was no kitchen, consequently no cooking or washing facilities. However, Iris was not fazed. During our visit she provided an excellent meal for Henry and me cooked on an electric hotplate and served on the bed. She washed our shirts and underclothes, using what Joe called an "automatic" washboard, the clothes being propelled by Iris's hands.

For the installation of the processing machinery Joe had a team of three Mackie erectors, who stayed in a separate hotel some distance from the factory. I considered it appropriate to visit them at their "digs" so Henry and I did so on a Sunday afternoon accompanied by Joe. It was a hot day so we found the "boys" stripped to the waist sitting on the balcony outside their rooms and quaffing beer. Despite the fact that their surroundings were primitive and there was no form of entertainment the erectors seemed to be reasonably happy. Mackie erectors learned to be very versatile and generally speaking were willing and able to adapt to any conditions within reasonable limits. The job was also progressing well and there were no complaints from the management.

Over ensuing months it was necessary for me to visit S.R.V. on several occasions but I will refer to only one more. For some financial reason, I can't recall the problem precisely, I had to accompany Peter Heroys, the banker, on a visit to Hanoi. For some reason we did not share the guest room at the Ambassador's residence as Henry and I had done during previous visits. Peter stayed above the Embassy and I at the residence. During our stay our Vietnamese hosts informed us that we were being taken to a mountain resort for a couple of days. It was not an invitation or a suggestion, but a statement of fact. On yet another occasion we found our hosts' plans rather puzzling. It was our desire to conclude the business on the agenda as quickly as possible so that our stay would not be unnecessarily protracted. Once again no questions asked and the Ambassador's advice taken to acquiesce!! For some inexplicable reason it was not opportune for Peter and I to be in Hanoi.

Perhaps our hosts noticed our hesitancy as they went out of their way to assure us that we were going to a popular mountain resort and would stay in a nice hotel where we could relax. Due to our previous experiences all these assurances were taken with a "pinch of salt". Right from the outset our misgivings were justified. After a not particularly pleasant journey we arrived at the "Hotel" to find it occupied by an East German delegation who objected to two "Britishers" taking up residence. Yet again we were told not to worry as nearby there was a government Swiss type chalet which could be opened specially for us. "Swiss type" it might have been in design but certainly not hygienically. When the doors and shutters were opened out flew bats, and inside was a profusion of cobwebs and insects.

The bats and creepy crawlies did not worry Peter and I unduly but two other discoveries were rather alarming, one a hornets nest in the verandah door and two the lice infested beds. When we drew our host's attention to the former we were assured that hornets in Vietnam were harmless and did not sting. As to the bed lice they were, well they were not abnormal!! Off went our "friends" we knew not where!! They promised to return in the evening and take us elsewhere for dinner. Once again it was a question of making the best of it.

After a rather unappetizing dinner we returned to the "chalet" around 10 p.m. which was for us decision time. Peter said that having been in the British army bed bugs didn't worry him, so he spread his bath towel on one of the beds and lay down hoping to sleep. I was not so blasé so I put on all the clothes that I had brought in an attempt to keep warm, as it was quite cold up the mountain, with the intention of spending the night on one of the wicker chairs. As the night wore on sleep began to overtake me, so I gave in, spread my large towel on the other bed and lay down without a covering as the available blankets were probably also "crawling". However, as the temperature dropped both Peter and I decided to risk using the blanket. This had the desired effect of creating heat, but with disastrous results. The warmth enlivened the bugs and they began to attack. Almost simultaneously Peter and I jumped out of bed, he uttering some typical army jargon!! Yet again Jean Tesh the Ambassador's wife had risen to the occasion by providing an ice box containing some light refreshments for us. We rummaged through the contents and found a bottle of vodka. We decided some of the liquid would ease the pain, not by rubbing it on the bug bites, but as an internal medication!! The "prescription" certainly worked and quite quickly. It deadened the bites and if any bugs were still clinging to our skin they probably fell off inebriated from the vodka in our blood stream. In any event Peter and I survived till the morning without returning to the "moving" beds also without disturbing the hornets.

When our Vietnamese friends returned to take us for breakfast there were no enquiries as to how we had slept or about our general welfare. They simply told us that we would be returning to Hanoi and left us wondering why they had insisted that we should make that pointless trip. This was another of several inscrutable decisions made by the Vietnamese which taught one to curb one's curiosity in certain countries.

Shortly after this visit the British Ambassador who we had come to know so well was transferred to Ethiopia. He was temporarily replaced by a Lady Charge d'Affaires who befriended only one of the Taylor Woodrow building engineers and was of no help whatsoever to the Mackie erectors. That of course was her business, but what annoyed me immensely was that she recommended the Taylor Woodrow man for an award from the Queen, which should have gone to Joe McClelland. Fortunately we no longer needed diplomatic help having established our own contacts in all sections of the commercial life in Hanoi, also with the Tang Loi hotel so had no problem in securing accommodation.

The negotiations and implementation of the Vietnamese contract were sometimes perplexing but also very challenging. Unfortunately, the Vietnamese government did not honour their financial commitments so the British Treasury had to step in.

It was fascinating for me as I conclude the chapter to listen to the programme on BBC Radio 4, "From Our Own Correspondent", this morning, the first Saturday of 2006. One of the correspondents was reporting from Ho Chi Minh City (Saigon) about the changes that have taken place in that country over the past thirty years, despite the fact that the government is still communist in its basic policies.

I was already aware that a team from the U.S.A. had been allowed to enter the country and to search the former war zones in an attempt to locate the remains of American soldiers who died during the war and whose bodies had not been recovered. However, there have been other significant improvements in U.S. – Vietnam relations. Very recently President Bush has announced that trade relations between the two countries would be normalised thereby enabling S.R.V. to become a member of the World Trade Organisation (W.T.O.). This will also mean that U.S. companies will have more freedom to invest in the S.R.V. Indeed the BBC reporter stated that there was now more foreign investment in Vietnam than in either India or China, which really surprised me!!

The government of Hanoi has to some extent relaxed its opposition to private enterprise, perhaps having observed the success of China in doing so. One example was cited of a Vietnamese who as a young man had been evacuated from the roof of the U.S. Embassy by helicopter as a refugee, but who had returned to his native country when things had settled down. He is now one of the biggest private entrepreneurs in the country.

After the war the S.R.V. had to import rice, one of its staple diets, because the conflict had seriously damaged its agricultural framework. It has now overtaken Thailand as the world's largest rice exporter. It also exports steel, computer components and other industrial products. The new prosperity is demonstrated by the thousands of mopeds that weave their way through the streets of Ho Chi Minh City, many of them carrying complete families. The BBC reporter expressed concern that the mopeds would soon be replaced by cheap cars and that the thought of thousands of Vietnamese flying about in metal boxes was frightening. Indeed similar to Chinese cities, Ho Chi Minh, Hanoi and other large towns could become gridlocked. Prosperity has its plusses and minuses!!

One cannot help but wonder why so many U.S. lives were sacrificed. Had the U.S.A. and the Western Nations in general adopted a different political approach to Ho Chi Minh he may not have become an extreme communist. As a non-political observer one has witnessed the outcome of many blunders made by Western Nations in the Middle and Far East!!

REPUBLIC OF THE PHILIPPINES

The country of over 7,000 islands

THE COUNTRY WAS NAMED "Las Islas Filipinas" (The Philippine Islands) by Ruy Lopez de Villalobos after King Philip II of Spain. Spanish colonial rule began in 1565 and lasted about three centuries until the Philippine Revolution of 1896.

The United States gained possession of the Philippines after the Spanish-American War in 1898 and the Philippine-American War in 1899. The U.S. ruled the country for about five decades. Philippine culture has many affinities with the West. Roman Catholicism is the predominant religion and Filipino and English are the official languages. After the Japanese were defeated in 1945, the Philippines achieved independence from the United States on July 4, 1946.

Early in 1968 while I was still based in Calcutta the Company requested me to visit the Philippines to assess an enquiry relative to the setting up of a small jute mill. The enquiry emanated from a privately owned company, Dacay Enterprises, based in Cebu City, the capital of one of the smaller islands of the Republic, having the same name as the City, Cebu, and located approximately 500 Km. (300 miles) south of Manila. It is reckoned that there are over 7,000 islands in the Group, which is more than twice as many as Indonesia. However, only 462 have an area of one square mile or more!

My first visit took place in April 1968. I flew from Hong Kong to Manila where I was met by a representative of Dacay Enterprises, who had booked a room in the Manila Hilton Hotel where I stayed one night. The next morning I travelled by Philippines Airlines (PAL) internal flight to CEBU, a flight of about one hour. On this route PAL operated a British built jet, a BAC 111 and in all respects but one the flight was quite normal. The exception was quite a shock to a new arrival in the country. Before take-off the stewardess made the usual announcements in English, which is one of the official languages, but added the following codicil; "would all passengers carrying firearms please hand them to the steward". Her male colleague then walked down the aisle with a tray on which the passengers laid their revolvers, pistols etc, which was then taken to the flight deck. The Philippines, I understand, is still a "trigger happy" country!! I will say more about this later.

The proprietor of the Company in Cebu was a Philippine National of Chinese origin who had adopted a Filipino name, Ernesto Dacay. He was a placid person with a very quiet manner which belied his sharp business brain. At that time there were three companies in his group, one investment, the second industrial and the third marketing. He had two sons in their late teens. The older one, Henry, was a real academic not in the least interested in business. The younger boy, Benson, had a very pleasant disposition, like his father, and was intensely keen on learning all aspects of his father's business. It was he who visited Belfast after the signing of the contract.

Negotiations with Mr. Dacay were very straightforward, as he knew exactly what he wanted, so during my first visit we quickly agreed on the machinery required for the production envisaged. Indeed a very good relationship was established and most day's I had lunch at his home with the family. The food was basically Chinese and very appetising. It was then a matter of having a detailed proposal and contract prepared. I cannot recall whether I requested Belfast to prepare these documents or did the necessary work in Calcutta. In any event a contract was negotiated and signed in a matter of months.

An artist's impression of the mill. Mr. Dacay and author.

Signing of the contract.

Inevitably it was necessary for me to visit the Philippines periodically over the subsequent months so I became a close friend of the Dacay family and enjoyed their hospitality and greatly appreciated Mr. Dacay's confidence in me. This was a valuable relationship as Mr. Dacay was a supporter of the then President Ferdinand Marcos, whose wife Imelda was famous for her wardrobe of shoes, for which she had an obsession. Possibly there was an element of risk in this relationship with the President as Mr. Dacay always carried a loaded revolver which he handed to his driver to lock in the glove compartment of the car, before going into a hotel or restaurant. Come to think of it he must have had great confidence in his driver. As was the case in most countries I visited there were numerous interesting experiences in the Philippines but I will cite only a few which I think will be of interest. On one occasion I was spending a night in the multi storey Manila Hilton Hotel and I had a room near the top. There had been a series of earth tremors previously which didn't particularly worry me. However, the following morning at around 6 a.m. I was wakened by the bed sliding around, and I opened my eyes to see the pictures swinging on the walls. The hotel building seemed to be rotating on its axis. Fortunately it was built with a steel structure to permit it to do so without collapsing. I jumped out of bed, opened the door, and looked along the corridor to see other residents running for the stairway in all sorts of dress and undress. The hotel staff reacted very quickly and reached our floor in a matter of minutes. I took the advice of the staff member to remain calm, get dressed, and proceed to the coffee shop in the ground floor. I left for

Above: *Meal with Mr. Ernesto Dacay (Mill owner) and staff.*

RP Industrial Potential Cited

There is plenty of potential for the industrial and economic development of the Philippines.

This observation was made by W.H.S. Jebb, senior technical consultant of James Mackie & Sons Ltd. for Far East Asia who is now in Cebu to oversee the construction of a textile mill operated by Mackie Industries Corporation in Pakna-an, Mandaue.

Jebb's home company, considered the biggest family corporation in the United Kingdom, is in Belfast, Northern Ireland, but he is based in Calcutta, India.

Comparing the Philippines to less-developed countries like India, Jebb expressed surprise as to why there are not so many industries in the country. He noted that engineering goods and equipment still have to be imported from abroad despite the abundance of natural resources here to support industry.

Jebb pointed out that there is no reason the Philippines should not manufacture even simple machine tools like India is doing. The people of the Philippines, Jebb observed, are highly intelligent and educated, and that the technical as well as academic standards of education here are higher than that in other countries.

At the same time, Jebb saw a bright future for closer economic cooperation between the Philippines and Great Britain. He said there is no question that British capital would come into the country if the facilities and other considerations like the repatriation of profits are sufficiently attractive.

He said there are more reasons for the Philippines to have closer economic ties with Europe than anywhere else considering the country's association with Spain. He also pointed out that Ireland and the Philippines have many things in common, one of them being religion.

Left: *Write-up in local newspaper in Cebu City.*

Cebu as scheduled at 9 a.m. so did not experience the after shocks which occurred in Manila.

After several days I returned to Manila and booked into the same hotel. I was allocated a twin-bedroom and when I entered it I immediately noticed that the dividing wall between the bathroom and the bedroom was badly cracked. I hit it with my fist to test its stability and huge chunks fell on the bed alongside. Without any ado the porter, who had brought in my bags, lifted the phone and called the reception. Within a few minutes two men arrived with a wheelbarrow, a brush and a shovel to remove the debris. I was told that all available rooms were in a similar condition so I didn't remonstrate any further. Needless to say, I slept in the bed furthest from the wall. Just another incident in a rather exhilarating life.

During one of my stays in Manila I had time to do a little sightseeing. One of the places of interest recommended was the museum where the vintage cars of former Presidents were on display. It certainly proved to be fascinating as there were around a dozen limousines of different makes and vintage, quite a few open-topped, all typical American. There was, however, one unique feature; several were pockmarked with bullet holes, as a result of a demonstrator having taken pot-shots at a President. No doubt like the U.S.A. the Philippines has learned a lesson and now provides the President with a bullet-proof, enclosed limousine, nevertheless, it is still dangerous to be a politician in the Philippines. I have watched Senators arriving at the Hilton Hotel with their families to attend functions. When the car draws up at the entrance two guards armed with automatic rifles jump out and position themselves at the ready on each side of the door. Only then does the Senator and his family emerge from the car.

Now to get back to the new factory. When it came to naming the company Mr. Dacay thought he was honouring the Belfast Company by calling it Mackie Industries Corporation. Knowing how conservative our Company and indeed the Mackie family was I tried to discourage him but he could not be dissuaded.

It was towards the end of 1969 when the installation of the machinery commenced, and once again I was fortunate that our most competent erection engineer, Joe McClelland, was available. I can recall that Joe met me in Bangkok to be briefed on the job. We both stayed at the Dusit Thani Hotel which was built in a triangle with a garden and swimming pool in the centre. The enclosure was a sun-trap in good weather but could be otherwise when the wind sprang up. On a lovely morning Joe and I decided to take advantage of the sun by having our discussions by the pool. We found a suitable table and spread out the drawings and other technical papers. We hadn't got very far when the palm trees began to rustle and as the wind increased we had to grab our papers and run for cover. We had just got inside when the sun umbrellas, tables and chairs became airborne and swirled around the enclosed space. Maybe someone in Belfast had heard about the staff members "relaxing" in the sun, and sent the storm!!

When the time came to commission the Plant I decided to visit Cebu once again, to give Joe McClelland some moral support, as he certainly did not need any technical assistance. The Mill Manager who had been appointed was a Filipino of Chinese extraction. He was an eccentric or should I say weird person who indulged in black art. His desk was like an Ouija board with tumblers containing different coloured liquids, also glass "ornaments" of varying shapes. Apparently he moved these objects around on the glass-topped table when he was seeking the guidance of "the spirits". When he learned that the commissioning was about to take place he called me into his office to tell me that he would decide on an auspicious day and date on which the wheels should start turning as guided by "the spirits". In response I told the manager politely but firmly that the decision would be mine as the machinery was still under Mackie's control. He then became quite angry and told me, "without batting an eyelid" that if I precipitated his advice I would die. My retort was that I was quite prepared to take that risk. I then went into the factory and told Joe and his colleagues to set the wheels in motion without delay. The Plant was started-up without any hitch and I'm still alive to tell the tale!

Paradoxically although Mr. Dacay was a devout Roman Catholic and did not indulge in alcohol, or fraternise with the opposite sex, on some evenings he liked to go to a club, sit and sip coca-cola and watch the goings-on. If one of the "hostesses" joined him it was purely for a chat, and an occasional dance. He often invited Joe McClelland to join him. Joe felt it was one way to show his appreciation of Mr. Dacay's kindness. However, as he strictly maintained the same moral standards as Mr. Dacay they must have appeared a rather sober pair among the other guests. The two most popular clubs in Cebu City were the "After Six" and "The Other Place". I understand that these were favourite haunts of the Mackie erectors.

In pursuit of his business Mr. Dacay had to periodically visit Manila. On one occasion when his visit coincided with my stay in the capital, he invited me to join him and several of his Manila staff for a dinner. Inevitably we landed up in a club and the other men called for female companions. Yet again keeping in mind my reputation and that of the company I declined, and said truthfully that I wished to return to my hotel early. Obviously Mr. Dacay mistakenly thought it was shyness on my part and had a word with the "Mama-Saw" (Mother to the Girls). In any event a very attractive beautifully dressed lady pulled up a chair beside me and introduced herself as Gigi. She proved to be highly intelligent and a good conversationalist, so I enjoyed talking to her, and she was quite happy when I made it clear that I had no ulterior motives in mind. I later learned that her full name was Gigi Santiago as many Filipinos have for obvious reasons Spanish names.

The Mackie Industries Jute Mill eventually became the responsibility of the younger son Benson and proved to be a good investment. During one of my visits to Cebu City I was interviewed by a local newspaper and as a matter of interest I've included a copy of the article he wrote.

Sadly I have lost contact with the Dacay family and recent efforts to re-establish correspondence have been futile, nevertheless, I have many happy memories of that country.

THE REPUBLIC OF KOREA

The land of the Yangban

Preface

ANYWHERE YOU GO, YOU may meet a man who will say "I am a yangban. My ancestors were the family of Lee Song-Ke, the founder of the Yi Dynasty". On the other hand, the Kims and Parks will have a similar story in which their forefathers were the Prime Ministers of the provincial governors, etc., in the Yi Court. The point is that all Koreans seem to have names like Kim, Park or Lee. These surnames represent Korea.

One will wonder what a "yangban" in the old days was. To explain briefly, the yangban were one of the classes which existed in the Yi Dynasty and indicated a family which held a title and position in the court or was given a peerage due to a loyal deed. The yangban were, therefore, directly linked to the monarchs, and were associated primarily with loyalty. To say it with one word, the yangban were the ruling class in the old days.

Nowadays, yangban implies the blood of one's family which often becomes an issue when marriage talk begins. The opposite to yangban was sangin which meant lower class and chungin, middle class or commoners.

Koreans who call themselves yangban support their claim by the chopku (family record) and by the sonyong (private cemetery). Everyone has these two in addition to land owned by the family. The land ownership is no longer considered as a criterion of being a yangban since the Land Reformation Law of 1946.

—∞—

During the thirty years I was involved in Mackie business in the Far East no orders for our machinery were secured from Korea. This may have been attributable to the fact that most of the textile factories in that country were processing wool, which was one of the two natural fibres for which Mackie did not manufacture machinery, the other being cotton. However, there was one flax mill which had installed Mackie equipment around 1950, which was before my time. According to one of my younger colleagues, Gilbert Watt, who is still involved in the textile machinery business, this company purchased some Wet Ring Spinning around 1990. At approximately the same time, a new company named Dong Yang Textiles, purchased some modern Preparing and Wet Spinning machinery.

During the lean period, in fact in early 1967 it was proposed that I should visit Korea to see if that market could be revived.

My visit took place in April 1967 and was of a week's duration, during which I contacted as many as possible of the dozen Textiles Companies then in operation. Korea was not then industrialised to the extent that it is today nor had it opened up to Western Companies or tourists on the scale which has prevailed in the late 1990's and the early 2000's. The Capital Seoul (Soul) was also a relatively small city with very few large international hotels.

All correspondence with Korea was channelled through a Trading Company in Seoul, which had the English name of Claggett Nolan Co., Incorporated. I'm not aware of the history of that Company, but it could well have been the overseas branch of a U.S. or British Company, more likely the former as at the time of my visit the General Manager was a businessman of German extraction. He had two assistants, a Mr. Woo Yong Hahn and a Mr. C. S. Park, the former being the senior of the two. I was looked after by Mr. Hahn who spoke excellent English.

Direct flights from Hong Kong to Seoul were then not as frequent as now so I flew via Tokyo. I stayed overnight at an airport hotel, so did not see anything of that large metropolis. Furthermore, I did not otherwise have an opportunity of visiting Japan as that country was under the jurisdiction of David Chamberlain, and Mackie had not only a local agent but also a resident engineer by the name of Sammy Spratt.

In Seoul Mr. Hahn had booked a room for me in one of the smaller hotels. After meeting me at the airport and seeing me ensconced in the hotel, Mr. Hahn discussed our programme and left me to unpack and rest. I had just got organised and was about to settle down for the night when there was a knock on the bedroom door. When I opened it I found a young Korean "Lady" standing there who proceeded to offer her services, which were firmly, but I hoped politely declined. Korea was the only country in all my travels where such services came to the bedroom door on their own initiative.

Visits to the offices of a considerable number of companies were arranged by Mr. Hahn. Friendly and interesting discussions took place but no business resulted. Several years after Bryan Hall decided that a former member of the Calcutta Staff, Eric Totten, should be based in Hong Kong so that a more concentrated effort could be made in countries in that area, including Korea, to secure business particularly for what Mackie termed their Semi-Worsted Machinery. That also did not result in any substantial orders.

My host Mr. Hahn was very friendly and hospitable as indeed I found most Koreans. He asked if one evening I would like a really authentic Korean meal, and of course I was most enthusiastic about the suggestion being always keen on any new experience. On entering the restaurant chosen by Mr. Hahn we were shown to a downstairs room of around twenty-five square metres. There was no furniture apart from a low table, which could be described as a coffee table. The floor was covered with what appeared to be wax paper which was highly polished and spotlessly clean. It was explained that I should sit cross-legged on the floor, which I could then do with relative ease, as I was only in mid-life. It was otherwise very comfortable there being under-floor heating.

Naturally I left it to Mr. Hahn to choose the dishes. The food was served by two very attractive Korean young ladies and I use that term meaningfully, as they had impeccable manners and spoke English fluently and correctly. They were dressed in beautiful traditional costumes which according to fashion experts cannot be compared to women's dresses in any other part of the world. The long skirt covering the ankles and the short blouse tied with bows on the chest are charming and different. The Korean names for the three parts of the ladies' costume are Chagori, Chima, and Trumagi respectively. For many years Korean girls have been taught in the home the art of dressmaking and other needle-work such as making embroidered pictures and a variety of household items. Nowadays this training generally speaking no longer takes place in the home but is part of the curriculum in Girls' High School.

Now to get back to the restaurant, and the two hostesses. It was quite clear to me that these girls were not there for any ulterior purpose and should be treated with the greatest decorum, not that I had the intention of doing otherwise. They brought each course and daintily served the food sitting on the floor beside us.

They also entertained us by singing and when they learned I was from Ireland, one of them sang "When Irish Eyes are Smiling" in a beautiful melodious voice. I cannot recall the meal precisely, but no doubt there was kimichis, which is a shrimp dish highly spiced, also pugoki which means marinated beef. The cooked beef is usually dipped in soya sauce. There is also another dish which is very popular called simsollo which could also be described as Korean stew as it contains meat, a wide selection of vegetables and a variety of nuts. Korean food is unique but very tasty and nourishing.

The evening was so enjoyable that I felt a token of appreciation to the girls other than money was called for. I asked Mr. Hahn if an invitation to join us for lunch the following day would be misunderstood and he assured me that such an invitation would not be misinterpreted, on the contrary would be appreciated, so arrangements were made for the four of us to meet at lunchtime the next day. The two young ladies turned up again beautifully attired, but on this occasion in Western costumes. We had an excellent and a most interesting conversation and I looked back on it as one of the most pleasant experiences of my travelling life.

I left Korea unfortunately with no business prospects but with very pleasant memories.

Korean delegation on visit to Belfast, April 1977.
Mackie staff in photograph.
Extreme left – Major John McConnell, assistant sales director.
Fourth from left – Desmond Morgan – head of wool and semi-worsted sales.
Sixth from left - Nigel Shannon - semi-worsted sales.
Extreme right – Bertie Hunt – research and development.

HONG KONG AND MACAU

Preface
Hong Kong

FORMERLY A BRITISH CROWN Colony, dependency of the United Kingdom, and member of the Commonwealth of Nations, Hong Kong consists of three main areas of land – the island of Hong Kong (29 square miles), the peninsula of Kowloon (3.5 square miles), and the adjoining New Territories (365.5 square miles) which border the People's Republic of China – as well as Stonecutters' Island and hundreds of small islands (mostly uninhabited), altogether totalling some 400 square miles. Between the island and the mainland lies the magnificent and almost land-locked harbour.

After the vicissitudes of the Anglo-Chinese ('Opium') wars, Hong Kong Island was formerly ceded to the British in 1842; in 1860 Kowloon was added; in 1898 a 99-year lease was granted to Britain for the New Territories. For almost fifty years Hong Kong remained a sleepy colony, of late-Georgian and Victorian buildings, of graceful villas set in rich, bright gardens, with tree-lined streets along which sedan chairs and rickshaws passed at a leisurely pace. As time went on, the protection of the Royal Navy and the establishing of British commercial practice and free trade began to attract great numbers of Chinese merchants and skilled workers to the area. At the Colony's foundation the population was a meagre 5,000; by 1898 it had reached the 250,000 mark; in 1921 it was over 600,000; by 1941 it had grown to over 1.5 million. Then came the Japanese occupation (Christmas 1941) and surrender (August 1945). The war severely disrupted public services and brought commercial activity to a standstill but the British administration took control again, and began a programme of recovery. Artisans, traders, and other Chinese from surrounding areas came to the Colony in ever-growing numbers.

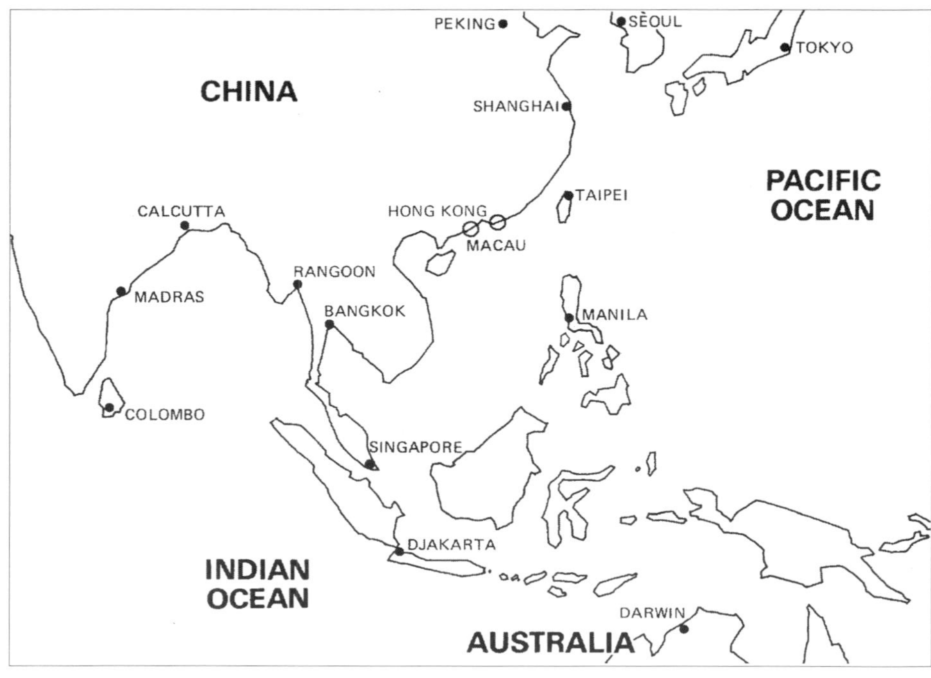

During the past two decades refugees from China have poured in by tens of thousands (Hong Kong's population today is over 4 million). The result of efforts to accommodate them and to provide suitable facilities for expanding trade in such a small area could have been depressing, but Hong Kong is a model of social order and architectural ingenuity, where every skyscraper has to be worthy of its space (some, such as the Mandarin Hotel and Prince's Building, must be among the most elegant of their kind in the world).

Macau

A two-square mile peninsula attached to the Chinese district of Cheung Shan (famous as the birthplace of Sun Yat-Sen) and the islands of Taipa and Colane, totalling six square miles, make up this overseas province of Portugal, which lies on the western side of the Pearl River estuary. It is the oldest remaining European settlement in the Far East.

The first European to visit the area was a Portuguese, travelling as a passenger on a Chinese vessel from Malacca, and it was first settled by the Portuguese in the 1550's. The name Macau is derived from A-Ma, the local goddess of sailors and fishermen; A-Ma-Kao means 'Bay of A-Ma'. Once the main Portuguese trading post in the Far East, serving as an entrepot for trade with India, Japan and China, Macau was for many years a storehouse

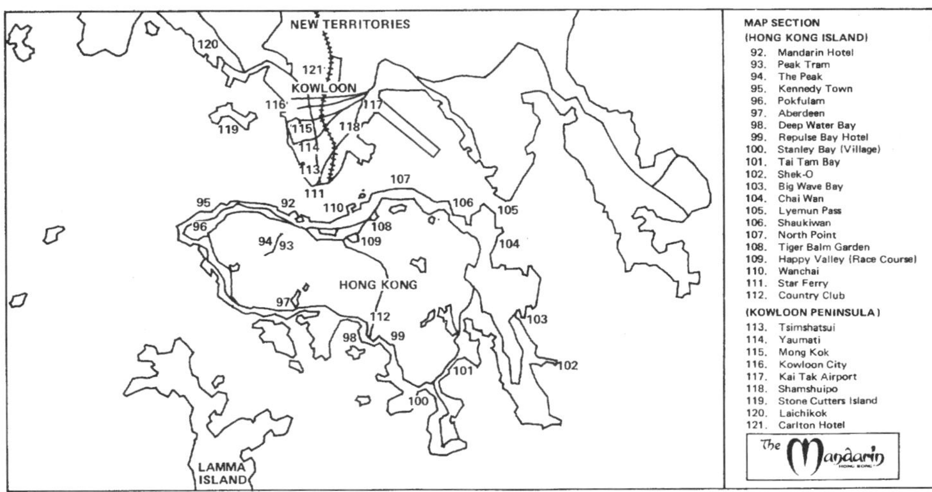

Map of Hong Kong, Kowloon and surrounding islands.

of oriental treasures. Today its income is derived from gambling, tourism, and light industries (teak and camphorwood furniture, cigarettes, matches, firecrackers, incense etc.). Out of a population of 270,000, 97% are Chinese, and only 8,000 are citizens.

Outwardly Macau has the appearance of a charming Mediterranean resort, with its colour-washed houses, stately public buildings, wrought-iron balconies, commemorative statues, public squares, and tree-lined avenues. It is only when one looks closer – along the narrow cobbled side-streets (the cobbles were brought in as ballast by ships which took back oriental goods to Europe), and alleyways seething with people; down by the waterfront where scores of junks lie at anchor; across the narrow reach of water to China, that one becomes aware of its unique and incongruous situation.

The contrast of Old Portugal and new China, the romantic background, the very fact of its existence, give Macau a unique fascination. While you are in Hong Kong it is well worth making the 40-mile trip across the water. A day-tour is better than nothing, but if you have time, you should spend a day or two here to look at the province and to enjoy the casinos.

—∞—

Inevitably during my traversing of the Far East, I visited Hong Kong on numerous occasions, frequently in transit to other destinations, other times on business, and in some instances, for a short break. Almost without exception I stayed on Victoria Island, as did most other business executives, this due to the fact that the important banks and commercial houses were located on the Island rather than in Kowloon, while tourists probably had a preference for Kowloon.

The most famous hotel in the colony was the Peninsula in Kowloon, which was the old colonial type, and although modernised in recent years, has retained its exterior architecture and its interior décor. On the majority of occasions I stayed in the Mandarin Hotel on the Island, which was nominated as one of the world's top ten hotels. Despite its status the rates were remarkably reasonable by today's standards. My choice was influenced by its location in the commercial area. I usually requested a room on the left hand corner of one of the upper floors from which there was a superb view across the harbour to Kowloon, also of the Hong Kong cricket grounds and the governor's residence.

During my early visits to cities in the Orient most were relatively small compared to today and Hong Kong was no exception. The Mandarin Hotel was virtually on the water front, and just opposite the star ferry which plied between the Island and Kowloon. This was important as the road tunnel had not then been built. For a period there was also a helipad near the hotel from which a helicopter service operated to Kai Tak Airport, which was a most convenient way of avoiding traffic jams and of having to manhandle one's luggage on and off the ferry. Due to the extensive land reclamation schedule the Mandarin Hotel is now well back from the shore and its view has been spoilt by the springing up of multi storey buildings in front of it.

Apart from business associates, right from the outset I had a good contact in Hong Kong, a person called Mark Milliken, a boyhood friend. Our lives had been remarkably similar. We both had been born in South Belfast into working class families and had a very basic education, in what was then known as a public elementary school. At the specified age of sixteen we both commenced apprenticeships as fitters, Mark in "The Yard", which was the common name for Harland and Wolff's Shipyard, while as explained earlier, I spent the requisite five years between three companies, ending up in Mackies. Mark and I, when boys, went to the same Sunday school, and as adults, became members of the same church.

Through a series of events which are not relevant to this book, Mark was offered and accepted a job as a representative in Hong Kong of a well known British engineering company, Gardiner Diesels. He took up his appointment in 1954 a few months earlier than I went to Calcutta. Our paths crossed periodically in the Far East, particularly in China, but I will refer to that fact in more detail later. Of course in my extensive travelling I had got to know a number of the Chinese stewardesses who worked for the airlines which operated on the Hong Kong/Calcutta sector.

Personal friend, Mark Milliken from Belfast, who represented the Hong Kong based Dodwell & Co, at the Mackie stand, Beijing.

My visits to Hong Kong became more frequent when a company in the colony was appointed Mackie's agent for Cambodia, as mentioned in the section on that country. In addition to becoming friendly with the proprietor Maurice Green and his wife Louisa, I got to know their son Michael and his wife Judy very well. Judy, whose maiden name was Salmoun, was originally from South Africa and had spent a considerable number of years in the colony as her father was Chairman of the Hong Kong Tramways Company, so she knew her way around extremely well and saved me lots of money by accompanying me on shopping expeditions. Most visitors would go to reputable British owned shops, which were inevitably relatively expensive, whereas Judy would guide me down side streets to Chinese stores where exactly the same make of clothing and other items were available at much lower prices. Furthermore, Judy was a more effective bargainer, due to being able to speak basic Cantonese.

Judy was an attractive young lady in every way with good looks and a charming personality, and could express herself very well, consequently she was asked from time to time to compere fashion shows in the up-market shops, Often these shows took place at lunchtime, and one was delighted to be asked to be her escort when Michael her husband could not get away from business. As a result of the contract for the jute mill in Cambodia, Arnold and Company were put on a firmer financial basis than previously. Furthermore, when Michael qualified as an electrical engineer, he joined

Top: *Maurice and Louisa Green. Maurice was proprietor of Arnold & Co. Mackie's agent for Cambodia.*

Bottom: *Michael Green (son of Maurice and Louisa) and his wife, Judy.*

his father Maurice and together they were successful in a bid to supply equipment to the Hong Kong Electrical Supply Company. So Arnold's, although a relatively small company, became very profitable.

The parents, Maurice and Louisa Green, lived in an attractive apartment in one of the Island's many beautiful bays, while Michael and Judy had an impressive residence up the peak, which was one of the most select areas in the colony! In addition to the latest model cars, the latter had a motorised Chinese Junk, on which they could relax at the weekends and also entertain guests. I really enjoyed their hospitality!!

My shopping expeditions in Hong Kong were not exclusively on my own behalf. Unlike today, ladies' underwear of good quality was not then available in India, so when the wives of the Mackie and Lagan staff members learned that I was bound for Hong Kong, I was provided with a list of bras, panties and other ladies' requisites to bring back with me. When Judy Green was not available to help me out, I would go to the well known store of Lane Crawford and solicit the help of one of the lady assistants. Naturally they were quite amused, but when I explained that I was a bachelor, there was always one delighted to choose suitable items. Fortunately, I was well known to several of the custom officers at the Calcutta airport, so my bags were opened only if they thought a superior was watching.

There were several South African families resident in Hong Kong among

Dinner party with Greens during visit of Bryan Hall – third from right.

whom Judy had a good chum. I cannot recall her name, but for simplicity I will refer to her as Jacqui. She had a somewhat similar background with the exception that Jacqui's father was a diamond merchant in South Africa and was evidently quite wealthy. Jacqui's husband had been sent to the colony to represent the diamond company in S.E. Asia. It was obvious that his son in law was well paid by the company and that father ensured that Jacqui was not short of cash as they had a fairly lavish life style in Hong Kong.

Macau was popular not only with tourists but also for many Hong Kong residents, the main attraction being the casinos. The Chinese, when not restricted, are inveterate gamblers. As one walked the streets of the colony in the evenings, the click, click of mah-jong tiles would be heard through the open windows of many buildings as games were in progress with no doubt bets at stake. Frequently games continued all night. When mah-jong was played by westerners the games were very slow as they found it necessary to look at each tile to identify it, and in doing so had to keep the tile hidden from their opponents. The experienced Chinese mah-jong player can identify each tile by feel, so can keep the tile upside down until he or she decides to place it, so the game is played at rapid speed. The more wealthy Chinese go for bigger stakes either at the horse racing in Happy Valley or on frequent visits to the casinos in Macau.

Of course many westerners also liked a flutter, so a trip to Macau by hydrofoil was very popular. As mentioned in the preface to this section, the trip took 15 minutes each way so a day trip was quite practical. During one of my visits to Hong Kong, Judy, Michael and another couple decided to have a day out in Macau and kindly invited me to join them, I readily accepted. Their purpose was not to sightsee or shop but to spend most of the time in a casino. I was not in the least interested in gambling but felt it proper to stick with my friends while they had a "flutter". I wandered around watching the goings on. Despite the fact the Greens and their friends did not place large bets, after a couple of hours or so they had lost a considerable amount, as they put it "lady luck" was not on their side!!

As I wandered around I stopped at a table and watched a little Chinese placing her "chips". I still haven't a clue as to what type of game she was playing, but she was raking in the money. On the spur of the moment, I bought some chips for a few Hong Kong Dollars and wherever she placed her "chips" I set some alongside. To my surprise on each occasion I won and very quickly recovered the money my friends had lost plus a profit. When my friends came along they were absolutely amazed and thought I should continue while on the winning streak, but I could not be persuaded. That was the only time I had ever engaged in gambling and was never tempted to do so again.

While writing about Hong Kong, I consider it appropriate to refer to my close friend and colleague, Eric Totten. When I arrived in Calcutta in August 1954, Eric was already there as an erection engineer, supervising the installation of machinery in a Calcutta Jute Mill. Eric lived in a small bungalow near to the apartment where I resided, so apart from work we met fairly frequently and Eric was able to give me good advice about living in India.

At that time neither Eric nor I could drive. The Company had provided a standard Vanguard station wagon for my use, also a driver who had been given the name of "Mickey" – which was not particularly appropriate for a Moslem!! It was however expected that when not on business, one would drive oneself. Eric and I took the car out on a Sunday before the traffic build-up and, by trial and error, learned how to handle a car. Fortunately we had no accidents.

Eric was eventually promoted to the Sales Staff, and was initially posted to Dacca (now Dhaka) to assist Colin Metcalfe. After a relatively short period, he was transferred to Hong Kong in mid 1967 to endeavour to promote the sales of semi-worsted machinery in the Crown Colony, also in Taiwan, Japan, Korea and the Philippines. Until then a French company, Schlumberger, had monopolised this market. Against keen competition Eric was successful in getting a foothold for Mackie semi-worsted machinery particularly in Taiwan and Japan.

Eric and Kaye Totten who were based in Hong Kong for a couple of years.

The sale of worsted machinery was a different proposition, as Mackie did not manufacture combing equipment, which was an essential part of processing worsted yarns.

For some reason of which I am unaware, Eric was recalled to Belfast in 1970. Having spent so many years abroad, Eric and his wife Kaye could not settle in Northern Ireland – so they were very happy when Eric was offered a managerial post with Consolidated Textiles Limited in Durban, Republic of South Africa. When that company closed down on the death of its proprietor, Eric had no difficulty in procuring other even more attractive jobs. Consequently he and Kaye never returned permanently to Northern Ireland. We do however keep in close contact and when they return to Belfast on holiday they stay at our home.

PEOPLE'S REPUBLIC OF CHINA

A mind-boggling country historically, geographically and economically

Preface

THE PEOPLE'S REPUBLIC OF China, also know as China, P.R.C. and PRC, is a country located mostly in East Asia, with a smaller proportion of its area located in Central Asia. The PRC has a coastline of 14,500 kilometres (9,010 miles), and borders (clockwise from south to northeast) Vietnam, Laos, Myanmar, India, Bhutan, Nepal, Pakistan, Afghanistan, Tajikistan. Kyrgyzstan, Kazakhstan, Russia, Mongolia, North Korea and located on the west of East China Sea and north of South China Sea. The PRC is a socialist republic, with its capital in Beijing.

At over 3.7 million square miles (over 9.5 million Km^2), the PRC is the third or fourth largest country by area. China's landscape is varied with largely desert on the north and humid and mountainous on the east and largely dry on the western part of the country. It is also the world's most populous nation, with over 1.3 billion citizens and borders the most countries in the world with 14 independent countries.

The present day location of PRC was the birthplace of the Chinese civilization that dates back to at least 18th century BC. The PRC was officially founded as a state on October 1, 1949 in Beijing during the closing stages of the Chinese Civil War.

The PRC is currently the world's fourth largest economy and second largest at purchasing power parity, third largest exporter and importer, consumes a third of the world's concrete and almost half of the world's steel, and represents China as a permanent member of the UN Security Council and APEC (Asian Pacific Economic Co-operation). China is also the largest trading partner of every country in East Asia. Due to its large and stable population, its rapidly growing economy (+9.4% annually), its large research and development investments ($136 billion annually)

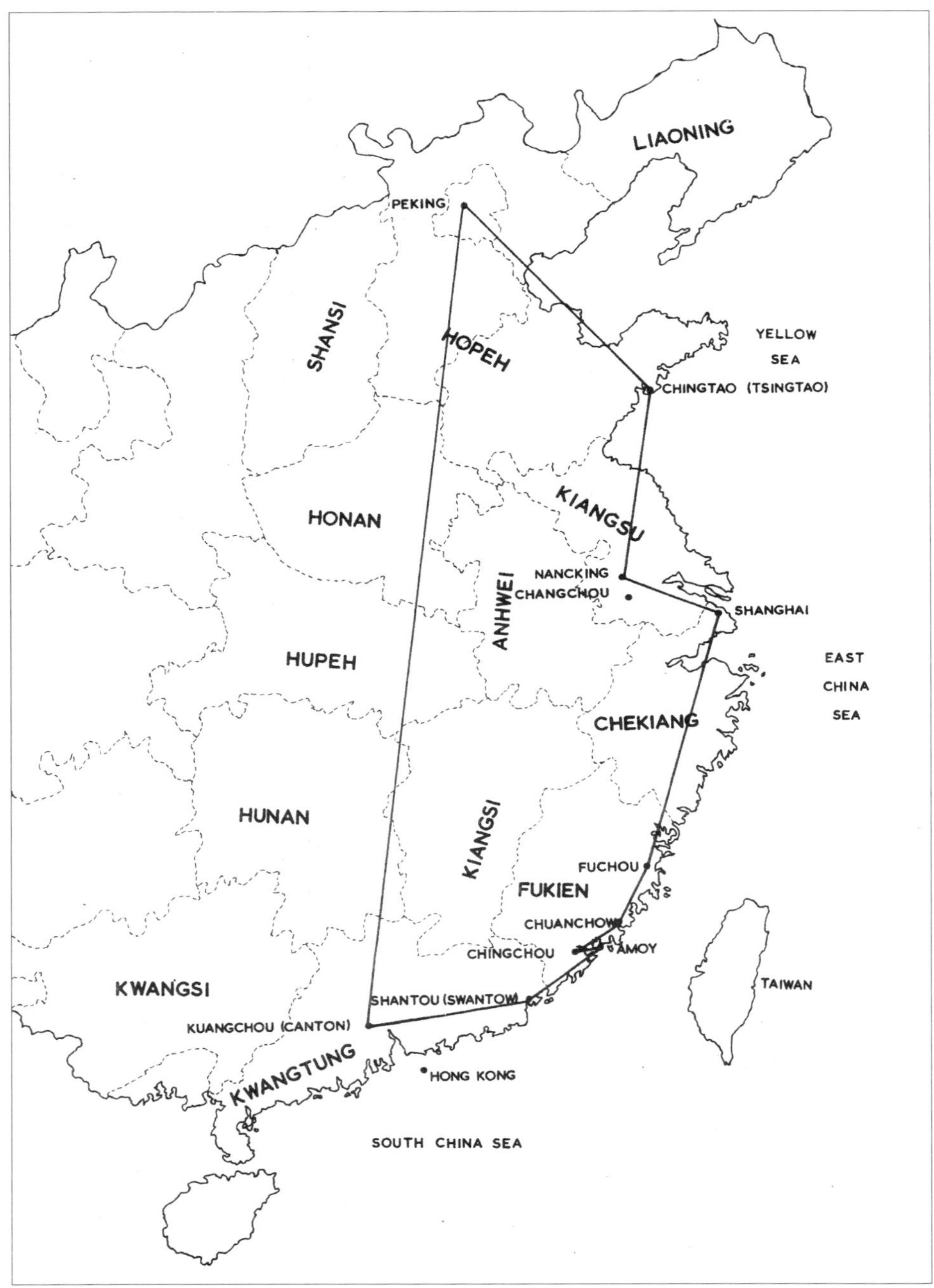

and military spending ($84.4 billion annually), and other capabilities, the PRC is often considered by analysts and commentators as an emerging superpower.

Background

Around the time it was officially founded, the previous government of China, the Republic of China (R.O.C.), retreated to the island of Taiwan, where it currently remains. Since then, the People's Republic of China (PRC) has claimed sovereignty over Taiwan and some nearby islands, which are administered by the Republic of China (R.O.C.), and asserts that the PRC has supplanted the R.O.C. in its legitimacy to govern all of China. The R.O.C. on Taiwan rejects these claims, and administers itself as a sovereign state with a democratically elected government and president. Until 1991, Taiwan also claimed to be the sole leader of all of China, as well as Mongolia. The term "mainland China" is sometimes used to denote the area under PRC rule, but usually excludes the two Special Administrative Regions: Hong Kong and Macau. The Communist Party of China (CPC) has led the PRC under a one-party system since the country's establishment in 1949. Despite this, nearly half of the PRC's economy has been privatized in the past three decades under "Socialism with Chinese characteristics".

Market-based economic reforms started since 1978 helped lift millions of people out of poverty, bringing the poverty rate down from 53% of population in 1981 to 8% by 2001. Today, China is the world's largest producer of steel and concrete, and consumes a third of the world's steel, over half of the world's concrete, and is the second largest importer and consumer of world oil.

However, due to this mixing of market and planned economies, the PRC is faced with a number of problems associated with each, including unemployment and an increasing rural/urban income gap. Despite these shortcomings, greater prosperity has led to growing Chinese influence in global, economic, political, military, scientific, technological, and cultural affairs.

History

The Chinese Civil War ended in 1949 with the Communist Party of China in control of the mainland, and the Kuomintang retreating to Taiwan and some outlying islands of Fujian. On October 1, 1949 Mao Zedong proclaimed the People's Republic of China, declaring "the Chinese people have stood up."

Following a series of dramatic economic failures, like the famous Great Leap Forward, Mao stepped down from his position as chairman in 1959, with Liu Shaoqi, elected by the National People's Congress, as successor. Mao still had huge influence over the Party, but was removed from day-to-day management of economic affairs, which came under the control of a more moderate leadership consisting of Liu Shaoqi, Deng Xiaoping, and others who initiated economic reforms.

In August 1966, Mao and his allies launched the Cultural Revolution, which is viewed by many analysts and historians as an attempt to purge the moderate leadership and strike-back at Mao's rivals by mobilizing the population in support of his thought. Mao's sympathizers argued it as an experiment in direct democracy and a genuine attempt at fighting corruption and other negative influences within Chinese society. However, Mao's personality cult at the time and the hierarchical structure of the "Red Guard," as well as the economic reconstruction needed after these events, tend to contradict this.

—∞—

My interest in China was stimulated in mid 1972 when I was requested by Bryan Hall, the then Mackie Sales Director, to assume the responsibility of organising a stand of Mackie exhibits for the forthcoming British Industrial Technology Exhibition which was scheduled to take place the following year in Peking now Beijing. The British Textile Machinery Association (BTMA) had approached Mackie's about participating in the exhibition and company directors decided it would be beneficial to do so. Perhaps it would be interesting to give a brief report on that exhibition before describing the experiences of myself and my colleagues.

The British Industrial Technology Exhibition, which took place between 26th March and 7th April 1973, was conceived to show the Chinese the wide range of products and services which Britain could offer in the field of advanced technology, with a view to increasing the size of Britain's contribution to the development of China's economy in the years ahead. British business as well as the UK government saw the exhibition as Britain's opportunity to drive forward, hard and fast, its relationship with China, and the resulting business. It was recognised that Britain's lead position in China would be short-lived.

The organisers were SBTC (Sino-British Trade Council) and Industrial & Trade Fairs, with DTI sponsorship. From the beginning, all concerned were determined that the exhibition would be a success. Preparations had begun more than a year earlier with a reconnaissance trip to Beijing in January 1972. British industry showed a great deal of interest in the project, which was the first major event for Britain in China since the 1964 exhibition.

The aim was to have an exhibition large enough to stimulate Chinese interest in British industrial goods as a whole, and to show British progress in technological fields in which China was specifically interested. With

364 companies taking part it was the largest exhibition seen in China to date (and one of the largest ever). Among the well known exhibitors which would later become some of the UK's biggest exporters to China were ICI, GEC, British Aircraft Corporation, Gullick Dobson and Rolls-Royce.

The influx into Beijing of over 900 British people posed some formidable problems for the organisers. For a start, the industrial and mining equipment to be exhibited weighed 5,000 tons. Shipping it to China began in the autumn of 1972. More than 200,000 invitations were issued to officials, technicians and end users, together with a 16-page guide to the exhibition. A 300-page catalogue with data sheets on hundreds of products was published, and issued to 10,000 visitors.

As will be appreciated a very considerable amount of preparation was required by Mackie's in Belfast. For this purpose a small committee was formed which was chaired by Bryan Hall and co-ordinated by me. A draughtsman named Ken Magee was appointed to organise the technical aspect of the Mackie stand although it had been decided not to take any complete machines. Accessories, components, and a wide variety of technical data had to be assembled. Ken was very suitable for this job, being very thorough in whatever he did.

A wide range of brochures and other literature had to be prepared and the obvious choice for that job was the head of the Mackie Advertising Department, Barry Pitman, a Welshman, married to a local girl. Barry had a great flair for designing attractive brochures and advertising material, so he relished the challenge of preparing literature for China, which of course involved having the technical data translated and printed in mandarin. For this purpose we engaged a London company recommended by BTMA. This resulted in a very interesting development.

For the purpose of mandarin translation the London Company engaged a number of resident Chinese. We, Mackie's, were most fortunate in having our work allocated to a Chinese gentleman, known as Terry Chang, who held a senior position in the BBC Chinese Department. We invited Terry Chang to visit Belfast to see Mackie machinery and to get a clear understanding of all technical terms. Terry turned out to be a very affable and cultured person and having been in England for over twenty years was fluent in English. Of course he had to be for the job he held!! I will revert to him shortly.

For the catering arrangements we naturally turned to the reliable and efficient Margot Wills. It must be remembered that in 1973 there were no Western hotels and no luxury goods or foodstuffs in the shops so Margot had to use her imagination. As usual she rose to the challenge and provided a mini bar and kitchen for the Mackie stand. These facilities were primarily for the Mackie staff, as apart from tea, coffee, and cold drinks, entertaining on the stand would not be permissible. We were eventually requested by Chinese officials to provide lunches for the local staff when it was not practical for them to get to nearby restaurants.

In addition to myself two other salesmen were chosen to go to the exhibition, Desmond Morgan, Head of the Wool and Synthetic Division, and Sammy McCoubrey, whose prime responsibility was Weaving, my niche being Jute Processing. In addition Bryan Hall decided that Hans Lowe, the head of Mackie's London Office, would be an asset due to his experience in Russia and East European countries, which were all still communist. The BTMA staff that was responsible for co-ordinating all arrangements for the exhibitors such as shipping, visas, travel bookings, were very helpful. Through the good offices of Hans Lowe we were able to meet and get useful advice from Sir John Keswick, the President of the Sino-British Trade Council.

It was decided that Desmond Morgan and I should travel to Peking as an advance party, to supervise the setting-up of the Mackie stand. The manual work was to be carried out by carpenters and other tradesmen provided by BTMA. We were to be followed by Sammy McCoubrey and Hans Lowe who were scheduled to arrive in time for the opening date.

Despite the fact that our hosts had undertaken to provide interpreters, I hit on the idea of taking Terry Chang as a member of the team if it could be arranged, as there were several obstacles to be negotiated. Firstly, Terry had to be released by his employers the BBC, then a visa for China had to be obtained. We did not know how the Chinese Foreign Office would react as Terry had been out of the country for twenty one years.

When I phoned Terry's boss at BBC London, his reaction was most favourable, particularly when I mentioned that it would give Terry the opportunity to see his aged mother after so many years. The BBC executive said he would be delighted to release Terry for the requisite time of three weeks. We were also pleasantly surprised when BTMA obtained a visa without any awkward questions being asked. Of course by this time Terry was a British citizen so had a British passport.

As planned, Desmond and I flew to Hong Kong with the idea of having just one night stop-over. If I recall correctly, Terry Chang took a separate flight and joined us in Hong Kong. A large number of the nine hundred British businessmen bound for the exhibition had assembled in the colony. Many of them, including the Mackie trio, had been booked on an early afternoon train to travel through the New Territories to the border post of Shenzhen where we had to disembark on the British side. The passengers then had to walk across the border and pass through the Chinese immigration and customs. It was fascinating to see the union flag flying a few hundred yards from the red flag of PRC. Everything went smoothly so we were soon on our way on the Chinese train to Canton, now Guangzhou.

The Chinese train was very basic but spotlessly clean and typical green tea was served in large mugs. The train was pulled by a traditional steam engine. The landscape through which we travelled was flat and was covered predominantly by paddy fields. At that time we passed through what could only be described as shanty towns, which I understand have now become relatively large cities with many modern buildings, including hotels, as a result of the industrial revolution that has taken place in the PRC. The city of Canton was also a drab place and the hotel in which we stayed was a large square – shaped barrack.

The air service between Canton and Peking in 1973 was rather limited, although China Airlines had just purchased a number of British built Trident aircraft. It was therefore stipulated that each British company should choose one representative to travel by air and the remaining staff would go by train, a journey which would take two days. It was decided that I should go by air, and Desmond Morgan and Terry Chang would follow by train, although Desmond did not really fancy the journey. Perhaps I should mention at this stage that BOAC, as British Airways was then called, had been permitted to operate one special flight from London to Peking to arrive on the 25th March. Fortunately BTMA were successful in booking two seats for Mackie's, which were allocated to Hans Lowe and Sammy McCoubrey. The airline chose a VC10 aircraft for the flight which was my favourite aircraft, with four engines mounted at the rear.

As already mentioned, there were no western style modern hotels in China at that time, even in Peking, indeed no hotels that could be described as "modern." Accommodation was provided by the Chinese authorities for the nine hundred plus British personnel at what was known as the Friendship Hotel, which was practical but had no luxuries. The suitcase label shown overleaf even enhances its appearance, and the few cars shown demonstrate the scarcity of transport, to which I will refer later. The rooms were en suite, that is, there was a basic bathroom attached to each. The bedroom itself was furnished with an old style spring bed, a wardrobe, and a chest of drawers all quite antiquated, but everything was spotlessly clean.

The hotel was located beside a military barracks, which could be considered an advantage or alternatively a liability. There were certainly no security risks in China in those days, so it did not make us feel more secure. The aspect I'm thinking of is the fact that the reveille was sounded every morning at 6 a.m. followed by the shouting of commands by the officers. Some of the British guests may have considered this as a benefit as there was no danger of sleeping-in while others may have preferred an extra hour in bed!!

Top and bottom: *Friendship Hotel, where British delegation stayed.*

Moving the furniture in the room was not permitted, which raised a problem when Hans Lowe and Sammy McCoubrey arrived. They had been allocated a twin bedroom, with an attached sitting room. Apparently Hans had a complex about sharing a room, and against my advice on checking in he proceeded to move one bed into the sitting room. When the chamber boy intervened and stopped him doing so, much to Hans' annoyance, it transpired that Hans preferred to wear a nightdress rather than pyjamas at night, which should not have caused him any embarrassment as I knew Jute Mill managers in India who preferred that night attire because it was much cooler in the hot season before air conditioning became the norm. However, according to Sammy McCoubrey, it was quite amusing when Hans donned his nightdress, lit up his cigar for his final puff before going to bed. He used to stand with his arms resting on the chest of drawers, looking into the attached mirror, and asked himself, "why did you leave your people to come out here?" This was a saying Hans often repeated when travelling abroad!!

The exhibition was held in a large hall which obviously had been built to house such events. It was located about twenty minutes drive from the Friendship Hotel. The distance could be covered quite quickly due to the paucity of traffic. There was very little public transport and only official cars plied the streets. A fleet of buses was provided to take the exhibitors to and from the hotel. Cars were laid on to take smaller groups to and from official functions. Some means of transport were very antiquated.

The organisers had an office at the exhibition hall to assist and advise exhibitors, also to handle mail, predominantly fax messages. They had also available a squad of British artisans. On arrival I immediately engaged the services of suitable tradesmen to erect the Mackie stand. This was not a big

Exhibition Hall, Peking (Beijing)

No traffic jams in 1973

undertaking as the stand was comparatively small and simple nevertheless attractive. Consequently, everything was in place by the time the other members of the team arrived.

The Chinese authorities provided two interpreters and two "explainers". The latter did not speak English, the idea being that the interpreters would explain the Mackie literature and equipment to the "explainers" so that they in turn could talk to casual visitors to the stand, while the interpreters helped the Mackie staff to deal with official visitors. We of course had the advantage of having the services of Terry Chang. The photo opposite shows all members of the Mackie team. The Chinese staff on our stand, indeed the vast majority of the Chinese people, were dressed in what could be described as "Mao Tse-Tung (Mao Zedong) Uniform", that was jacket and trousers made of blue denim, all jackets of course having "mandarin" collars. The clothes of the working class were made from cheap, low quality fabric while executives wore suits of finer and higher quality denim.

The day before the official opening of the exhibition a Chinese gentleman visited the Mackie stand. I purposely use the term "gentleman" as he was well dressed in the traditional suit, but of high quality denim, also spoke English fluently in quite a cultured voice. He stated that he had received some of his education in England and consequently was very interested in anything British. He gave the impression that he would be visiting other stands, but spent a lot of time on the Mackie stand asking quite intelligent questions. As he left he said he would see us again but

Front view of Mackie exhibition stand

Mackie team l to r. Author, Sammy McCoubrey, Bryan Hall, Jim Rodgers, Hans Lowe, Terry Chang and Desmond Morgan.

Top and bottom: *Visitors to Mackie stand.*

was very non-specific about when. It was not entirely surprising that the said gentleman turned up the following day and every day thereafter throughout the exhibition. We never did find out who the gentleman really was, but I'm sure your speculation is the same as that of the Mackie boys "big brother" watching us!!

For the opening ceremony on the 26th March 1973, each of the 364 British companies participating was requested to send one representative to a meeting in the assembly hall of the exhibition centre. At this meeting speeches were made by the Chinese Foreign Trade Minister, Comrade Bai Xianggno, also by the two British Ministers, Peter Walker and Michael Heseltine. I cannot recall if the British Ambassador or Sir John Keswick, President of the SBTC took part, but they and other senior British representatives were definitely on the platform. After the speech making the ribbon was cut by the Chinese Minister and the show was declared officially open.

During the twelve days of the exhibition there were various functions. The British guests were invited, indeed were expected to attend a cultural programme at one of Peking's leading theatres, at which there was traditional singing and dancing. All the songs, of course, eulogising the achievements and attributes of "The Great Leader" Mao Tse-Tung (Mao Zedong). Naturally all the attendees were expected to applaud enthusiastically and obliged.

The Chinese organised a banquet for their guests one evening and the British reciprocated a couple of days later. The etiquette at that time in China was that hosts should always be ten minutes early for a function and guests ten minutes late. For example, on the evening when the British were hosting the banquet, which was scheduled for 7 p.m., they all had to be at their tables at 6.50 p.m. and the Chinese guests did not arrive till 7.10 p.m. The idea was that the hosts could ensure that everything was as desired, while the guests would allow ten minutes grace in case something was amiss. Not a bad idea!

There were also smaller functions and I had a most interesting experience when organising a dinner party for representatives from the Chinese Textile Industry. I had all details nicely arranged for a dinner party of around twenty people including the Mackie team commencing at 7 p.m. on a Saturday evening, at the Big Peking Duck Restaurant. The day was chosen primarily because it was during the visit of the Mackie Chairman, Jim Rogers, and the Sales Director, Bryan Hall, who were in Peking for four days in the middle of the exhibition, although the former was not keen on such functions.

On the Saturday morning in question a Chinese government official came to our stand and told me that the timing of the proposed dinner had been changed and it would now commence at 5 p.m., which was two hours earlier than I had originally planned. By this stage, I had learned not to ask why, but there were several questions I had to ask. The conversation between the government official and me went something like this, what about our guests? They have been informed. What about the arrangements at the Big Peking Duck Restaurant? The management is aware of the change. What about the transport booked? It has been rearranged and all the Mackie people should be ready to leave the hotel at 4.30 p.m. I realised that I had to leave matters at that. However, our Chairman who liked everything cut and dry was rather agitated and I had some difficulty in calming him down and persuading him to accept the situation.

As expected by me the transport was waiting when we emerged from the hotel, and on arrival at the restaurant we found everything in order, so the meal proceeded smoothly. I was seated next to the government official who had rearranged things, with my Chairman on the other side. During the course of the meal, the Chinese gentleman became more communicative and told me that the changes had been made due to the fact that the Chinese Prime Minister, Zhou Enlai, had decided to visit the exhibition that evening and was scheduled to arrive at 7.30 p.m. Consequently it was important that we should be in attendance on our stand by 7.20 p.m. at the latest. When I conveyed this to Jim Rogers he again became even more agitated and certainly did not enjoy the excellent meal which included "real" Peking duck, which as its name suggested was the speciality of the restaurant. The Chinese gentleman must have noticed this fact as he asked me to assure our Chairman that everything was under control, in that we would finish the meal at 7 p.m. The bill would then immediately be presented to me for payment. We would proceed to the cars at 7.10 p.m. and be back in the exhibition hall at 7.20 p.m. As expected in China in those days everything went like clockwork, there being no risk of a traffic jam.

The premier of China was an interesting person. At the time of his visit to the B.I.T.E., Zhou Enlai had just turned 75 years of age having been born on 5th March 1898. He was the right-hand man of Mao Tse-Tung (or aka Mao Zedong) although an entirely different character. He was well educated and very cultured having studied at a university in Japan, also spoke several foreign languages including English and French. Zhou Enlai was appointed Prime Minister on the setting up of the People's Republic of China in October 1949 and held that post until his death on 8th January 1976. Although he and his entourage spent two hours in the exhibition hall he could not possibly visit the 364 stands, and Mackie's being one of the smallest was not honoured by a visit. He simply walked past with a casual glance. Had he unexpectedly stopped no doubt Jim Rogers and Bryan Hall would have had precedence in conversing with him!! We had a brief visit from Michael Heseltine, but not from the British Secretary for Trade and Industry.

The Saturday evening of the Chinese Premier's visit stands out in my memory for another and more unpleasant reason. All mail, including faxes, was channelled through a central office in the exhibition complex. That evening after the VIP's had left, for some reason which I cannot recall, I decided to check with the office before returning to the hotel, and I was handed a fax bearing very unpleasant news, particularly for Bryan Hall. A few words of explanation are necessary.

Visit of Michael Hesseltine to the stand.

The matron of one of the three large Belfast hospitals, Musgrave Park, was an English lady named Betty Chambers. This lady became friendly with the Hall family through Bryan's older sister, who until her rather untimely death, had been matron of the Purdysburn Hospital, on the outskirts of Belfast. After the death of Miss Hall, Betty Chambers became like a daughter to Bryan's mother. Indeed so much so that Bryan had purchased a bungalow with the idea that his mother and Betty could live there together after the latter's retirement which was fairly imminent and this would leave Bryan free to live his own life.

Periodically Betty Chambers visited England for a holiday, and found it most convenient to take her car by the Larne/Stranraer Ferry and motor down south. She had gone on such a trip prior to Bryan's departure for China and was scheduled to return before Bryan did. The fax conveyed the sad news that on the homeward journey Betty had been tragically killed on the A73 in Scotland, which was then a rather narrow, winding, and very dangerous road. On receiving the fax, I consulted our Chairman, Jim Rogers, who immediately took the message from me and said he would handle the matter on our return to the hotel, and in the meantime I should give no indication whatsoever of the tragic news. He surreptitiously took a bottle of "scotch" from the mini-bar on our stand, obviously with the idea that he could break the news to Bryan over a drink, also if Bryan so desired he could later "drown his sorrows."

It is intriguing that in non-Christian countries such as India and China, that Sunday is generally a holiday, so the Chinese authorities had made special arrangements for their British guests to visit the Great Wall of China the following day. Needless to say, Bryan did not put in an appearance. The most one can say about the "day trip" is that it was most interesting. The term enjoyable could not honestly be used. The buses provided were very basic and were certainly no way near the standard of "tour buses" in the west. The weather was cold and damp with occasional light snow showers. Most people have heard of the Great Wall of China and many could quote elementary details about it, such as its length which is approximately 6,400 Km. (4,000 miles), nevertheless the following brief history will be of interest to many readers.

The Chinese were already familiar with the techniques of wall-building by the time of the Spring and Autumn Period, which began around 8th century BC. During the Warring States Period from 5th century BC to 221 BC, the states of Qi, Yan and Zhao all constructed extensive fortifications to defend their own borders. Built to withstand the attack of small arms such as swords and spears, these walls were mostly made by stamping earth and gravel between board frames.

Qin Shi Huang conquered all opposing states and unified China in 221 BC, establishing the Qin Dynasty. Intending to impose centralized rule and prevent the resurgence of feudal lords, he ordered the destruction of the wall sections that divided his empire along the former state borders. To protect the empire against intrusions by the Xiongnu people from the north, he ordered the building of a new wall that connected the remaining fortifications along the empire's new northern frontier. Transporting the large quantity of materials required for construction was difficult, so builders always tried to use local resources. Stones from the mountains were used over mountain ranges, while rammed earth was used for construction in the plains. There are no surviving historical records indicating the exact length and course of the Qin Dynasty walls. Most of the ancient walls have eroded away over the centuries, and very few sections remain today. The Han, Sui, Northern and Jin dynasties later in history have all repaired, rebuilt, or expanded sections of the Great Wall at great cost to defend themselves against invaders from the north.

The Great Wall concept was revived again during the Ming Dynasty, following the Ming army's defeat by the Mongols in the Battle of Tumu in 1449. The Ming had failed to gain a clear upper-hand over the Mongols after successive battles, and the long-drawn conflict was taking a toll on the empire. The Ming adopted a new strategy to keep the Mongols out, by constructing walls along the northern border of China. Acknowledging the Mongol control established in the Ordos Desert, the wall followed the desert's southern edge instead of incorporating the bend of the Huang He.

Unlike the earlier Qin fortifications, the Ming construction was

Top and bottom: *Visit of Mackie chairman and staff to Great Wall of China*

stronger and more elaborate due to the use of bricks and stone instead of rammed earth. As Mongol raids continued periodically over the years, the Ming devoted considerable resources to repair and reinforce the walls. The sections near the Ming capital of Beijing were especially strengthened.

Towards the end of the Ming Dynasty, the Great Wall helped defend the empire against the Manchu invasions that began around 1600. Under the military command of Yuan Chonghuan, the Ming army held off the Manchus at the heavily fortified Shanghai Pass, thus preventing the Manchus from entering the Liaodong Peninsula and the Chinese heartland. The Manchus were finally able to cross the Great Wall in 1644, when the gates of the Shanghai Pass were opened by Wu Sangui, a rebel Ming border general. The Manchus quickly seized the Ming capital of Beijing, and subsequently defeated the remaining Ming resistance to establish the Qing Dynasty.

Construction and repairs of the Great Wall were discontinued under the Qing rule, as China's borders extended beyond the walls and Mongolia was annexed into the empire.

While during the various dynasties there were evidently great achievements, at the time of one's visit in early 1973 things in China could only be described as primitive or antiquated. Nevertheless the Chinese officials were very proud of their achievements since the communist take-over in 1949, consequently they were anxious to show their British guests various aspects of the country's educational, industrial, and cultural systems. Groups were taken on visits to primary schools, textile factories and cultural centres, of course not forgetting the Peking Zoo to see the famous pandas.

Visits were also made to historical places such as Tiananmen Square, The Forbidden City, and the Great Hall of the People. The following is a brief history of the famous Square and its surrounding buildings and monuments.

Tiananmen Square (Simplified Chinese); Traditional Chinese: Pinyin: Tian'anmen Guangchang) is the large plaza near the centre of Beijing,

Visit to Primary school

Bryan Hall and author visiting Cotton Mill, Beijing.

China, named after the Tiananmen (literally, Gate of Heavenly Peace), which sits to its north, separating it from the Forbidden City. It has great cultural significance as a symbol because it was the site of several key events in Chinese history. Outside of China, the square is widely known for the Tiananmen Square protests of 1989.

The square is 880 metres south to north and 500 metres east to west, a total area of 440,000 square metres, which makes it the largest open-urban square in the world.

History

The Tiananmen was built in 1417 in the Ming Dynasty. In 1699 (early Qing Dynasty), the Tiananmen was renovated and renamed to its present form. During the Ming and Qing eras, there was no public square at Tiananmen, and instead the area was filled with offices for imperial ministries. These were badly damaged during the Boxer Rebellion and the area was cleared to produce the beginning of Tiananmen Square.

Near the centre of today's square, close to the site of the Mao Tse-Tung (Mao Zedong) Mausoleum, once stood one of the most important gates of Beijing. This gate was known as the "Great Ming Gate" during the Ming Dynasty. "Great Qing Gate" during the Qing Dynasty, and "Gate of China" during the Republic of China era. Unlike the other gates in Beijing, such as the Tiananmen and the Qianmen, this was a purely ceremonial gateway, with three arches but no ramparts, similar in style to the ceremonial gateways found in the Ming Dynasty Tombs. It normally remained closed, except when the Emperor passed through. Commoner traffic was diverted to two side gates at the northern and eastern ends of today's square, respectively. Because of this diversion in traffic, a busy marketplace, called Chessgrid Streets developed in the big, fenced square to the south of this gate.

In the early 1950s, the Gate of China (as it was then known) was demolished along with the Chessgrid Streets to the south, completing the expansion of Tiananmen Square to (approximately) its current size.

Features

Enlarged in 1949 to the current size, its flatness is broken only by the 38 metre high Monument to the People's Heroes and the Mausoleum of Mao Tse-Tung (Mao Zedong). The square lies between two ancient, massive gates: the Tian'anmen to the north and the Zhengyangmen, better know as Qianmen; Pinyin: Qianmen; literally ("Front Gate") to the south. Along the west side of the Square is the Great Hall of the People. Along the east side is the National Museum of China. Chang'an Avenue, which is used for parades, lies between the Tian'anmen and the Square. Trees line the east and west edges of the Square, but the square itself is open, with neither trees nor benches.

The Square is lit with huge lamp posts which also sport video cameras. It is heavily monitored by uniformed and plain clothes policemen.

Events

Tiananmen Square has been the site of a number of political events such as the proclamation of the People's Republic of China by Mao Tse-Tung (Mao Zedong) in October 1, 1949, for annual mass military displays on all subsequent National Days until October 1st 1959, plus the 1984 military parade for the 35th anniversary of the People's Republic of China and the 50th anniversary in 1999 plus for mass rallies during the Cultural Revolution. It has also been the site of a number of protest movements, most notably the May Fourth Movement of 1919 for science and democracy, protests in 1976 after the death of Zhou Enlai, and the Tiananmen Square protests of 1989.

The protests of 1989 resulted in the killing of Chinese protesters in the streets to the west of the square and adjacent areas. Some western reporters who were on the square during the unfolding events reported that they saw no one actually die on the square itself, though did see bloodied people but could not confirm whether they were either dead or injured. However, Chinese expatriates who left the country after the killings said

Tiananmen Square and Great Hall of the People

that the total number of deaths ended up being in the thousands. This was a combination of the hundreds killed on the spot and the "miniature" purge that followed.

As the exhibition drew to a close it was decided that Sammy McCoubrey and Hans Lowe, who were booked on the special BOAC return flight, should remain on site to supervise the dismantling and packing of the Mackie stand and its contents, while the other team members should head for their respective destinations. For example, Desmond Morgan was ironically scheduled to go to Taiwan, of course not directly but via Hong Kong. He also had a second passport containing his Taiwanese visa. He certainly would not have been welcome in "the other China" had he produced a passport with P.R.C. Immigration Stamps!! Having been responsible for taking Terry Chang to P.R.C., I felt it was incumbent upon me to ensure that he got safely out of the country, so he travelled along with me to Hong Kong via Canton. Fortunately, there were no hiccoughs on the journey!! I eventually saw Terry safely on a flight at Kai Tek Airport bound for the U.K., after which I proceeded to Nepal via Calcutta.

Mackies were not really surprised when no business resulted from their participation in the exhibition. The reason for this will become obvious later. Furthermore, the prospect of future business was very slim; consequently I concluded that there would be no further visit to the P.R.C. for me, certainly as Mackie's representative. This proved to be a wrong conclusion, as early in 1977, an overseas Chinese businessman, who had very substantial interests in Singapore and Hong Kong contacted Mackies. This gentleman's request was that a competent technician should be provided to accompany several of his own staff members on an exploratory tour of China, at his expense. Before going into further details about the outcome of this idea, a word of explanation would be appropriate, about the attitude of wealthy overseas Chinese businessmen towards their "homeland", even when the P.R.C. was still virtually a closed country.

The Chinese have a similar tradition to the Indians. Almost every Indian, even the poorest and those of the "dalat" caste, who come to the cities to find employment, has an ambition not simply to subsist but to earn sufficient to save enough to one day do something for his home village or town, primarily to eventually purchase a piece of land and build a house there. The same ambition seems to be in-built into the overseas Chinese even the most wealthy. Even though they don't intend to return to reside in China, they have the desire to do something for the village or town from which they or their forbearers came.

In view of my previous experience in the P.R.C. I was asked by Bryan Hall to undertake the proposed tour, which I was most willing to do. Incidentally I never got into the habit of keeping a diary so the vast majority of my reminiscences in this book are from memory. However, on this occasion, I obviously made an exception as I've just turned up an old notebook containing daily details of this trip. The tour turned out to be very extensive as will be seen from the attached map, and was of more than a month's duration, consequently it is my intention to highlight only the most interesting experiences, otherwise a separate book would be required.

It was arranged that I should meet the Chinese businessman in question, Mr. Ho Yeow Hoon at his Hong Kong office, namely Latimer

Trading Co., Ltd., that was obviously a family concern, as both his son and daughter were present at the meeting. This meeting took place on 29th July 1977. At the outset Mr. Ho explained that as a result of changes in the Chinese government policies and attitudes towards foreign trade, he considered there was potential for what he termed "compensation trading" with the P.R.C. He went on to say that he had already been in touch with the companies on the mainland, namely Canton Investment Co., and Fukien Investment Co., which, despite their names, were government organisations. To put it briefly, it was Mr. Ho's desire that I should survey the existing jute industry and determine if it would be viable to set up a jute processing plant in his "home town". This would involve visiting a reasonable number of existing jute mills, and Mr. Ho said he had already obtained official permission for me to do so.

Although I had visited Hong Kong on many occasions previously I had not up until then experienced a typhoon. Very early on the 2nd August the warning balloons were hoisted as typhoon "Hope" approached the colony and all small boats headed for the typhoon shelters while the larger ships moved out into the centre of the bay and battened down the hatches. The Excelsior hotel in which I was staying on this occasion had large plate glass windows around the lobby, so workmen were engaged to cover these with large sheets of plywood about one inch (25 mm) thick. Towards lunchtime the red balloons went up, the sky darkened, and deathly silence settled over the colony.

The hotel guests were warned, not only to stay inside, but also to stand well back from the entrance and the windows. Rather stupidly some tourists primarily Americans wanted to take photographs, a ludicrous idea! Despite the efforts of the doorman who was a big Sikh some folk pushed their way out on to the sidewalk. Suddenly there was a "whirring roar", the only way I can describe it, and the would be "photographers" lost their courage and beat a hasty retreat. "Hope" went as quickly as she had arrived, but not before venting her fury by lifting a 7,000 ton ship out of the water and leaving her bow on the jetty, also throwing cars and other loose objects around. A rather scary experience!!

During the week spent in Hong Kong frequent meetings took place with Mr. Ho and his company executives. High on the agenda was how the project in China would be financed should it prove attractive to implement the idea of setting up a jute mill. Mr. Ho mentioned several reputable banks, including the Bank of China, with which he had previous dealings and had established good relations. However, I felt it appropriate to introduce him to Grindlay Brandts Asea Ltd., as Mackies had done considerable business with that bank's parent company in the U.K., and it so happened that I had already met the senior manager in Hong Kong, a Mr. Graham Hartley. At a meeting which I arranged between the two parties the reaction of Mr. Hartley and his colleague Ken Hughes was favourable but it was mutually agreed that no concrete steps could be taken until a firm proposal had been prepared by Mackies.

From the outset it was very obvious that Mr. Ho had made very thorough preparations for my visit to China. As already mentioned, he had obtained official permission for me to visit jute mills in many parts of the country, which in those days was not readily granted. He also supported my visa applications resulting in a visa being issued in record time. Furthermore, he arranged that I should be accompanied by two of his young executives, one from the Singapore office and the other from Hong Kong, both of whom spoke English fluently. In addition he requested an older associate, who had practical experience of business in communist China to go along as mentor. On receipt of the requisite visas, bookings were made for the foursome to travel on the through train to Canton (Changzhou) on Tuesday 7th August 1977. Evidently I did not get to bed until late the previous night as the photo below would indicate. The other person in the photograph is Mr. Lee, our mentor, who on the tour came to be known respectfully as "Uncle Lee". The two young men were Mr. Chang from Singapore and Mr. Tsang from Hong Kong. We clicked from the outset and so formed a very effective team.

The outward journey from Canton (Changzhou) to Peking (Beijing) was by train and as I've said already it was quite a lengthy trip. According to a rough calculation it covered nearly 3000 Km. (1864 miles). At that time coal fired steam engines were being used and the carriages were of the traditional design, including a "sleeper". We had a four-berth compartment, which was by no means luxurious, but was adequate and clean, sheets and pillows being provided. We had the service of a conductor, in our case a girl in her twenties. She was also responsible for security and permitted only passengers who had the proper ticket into the carriage, so we had no worries about our belongings. My companions, although westernised, travelled in loose fitting Chinese trousers and jacket, so I took the liberty of travelling in my pyjamas and nobody paid any attention even when I got out on to the platform. Of course, we dressed appropriately for business appointments, I generally in a safari suit.

I very quickly adapted to the basic toilet facilities and "coughed and spluttered" along with my fellow passengers as we washed at the tin basins mounted on the corridor wall. The lavatory was a "hole in the floor" with four pads to guide the passenger to "hunker" in the right position to hit the bull's eye! Of course one had to take extra care as the train rattled along or there would have been a "mis-hit". Exclusively Chinese food was served in the dining car which I thoroughly enjoyed as it was well prepared and tasty.

I've frequently been asked if in all my extensive travels I ever encountered a dish I could not eat. I have a standard reply to that question. I refer to the advertisement about a dog for sale. After listing several good qualities the seller went on to say; "will eat anything, very fond of children". Some of the delicacies I enjoyed in China were "Peking Duck", "Bird's Nest Soup" and "100 year old eggs", not forgetting suckling pig.

We stopped off at eight towns/cities. At each we visited one or more jute mills and other textile factories. Meetings also took place at various government departments. At each place we were welcomed by senior executives from the jute mills in the area and treated as honoured guests. Indeed I had so many multi-course Chinese meals that by the time I reached Peking my waist had increased at least a couple of inches. Probably the hospitality was extended not because we were considered vitally important but rather it afforded an opportunity for our hosts to live it up at their government's expense. I was surprised that there were no obvious restrictions placed on us. Indeed at one factory I was taken literally underground and shown an extensive atom bomb shelter, which was a labyrinth of tunnels with requisite living facilities.

On one sector of the train journey I had a particularly interesting experience. A T.V. camera crew in the process of shooting a travelogue on China's railway network came aboard. The producer was a rather attractive young lady who spoke English fluently. She was obviously quite

Mr Ho and author on train from Hong Kong to Changzhopn (Cantau). Even the Chinese tea could not keep author awake!

surprised to find a westerner sitting in a compartment with three Chinese companions. She asked me if I would be willing to participate in the film. I told her I would be pleased to do so provided I was given time to change from my pyjamas to a safari suit. When I was properly attired the little conductor was brought in to ask me questions through translation while the camera whirred in the corridor. Unfortunately the producer didn't keep her promise to send a copy to me, or possibly red tape prevented her from doing so.

It was no surprise to me to find all the jute mills equipped with Mackie design machinery, which had been manufactured indigenously. In one instance a machine was giving trouble so the management asked my advice. I could have solved the problem on the spot, but made the excuse that it would have to be thoroughly investigated. This afforded me the opportunity to examine the machine in detail and I found that the Chinese manufacturer had done a remarkably good job. Ironically as I write this a large proportion of jute processing machinery of Mackie design is manufactured in the P.R.C. by a company called Golden Eagle Mackie Ltd. In view of this situation, even if it had been viable for Mr. Ho Yeow Hoon to set up a jute mill in the P.R.C. he would have to do so with locally made machinery. Apart from that, taking all factors into consideration I could not in all honesty, recommend investment in China to Mr. Ho. Despite this fact the tour of the country was beneficial in that it gave me a great insight into life in the P.R.C. as it then prevailed but, of course since then the country has changed beyond all recognition.

Now in 2008 I have quite a few Chinese friends who are students at Queen's University, Belfast, who find incredible some of the things I tell them about their country thirty years ago, particularly the girls who dress like other modern young folk, in brightly coloured clothes, with attractive jewellery and accessories. What a contrast to 1973 when they would have had to wear "Mao Zedong" uniforms, all dark blue, and certainly very simple jewellery if any. Furthermore, judging from photographs they show me, some live in quite modern apartments.

Incidentally, the Chinese company which now manufactures machinery considers it appropriate to maintain an office in Belfast under the name of Golden Eagle Mackie (UK) Ltd. Three former Mackie members, who are considerably younger than me, are Directors of that company. A young lady, formerly on Mackie's secretarial staff, is secretary of the company, so in some way the name Mackie is still to the fore in the jute world.

TAIWAN – REPUBLIC OF CHINA (ROC)

Survival by adaptabiltiy
The economic miracle

Preface
Political Status

THE POLITICAL STATUS OF the Republic of China is a contentious issue. The PRC claims that the ROC government is illegitimate, referring to it as the "Taiwan Authority", while the ROC views itself as an independent sovereign state. The ROC actively claimed to be the sole legitimate government of all China since its retreat to Taiwan in 1949 until the lift of martial law in 1987. Although the administration of pro-independence President Chen Shui-Bian does not actively claim jurisdiction over all of China, the national boundaries of the ROC have not been redrawn and its outstanding territorial claims from the late 1940s have not been revised. Thus, the claimed area of the ROC continues to include Mainland China, several off-shore islands, Taiwan, Outer Mongolia, northern Myanmar, and Tuva (now Russian territory).

The political environment is complicated by the potential for military conflict should overt actions toward independence or reunification be taken. It is the policy of the People's Republic of China to use force to ensure reunification if peaceful reunification is no longer possible, as stated in its anti-secession law, and there are substantial military installations on the Fujian coast for this reason. As a result of Cold War politics, the United States has provided military training and sold arms to the ROC armed forces. However, the current status quo, as defined by the US, is supported on a quid pro quo basis between both Chinese states. The PRC is expected to "use no force or threat[en] to use force against Taiwan" and the ROC is to "exercise prudence in managing all aspects of cross-strait relations." Both are to refrain from performing actions or espousing statements "that would unilaterally alter Taiwan's status."

Within the ROC, opinions are polarized between those supporting

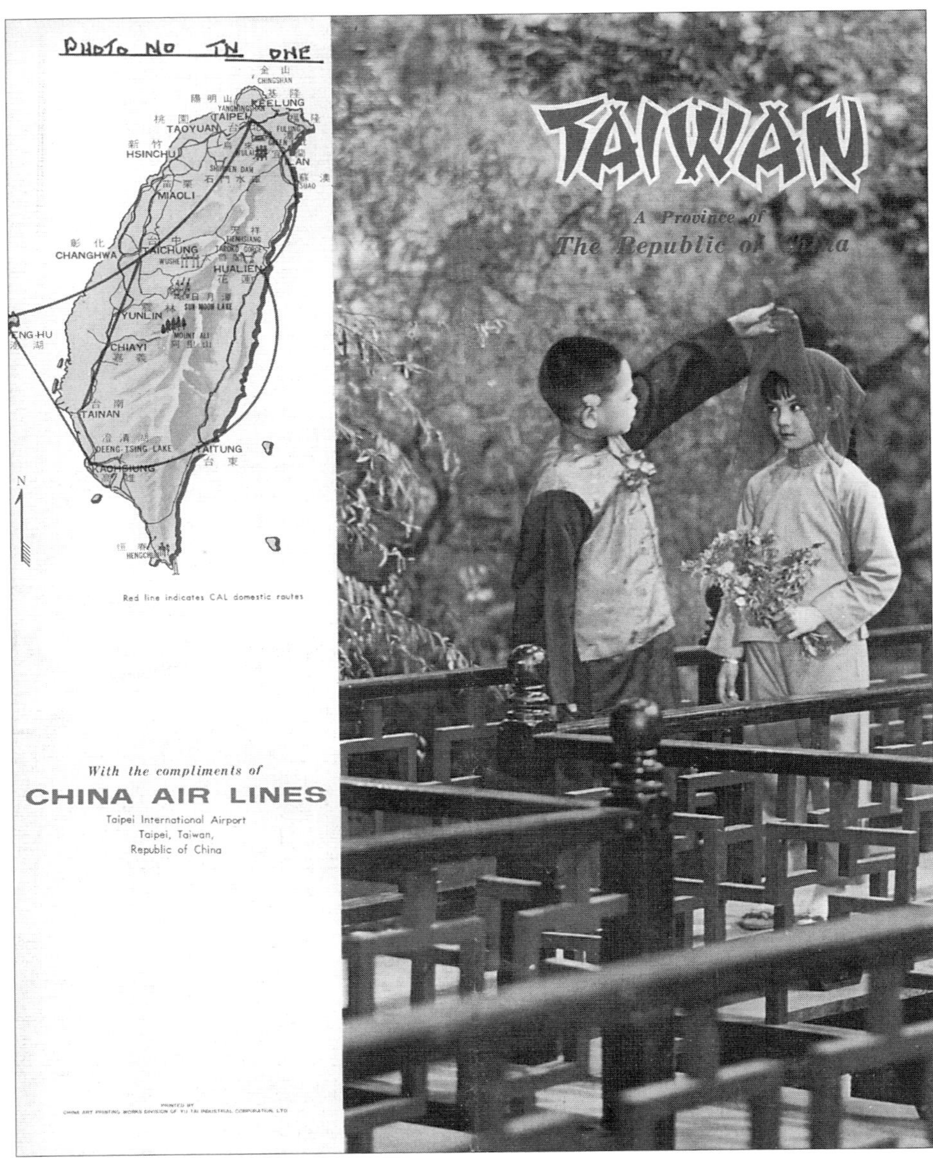

Promotional brochure of China Airlines.

unification, represented by the Pan-Blue Coalition of parties, and those supporting independence, represented by the Pan-Green Coalition of parties. The Kuomintang, the largest Pan-Blue party, supports the status quo for the indefinite future with a stated ultimate goal of unification. However, it does not support unification in the short term with the PRC as such a prospect would be unacceptable to most of its members and the public. Ma Ying-Jeou, former chairman of the KMT and frontrunner for the 2008 presidential election, has set out democracy and economic development to a level near that of the ROC, also equitable wealth distribution as the conditions that the mainland must fulfil for reunification to occur. The DPP, the largest Pan-Green party, also supports the status quo because the risk of provoking the PRC is unacceptable to its members. However, President Chen Shui-Bian of the DPP has stated that no matter what, any decision should be decided through a public referendum of the people of the ROC. Both parties' current foreign policy positions support actively advocating ROC participation in international organisations, but the KMT accepts the "One-China" principle and the DPP encourages economic ties with countries other than the PRC for security reasons.

For its part, the People's Republic of China appears to find the retention of the name "Republic of China" far more acceptable than the declaration of a de-jure independent Taiwan. However, with the rise of the Taiwanese independence movement, the name "Taiwan" has been employed increasingly more often on the island itself. The PRC has stated that any effort in Taiwan to formally abolish the ROC and replace it with a Republic of Taiwan would result in a strong and possibly military reaction. The current position of the United States is that the Taiwan issue must be resolved peacefully and unilateral action by either side is condemned; neither an unprovoked invasion by the PRC or a formal declaration of independence by Taiwan would be acceptable.

Citing its One-China policy, the PRC requires other countries to give no official recognition to the ROC as a condition of maintaining diplomatic relations. As a result, there are only 24 countries that have official diplomatic relations with the Republic of China. However, most countries have unofficial representative offices in the ROC. The United States maintains unofficial relations with the ROC through the instrumentality of the American Institute in Taiwan. The ROC maintains similar de-facto embassies and consulates in most countries called "Taipei Economic and Cultural Representative Offices" (TECRO), with branch offices called "Taipei Economic and Cultural Offices" (TECO). Both TECRO and TECO are "unofficial commercial entities" of the ROC in charge of maintaining diplomatic relations, providing consular services (i.e. Visa applications), and serving the national interests of the ROC in other countries in basically the same way as an Embassy or Consulate.

Also due to its One-China policy, the PRC only participates in international organisations where the ROC is not recognized as a sovereign country. In 1945, the ROC, as representative of all the territory of China, was one of the founding nations and Security Council member of the United Nations, however, in 1971, with the passage of United Nations

General Assembly Resolution 2758, it was replaced by the PRC. Each year since 1992, the ROC has petitioned the UN for entry but has been unsuccessful. Most member states, including the United States, do not wish to discuss the issue of the ROC's political status for fear of souring diplomatic ties with the PRC. However, both the US and Japan publicly support the ROC's bid for membership in the World Health Organisation as an observer. Although the ROC has applied for WHO membership every year since 1997 under various denominations, their efforts have consistently been blocked by PRC. Also, the Republic of China is pressured to use the politically neutral name "Chinese Taipei" in international events such as the Olympic Games when the PRC is also a party. The ROC is typically barred from using its national anthem and national flag in international events due to PRC pressure and ROC spectators attending events such as the Olympics are often barred from bringing ROC flags into venues. The ROC is able to participate as "China" in organisations that the PRC does not participate in, such as the World Organisation of the Scout Movement.

The relationship with the PRC and the related issues of Taiwan independence and Chinese reunification continue to dominate ROC politics. For any particular resolution public favour shifts greatly with small changes in wording, illustrating the complexity of public opinion on the topic.

Taiwan Miracle

Taiwan's quick industrialisation and rapid growth during the latter half of the twentieth century, has been called the "Taiwan Miracle" or "Taiwan Economic Miracle". As it has developed alongside Singapore, South Korea and Hong Kong, the ROC is one of the industrialised developed countries known as the "Four Asian Tigers".

Japanese rule prior to and during World War II brought forth changes in the public and private sectors of the economy, most notably in the area of public works, which enabled rapid communications and facilitated transport throughout much of the island. The Japanese also improved public education and made the system compulsory for all ROC citizens during this time.

When the KMT government fled to Taiwan it brought the entire gold reserve and the foreign currency reserve of mainland China to the island which stabilized prices and reduced hyperinflation. More importantly, as part of its retreat to Taiwan, KMT brought with them the intellectual and business elites from the mainland. This unprecedented influx of monetary and human capital laid the foundation for Taiwan's later dramatic economic development. The KMT government instituted many laws and land reforms that it had never effectively enacted on mainland China. The government also implemented a policy of import-substitution, attempting to produce imported goods domestically. Much of this was made possible through US economic aid, subsidising the higher cost of domestic production. Native Taiwanese were largely excluded from the mainlander dominated government, so many went into the business world.

In 1962, Taiwan had a per capita gross national product (GNP) of $170, placing the island's economy squarely between Zaire and Congo. By 2005 Taiwan's per capita GNP, adjusted for purchasing power parity (PPP), had soared to $29,000 (2006 est.), contributing to a Human Development Index equivalent to that of European countries such as Greece.

According to economist Paul Krugman, the rapid growth was made possible by increases in capital and labour, but not an increase in efficiency. In other words, the savings rate increased, and work hours were both lengthened and many more people, such as women, entered the work force.

Dwight Perkins and others cite certain methodological flaws in Krugman's (and Alwyn Young's) research, and suggest that much of Taiwan's growth can be attributed to increased productivity. These productivity boosts were achieved through land reform, structural change (urbanisation and industrialisation), and an economic policy of export promotion rather than import substitution.

Present

Today the Republic of China has a dynamic capitalist, export-driven economy with gradually decreasing state involvement in investment and foreign trade. In keeping with this trend, some large government-owned banks and industrial firms are being privatized. Real growth in GDP has averaged about eight percent during the past three decades. Exports have provided the primary impetus for industrialisation. The trade surplus is substantial, and foreign reserves are the world's third largest. The Republic of China's current GDP per capita (PPP) is equal to the average of EU Countries. The Republic of China has its own currency: the new Taiwan Dollar.

Agriculture constitutes only two percent of the GDP, down from 35 percent in 1952. Traditional labour-intensive industries are steadily being moved offshore and with more capital and technology-intensive industries replacing them. The ROC has become a major foreign investor in the PRC, Thailand, Indonesia, the Philippines, Malaysia, and Vietnam. It is estimated that some 50,000 Taiwanese businesses and 1,000,000 business people and their dependents are established in the PRC.

Because of its conservative financial approach and its entrepreneurial strengths, the ROC suffered little compared with many of its neighbours from the Asian financial crisis in 1998 – 1999. Unlike its neighbours

South Korea and Japan, the Taiwanese economy is dominated by small and medium sized businesses, rather than the large business groups. The global economic downturn, however, combined with poor policy coordination by the new administration and increasing bad debts in the banking system, pushed Taiwan into recession in 2001, the first whole year of negative growth since 1947. Due to the relocation of many manufacturing and labour intensive industries to the PRC, unemployment also reached a level not seen since the 1970's oil crisis. This became a major issue in the 2004 presidential election. Growth averaged more than 4% in the 2002-2006 periods and the unemployment rate fell below 4%.

The ROC often joins international organisations under a politically neutral name. The ROC is a member of governmental trade organisations such as the World Trade Organisation under the name Separate Customs Territory of Taiwan, Penghu, Kinmen and Matsu since 2002.

—∞—

During my extensive travelling in the Far East I was called upon to visit Taiwan only once. Due to the fact that the jute industry in that country was very small, the textile industry as a whole was relatively large, there being thirty factories but only two jute mills. The other twenty eight processed predominantly wool and synthetic and consequently came under the umbrella of my colleague Desmond Morgan, the head of the Wool and Synthetic Department.

Author with tourist guide.

I recall being very impressed by the economy of Taiwan. The centre of the island is mountainous and only 10% of the land is arable, which is in the form of a belt on the coast around the mountains. This belt is very narrow on the East, the widest parts being on the North and South West of the Island, consequently the large cities and towns are located in those areas, the capital Taipei (Taibei) being in the North. At the widest part the belt would be approximately 80 Km (50 miles) from coast to the mountains. Amazingly the population of nearly 23 million live in this area and only a small percentage in the mountainous area, the population density being 633 per Km^2 (1639 per sq. mile).

Regrettably I did not keep a personal record of other facts that I learned during my visit. I did write a detailed report to Belfast, which must have been very informative as Bryan Hall complimented me on it and said that as he read it he felt he was in the country. Unfortunately I did not put a copy in my personal file and the company file has been destroyed, another regret!! Nevertheless Taiwan (ROC) stands out in my mind as a fascinating and an impressive country.

Author enjoying the sights.

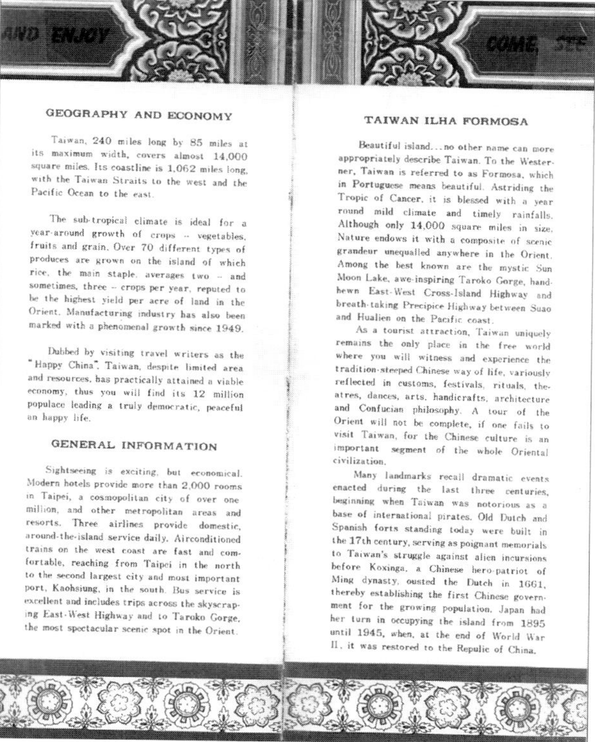

GEOGRAPHY AND ECONOMY

Taiwan, 240 miles long by 85 miles at its maximum width, covers almost 14,000 square miles. Its coastline is 1,062 miles long, with the Taiwan Straits to the west and the Pacific Ocean to the east.

The sub-tropical climate is ideal for a year-around growth of crops -- vegetables, fruits and grain. Over 70 different types of produces are grown on the island of which rice, the main staple, averages two -- and sometimes, three -- crops per year, reputed to be the highest yield per acre of land in the Orient. Manufacturing industry has also been marked with a phenomenal growth since 1949.

Dubbed by visiting travel writers as the "Happy China", Taiwan, despite limited area and resources, has practically attained a viable economy, thus you will find its 12 million populace leading a truly democratic, peaceful an happy life.

GENERAL INFORMATION

Sightseeing is exciting, but economical. Modern hotels provide more than 2,000 rooms in Taipei, a cosmopolitan city of over one million, and other metropolitan areas and resorts. Three airlines provide domestic, around-the-island service daily. Airconditioned trains on the west coast are fast and comfortable, reaching from Taipei in the north to the second largest city and most important port, Kaohsiung, in the south. Bus service is excellent and includes trips across the skyscraping East-West Highway and to Taroko Gorge, the most spectacular scenic spot in the Orient.

TAIWAN ILHA FORMOSA

Beautiful island...no other name can more appropriately describe Taiwan. To the Westerner, Taiwan is referred to as Formosa, which in Portuguese means beautiful. Astriding the Tropic of Cancer, it is blessed with a year round mild climate and timely rainfalls. Although only 14,000 square miles in size, Nature endows it with a composite of scenic grandeur unequalled anywhere in the Orient. Among the best known are the mystic Sun Moon Lake, awe-inspiring Taroko Gorge, hand-hewn East-West Cross-Island Highway and breath-taking Precipice Highway between Suao and Hualien on the Pacific coast.

As a tourist attraction, Taiwan uniquely remains the only place in the free world where you will witness and experience the tradition-steeped Chinese way of life, variously reflected in customs, festivals, rituals, theatres, dances, arts, handicrafts, architecture and Confucian philosophy. A tour of the Orient will not be complete, if one fails to visit Taiwan, for the Chinese culture is an important segment of the whole Oriental civilization.

Many landmarks recall dramatic events enacted during the last three centuries, beginning when Taiwan was notorious as a base of international pirates. Old Dutch and Spanish forts standing today were built in the 17th century, serving as poignant memorials to Taiwan's struggle against alien incursions before Koxinga, a Chinese hero-patriot of Ming dynasty, ousted the Dutch in 1661, thereby establishing the first Chinese government for the growing population. Japan had her turn in occupying the island from 1895 until 1945, when, at the end of World War II, it was restored to the Repulic of China.

Write up – interesting facts

IRAN (PERSIA)

The land of the Shah and the Ayatollah

Preface

OFFICIALLY THE ISLAMIC REPUBLIC of Iran, formerly known internationally as Persia, is a Southwest Asian country located in the geographic territories of the Middle East, Southern Asia, Central Asia and the Caucasus. Shi'a Islam is the state religion and Persian the official language.

The 18th largest country in the world in terms of area at 1,648,000 square kilometres, Iran is about the size of the United Kingdom, France, Spain and Germany combined. It has a population of over seventy million people.

Iran borders Armenia, Azerbaijan, and Turkmenistan to the north; Afghanistan and Pakistan to the east; and Turkey and Iraq to the west. In addition, it borders the Persian Gulf, an important oil-producing area, Gulf of Oman, and the Caspian Sea. Because of its geographically central location it also has a proximity to Europe, Africa, South and Central Asia and is therefore considered to be of geographical importance.

The political system of Iran comprises several intricately connected governing bodies. It is based on the 1979 Constitution. The highest state authority is the Supreme Leader, currently Ayatollah Ali Khomeini.

Iran is one of the world's oldest continuous major civilisations, with historical and urban settlements dating back to 4000 BCE, making it a possible candidate for the earliest human civilisation. Throughout history Iran has been of geostrategic importance because of its central location in Eurasia. Iran is a founding member of the UN, NAM, OIC, OPEC, ECO, and seeks to join the SCO.

It occupies an important position in international energy security and world economy due to its large reserves of petroleum and natural gas. The country is known for its independent stances in the global arena. Iran is currently a regional power. The name Iran is a cognate of Aryan, and literally means "Land of the Aryans".

Persia suffered several wars with Imperial Russia during the Qajar era, resulting in Persia losing almost half of its territories to Imperial Russia and the British Empire via the treaties of Gulistan, Turkmenchay, and Akhal. Repeated foreign intervention and a corrupt and weakened Qajar rule led to various protests, which by the end of the Qajar period resulted in Persia's constitutional revolution establishing the nation's first parliament in 1906, within a constitutional monarchy.

Famine in 1870-1871 is believed to have caused the death of 2 million people. During the 1917-1919 famine, as much as 1/4 of the population living in the north of Persia died.

From the Pahlavi era to the Iranian Revolution (1921 – 1979)

With the rise of modernisation and encroachment of stronger Western powers in the late nineteenth century came the Persian Constitutional Revolution of 1905-1911. Reformers hoped the constitution would strengthen Iran against Imperial Russia and Britain by centralising and modernising it. Ultimately the constitution became law, but its provisions were seldom followed during most of its history.

In 1921, an army officer Reza Khan of Mazandarani and Persian descent (known as Reza Shah after assuming the throne) staged a coup against the weakened Qajar dynasty. An autocrat and supporter of modernisation, Reza Shah initiated the development of modern industry, railroads, and establishment of a national education system. Reza Shah sought to balance the influence of Russia and Britain by seeking out assistance and technology from European powers traditionally not involved in Iranian affairs, but when World War II started his closeness to Germany alarmed allied powers Russia and Britain, Germany's enemies.

In the summer of 1941, Britain and the USSR invaded Iran to prevent Iran from allying with the Axis powers. The Allies occupied Iran, securing a supply line to Russia, Iran's petroleum infrastructure, and forced the Shah to abdicate in favour of his son, Mohammad Reza Pahlavi. In 1951, a nationalist politician, Dr. Mossadegh, rose to prominence in Iran and was elected Prime Minister. As Prime Minister, Mossadegh became enormously popular in Iran by nationalising the Anglo-Iranian Oil Company (later British Petroleum, BP) which controlled the country's oil reserves. In response, Britain embargoed Iranian oil and began plotting to depose Mossadegh. Members of the British Intelligence Service invited the United States to join them; convincing U.S. President Eisenhower that Mossadegh was reliant on the Tudeh (Communist) Party to stay in power. In 1953, President Eisenhower authorised Operation Ajax, and the CIA took the lead in overthrowing Mossadegh and supporting a U.S.-friendly monarch; and for which the U.S. Government apologised in 2000.

The CIA faced many setbacks, but the covert operation soon went into full swing, conducted from the U.S. Embassy in Tehran under the leadership of Kermit Roosevelt, Jr. Iranians were hired to protest against Mossadegh and fight pro-Mossadegh demonstrators. Anti- and pro-monarchy protestors violently clashed in the streets, leaving almost three hundred dead. The operation was successful in triggering a coup, and within days, pro-Shah tanks stormed the capital and bombarded the Prime Minister's residence. Mossadegh surrendered, and was arrested on 19 August 1953. He was tried for treason, and sentenced to three years in prison.

Mohammed Reza Pahlavi returned to power greatly strengthened and his rule became increasingly autocratic in the following years. With strong support from the U.S. and U.K., the Shah further modernised Iranian industry, but simultaneously crushed all forms of political opposition with his intelligence agency, SAVAK. Ayatollah Ruhollah Khomeini became an active critic of the Shah's White Revolution and publicly denounced the government. Khomeini, who was popular in religious circles, was arrested and imprisoned for 18 months. After his release in 1964, Khomeini publicly criticised the United States government. The Shah was persuaded to send him into exile by General Hassan Pakravan. Khomeini was sent first to Turkey, then to Iraq and finally to France. While in exile, he continued to denounce the Shah.

Iranian Revolution and Iran-Iraq War (1979-1988)

The Iranian Revolution (also known as the Islamic Revolution) transformed Iran from a monarchy under Shah Mohammad Reza Pahlavi, to an Islamic republic under Ayatollah Ruhollah Khomeini, the leader of the revolution and founder of the Islamic Republic.

The revolution began in January 1978 with the first major demonstrations against the Shah. After strikes and demonstrations paralysed the country, the Shah fled the country in January 1979. On February 1, 1979 Ayatollah Khomeini returned from exile to Tehran, enthusiastically greeted by millions of Iranians. The Pahlavi dynasty collapsed ten days later on February 11 when Iran's military declared itself "neutral" after guerrillas and rebel troops overwhelmed troops loyal to the Shah in armed street fighting. Iran officially became an Islamic Republic on April 1, 1979 when Iranians overwhelmingly approved a national referendum to make it so. In December 1979 the country approved a theocratic constitution, whereby

Khomeini became Supreme Leader of the country. The speed and success of the revolution surprised many throughout the world, as it had not been precipitated by a military defeat, a financial crisis, or a peasant rebellion. It produced profound change at great speed. It overthrew a regime thought to be heavily protected by a lavishly financed army and security services. And it replaced a monarchy with a theocracy based on Guardianship of the Islamic Jurists (or velayat-e faqih). Although both nationalists and Marxists joined with Islamic traditionalists to overthrow the Shah, it ultimately resulted in an Islamic Republic "under the guidance of an 80-year old exiled religious scholar from Qom," Ayatollah Ruhollah Khomeini.

Iran's relations with the United States became deeply antagonistic during the revolution. On November 4, 1979, Iranian students seized US embassy personnel, labelling the embassy a "den of spies." They accused its personnel of being CIA agents plotting to overthrow the revolutionary government, as the CIA had done to Mohammad Mossadegh in 1953. While the student ringleaders had not asked for permission from Khomeini to seize the embassy, Khomeini nonetheless supported the embassy takeover after hearing of its success. While most of the female and African American hostages were released within the first months, the remaining fifty-two hostages were held for 444 days. This is often considered a violation of the long-standing principal of international law that diplomats are immune from arrest (diplomatic immunity). The students demanded the handover of the Shah in exchange for the hostages, and following the Shah's death in the summer of 1980, that the hostages be put on trial for espionage. Subsequent attempts by the Jimmy Carter administration to negotiate or rescue were unsuccessful until January 1981 when the Algiers declaration was agreed upon. The U.S. promised (among other things) in the accord to release Iranian assets that had been frozen, but as of 2007 those assets still remain frozen.

Iraqi leader Saddam Hussein decided to take advantage of what he perceived to be disorder in the wake of the Iranian Revolution and its unpopularity with Western governments. The once-strong Iranian military had been disbanded during the revolution, and with the Shah ousted, Hussein had ambitions to position himself as the new strong man of the Middle East. He also sought to expand Iraq's access to the Persian Gulf by acquiring territories that Iraq had claimed earlier from Iran during the Shah's rule. Of chief importance to Iraq was Khuzestan which not only boasted a substantial Arab population, but rich oil fields as well. On the unilateral behalf of the United Arab Emirates, the islands of Abu Musa and the Greater and Lesser Tunbs became objectives as well. With these ambitions in mind, Hussein planned a full-scale assault on Iran, boasting that his forces could reach the capital within three days. On September 22,

1980 the Iraqi army invaded Iran at Khuzestan, precipitating the Iran-Iraq War. The attack took revolutionary Iran completely by surprise.

Although Saddam Hussein's forces made several early advances, by 1982, Iranian forces managed to push the Iraqi army back into Iraq. Khomeini sought to export his Islamic revolution westward into Iraq, especially on the majority Shi'a Arabs living in the country. The war then continued for six more years until 1988, when Khomeini, in his words, "drank the cup of poison" and accepted a truce mediated by the United Nations.

Tens of thousands of Iranian civilians and military personnel were killed when Iraq used chemical weapons in its warfare. Iraq was financially backed by Egypt, the Arab countries of the Persian Gulf, the Soviet Union and the Warsaw Pact states, the United States (beginning in 1983), France, the United Kingdom, Germany, Brazil, and the People's Republic of China (which also sold weapons to Iran).

There were more than 100,000 Iranian victims of Iraq's chemical weapons during the eight-year war. The total Iranian casualties of the war were estimated to be anywhere between 500,000 and 1,000,000. Almost all relevant international agencies have confirmed that Saddam engaged in chemical warfare to blunt Iranian human wave attacks; these agencies unanimously confirmed that Iran never used chemical weapons during the war.

Government and Politics

The political system of the Islamic Republic is based on the 1979 Constitution called the "Qanun-e Asasi" ("Fundamental Law"). The system comprises several intricately connected governing bodies. The Supreme Leader of Iran is responsible for delineation and supervision of "the general policies of the Islamic Republic of Iran". The Supreme Leader is Commander-in-Chief of the armed forces, controls the military intelligence and security operations, and has sole power to declare war. The heads of the judiciary, state radio and television networks, the commanders of the police and military forces and six of the twelve members of the Council of Guardians are appointed by the Supreme Leader. The Assembly of Experts elects and dismisses the Supreme Leader on the basis of qualifications and popular esteem. The Assembly of Experts is responsible for supervising the Supreme Leader in the performance of legal duties.

—∞—

During the 1970's I visited Iran frequently and spent relatively long periods there. It was one country in which I never felt entirely at ease, although I did make numerous good friends. After the Islamic Revolution in 1979, I paid my last visit in March 1982, which was rather scary. The changes that had taken place in the two years after the overthrow of the Shah were awesome. Islamic rules were stringently enforced by Ayatollah Khomeini, the Supreme Leader and his cohorts. Initially the army and the police remained somewhat neutral, but a separate force was formed called the Revolutionary Guards, the members of which were extremists and were greatly feared. They treated the general public ruthlessly, and the army and police with distain. I will return to this subject later.

My first visit to Iran took place in April 1972. At that time Mackie had not appointed an official agent and were provisionally represented by a Jewish company, Iracont Textile Machinery Co. Ltd. The staff member delegated to look after our interests was a young Jewish man by the name of John Sueke, who hailed from Manchester. He had been involved in the cotton industry in that city. I'm not aware of the circumstances, but he met and married a very attractive Iranian Jewish girl called Mina and decided to seek his fortune in Iran. He talked glibly about becoming a millionaire in a matter of a few years, but I don't think John ever achieved his ambition.

In 1972, there was a sizeable textile industry in Iran but only three jute mills, one of which was very small. All were equipped with out-of-date machinery, but strangely, there were no serious plans for modernisation. The government was more interested in expansion of the industry. Plans for industrial expansions in the public sector came under the control of a department called the Industrial Development and Renovation Organisation (IDRO). The gentleman with whom we dealt in that organisation was a Mr. Tamaddon. Strangely enough this gentleman was not a Muslim but a devotee to the Bahá'í Faith. The following excerpt on this religion may be of interest.

What is the Bahá'í Faith?

Founded a century and a half ago, the Bahá'í Faith is today among the fastest-growing of the world's religions. With more than five million followers, who reside in virtually every nation on earth, it is the second-most widespread faith, surpassing every religion but Christianity in its geographic reach. Bahá'ís reside in more than 100,000 localities around the world, an expansion that reflects their dedication to the ideal of world citizenship.

The Bahá'í Faith's global scope is mirrored in the composition of its membership. Representing a cross section of humanity, Bahá'ís come from virtually every nation, ethnic group, culture, profession, and social or economic class. More than 2,100 different ethnic and tribal groups are represented.

Since it also forms a single community, free of schism or factions, the

Bahá'í Faith comprises what is very likely the most diverse and widespread organised body of people on earth.

The Faith's Founder was Bahá'u'lláh, a Persian nobleman from Tehran who, in the mid-nineteenth century, left a life of princely comfort and security and, in the face of intense persecution and deprivation, brought to humanity a stirring new message of peace and unity.

Bahá'u'lláh claimed to be nothing less than a new and independent messenger from God. His life, work, and influence parallel that of Abraham, Krishna, Moses, Zoroaster, Buddha, Christ and Muhammad. Bahá'ís view Bahá'u'lláh as the most recent in this succession of divine Messengers.

The essential message of Bahá'u'lláh is that of unity. He taught that there is only one God, that there is only one human race, and that all the world's religions represent stages in the revelation of God's will and purpose for humanity. In his day, Bahá'u'lláh said, humanity has collectively come of age. As foretold in all of the world's scriptures, the time has arrived for the uniting of all peoples into a peaceful and integrated global society. "The earth is but one country, and mankind its citizens," he wrote.

I will return to the subject of Mr. Tamaddon and IDRO in due course.

In 1974 the Iranian authorities decided to hold an exhibition of industrial equipment in which a considerable number of British companies, including Mackie, participated. As we saw a potential market for both jute and synthetic processing machinery, it was decided to exhibit an S4 Semi-Circular Weaving Machine for jute and a D.A.S.N. Spinning Frame for synthetic fibres. We also displayed what were termed "furnishings", i.e. ancillary components. As usual, Barry Pitman of the Publicity Department designed the stand, which as always, was serviceable and attractive. Of course the catering facilities were planned and provided by Margot Wills who again did a superb job. Indeed, the Mackie stand was the envy of the other exhibitors to such an extent that I had to make it clear, that while we were willing to provide the occasional refreshing drink, the facilities were primarily for our staff and visitors. We did, however, make an exception for a young Austrian lady, Margarete Preis, who represented a small British company, which had provided no facilities whatsoever for her. Real Irish hospitality was provided for her!!

At all exhibitions it is not only necessary but also appropriate to employ some local personnel and it is advantageous to include a couple of attractive young ladies. In this instance, we engaged John Sueke's sister-in-law, Norah, and a friend recommended by her, both Jewish. This did not present any problem, as when Shah Reza Pahlavi was in power, there was a substantial Jewish community in Iran, and according to my colleague, Desmond Morgan, there were eighty Jewish members of Parliament. Relations between Iran and Israel were such that El Al Airline and Iran Air operated

Mackie exhibition stand showing the two Iranian (Jewish) ladies – Norah and Rebecca, dressed in Irish linen discussing technical brochures with author and Norman Howie, sales consultant.

frequent flights between Tehran and Tel Aviv.

Another idea of Margot's was also adopted for the Mackie stand. Lengths of Irish linen, in three different colours, were sent from Belfast. Naturally the Irish colour of green was chosen as the basic one. The second was a "tartan" design of green and white, while the third was plain white. A local tailor was engaged to produce "co-ordinates" for the girls i.e. jackets, shirts, and trousers, which could be "mixed and matched". These costumes fulfilled a dual purpose, as they were an added attraction on the stand, and being Irish linen, they were a form of advertising. It could be pointed out that the flax yarn, from which the fabric was woven, had been produced on Mackie equipment, thereby informing textile industrialists that we could offer also that type of machinery, in addition to that on display.

Technically the stand was manned by two Mackie erection engineers. On the sales side by Norman Howie from the Wool and Synthetics Department, and myself from the Jute Division. There were also two young Iranian men for liaison purposes. We were joined for several days by Bryan Hall, who as Sales Director, wished to assess the potential business for Mackie in the Iranian market. Recalling Bryan's visit brings back a rather unpleasant memory. He had arrived hoping to attend the official opening of the show by the Shah, indeed knowing Bryan, I think he may have had in his mind the possibility of meeting his majesty to add to the list of the other Heads of State he had previously met. The first expectation was reasonable, as in other countries, even in China, at least one representative from each exhibiting country is invited to such a ceremony, and as the most senior Mackie executive, Bryan would have been given preference, however, Iran was unique in several ways.

As mentioned in the preface, the Shah protected his position by strong arm tactics through his intelligence agency "SAVAK". Wherever he or close members of his family went, very stringent security measures were imposed, and the Shah dictated unreasonable measure to suit his own interests. For example, on one occasion when my colleague Desmond Morgan was on a visit to Tehran, he was staying in the Inter-continental hotel. One day, when he returned to the hotel after being out on business, as usual went to the reception to collect his key, only to be told to collect his suitcases and move out, as on the orders of the Shah, all rooms had been commandeered to accommodate his guests who were about to arrive in Tehran for an important function hosted by the Shah. No objection or argument made any difference! It can be appreciated how difficult it was to find alternative accommodation.

This situation was made worse by the fact that the Mackie Deputy

Team of British and Iranian personnel who manned the stand, i.e. two Mackie consultants, two Mackie engineers and three Iranian. Desmond Morgan – Technical consultant for wool and synthetics arrived later.

Sales Director, John Mc Connell, was about to arrive to join Desmond. Eventually rooms were secured in a two star hotel, which did not please John, despite the fact that he was a very understanding person.

To get back to the exhibition. John Sueke and the other Directors of the Iracont Company pulled out all the stops and used their considerable influence in an attempt to obtain at least one entry permit to the opening ceremony but all to no avail. Much to Bryan Hall's annoyance, which was expressed in no uncertain terms at a luncheon party hosted by Iracont Directors in Bryan's honour. It was all very embarrassing for me as I felt our Iranian friends had done their very best under the circumstances, nevertheless it put paid to any chance of Iracont being appointed as the Mackie agent for Iran, which left poor John Sueke rather disillusioned!! However, he being an ebullient character soon got over this hurdle and continued to solicit business for Mackies primarily in the wool and synthetic field, as the sale of jute machinery was subsequently channelled through another party.

During the exhibition no firm business was secured but the Mackie name was certainly brought to the attention of government officials and Irish industrialists. This probably attributed to some extent to the substantial orders received over the following five to six years for both jute and synthetic processing machinery. At the exhibition the Mackie staff and their Iranian colleagues worked very hard and put on an excellent show. So, in recognition of their efforts, I decided to arrange a night out. A Greek restaurant was chosen for the event, probably on the recommendation of Norah. The boys enjoyed not only the Greek cuisine, and of course the beverages, but the Greek custom of smashing the plates and other dishes after each course. They wholeheartedly indulged in this exercise.

Very sensibly cheap delph and crockery are used and the floor is tiled. The restaurateur expects diners to enjoy themselves and the Mackie boys and friends did not disappoint him, particularly Norman Howie, who at the best of times is a "wag" was the most enthusiastic, more so after he had a few "tipples"! By the end of the evening the restaurant floor was covered by broken crockery to a depth of several inches. However, there was no misbehaving and a good time was had by all.

In mid 1975 the situation in the jute machinery field changed by the arrival on the scene of a Mr. Bernhard Litscher, the proprietor of a very successful Swiss trading company based in Geneva. By this time Bernhard had had a long association with Mackie, securing business for the company primarily in West Africa. He was a very astute businessman who presented an excellent image in dress and deportment. His company in Switzerland, Altrom Ltd., represented several very reputable organisations such as Bosch and had very good relations with Mercedes Benz. He was ably assisted by his nephew Bernhard Lippuner. Both of these gentlemen spoke English,

Author with John Sueke and sitting opposite, his wife Mina.

French and German fluently and of course Switzer Deutsch. Their names will arise relatively frequently in the future, so to differentiate between them and for brevity, I will refer to the former as Bernhard Lt. and the latter as Bernhard Lp.

After his dispute with the Iracont Company, Bryan was still considering the agency problem when he was contacted by Bernhard Lt., who told them that he had a very good "middleman" in Tehran who had access to the right people in government and private circles. That person turned out to be an Armenian named Uahe Hovesepian, who ran a small merchandising company in the city. Uahe was what I term a "wheeler-dealer" with really no business acumen, but a person who could work behind the scenes who could wheedle his way into offices, influence people and get the right information. He left office work to his assistant and spent his time either on the phone or driving from one source of information to another. Despite his unorthodox method of operation, I formed a good relationship with Uahe and periodically had dinner at his home.

From the outset of our acquaintance Bernhard Lt. and I hit it off. Although I say it myself, we did make a good team. He as the smooth but shrewd businessman, and I with my down to earth approach and technical knowledge and experience, complemented each other. I will say more later about the friendship that developed not only with Bernhard Lt. but with his lovely wife Dagmar and his family.

The first contract the trio, Bernhard Lt., Uahe Hovesepian and I were successful in securing, was with IDRO, the organisation already mentioned, which was represented by Mr. Tamaddon and a colleague Mr. Rasoullin. Both these gentlemen were experienced negotiators who drove a hard bargain, so after I had laid the ground work I was joined on our side by Bernhard Lt., Bryan Hall, and the Mackie Contract Manager, Jim Mawhinney, to negotiate the final hurdle. We all assembled one morning around 10 a.m. at the IDRO office. After a couple of hours bargaining the two parties shook hands on the deal. As was frequently the case with clients, when terms were agreed the two IDRO men desired to have the contract signed with the least possible delay, probably having in mind their "cut", in fact they suggested 2.30 p.m. that afternoon.

I can still see the look of consternation on Bryan Hall's face. Around three hours to have the requisite documents drawn up and typed!! The situation was exacerbated by the fact that, after cutting ties with Iracont, Mackie had no typing facilities in Tehran. Bryan looked at me in despair, but as mentioned earlier, I had learned to anticipate the unexpected and to improvise when necessary. I told him and Bernhard Lt. to go back to the hotel, relax and have lunch, then to return to the IDRO office at the appointed time.

I recalled that a young Iranian lady who had typed for me previously worked in a nearby office, so I decided to chance my arm. Accompanied by Jim Mawhinney, I found my way to the office in question and was greatly relieved to find the young lady at her desk. When I explained to her our quandary, she quite rightly pointed out that on previous occasions she had worked for me after hours, while now she was on her permanent job and her boss had just given her some work. On my suggestion she contacted her boss saying a very persuasive man wished to speak to him. A few minutes later a very pleasant gentleman came into the room. When I explained my problem so to speak he rubbed his hands and said "that's a good excuse for me to have a round of golf"! He then turned to his secretary and said; "look after these gentlemen, order some sandwiches and coffee for their lunch, then get cracking on the typing." And so the wheels were set in motion. As the young lady was an excellent typist the job was completed in good time and the contract was signed as desired by the clients, and we had a celebratory dinner in the hotel that evening. Naturally the young lady was handsomely rewarded.

Mention of the hotel brings some interesting facts to mind. At that time there were only two hotels of international standard in Tehran, the Hilton and the Intercontinental. I preferred the latter because of its location downtown and near the office I had to visit. Both hotels were always fully booked so one had to make contingency plans. This I did by cultivating a good relationship with the Reservations Manager of the Intercontinental, a Mr. Munasian, and perhaps indulging in a little bribery by taking him some "duty free" on each visit. Consequently, I only had to send a fax informing him of the date of my arrival and he always reserved a suitable room for me.

Most flights from Europe arrived in Tehran in the evening, so between 7 and 8 p.m. on most evenings, there was what I called "the battle of the bookings" at the reception counter as business people claimed they had reservations and waved faxes at the staff only to be told there were no rooms available. My arrival was quite a contrast as I was greeted by Mr. Munasian; "welcome back Mr. Jebb your usual room has been reserved". The bell boy was called who carried my suitcases to the room and returned with a parcel!! I also made appropriate arrangements at the fax office, there being no emails in those days. Most evenings there was a queue of residents demanding that their faxes should be sent without delay only to be told they would have to take their turn. I simply wrote my message, folded the paper, inserted a 200 Riel note, and said dispatch that as soon as you have time. Thereafter I waited in the lobby not more than ten minutes to receive a copy of the fax that had been sent. Just a token of appreciation did the trick!!

In the days of the Shah many overseas companies had representatives in Tehran and quite a few made the Intercontinental hotel their base. Despite the fact that there was a variety of nationalities, they were inclined to consort with one another, particularly around the swimming pool on Thursday afternoon and Friday, the "weekend" in Iran the country being predominantly Muslim. Initially I was inclined to keep myself to myself until a friendly German lady, noticing this, insisted that I join the "club", and I soon entered into the "spirit of the party", which came to the attention of a local newspaper correspondent resulting in an article in his paper. As a group we also experienced the extent to which the security authorities went. Frequently on a Friday when relaxing by the pool we were joined by a bearded gentleman, an Iranian, who claimed to be Development Manager for the Intercontinental Hotel Group. Normally, only residents and their friends were permitted to use the swimming pool facilities, but this man, although in neither category, seemed to come and go freely. Somehow one of our group found out that he was in fact a member of SAVAK the Secret Service Agency. This did not in any way curtail our activities, in fact, some of the foreigners were inclined to lead him on!! Our position was further safeguarded by the fact that he took a fancy to Alice Anders, the Danish singer and guitarist, and paid more attention to her!

To revert to the contract signed with IDRO, a suitable site for the factory had been acquired by Mr. Tamaddon at a place called Rasht 230 Km (144 miles) north west of Tehran near the Caspian Sea. It had been decided to name it Kanaf Kar Company (Kanaf being the Iranian name for kenaf fibre). More money was spent on the factory building than I would have recommended, but that was up to Mr. Tamaddon. I can guess why!

When the project got under way, Bernhard Lt. arranged for a young Swiss man called Hans Burkhard to reside in Tehran and handle the day to day practicalities of the Kanaf Kar project and other Altrom business interests. A car was provided for Hans, which in fact he drove all the way from Switzerland, which did not fizz on Hans as he was a well built six-footer. He acted as my chauffeur when journeys up country were necessary. We quickly became "partners in crime" and very good friends, a friendship which continues. He now has his own small trading company in Zurich.

Some of the glamour that frequented the swimming pool at the Tehran Intercontinental Hotel.

I was successful in negotiating a contract with another government department for the expansion of an existing jute mill, located in a town called Shahi (Ghaemshar) also on the southern shore of the Caspian Sea, around 250 Km (150 miles) east of Rasht and about the same distance north east of Tehran. The management of that company desired to add a plant to produce jute wall covering. Drawing up a proposal for a suitable plant was a new challenge for me as the spinning machinery had to be capable of a very fine jute yarn of high quality. The manufacture of suitable equipment did not present any problem to Mackie, but what in the trade was called the finishing equipment, was entirely different from that in a standard jute mill. For the production of wall covering, the jute fabric has to be dyed or printed with patterns, laminated to paper backing, and cut into the requisite width. Machinery for these processes did not come within the ambit of Mackie manufacture, so I had to contact companies which specialised in these procedures and also acquaint myself with the necessary techniques. When it came to commissioning the plant, I, as always, turned to the ever capable Joe Mc Clelland, however, let me outline the complexities of negotiations.

Unlike the previous contract there were only two persons involved in the negotiations, the head of the government department, a Dr. Sabeti and myself. The usual bargaining took place but the doctor was tenacious and whittled the price down to the limit to which I could go on my own initiative. He was obviously serious as the final session took place on a

Friday, the weekly holiday, when Dr. Sabeti told me that if I gave a further two and a half percent he would sign the contact. As I refused to give way he told me to sleep on it and come to his office the following morning to finalise the deal. Having made up by mind not to carry the can myself, I decided on the following morning to consult Bryan Hall by phone. It being Saturday I called his home "Tara Lodge".

When there was no reply I decided to try the phone number of the Assistant Sales Director, John Mc Connell, a Ballymena man who was known as "The Major", having been in the British army. Fortunately John was available so I explained the situation to him and asked him how Bryan could be contacted as an immediate decision was essential. When he told me that it might not be possible to do so as Bryan was going that morning on a complimentary flight for VIP's on the Concorde, which was about to be introduced into service by British Airways and Air France, so he had probably already left home. When I heard this I "saw red" and "blew my top" over the phone.

Poor John bore the brunt of my pique. I told him that while I was "slogging my guts out" trying to get business for the company, the sales were sitting in luxury sipping champagne. Furthermore, if I didn't have an answer within a couple of hours, I would pack my bags and take the next flight home!! John would have been quite justified in telling me to cool it and to remember to whom I was speaking, but John being John, a real gentleman to me, he would see what could be done. I learned later from Desmond Morgan that John Mc Connell didn't take time to change from his bedroom slippers, but jumped into his car and drove like fury to Aldergrove, the Belfast International Airport. Apparently he arrived just in the nick of time so caught Bryan as he was about to go through the boarding gate. During a brief exchange Bryan said; "tell Stanley to take his own decision". Consequently John called back well within the specified time. I can't recall if I apologised to John for my arrogance, but I certainly should have done so!!

Later that morning when I arrived at Dr. Sabeti's office he did not, as I expected, enter into further negotiations. He simply pushed across his desk a signed Letter of Intent at the lower price and more or less said; "you cannot look a gift horse in the mouth" please countersign. After some hesitation and assumed reluctance I put my signature to the document. The implementation of this contract was quite an undertaking but I will refer to that later.

Quite unexpectedly I renewed contact in Iran with a large industrial family with whom Mackies had done substantial business in Pakistan, the Isphahanis. This family had very considerable investments in Burma but lost everything during the anti Indian uprising after that country gained independence. They then invested in a jute mill and other industries in East Pakistan only to be forced out of that country when it became independent Bangladesh. One of the younger generation, Isky Isphahani, had a look at Iran in the mid 1970's and decided it was a safe place to invest so we were successful in selling him a jute mill plant for the manufacture of jute carpet backing.

The company was called Iran Kanaf Ltd., and the factory was set up near the town of Rasht, an area, which for some reason I was not able to determine, was favoured by industrialists. I was not asked for my opinion but I felt that this, if anything, was more risky than the family's previous investments for several reasons. The main one's being the uncertainty of the political future of Iran and the volatility of the carpet backing market. Unfortunately my hunch proved to be correct so Isky must have again lost a packet!

I will refrain from going into the boring details of other contracts in which I was directly or indirectly involved. I will conclude my recollections of Iran by citing interesting experiences which stand out in my mind. During my visits to Iran it was necessary for me to make a round trip, in fact, it was more precisely a triangular journey, going north west to Rasht, then east along the southern edge of the Caspian Sea to the town of Shahi, now Ghaemshar, and finally south west back to Tehran. The purpose of this trip was to visit the various jute mills, not only when the Mackie engineers were engaged in installation of the machinery, but also after commissioning as part of the after sales service, in which Mackies excelled.

On one trip I again proved the truth of the saying; "the world is a small place"! If accommodation was not offered at any of the mills in the Rasht area it was advisable to go on to Ramsar, a distance of about 80 Km (50 miles). Ramsar was a popular Caspian Sea holiday resort for the better off Iranians, there being a casino attached to one of the hotels. On this occasion I was accompanied by Hans Burkhard and his fiancée Annick, so a mill management could not be expected to provide accommodation for three persons. After concluding our business at the Rasht mill, we proceeded to Ramsar and booked into a hotel there. After dinner with Hans and Annick I decided not to be a gooseberry but to leave them to their own devices, or should I say "vices"? As it was still early in the evening I wandered over to the casino out of curiosity, with no intention of gambling. Due to it being the middle of the week the clientele were few, so after having a look around I went to the bar and ordered a cold drink. At that time I didn't think that I had a particularly pronounced Belfast accent, but the young lady behind the bar, a "croupier", served up the drink and then asked me "from what part of Belfast do you come"? I replied originally from Stranmillis, and she then said; "I come from the Shankill Road". Needless to say there was an immediate rapport and we chatted freely. Two people from Belfast meeting in a casino in Northern Iran, and one a non gambler!!

On another occasion during the Iranian winter it was necessary to visit Shahi Jute Mill, later given an Iranian name Gunibafi Ghaemshar, literally translated means Ghaemshar Bag Factory. I finished the necessary business around 5 p.m. and decided, much against the advice of the factory manager and his colleagues, to head back to Tehran that evening. They warned me that I was taking a considerable risk as the road led over a mountain pass, nevertheless I hired a taxi and set out. In less than an hour it began to snow heavily. Very shortly thereafter, as darkness had also fallen, the police began stopping the traffic, particularly the trucks, and telling the drivers to park at the side of the road against the cliff side for the night. Fortunately I was not aware at the time I left that there was a rather narrow width of road between the parked vehicles and a shear drop into the valley below.

I was waiting for the police to stop the taxi and tell the driver to park. This would have meant spending the night in the back, which would have been a very uncomfortable and unpleasant experience, as we were well away from any source of food, hot drinks, or even a blanket. I don't know if the taxi driver bribed the police but in any event they did not intercept us. Despite slipping and sliding all over the road, the driver kept pressing on and "navigated" all obstacles. It goes without saying that I was greatly relieved when the taxi drove into the forecourt of the Intercontinental hotel around 9 p.m. I paid the taxi driver handsomely then went into the hotel and had a good stiff drink. Most people would say I was very lucky but I'm convinced there was divine protection. I became even more certain of this when I later did the journey by daylight. It was also evident how foolish I had been in embarking on the journey late in the day.

Perhaps it is regretful that I did not see more of the country and visit some of the historical sites, for as most people know, Iran (Persia) has a rich history, but after all my first responsibility was business. I did, however, see something of the country's heritage. In the centre of Tehran there is a government vault where what could be termed the crown jewels are kept. I don't know if it is still maintained, but during the reign of the Shah it was open to the public and the exhibits were breathtaking!! They included the Peacock Throne and displays of invaluable precious stones such as rubies, emeralds, and diamonds. These were literally in piles in glass cases, obviously the glass being a special type about 100mm (4") thick. There was also on display a series of ensemble including shoes, gloves, and handbags, worn by the Empress on state and special occasions. Apparently Empress Farah Diba had simply to tell her lady-in- waiting the number of the ensemble she wished to wear on a certain occasion and it would be brought from the vault under strict security.

As is well known Persian carpets are considered the best in the world in design, quality and value, so it is appropriate that there should be a museum in Tehran in which a great variety of carpets and rugs are beautifully displayed. It was on my last visit to Iran that I spent a fascinating afternoon going round the museum, which was situated a short distance from the Intercontinental hotel. The exhibits were most attractively laid out on platforms, which are angled and illuminated to show to the best advantage the design, pattern, textile and colour of each carpet and rug. The contents of the museum are invaluable and probably irreplaceable. An afternoon was really too short to adequately appreciate the display, its beauty and value.

That visit took place in March 1982, which as mentioned earlier, was after the revolution. It was evident, even before my arrival in Tehran, that I was about to visit a radically changed country. One of the international airlines still flying to Iran was Lufthansa. There were a considerable number of Iranian couples on the outward flight on which I was a passenger. At the outset, almost all the ladies were beautifully attired in western dresses, bedecked with jewellery, and had attractively coiffured hair, but not wearing headscarves! Over an hour before ETA in Tehran, it was well nigh impossible for males to get to the toilets, as the Iranian ladies were queued up to use the closets as changing rooms. Each one emerged wearing long dresses of dull colours and headscarves of a size to completely cover her hair. The wearing of the Burka (traditional Islamic gown) or Hijab (headdress covering the face) is not strictly enforced in Iran.

On landing at Tehran airport, the same ladies sat down demurely while their husbands undertook immigration and custom procedures. One man noticed that a lock of his wife's hair was sticking out of her headscarf and he took the precaution of pushing it in underneath. It must have been very painful for Iranian ladies who were very fashion conscious, and college girls who were accustomed to wearing western style uniforms, jeans, bush shirts, and similar gear to change their habits. Indeed, I know that many professional girls went to private offices in the acceptable garb and changed as soon as they got inside. Of course they were taking a risk, and probably kept their office and their other outfit close at hand.

As previously, I booked accommodation in the Intercontinental hotel, but what a shock I got on walking in to the lobby. What on previous occasions was bright and welcoming was now dimly lit and depressing. Where there had been a hub-bub of voices and a hive of activity there was now a depressive and deserted atmosphere. Furthermore, across the lobby was printed in large letters "Death to America"!! A shiver ran up one's back!! To my surprise, my friend, Mr. Munasian, was in his usual place behind the reception counter, but there was a noticeable change in his dress and deportment. Instead of being immaculate in a dark suit, white shirt and colourful tie, his suit appeared to be crumpled, and he was not permitted to wear a tie, which is considered to be a symbol of decadence. When I quietly asked Mr. Munasian how things were he did not lift his head, but almost in a whisper he said "terrible". There was no bar in the hotel as they had all been smashed to pieces by the revolutionary guards. The swimming pool was empty and altogether the hotel was a dismal place.

Once again I did my circular or "triangular" tour, the main object being to visit Joe Mc Clelland who was working at the Shahi Jute Mill endeavouring to sort out some problems on the laminating machine so that good quality wall covering could be produced. Only Joe would have stuck the conditions in which I found him living, there being not even a basic western type hotel in Shahi. He was staying in a small two bedroom apartment with no "mod cons" at all. The only means of heating was an electric fire on which only one bar was working. Again, in keeping with his character, Joe insisted that I should have the fire in my room the night I stayed over. I have told Joe that he should write a book primarily recording the circumstances and conditions in which he and his wife Iris have lived in many volatile parts of the world.

On a visit to another jute mill in the same area, North East Iran, near a town called Amoul (Amol), Joe accompanied me. This gave Joe a short break as surprisingly, we found a newly built modern hotel. What motivated any party to invest in a hotel in that town I don't know, but Joe and I were certainly glad of the comfort. While staying there we had an experience which stands out in my mind. One evening Joe called me from his room to say that a group of men wished to meet us in the hotel lobby, and he added as to why he hadn't a clue. This, under normal circumstances, would have caused no alarm, but events in Iran were very unpredictable. On entering the elevator we were somewhat apprehensive and were more so when we emerged into the lobby. There were at least five men with black bushy beards, wearing turbans, and Islamic robes, waiting for us. I think Joe and I jumped to the same conclusion, that either Bin Laden and his cohorts had come to enlist us, or a squad of the revolutionary guards had come to arrest us!! The purpose for the visit was much more elementary and understandable, although why five men were required beats me!! Perhaps it was due to the prevailing climate of suspicion in Iran.

The delegation had come from the old jute mill in Rasht to meet Joe McClelland. Joe's reputation as an engineer-cum-jute technologist had obviously spread throughout the whole industry in Iran. They discussed the problems being encountered at the factory in Rasht, and then requested Joe to visit the plant and advise how it's efficiency could be improved. Joe expressed his willingness to do so, but only after the job at Shahi had been completed.

Mackie staff with Iranian colleague

One of the Shahi factory managers accompanied me on my return to Tehran. He was a jolly type and certainly did not conform to the strict Islamic rules. On the way he told me that he and I had been invited to a dinner party that evening. I thought such events were a thing of the past, or if held, would be a rather dour affair, but I was in for a surprise. As arranged, he picked me up at the hotel at 7 p.m. and drove to a private house in a selective area of Tehran. On arriving at the door he seemed to give a special signal on the bell. In response the door was opened by a very suave gentleman dressed in a Saville Row suit with a co-ordinated shirt and tie. He greeted me in Oxford English and as soon as we got inside he closed and locked the door. When my friend and I were ushered into a large room we found probably a dozen guests, the other men equally as well dressed as the host, and their wives beautifully attired in western dress and bedecked with expensive jewellery.

Several more surprises awaited me! We were seated around a large coffee table on which there were bottles of coca cola. I was surprised that the name of the drink, being American, had not been changed! When the host started to pour the drinks, his hand went under the long tablecloth and out came a large stone jar containing vodka. I can't recall any of the guests declining to indulge!! As the evening wore on everybody became more relaxed and western music, which was strictly forbidden, was played. I noted that there were very thick curtains on the windows and that these were tightly closed. When I recently described the scene to a Muslim friend, she said "what a sham"! I felt it was also a shame!!

When it came to the homeward flight by Lufthansa, passengers were told to check-in at 4 a.m., although the scheduled time of departure was not until 7 a.m. That may not seem abnormal at the present time, but then, one hour prior to the expected time of departure was the norm. All the passengers were looking forward to getting out of Iran, so if anything, got to the airport earlier than stipulated. When we cleared customs and immigration and reached the embarkation lounge, we were informed that the flight would be delayed. No one could give even an approximation of the extent of the delay. The passengers who were already "up tight" became even more so, and there was no bar at which they could get a stiff drink to steady their nerves.

As 7 a.m. passed, then 8 and finally 9 without any definite information, my fellow passengers and I became more and more on edge and restlessly walked to and fro in the lounge. Eventually it was announced that the flight would take off at 10 a.m. When the call came to board I think everyone, including me, felt like making a dash for the aircraft and restraint required a major effort. At long last the doors were closed and the plane took off. Even when airborne the stewardess in the first class had to calm down mature business travellers and tell them that no alcoholic drinks could be served until the flight was out of Iranian airspace. When the imaginary line was crossed the stewardess brought a large tankard of beer to a German man seated across the aisle from me. He consumed it so quickly that most of it went round him rather than down his throat. After downing about four tankards he relaxed and enjoyed a good breakfast!! While the other passengers appeared to be more composed undoubtedly inside they felt the same and indulged in their own relaxant. I certainly did! I think this was the most nerve-racking experience of all my travels. Of course, I must not let it blot out the memories of many happy experiences in Iran, and I sincerely hope and pray that normality will one day return to that country. However, I feel that ex-Empress Farah Diba and her son, who are now living in exile in Egypt, are hoping in vain that this will take place in their lifetime.

As I complete the text for this book (June 2009) there is much unrest in Iran following recent elections which the opposition candidates claim were rigged to ensure the return to power of the previous President Mahmoud Ahmadinejad who is an extremist and is supported by Iran's supreme Leader Ayatollah Ali Khomeini. Many thousands have taken to the streets demanding fresh elections, but so far the supreme leader has been inflexible in his reaction. Perhaps he feels secure having the support of the army, the police and more sinister, the revolutionary guard. The situation is so volatile that even the most experienced Iran observer would not hazard a guess to the ultimate outcome. What a pity!! A country with a rich history and great potential is floundering in political confusion.

THE REPUBLIC OF PAKISTAN

Dictatorship v Democracy
The country of many Presidents and Prime Ministers

Preface
Creator of Pakistan

MOHAMMAD ALI JINNAH WAS born in 1876 and became a leader in India's struggle for independence from Britain. He originally was dubious about the practicability of the idea of an independent Pakistan that Sir Muhammad Iqbal propounded to the Muslim League Conference in 1930. However, before long he became convinced that a Muslim homeland on the Indian Subcontinent was the way of safeguarding Muslim interests and the Muslim way of life.

As is well known, the country of Pakistan came into existence on 15th August 1947.

Liaqat Ali Khan, was the first interim Prime Minister of Pakistan, though few of us appreciate this fact. Pakistan had a provisional Constituent Assembly of 69 members, indirectly elected by the Muslim members of the Provincial Assemblies of the British-held 1946 elections from the areas that came to be Pakistan in 1947. In the absence of a constitution and a legislature, Liaqat was made an interim Premier to run day to day affairs, in the pious hope that the Constituent Assembly would be able to frame a constitution in a year and dissolve itself, to be replaced by a national legislature duly elected by a direct franchise. An elected Prime Minister could thus have been chosen by 1949 or so. Yet, as fate would have it, he was still an interim Prime Minister till an assassin's bullet killed him in October 1951.

The Governor General Khwaja Nazimuddin manoeuvred to come one step down and lead the Cabinet. Nazim's fascination with his former protégé and then handpicked boss Ghulam Mohammad ended, when the latter dismissed him on 17 April 1953, accusing him of incompetence. The choice fell on the unsuspecting Ambassador to the United States who was recalled to be crowned. History has repeated itself many times ever since.

The first Constituent Assembly never made a constitution and was dissolved in 1954, on the plea that it had converted itself into a "perpetual" assembly. The new indirectly elected 80-member House voted for a veteran Civil Servant Chaudhry Mohammad Ali, as the fourth Prime Minister whose singular achievement was to give the nation its first Constitution of 1956. The constitution, as is the case with such legal documents, dared to provide for general elections, which were never to come. Another civil servant-turned President Iskandar Mirza, continued palace intrigues to discredit and dismiss Prime Ministers and there were three more in a span of two years, i.e. 1956-8, namely, Hussain Shaheed Suharwardy, Ibrahim Ismail Chundrigar and Feroze Khan Noon.

In 1958, a bloodless military coup overthrew the civilian dispensation, which had had the blessing of the then President Iskandar Mirza, who nominated General Ayub as his military Prime Minister. After three days, the eighth Prime Minister of Pakistan deposed and deported Iskandar to the UK and took over as the President himself, and during the 11 years of General Ayub's rule, he did not need a Prime Minister.

He was replaced by General Yahya Khan, in a palace coup in 1969, who also did not like to share power with anyone. First, he did not nominate a Prime Minister, arguing that it was the right of the people, and when in 1970, the people of Pakistan gave their majority verdict in favour of Sheikh Mujib-ur-Rahman, Yahya prevaricated and dithered saying that he wanted to secure the rights of the people of Pakistan. Good! An unelected dictator fighting for the rights of the people by denying government to the man they elected! During the 1971 war, the torpedoing of democracy came into the world spotlight which had precipitated the civil war and then the war. Yahya picked veteran East Pakistani politician Dr. Noor-ul-Amin as the ninth civilian Prime Minister of Pakistan. Yahya had little choice since he was the one and only non-Awami League legislator from the Eastern wing. Amin remained Prime Minister for 13 days only, since the country broke up and the province he came from seceded to become a new country (Bangladesh) and a defeated Yahya was kicked out. Zulfiqar Ali Bhutto took over as President and the Chief Martial Law Administrator in December 1971, since there was no constitution in place.

A constitution was then framed which was parliamentary in nature. The Constituent Assembly became the National Assembly for a period of five years with effect from the 14th August 1973. Bhutto took over as the tenth Prime Minister of Pakistan, and was supposed to hold office as such for five years, till August 1978. He chose mid term elections in March 1977, more than a year ahead of schedule to surprise and outsmart a divided opposition. The opposition rather surprised him by putting up a united front against him. He nevertheless won the disputed elections and took oath as the 11th Prime Minister on 25th March 1977. He was overthrown that July in a military coup and later executed in 1979.

After eight years of the most ruthless dictatorship, marked by arbitrary executions and public floggings, General Zia managed to create a dummy parliament in 1985, through a party-less election that was boycotted by all political actors of the country. Jonejo was picked and nominated as the 12th Prime Minister of Pakistan but he never enjoyed power. Strings were pulled from somewhere else, and following an uneventful period, he was sacked and withdrew into oblivion from where he has not emerged.

During 1988 to 1998, a ping pong between Benazir Bhutto and Nawaz Sharif continued. Each was pulled out by intrigue and the other entered through the back door. Both enjoyed two stints with four Caretaker Prime Ministers in between. Thus the Prime Ministership changed faces as follows; Benazir Bhutto (13th), Ghulam Mustafa Jatoi (14th), Nawaz Sharif (15th), Balkh Sher Mazari (16th) Moin Qureshi (17th), Benazir Bhutto (18th), Malik Meraj Khalid (19th) and Nawaz Sharif (20th). Now, during Pervez Musharraf's theatre democracy, three faces have changed so far, Zafarullah Jamali (21st), Chaudhry Shujaat (22nd) and Shaukat Aziz (23rd).

Due to the frequent political changes in that country, the founding and most notable Prime Minister of India, Pandit Nehru, once quipped that "he could not change as many trousers as Pakistan changed Prime Ministers"!!

—∞—

Pakistan

As Pakistan had played a relatively small part in my career, it was initially my intention to omit it from my recollections, but as recent events, particularly the assassination of Benazir Bhutto on 28th December 2007 brought this country very much to the fore, and resurrected some memories for me, I decided a brief chapter could be of interest.

In April 1979, I was in Karachi, the then capital of Pakistan. As usual I had breakfast served in my hotel room. When I opened the newspaper on my breakfast tray; "The Dawn" bold headlines hit me, stating "Bhutto Hanged"!! Thereby ended the life of Zulfiqar Ali Bhutto, the head of an influential political family, perhaps one of the most powerful and well known in Pakistan's history. Bhutto had been Prime Minister from the 14th August 1973 until 5th July 1977, when he was deposed by an army coup. He had been an autocratic leader.

Knowing the volatility of the Pakistanis, I concluded there could be a violent reaction on the streets, so, "discretion is the better part of valour" and that I should exit the country A.S.A.P. There was also no valid reason for me to stay as my business had been completed. After breakfast I made my way to the British Airways office by taxi and booked a seat on a London bound flight that evening. The streets were ominously quiet, indeed to me it seemed to be "the calm before the storm"! As it transpired there was no demonstration as the military ruler had obviously planned things very shrewdly and would have ruthlessly crushed any uprising. Furthermore, the hanging had been carried out well away from the metropolis in the Rawalpindi Jail in North East Pakistan.

I made one visit to North West Pakistan but greatly regret that it was not possible to go even a short distance through the Khyber Pass. Perhaps I could have made time but security was as strict then as it is now. However, it was most interesting to visit the towns of Rawalpindi and Peshawar and to see the contrast in dress and culture to the other parts of the country. On this visit to the North West I was accompanied by a colleague from the Wool and Synthetic Department, Nigel Shannon, who unfortunately later died relatively young. I still keep in touch with his wife Roberta, who also had the privilege of working in Mackies in a secretarial capacity. Actually on that trip we were a trio, the third person being our agent, a Mr. Zainul Abidin, who owned a trading company called Alliance International Limited. I understand that Zainul is still alive, although retired. He keeps in touch with my long time colleague and friend, Sammy McCoubrey, with whom I worked in the late 1940's installing flax processing machinery in Barbour Linen Mills, in Hilden on the outskirts of Belfast.

Our purpose for being in Peshawar was that Nigel Shannon was negotiating the sale of a Carpet Yarn Plant, while I was trying to promote the sale of a Jute Mill Plant. My recollection is that the negotiations were very pleasant as we were dealing with a very cultured and wealthy family. A father and three highly educated sons, all of whom spoke "Oxford" English. We were invited to have dinner at their home one evening, which needless to say was a most pleasant and enjoyable event. We might as well have been in an upper class British home! Our hosts were immaculately dressed in western suits, and we, the Mackie trio, knowing what to expect, had put on our best "bib and tucker"! Aperitifs were followed by an excellent dinner served on an attractively appointed table. As far as I can recall, Nigel eventually signed a contract for the Carpet Yarn Plant, while another salesman finalised the contract for the Jute Mill Plant, consequently Mackies did substantial business with that family.

My experience with another business family in Pakistan was a stark contrast. It would of course be unwise and unethical for me to mention

Sammy McCoubrey – Mackie consultant, in discussion with Major General G.S.Butt, President of Pak Oil and serving government minister.

Sammy McCoubrey in consultation with Mr. Chowdury Habib-Ur Rahman who purchased two jute mills and was the person through whom Mackie liaised with the Pakistan government.

Signing of contract documents between Sammy McCoubrey – Mackies, and Suhail Shaikh – Suhail Company.

Informal discussion between Mackies' agent – Zainul Abidin (in light suit) and Major General G.S.Butt.

names of places and persons, so I will restrict myself to the bare facts. The negotiations were with a father and son, both obviously devout Muslims and dressed accordingly to which of course I had no objection. The meeting took place in a sparsely furnished office, the father sat on one side of the desk and the son and I on the other side. It was evident that the son was learning the business as he participated only occasionally in the conversation.

The meeting commenced in the early afternoon so no doubt Mr. S. as I will call him, had engaged in the noon prayers. Initially the technical aspects of the Mackie proposal were discussed and were mutually agreed without any acrimony, and then the bargaining, or perhaps a more appropriate word would be haggling, over prices began. The usual "toing and froing" took place as Mr. S. endeavoured to whittle down the prices. An agreement had not been reached by mid-afternoon so the call to prayer again came. Without any ado, Mr. S. got up from his desk, washed his hands at the wash hand basin, fitted in the office no doubt for that purpose. He then spread his prayer mat, got down on his knees and proceeded to bow and pray towards Mecca. I noted his son did not join him, but I won't speculate why. There was of course silence in the office. Suddenly I was startled as Mr. S., even before he was off his knees, began where he had left off before prayer!! I think I'm safe in concluding that his mind was not really on his prayer, but rather on how much discount he could squeeze out of me!! In any case, an agreement was reached shortly afterward and a contract secured.

The life of a Mackie sales consultant was never monotonous due to the wide variety of experiences! I've cited what could be termed a sedate event with a cultured family, then a sales tussle with a merchant type, and now I come to possibly the most relaxed and enjoyable of the three, a social meeting with friends. One of my visits to Pakistan in the late 1970's afforded me the opportunity to renew acquaintance with a member of the major industrial family, the Adamjees, who had set up the largest ever Jute Mill in the world in East Pakistan, now Bangladesh. I had done business with Hanif Adamjee in Thailand resulting in the establishment of Khon Kaen Jute Mill, also in Malaysia, where Hanif invested in Gilani Jute and Textiles at Butterworth on the mainland opposite Penang.

Hanif and I had become good friends and met socially from time to time when our paths crossed in Bangkok, London and elsewhere. He could in no way be described as an eccentric but he had certain likes and dislikes. For example, when booking a room in a hotel he requested one in which the air conditioning could be adjusted as he slept most soundly in a cold room. Furthermore, he stipulated that the room should be on the side of the hotel facing the main road, as he liked the sound of traffic.

When I met Hanif in Karachi his business life had entered a new phase. The Adamjee family had lost a substantial amount of investment when the "Indians" were forced out of Burma, now Myanmar. The same happened when East Pakistan became Bangladesh. I understand that the jute mill in Malaysia was also not a profitable investment due to the government nationalist policy. As a result of these experiences, Hanif told me that he no longer invested in industry but in commercial ventures, the assets of which could be carried in a brief case. Furthermore, he worked only half a day and socialised in the afternoons either in a club or at home.

On the day on which we met in Karachi, he picked me up at my hotel in his chauffeur driven shiny Mercedes shortly after midday. He obviously had not engaged in "noon prayers"!! Lunch was laid on at his modern and quite westernised home. We were joined by several of his friends who like Hanif were semi-retired. Although all were Muslims, they enjoyed their "chota pegs" (scotch with soda or water), so it was around 3 p.m. before "tiffin" (lunch) was served, but altogether it was a very pleasant afternoon.

The reader may recall my story about showing two British Airways stewardesses a typical Calcutta house party at the home of Adrian Gubbay. Some months thereafter I booked to fly home from Karachi on a British Airways evening flight. Our agent took me to the airport relatively early and after I had checked in we were sitting chatting when the flight crew passed. I thought one of the stewardesses was familiar and said so to our agent. Later when we were airborne the stewardess in question came round with the tray of sweets, which was the custom in those days. When she came to where I was seated, she stepped back and said; "excuse me if I'm wrong, but would you be Stanley from Calcutta"? She was very pleased when I confirmed my identity. It so happened that the crew members were scheduled to "slip", the jargon in the airline business, at Beirut, where I had planned to stay for a few days, so I arranged to meet her for lunch the following day.

The next morning I had a phone call from another British Airways stewardess, Reeta Roy, Bryan Hall's friend. She had been unwell and had been marooned in Beirut for several days, but having recovered she was "champing at the bit" to get out of the hotel, and it would have been unwise to walk around on her own. Consequently, she was delighted to join the other girl and me for lunch. The following day we were also joined by a third British Airways stewardess, also an Indian, but in this instance a Muslim, so during my relatively short stay sightseeing in Lebanon, I had the company of three young ladies of different religions, at least nominally; a Christian, a Hindu, and a Muslim. I recall that in the "Indian Section" I mentioned the most senior stewardess of the Airline's Asian flight staff who was a Parsee. This demonstrates one of the many wonderful aspects of my job, the opportunity to make a great variety of friends from different backgrounds, cultures, religions and professions!!

As I conclude my reminiscences on Pakistan another round of elections is scheduled to be held within twenty four hours, which I hope will bring some political stability to the country, but the omens are not good as there has been considerable violence already. It is possible the People's Party of Pakistan (P.P.P.) will attempt to avenge the death of their late leader Mrs. Benazir Bhutto.

Since I wrote the foregoing, the People's Party of Pakistan has emerged from the elections as the party with the most seats in the new parliament, and subsequently Mrs. Bhutto's husband, Asif Ali Zardari has been chosen as the President of Pakistan.

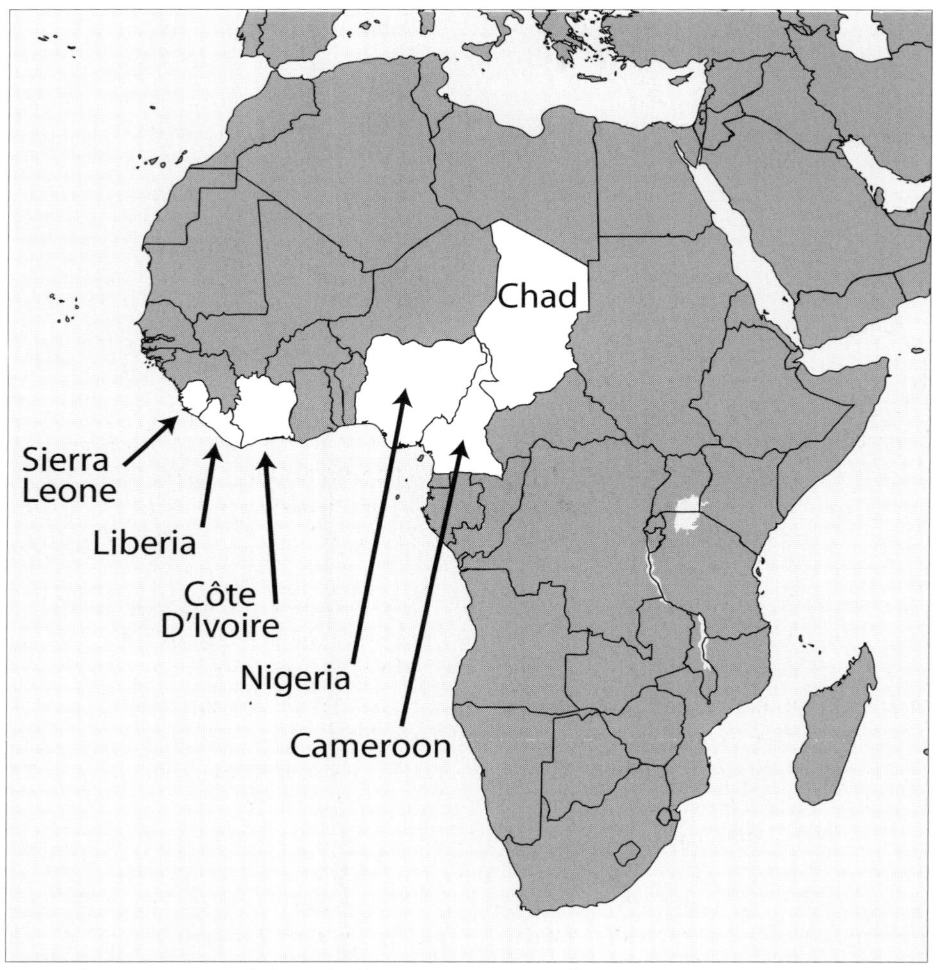

Map of various West and Central African countries visited.

VARIOUS WEST AND CENTRAL AFRICAN COUNTRIES

Republic Of Chad

Preface

CHAD, OFFICIALLY THE REPUBLIC of Chad, is a landlocked country in central Africa. It is bordered by Libya to the north, Sudan to the east, the Central African Republic to the south, Cameroon and Nigeria to the southwest, and Niger to the west. Due to its distance from the sea and its largely desert climate, the country is sometimes referred to as the "Dead Heart of Africa". Chad is divided into three major geographical regions: a desert zone in the north, an arid Sahelian belt in the centre and a more fertile Sudanese savanna zone in the south. Lake Chad, after which the country is named, is the largest wetland in Chad and the second largest in Africa. Chad's highest peak is the Emi Koussi in the Sahara, and the largest city by far is N'Djamena, the capital. Chad is home to over 200 different ethnic and linguistic groups. French and Arabic are the official languages. Islam is the most widely practiced religion.

While many political parties are active, power lies firmly in the hands of President Déby and his political party, the Patriotic Salvation Movement. Chad remains plagued by political violence and recurrent attempted coups d'état, and is one of the poorest and most corrupt countries in Africa. Most Chadians live in poverty as subsistence herders and farmers. Since 2003 crude oil has become the country's primary source of export earnings, superseding the traditional cotton industry.

—∞—

At the beginning of 1973, Jack Bunting, the head of the Jute Machinery Department and I did a tour of several West African countries. On the outward and homeward sectors we travelled on Caledonian, a Scottish owned airline on which the female cabin crew wore tartan uniforms, which was subsequently taken over by British Airways. We flew firstly to Fort Lamy, now called N'Djamena, the capital of Chad, a Republic situated right in the centre of North Africa between Sudan on the east and Niger on the west. There we met up with Bernhard Litscher, the proprietor of Altrom Limited of Geneva, about whom I gave details in the Iran section.

The purpose of our visit to Chad was to explore with the country's government the viability of processing the fibre from the Dum (Cor Doum) palm, which grows profusely around the perimeter of the Sahara Desert. The practicability of cultivating this plant and processing its fibre had been enthusiastically pursued by Jack Bunting over several years. He was convinced that if implemented properly the project would be beneficial in several ways to Saharan countries. Firstly, organised cultivation of the Dum palm would create jobs for the farming community. Furthermore, if grown in sizeable areas on the edge of the Sahara, they could be a barrier to the incursion of the desert sands. Of course, the extraction of the fibre from the young shoots would have to be carefully controlled to ensure the survival of the plants. The extracted fibre could then be processed into sacks and other heavy duty fabrics, thereby creating a small scale industry in which largely unskilled labour could be employed.

Author with Bernhard Litscher of Altrom Ltd., Geneva. The latter is about to leave for home.

As far as I personally am aware there was only one serious attempt to exploit this potential. That was in Eritrea in East Africa. I discovered the following extract about this project in one of my note books.

Dum

"A considerably coarser fibre than Musa, is extracted from the young shoots of the Dum palm. These Dum palms grow on dry water courses. There is a factory extracting fibre in the Erota district of Eritrea and the Concessionaire of this area is starting a spinning mill and bag-making factory in the near future. It would appear that there is a vast quantity of Dum which can be extracted, and this extraction is in the form of decortication. The Dum fibre will spin an 18 lb. yarn very satisfactorily. The other point that should be understood regarding Dum is that the Concessionaire for the main Dum palm areas will also be a manufacturer of sacks."

While in Chad, Jack Bunting and I hired a jeep and travelled down into the desert and had a good look at Dum palms growing wild. As mentioned above, these plants grow on dry water courses, so flourish in desert areas. The villagers in the areas visited were used to seeing French nationals so the appearance of two European men did not raise their curiosity!! The government officials whom we met expressed keen interest in our ideas, but that was as far as it got. As is the case in many African countries, so it was in Chad. There needs to be a "financial incentive" to make government officials move. It is also a great pity that the United Nations Industrial Development Organisation (UNIDO) did not consider it viable, but it was obviously too insignificant to be of interest. As usual, Bernhard Litscher of Altrom gave us his full support so it was not merely a Mackie effort.

The locals appreciated the utility of dum fibre so put it to many practical uses. It provided them with twine, ropes, thatching materials and was used in a wide variety of ways domestically. Of course all processes like decortication, spinning, twisting were carried out by hand. The journey into the countryside enabled Jack and I to see basic rural life.

Author examining dum palm.

Those who knew Jack Bunting will agree that he was a delightful person, always smiling, and not easily ruffled. Generally speaking, wherever he went there was an amusing incident and the visit to Chad was no exception. The hotel in which we were staying was a two storied building, and each bedroom opened on to a balcony, but a resident had to be careful as the door from the bedroom to the balcony was fitted with a spring-loaded closing device and an automatic lock, so when a resident went out on to the balcony it was essential to "snib" the lock in the open position. One evening, Bernhard, Jack and I had dinner in the hotel dining room, then retired to our respective

Jack Bunting examining 'sticks' from which fibre is extracted.

Bundles of 'rough' dum fibre in village. Jack Bunting discussing its various use with villager.

bedrooms. All our bedrooms were on the first floor, but Bernhard's and Jack's were on one side and mine on the other.

Having stripped to his underpants, Jack decided to go on to the balcony to stretch and get some "fresh" air, but forgot to set the lock in the open position. Inevitably the door banged closed behind him, so there he was marooned on the balcony in his underpants!! Of course, as I've already said, it took a lot to non-plus Jack. It would have been quite dangerous to attempt to climb down to the ground, so he didn't consider that. Recalling that Bernhard was a couple of rooms along the corridor he decided to do a James Bond stunt and swing himself hand over hand along the wrought iron railings. This he did successfully and climbed on to the balcony of Bernhard's room. He was about to rap the window when he remembered that Bernhard, when in Africa, slept with a loaded pistol below his pillow. Security on air travel was not then as strict as it is now so a gun could be carried in one's luggage! The balcony window was of standard design with a solid wall projecting at each side. Jack proceeded to stand behind one of these projections, lean forward, knock the window, and shout; "it's me, Bernhard, don't shoot". Realising something was wrong, Bernhard got up and let Jack into his room, but he flatly refused to go down to the reception and get the master key for Jack's room, so poor Jack had to do so in nothing but his underpants. So the story goes but I assume that he borrowed at least a bath towel. In any event, as I recently said to a friend, an observer would probably have noticed Jack's broad grin, rather than his state of undress. As the saying goes, "all's well that ends well", and so here ends my write-up on Chad!

Village market in Chad.

UNITED REPUBLIC OF CAMEROON

(Cameroun)

Preface

On 1 January 1960, French Cameroun gained independence from France under President Ahmadou Ahidjo, and on 1 October 1961, the formerly-British Southern Cameroons united with its neighbour to form the Federal Republic of Cameroon. Ahidjo used the ongoing war with the UPC and fears of ethnic conflict to concentrate power in the presidency, continuing with this even after the suppression of the UPC in 1971. His political party, the Cameroon National Union (CNU), became the sole legal political party on 1 September 1966 and in 1972, the federal system of government was abolished in favour of a United Republic of Cameroon, headed from Yaoundé. Ahidjo pursued an economic policy of planned liberalism, prioritising cash crops and petroleum exploitation. The government used oil money to create a national cash reserve, pay farmers, and finance major development projects, however, many initiatives failed when Ahidjo appointed unqualified allies to direct them.

Despite 20 years of repressive government under President Ahmadou Ahidjo, Cameroon saw investment in agriculture, education, health care and transport.

Ahidjo stepped down on 4 November 1982 and left power to his constitutional successor, Paul Biya. However, Ahidjo remained in control of the CNU and tried to run the country from behind the scenes until Biya and his allies pressured him into resigning. Biya began his administration by moving toward a more democratic government, but a failed coup d'état nudged him toward the leadership style of his predecessor. An economic crisis took effect in the mid 1980's to late 1990's as a result of international economic conditions, drought, falling petroleum prices, and years of corruption, mismanagement, and cronyism. Cameroon turned to foreign aid, cut government spending, and privatised industries. With the reintroduction of multi-party politics in December 1990, Anglophone pressure groups called for greater autonomy, with some advocating complete secession as the republic of Ambazonia.

Faced with popular discontent, Mr. Biya allowed multi-party presidential elections in 1992, which he won.

In 1994 and 1996 Cameroon and Nigeria fought over the disputed, oil-rich Bakassi Peninsula. Nigeria withdrew its troops from the area in 2006 in line with an international court ruling which awarded sovereignty to Cameroon. In November 2007 the Nigerian senate passed a motion declaring as illegal the Nigeria-Cameroon agreement for the Bakassi Peninsula to be handed over to Cameroon.

Internally, there are tensions over the two mainly English-speaking southern provinces. A secessionist movement, the Southern Cameroon National Council (SCNC), emerged in the 1990's and has been declared as illegal.

Cameroon has one of the highest literacy rates in Africa. However, the country's progress is hampered by a level of corruption that is among the highest in the world.

—∞—

The writer has a very good memory for details but I cannot recall why Jack Bunting and I didn't obtain all visas for our West African trip in London before embarking on our journey, which was the normal procedure. We obviously obtained a visa for Chad, also one for Cameroon. Furthermore, I'm at a loss to remember why the additional visas could not be obtained in Fort Lamy (N'Djamena). Perhaps the countries to which we intended to travel had no embassy or consulate in that city. In any event, we found it necessary to transit in the Cameroon.

Travel arrangements were not difficult as Cameroon Airways operated regular flights between Fort Lamy and Yaoundé, the capital of Cameroon, with Boeing 737's. This part of our itinerary seemed to be fraught with complications, as on arrival at Yaoundé we learned that it would be necessary to go to Douala, the second city in the country to get a visa for Sierra Leone. Being well experienced, Jack and I were not easily fazed, so, without any ado, set about making the necessary arrangements.

As the distance between the two cities was only around 200 Km. (125 miles), the connecting road was reasonable and the weather temperate, we opted to travel by car, so hired a suitable vehicle. I also found suitable headgear for the journey. As there was no timetable to keep, and Cameroon is a pleasant country, we journeyed leisurely and took the opportunity to stop frequently, talk to the local people, and see various aspects of life in the countryside.

The people of Cameroon are very friendly and ready to talk, particularly to foreigners, and as English is one of the official languages, we found

Top: *Journey between Yaounde and Douala.*
Bottom left: *Author in suitable attire for journey.*
Bottom right: *Refreshments by roadside.*

Products of country – timber and cotton.

conversation very easy. Many of the girls are very good looking and dress attractively. Obviously some of the Cameroonians have Irish tastes!!

Our final experience in Cameroon was not too pleasant. Generally speaking before 9/11 security checks at airports were rather superficial. As stipulated in those days Jack and I reported at the Yaoundé Airport one hour before E.T.D. "Expected time of departure" is an appropriate term! We were in for quite a surprise, indeed a shock. The security check carried out was so thorough that the flight was delayed for almost three hours, in fact it was the most rigorous that either Jack or I had ever experienced on our extensive travels. The security officers left nothing to chance. They went through our pockets and luggage, as the saying goes; "with a fine tooth comb", and removed all items that were metal or sharp, no matter how small. The confiscated items were put in plastic bags, labelled and taken to the flight deck (cockpit), which must eventually have looked like a second-hand market. Despite being seasoned travellers Jack and I were greatly relieved when the flight eventually was airborne and we could wave goodbye to Cameroon.

Inevitably all the passengers wondered why security had been so strict. The rumour circulated during the flight that there was an Israeli Government Minister on Board. I took that "with a pinch of salt" as I doubt that such a person would have travelled on a normal scheduled flight.

A Cameroonian beauty.

A little bit of Ireland!

REPUBLIC OF LIBERIA

Preface

Liberia is Africa's oldest republic, but it became better known in the 1990s for its long-running, ruinous civil war and its role in a rebellion in neighbouring Sierra Leone.

Although founded by freed American and Caribbean slaves, Liberia is mostly made up of indigenous Africans, with the slaves' descendants comprising 5% of the population.

The West African nation was relatively calm until 1980 when William Tolbert was overthrown by Sergeant Samuel Doe after food price riots.

The coup marked the end of dominance by the minority Americo-Liberians, who had ruled since independence, but heralded a period of instability.

By the late 1980s, arbitrary rule and economic collapse culminated in civil war when Charles Taylor's National Patriotic Front of Liberia (NPFL) militia overran much of the countryside, entering the capital in 1990. Mr. Doe was executed.

Fighting intensified as the rebels splintered and battled each other, the Liberian army and West African peacekeepers. In 1995 a peace agreement was signed, leading to the election of Mr. Taylor as president.

The respite was brief, with anti-government fighting breaking out in the north in 1999. Mr. Taylor accused Guinea of supporting the rebellion. Meanwhile Ghana, Nigeria and others accused Mr. Taylor of backing rebels in Sierra Leone.

Matters came to a head in 2003 when Mr. Taylor – under international pressure to quit and hemmed in by rebels – stepped down and went into exile in Nigeria. A transitional government steered the country towards elections in 2005.

Around 250,000 people were killed in Liberia's civil war and many thousands more fled the fighting. The conflict left the country in economic ruin and overrun with weapons. The capital remains without mains electricity and running water. Corruption is rife and unemployment and illiteracy are endemic.

The UN maintains some 15,000 soldiers in Liberia and it is one of the organisation's most expensive peacekeeping operations.

—∞—

Our next port of call after Cameroon was Sierra Leone but there were no direct flights from Yaoundé so we had to transit at Monrovia, the capital of Liberia. For the first leg of the journey there was a suitable flight by the then international airline "Pan Am", which no longer exists but was at that time a reputable American air carrier. In fact "Pan Am" operated two flights, PA one and PA two, which circumnavigated the world continuously in opposite directions, one westward and the other eastward. In the early days when the airline had a fleet of DC6's, they had proper sleeping berths in the first class section. These pulled from the roof of the cabin, where the luggage racks are normally located. A portable ladder was provided to enable the passenger to climb into the bunk. I booked one on a couple of occasions on a flight between London and Calcutta. It was very comfortable provided a person was not claustrophic!

Another experience on "Pan Am" stands out in my memory. It was on an early morning flight between Calcutta and Bangkok. That sector during the monsoon season can be extremely turbulent, and even with the aid of radar the pilot can find it difficult to avoid the troughs, so the aircraft on this flight was rising and falling quite severely. We weren't far into the flight when a senior stewardess, a Scandinavian girl, approached me to ask a favour. She firstly said in the form of a statement as much as a question; "you're from Ireland". When I confirmed that to be so she said there was a young Irish girl on board as a supernumerary, and as this was her first flight

Author at Monrovia Airport.

she was very frightened, so as I was obviously a seasoned traveller, could I reassure the young girl. Naturally I said it would be a pleasure to do what I could. Opportunely there was a vacant seat beside me so Mary Murphy, as her name turned out to be, was brought and seated beside me. I felt like saying now Mary you're a good Irish Catholic and I'm a good Ulster "Prod", so if we pray together we will surely get to Bangkok safely, but of course I resisted the temptation. I simply told Mary that I had travelled that route very frequently and safely. Indeed to my knowledge there had never been an accident on that sector. Of course I also engaged her in conversation about our respective backgrounds, and before she was aware we had landed in Bangkok.

I've digressed considerably so must get back to West Africa. On arrival at Monrovia, Liberia, Jack and I booked a double room at a motel near the airport, as the onward flight was scheduled for early the following morning. It so happened that the "Pan Am" air crew were staying at the same motel. I mentioned this fact because two of the stewardesses found that they had been allocated a room right beside a large noisy air conditioning unit and they were very upset as due to the long delayed flight they were totally exhausted and needed a good night's sleep. The two Irishmen had been given a room some distance from the noise, so on hearing of the girls' quandary they gallantly offered to exchange rooms. Naturally the girls' gratefully accepted the offer. They must have slept well and decided to have a "lie-in" as we did not see them the next morning. However, Jack and I felt we had done the gentlemanly thing and had been good ambassadors for Ireland!!

REPUBLIC OF SIERRA LEONE

(Motto: "Unity – Freedom – Justice")

Preface

SIERRA LEONE, OFFICIALLY THE Republic of Sierra Leone, is a country in West Africa. It is bordered by Guinea in the north and east, Liberia in the southeast, and the Atlantic Ocean in the southwest and west. Sierra Leone covers a total area of 71,740 Sq. Km. (27,699 Sq. Miles) and has a tropical climate, with a diverse environment ranging from savannah to rainforests. Freetown is the capital, seat of government, and largest city.

Sierra Leone was first inhabited by the Sherbro, Temne and Limba peoples, and later the Mende, who know the country as Romarong. In 1462, it was visited by the Portuguese explorer Pedro da Cintra, who gave it its current designation, meaning 'Lion Mountains'. Sierra Leone became an important centre of the transatlantic slave trade, until 1787 when Freetown was founded by the Sierra Leone Company as a home for formerly enslaved African Americans and West Indians. In 1808, Freetown became a British Crown Colony, and in 1896, the interior of the country became a British Protectorate. In 1961, the two combined and gained independence. Political instability over the following decades eventually led to the Sierra Leone Civil War, which began in 1991 and was resolved in 2002 when the United Nations led by Britain defeated the rebel forces and installed a civilian government. Since then, almost 72,500 former combatants have disarmed and the country has re-established a functioning democracy. The Special Court for Sierra Leone was set up in 2002 to deal with war crimes and crimes against humanity committed since 1996.

Sierra Leone is the lowest ranked country on the Human Development Index and seventh lowest on the Human Poverty Index, suffering from endemic corruption, suppression of the press and the HIV/AIDS pandemic.

Colonial Era

In the early 20th century, Freetown served as the residence of the British governor who also ruled the Gold Cost (now Ghana) and the Gambia settlements. Sierra Leone also served as the educational centre of British West Africa. Fourah Bay College, established in 1827, rapidly became a magnet for English-speaking Africans on the West Coast. For more than a century, it was the only European-style university in western Sub-Saharan Africa.

During Sierra Leone's colonial history, indigenous people mounted several unsuccessful revolts against British rule and Krio domination. The most notable was the Bai Bureh rebellion against British rule in 1898. Bai Bureh was a man who refused to recognise the hut tax imposed by the British in 1893 in Sierra Leone. He did not believe Sierra Leoneans had a duty to pay taxes to foreigners, and he wanted all British to return to Britain and let the Sierra Leoneans solve their own problems. After he refused to pay his taxes on several occasions, the British issued a warrant to arrest him. In 1896 Bureh declared war on the British in Sierra Leone. He brought fighters from several Temne villages under his command, and from Limba, Loko, Soso, Kissi, and Mandinka villages. He had the advantage over the vastly more powerful British for several months of the war. Hundreds of British troops and hundreds of Bureh's fighters were killed. Bai Bureh was finally captured on November 11, 1898 and sent into exile to the Gold Coast (now Ghana).

Most of the 20th century history of the colony was peaceful. One notable event in 1935 was the granting of a monopoly on mineral mining to the Sierra Leone Selection Trust run by De Beers, which was scheduled to last 99 years. The 1951 constitution provided a framework for decolonization. Local ministerial responsibility was introduced in 1953, when Sir Milton Margai was appointed Chief Minister. He became Prime Minister after successful completion of constitutional talks in London in 1960. Independence came in April 1961, and Sierra Leone opted for a parliamentary system within the Commonwealth of Nations.

—∞—

The few days spent in this country were uneventful. We had meetings with various government officials, but all were very inconclusive. Indeed, as far as I'm aware, Mackie did not do any business in Sierra Leone.

There was time for a little sightseeing, not that I found Freetown a particularly attractive city, in fact I had a rather unpleasant experience as I took some photographs. The Volkswagen agent had a showroom in a five-storey corner building on the top of which was an eye catching feature. On the top corner of the building was perched a Volkswagen "beetle" which I decided would make an amusing photograph. As I raised my camera

Street scene in Freetown.

Unique advertisement for Volkswagon "Beetle" – see car perched on rooftop!

Landing stage for bus to airport.

An attractive beach near Freetown.

and took the shot, a tall well-built African man walked up to me in a very agitated mood. Thinking he was the subject being photographed, he was so angry that he threatened to smash my camera. Today being older and I hope wiser, I would simply have walked away, but being quite impetuous then I told him in no uncertain terms that I wouldn't waste a film on his "ugly mug". Fortunately he did not pursue the matter as had he done so, not only the camera but also I could have ended somewhat "worse for wear".

I also took another "abnormal" photograph, a city office building on fire. As my previous experience was still fresh in my mind, I decided it would be unwise to enquire if the fire had started accidently or as a result of arson, so I held my tongue and took the photos from a safe distance.

Our visit was confined to Freetown, except for the journey to the airport when we saw a rather attractive beach. Undoubtedly other parts of the countryside, which along with the beaches, could be exploited for tourism if the country were stable and peaceful.

I don't know what the situation is now, but at that time the airport serving Freetown was located on an island a mile or so off the coast opposite the city. A ferry and airline bus operated regularly between the two and although the journey was relatively short, passengers had to take this into account when calculating their reporting time. When Jack and I boarded the bus it was obvious that our timing was correct as the flight crew of Caledonian Airlines were on board.

The flight to London took off mid-morning so Jack and I spent the first hour or so comparing notes and drafting a report. Having done so Jack decided it was time to have an aperitif before lunch, so he ordered a G and T. I probably had a dry martini. I'm not aware of the reason but Jack had a rather amusing habit. He always had a somewhat polite accent and it became more pronounced after he had a few drinks. What was inexplicable, when on a flight Jack would call the stewardess, and ask most politely; "Miss would you possibly have any thin arrowroot biscuits on board?" This had happened when I had travelled with Jack on previous occasions, so I tipped off one of the stewardesses shortly after boarding, and she had brought a packet of biscuits. I don't think they were thin arrowroot but that didn't matter, and she put the packet in the pocket of the unoccupied seat behind Jack. Sure enough after a couple of G and T's and some wine with his lunch, Jack called the young lady and posed the usual question. There was a look of real surprise on Jack's face when she immediately produced the packet and said something to the effect "certainly Mr. Bunting we like to cater for the special tastes of our passengers!!" It was always a pleasant experience to travel with Jack Bunting.

Bus which plies between Freetown and airport.

FEDERAL REPUBLIC OF NIGERIA

Preface

A British sphere of influence

FOLLOWING THE NAPOLEONIC WARS, the British expanded trade with the Nigerian interior. In 1885 British claims to a West African sphere of influence received international recognition and in the following year the Royal Niger Company was chartered under the leadership of Sir George Taubman Goldie. In 1900 the company's territory came under the control of the British Government, which moved to consolidate its hold over the area of modern Nigeria. On January 1, 1901 Nigeria became a British protectorate, part of the British Empire, the foremost world power at the time.

In 1914 the area was formally united as the Colony and Protectorate of Nigeria. Administratively Nigeria remained divided into the northern and southern provinces and Lagos colony. Western education and the development of a modern economy proceeded more rapidly in the south than in the north, with consequences felt in Nigeria's political life ever since. Following World War II, in response to the growth of Nigerian nationalism and demands for independence, successive constitutions legislated by the British Government moved Nigeria toward self-government on a representative and increasingly federal basis. By the middle of the 20th century, the great wave for independence was sweeping across Africa.

Independence

Nigeria was granted full independence in October 1960 under a constitution that provided for a parliamentary government and a substantial measure of self-government for the country's three regions. From 1959 to 1960, Jaja Wachuku was the First black Speaker of the Nigerian Parliament – also called the "House of Representatives". Wachuku replaced Sir Frederick Metcalfe of Great Britain. Notably, as First Speaker of the House, Jaja Wachuku received Nigeria's Instrument of Independence – also known as Freedom Charter, on October 1, 1960 from Princess Alexandra of Kent – HM The Queen of United Kingdom's representative at the Nigerian Independence ceremonies.

The federal government was given exclusive powers in defence, foreign relations, and commercial and fiscal policy. The British Monarch was still head of state but legislative power was vested in a bicameral parliament, executive power in a prime minister and cabinet and judicial authority in a Federal Supreme Court. Political parties, however, tended to reflect the make up of the three main ethnic groups. The NPC (Nigerian People's Congress) represented conservative, Muslim, largely Hausa interests, and dominated the Northern Region. The NCNC (National Convention of Nigerian Citizens) was Igbo and Christian-dominated, ruling in the Eastern Region, and the AG (Action Group) was a left-leaning party that controlled the Yoruba west. The first post-independence National Government was formed by a conservative alliance of the NCNC and the NPC, with Sir Abubakar Tafawa Balewa, a Hausa, becoming Nigeria's first Prime Minister. The Yoruba-dominated AG became the opposition under its charismatic leader Chief Obafemi Awolowo.

Fourth Republic

The emergence of democracy in Nigeria in May 1999 ended 16 years of consecutive military rule. Olusegun Obasanjo inherited a country suffering economic stagnation and the deterioration of most democratic institutions. Obasanjo, a former general, was admired for his stand against the Abacha dictatorship, his record of returning the federal government to civilian rule in 1979, and his claim to represent all Nigerians regardless of religion.

The new President took over a country that faced many problems, including a dysfunctional bureaucracy, collapsed infrastructure, and a military that wanted a reward for returning quietly to the barracks. The President moved quickly and retired hundreds of military officers holding political positions, established a blue-ribbon panel to investigate human rights violations, released scores of persons held without charge, and rescinded numerous questionable licenses and contracts left by the previous regimes. The government also moved to recover millions of dollars in funds secreted in overseas accounts.

Most civil society leaders and Nigerians witnessed marked improvements in human rights and freedom of the press under Obasanjo. As Nigeria works out representational democracy, conflicts persist between the Executive and Legislative branches over appropriations and other proposed legislation. A sign of federalism has been the growing visibility of state governors and the inherent friction between Abuja and the state capitals over resource allocation.

The new President faced the daunting task of rebuilding a petroleum-based economy, whose revenues have been squandered through corruption and mismanagement. Additionally, the Obasanjo administration had to defuse longstanding ethnic and religious tensions if it hoped to build a foundation for economic growth and political stability. Currently there is unrest in the Niger delta over the environmental destruction caused by oil drilling and the ongoing poverty in the oil-rich region.

A further major problem created by the oil industry is the drilling of pipelines by the local population in an attempt to drain off the petroleum for personal use or as a source of income. This often leads to major explosions and high death tolls. Particularly notable disasters in this area have been: 1) October 1998, Jesse, 1100 deaths, 2) July 2000, Jesse, 250 deaths, 3) September 2004, near Lagos, 60 deaths, 4) May 2006, Ilado, approx. 150-200 deaths (current estimate).

Two militants of unknown faction shot and killed Ustaz Ja'afar Adam, a northern Muslim religious leader and Kano State official, along with one of his disciples in a mosque in Kano during dawn prayers on 13 April 2007. Obasanjo had recently stated on national radio that he would "deal firmly" with election fraud and violence advocated by "highly placed individuals." His comments were interpreted by some analysts as a warning to his Vice President and 2007 presidential candidate Atiku Abubakar.

In the 2007 general election, Umaru Yar'Adua and Goodluck Jonathan, both of the People's Democratic Party, were elected President and Vice President, respectively. The election was marred by electoral fraud, denounced by other candidates and international observers.

Nigeria is the most populous country in Africa. One in every four Africans is a Nigerian.

—∞—

Nigeria – Mackie Involvement

The Mackie family and consequently the Mackie company had a policy of keeping out of politics, avoiding publicity, and declining "Royal" honours, and they expected their senior executives to adhere to this policy. However, from time-to-time extenuating circumstances caused some of its itinerant salesmen and erection engineers to be involved in situations beyond their control. No one had more experience of this nature than our senior erection engineer, Joe McClelland, who I have mentioned on a number of occasions. I referred to his experiences in war torn Cambodia, and during the revolution in Iran, but undoubtedly his most noteworthy exploits were in Nigeria during the civil war, also known as the Biafran War. Before going into details about Joe McClelland's experiences, it would be appropriate to give the reader some idea of the war and the tensions that caused it.

While this is not a history book, a clear understanding of the conflict requires a fairly comprehensive explanation, so here goes.

The conflict was the result of economic, ethnic, cultural and religious tensions among the various peoples of Nigeria. Like many other African nations, Nigeria was an artificial construct initiated by European powers, which had neglected to account for religious, linguistic, and ethnic differences. Nigeria, which won independence from Britain in 1960, had at that time a population of 60 million people consisting of nearly 300 differing ethnic and cultural groups.

Of the ethnic groups that made up Nigeria, the largest was the mainly Muslim Hausa in the north, followed by the Yoruba in the half-Christian, half-Muslim southwest, and the Igbo (a variant spelling of Ibo) in the predominantly Christian southeast. With the independence of Nigeria, a political alliance was forged between the leading Hausa and Igbo political parties, which ruled Nigeria from 1960 to 1966. This alliance excluded the Yoruba, while the Igbos were considered by many to be the main beneficiaries of the alliance, taking most of the top jobs and leading business opportunities in the young country.

The Yoruba westerners had supported a left-leaning, reformist party, the Action Group, which was antipathetic to the conservative northern Muslim bloc. A "palace coup" by conservative elements in the west led to the formation of a more conservative Yoruba party, the Nigerian National Democratic Party (NNDP), which was prepared to go into alliance with the Hausa northerners. This new political alliance excluded the Igbo-dominated southeast from power, and threatened to roll back the gains of the Igbo elite.

The elections of 1965 witnessed the alliance of the Nigerian National Alliance of the Muslim north and the conservative elements in the west, against the United Progressive Grand Alliance of the Christian east and the progressive elements among the westerners. The Alliance of north and west won a crushing victory under Sir Abubakar Tafawa Balewa. There were many claims of widespread electoral fraud.

The military governor of the Igbo-dominated southeast, Colonel Odumegwu Ojukwu, citing the northern massacres and electoral fraud, proclaimed with the southern parliament the secession of the south-eastern region from Nigeria as the Republic of Biafra, an independent nation on May 30, 1967. Although there was much sympathy in Europe and elsewhere, only four countries recognised the new republic.

Civil War

The Nigerian government launched a "police action" to retake the secessionist territory. The war began on July 6, 1967 when Nigerian Federal troops advanced in two columns into Biafra. The right-hand Nigerian column advanced on the town of Nsukka, which fell on July 14, while the left-hand column made for Garkem, which was captured on July 12. But the Biafrans responded with an offensive of their own when on July 9, the Biafran forces moved west into the Mid-Western Nigerian state across the Niger river, passing through Benin City to reach Ore just over the state boundary on August 21, just 130 miles east of the Nigerian capital of Lagos. Although Benin City was retaken by the Nigerians on September 22, the Biafrans succeeded in their primary objective to tie down as many Nigerian Federal troops as they could. Four battalions of the Nigerian 2nd Infantry Division were needed to drive the Biafrans back and eliminate their territorial gains made during the offensive. But the Nigerians were repulsed three times and lost thousands of troops as they tried to cross the Niger during October.

However, reorganisation of the Nigerian forces, the reluctance of the Biafran army to attack again, and the effects of a naval, land and air blockade of Biafra led to a change in the balance of forces.

In June 1969, the Biafrans launched a desperate offensive against the Nigerians in their attempts to keep the Nigerians off-balance. They were supported by foreign mercenary pilots continuing to fly in food, medical supplies and weapons. Most notable of the mercenaries was Swedish Count Carl Gustav von Rosen who led five Malmö MF1-9 MiniCOIN small piston-engined aircraft, armed with rocket pods and machine guns. His force attacked Nigerian military airfields in Port Harcourt, Enugu, Benin City and Ughelli, destroying or damaging a number of Nigerian Air Force jets used to attack relief flights, including a few Mig-17's and three out of Nigeria's six Ilyushin Il-28 bombers that were used to bomb Biafran villages and farms on a daily basis. Although taken off-guard by the surprise Biafran offensive, the Nigerians soon recovered and held off the Biafrans long enough for the offensive to stall out. The Biafran air attacks did disrupt the combat operations of the Nigerian Air Force, but only for a few months.

War's End

The Nigerian federal forces launched their final offensive against the Biafrans on December 23, 1969 with a major thrust by the 3rd Marine Commando Division which succeeded in splitting the Biafran enclave into two by the end of the year. The final Nigerian offensive, named "Operation Tail-Wind", was launched on January 7, 1970 with the 3rd Marine Commando Division attacking, and supported by the 1st Infantry division to the north and the 2nd Infantry division to the south. The Biafran town of Owerri fell on January 9, and Uli fell on January 11. The war finally ended with the surrender of the Biafran forces in the last Biafra-held town of Amichi on January 13, 1970. Only a few days earlier, Ojukwu fled into exile by air to the republic of Côte d'Ivoire, leaving his deputy Philip Effiong to handle the details of the surrender to Yakubu Gowon of the federal army.

In 1967 a large jute mill was under construction in the city of Jos, the capital of Plateau State. The city is located high on the Jos Plateau. During British colonial rule it became an important centre for tin mining. An Ethiopian family by the name of Nasreddin had decided to invest in that factory and had wisely chosen Mackie machinery. In addition to supplying the processing machinery Mackies were requested to co-ordinate the complete project and Joe McClelland, the Mackie senior engineer, was selected to supervise the undertaking. The machinery and other equipment were assigned to Port Harcourt it being Nigeria's largest port. Due to the civil war this presented major problems as Port Harcourt was right in the middle of the troubled area and was part of the short-lived republic of Biafra. Consequently the operation of the port was severely disrupted and naturally the captains of foreign ships wanted to offload their cargo and get away as quickly as possible. Inevitably the consignments of Mackie machinery suffered as the packing cases were simply "dumped" on the dockside with no care whatsoever. As a result many packing cases were badly damaged and machinery components were scattered all over the place. The severity of the damage is visibly illustrated. The clearing agent obviously had abandoned his responsibility!!

According to Joe, the situation was exacerbated by the Nigerian army as some officers were suspicious about the undamaged packing cases. Thinking some might contain arms being smuggled in by the rebel forces, they proceeded to smash them open. Indeed they removed some packing to the military airport.

Of course there was another major problem in that normal transportation throughout the country had ceased. So even if the consignments of Mackie machinery were cleared from Port Harcourt there was no way of getting them overland to Jos, a distance of over 600 Km. (400 miles). The accumulative complications were inevitably felt at the factory site in that there was no machinery arriving for installation. The reader will have gathered from my previous comments about Joe McClelland, our senior engineer, that he did not take things lying down. I can't recall any miracle that he performed, but on many occasions he did what seemed impossible!! As usual, Joe rose to the occasion.

Despite the seriousness of the situation, particularly in the south of the country, Joe was willing to go to Port Harcourt in an attempt to sort things out but the question was how to get there, as no scheduled flights were operating, also no normal land transport. Even if it were possible to hire any sort of vehicle, the main roads were impassable having been bombed. Then something totally unexpected, indeed providential happened. Joe

Illustrates severity of damage to Mackie packing cases.

McClelland is in no way hyper-religious, but like myself he has a very basic and simple faith.

It is appropriate to mention again that Joe was in charge of the complete project so was responsible for the erection of the building, the installation of machinery and all ancillary equipment, the welfare of the four or five British erection engineers, the local staff and labour, also all aspects of security. His concern about the disruption can be understood.

One holiday when Joe and a couple of Mackie erectors were about to "tee off" at the Jos golf club, he was approached by a rather cultured gentleman, surprisingly a Britisher! The gentleman's request was simply to walk round with Joe and have a chat. Joe, being a friendly type, told him if he had a set of golf clubs he would be delighted to have him as a playing partner. The gentleman was very pleased to accept the offer and had no difficulty in acquiring a set of clubs. Right from the outset Joe noted that the locals, particularly the golf club staff, treated his friend with great deference, saluting and bowing to him. It transpired that in the time of the British rule he had been Governor of that area, and was now acting in a consultative capacity to the Nigerian government. Naturally the ex-Governor was very interested to learn what Joe and his colleagues were doing in Jos. Joe also made him aware of the problems caused by the civil war and of his desire to get down to Port Harcourt. This was all part of a general conversation which took place during the round of golf. Needless to say, Joe was quite surprised when he was asked if he was quite serious about going to Port Harcourt. When Joe confirmed that he could not be more so, the ex-Governor responded by saying that through his contacts in the government and military he could make suitable arrangements. The outcome was that Joe received permission to "hitchhike" on a military aircraft flying to Port Harcourt.

When Joe reached Port Harcourt he realised the immensity of the task he had taken on but there was no way of retracing his steps. Furthermore, there were no means of communicating with other parts of Nigeria, much less the outside world. As far as Mackies were concerned, Joe was lost for several weeks. For Joe personally the lack of proper food was the most distressing aspect. From being a well-built, robust six-footer, Joe became lanky, lean and rather skinny for his height!

The port had not only ceased to operate normally but was in a state of chaos. Cranes and other equipment had been damaged or stolen and large areas were decimated. Consequently there was no suitable lifting equipment in working order and it was totally impractical, indeed impossible to manhandle the heavier Mackie machinery parts. However, as I've said several times previously, travelling abroad for Mackies taught a person to improvise and Joe could rightly be called the "master of improvisation".

He soon located a broken-down forklift truck and found a Nigerian mechanic willing to repair it for more than a reasonable payment. Joe also employed other workers who were hanging around, so the job of repairing damaged packing cases and repacking loose machinery components soon got underway.

Joe McClelland on left – he is many kilos lighter than normal weight, due to hard work and poor diet.

That was only a start as the machinery when repacked had to be got out of Port Harcourt, and the only way to get it to the factory site at Jos was to have it transhipped to the port of Lagos. The original shipping company had given up, but again Joe was not stumped. In anticipation he had obtained new shipping documents from Belfast before coming to Port Harcourt and had also persuaded the representative of a Swiss clearing agency to take on the job. However, there was still a major hurdle to get over!! Could a ship's captain be found willing to take the cargo? Once again Joe's friendliness and initiative proved to be invaluable. While working on the repacking he had befriended a British captain whose ship was scheduled to sail to Lagos. He agreed to take the consignment, so an effective team was formed: Joe, the Swiss clearing agent, and the ship's captain. Working together they got the machinery loaded aboard.

Fine, the machinery would soon be on its way covered by the new shipping documents, but what about Joe? He had entered Port Harcourt "unofficially" on a military aircraft without either an entry or exit permit. If the ship were boarded between the two ports by the coast-guard or other "officials", the captain could be in serious trouble. However, the captain gallantly agreed to take Joe as a "stowaway", who in the event of the ship being boarded, would go to a designated hiding place. Fortunately no such necessity arose. On arrival at the port of Lagos, arrangements had to be made for transportation of the machinery to Jos a distance of over 860 Km. (560 miles), some by road and the rest by rail.

The reader may be asking "from where did the finance come to pay for all these services"? There was not only the prevailing civil war

L to R: British ship's captain, Swiss clearing agent and Joe McClelland.

but also the foreign exchange regulations, however, as usual Mackies working with Joe had the answer! The building contractor Taylor Woodrow (Export) Ltd. had several other contracts in Nigeria. For some reason, of which I'm not aware, they had accumulated a substantial sum of money which they could not get transferred to the U.K. This was lodged in one of the local branches of Barclay's Bank. The two companies had come to an arrangement whereby Joe could withdraw the cash he required and Mackies would reimburse Taylor Woodrow in the U.K. Perhaps not strictly legal but very practical!!

The involvement with Barclay's Bank led to Joe having yet another interesting experience. In those days British banks used to send young men to their branches abroad for practical experience. During Joe's spell in Jos, two young Britons were seconded to Barclay's branch in that city. Shortly after their arrival they clubbed together and purchased a car. Traffic in Jos was no different from that in other African towns and cities, it was chaotic! It was therefore almost inevitable that these two young men, if not extremely careful, would have an accident. The accident in which they were involved turned out to be rather serious, resulting in one of the young men suffering multiple fractures to one of his legs. Although the fractures were set and the leg put in plaster at the local hospital, the bank manager decided it was advisable for his injured staff member to return to the U.K. to ensure that the young man would get proper care and make a full recovery.

In the ordinary course of events only small aircraft called at Jos as the airport was certainly not international. Obviously the injured bank trainee had to travel on a stretcher by a small aircraft. This was impossible with all the seats in position, so the assistance of the Mackie senior engineer was solicited. Needless to say Joe was more than willing to help, and one of the Mackie erection engineers was brought along to remove the requisite number of seats, so the patient could have a comfortable journey to Lagos to connect with the international flight to London, probably by BOAC the previous name of British Airways.

On the surface there seems to be nothing extraordinary about this story so why do I include it? Let me give a few hints before disclosing the identity of the injured young man. The British High Commission staff, the Mackie boys and other British in Jos organised a variety of sports. They formed a soccer team, a rugby football team and a cricket eleven. The young man was interested only in the last mentioned, being a keen cricketer. The foregoing event took place in May 1967. On returning to the U.K. and after recovering from his accident, although he was left with a limp, he resigned from the bank and entered politics as a Conservative. Still in his early twenties in 1968, he was elected as a councillor for the Ferndale Ward of Lambeth. He continued to rise through the Tory ranks and won a seat as an M.P. at the 1979 general election. He continued to climb the Conservative ladder until he became Prime Minister in 1990. I speak of none other than John Major, if you have not already guessed. Little did Joe McClelland realise in 1967 in Jos, when he had a party in his house, that he was entertaining a future Prime Minster, and that he was instrumental in protecting or preserving his life. Many less worthy people than Joe McClelland have been knighted.

When Joe returned to Jos having brought his Port Harcourt "crusade" to a satisfactory conclusion, the antipathy between the Hausas and the Igbos had reached its zenith and the latter were being brutally murdered. The central government sent in large aircraft to evacuate the Igbos, which in the emergency managed to land at the Jos airport, but there were no suitable steps or ramps to enable the fleeing Igbos to board. To whom did the authorities turn for help? You have guessed correctly, Joe McClelland. Once again Joe rose to the occasion! He personally drove the forklift truck from the factory, got a table, turned it upside down and placed it on the forks of the truck. Thereby providing a platform on which quite a number of people could stand. Joe then drove the truck to the door of the aircraft and raised the forks to the required height so that the refugees could step into the aircraft from which seats had been removed. Joe must have gone through this routine repeatedly over a lengthy period of time as there were several hundred Igbos gathered at the airport.

Initially the Nigerian army did not assist Joe in the evacuation of the Igbos, indeed for some reason they tried to intimidate him. They didn't realise the sterling character they were up against!! When the intimidation was at its worst Joe instructed the four Mackie erection engineers to pack their bags. He also packed his suitcases fully intending that all the Mackie staff should leave Jos. When the military officer in charge learned what was happening he panicked and went to Joe to profusely apologise and

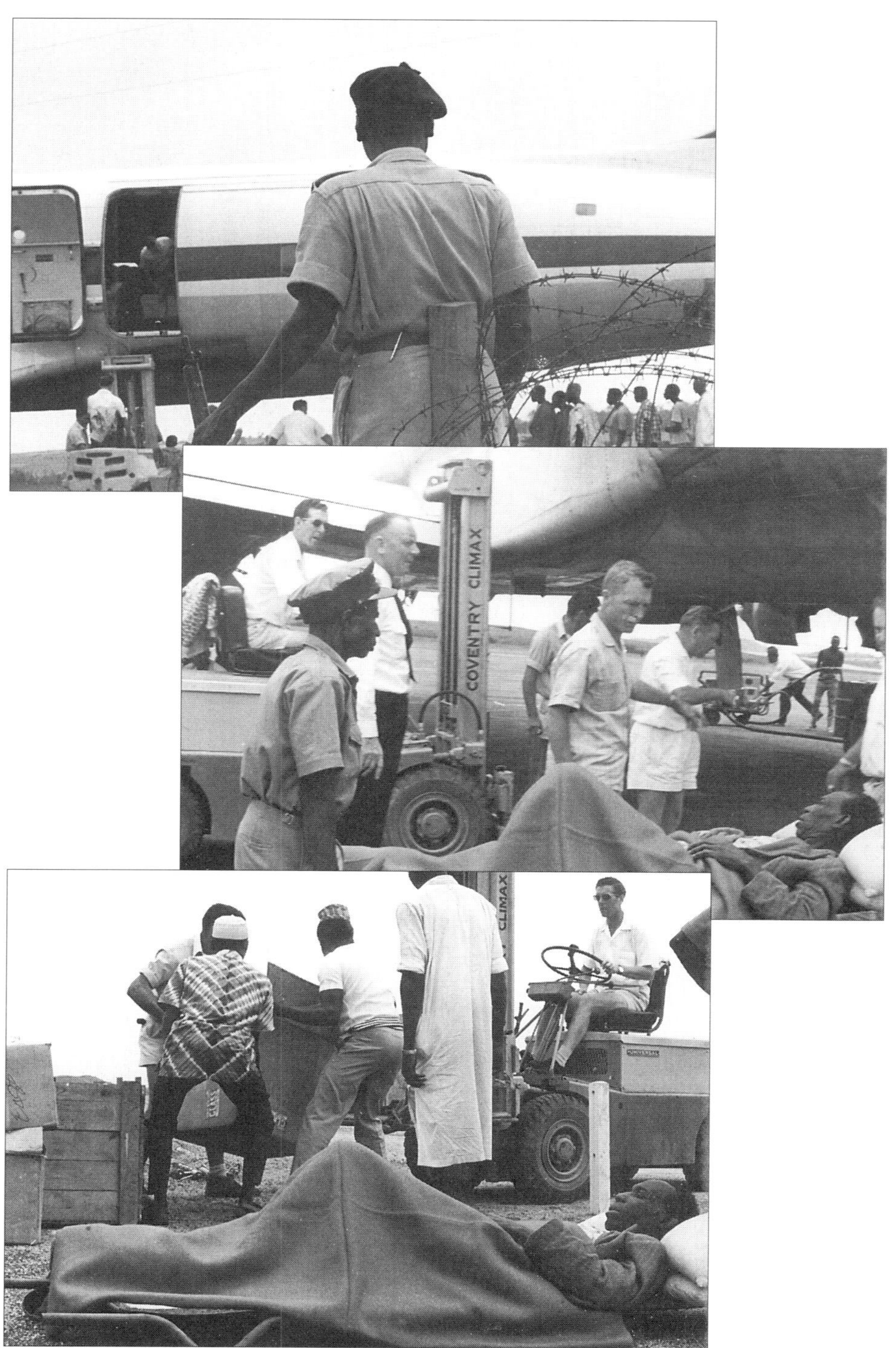
COVENTRY CLIMAX
CLIMAX

These pages:
Igbos being loaded on to plane to be flown out of Jos.

to assure him that he would get full military support. After that the army couldn't do enough for Joe. I personally learned early in our friendship, over 60 years, not to cross Joe McClelland.

Apparently U.K. newspapers reported Joe's exploits, as Mr. Jack Mackie came to know about them, but once again the British government failed to recognise Joe's initiative and courage in any way.

In the mid 1970's, Altrom Ltd. of Geneva was involved, not so much with existing jute mills, but primarily in an attempt to persuade the government that it would be an attractive proposition to set-up a new jute processing plant in the north west province, preferably within a reasonable distance of Sokoto the state capital. By then I had established an excellent working relationship with Altrom's owner, Bernhard Litscher and his nephew Bernhard Lippuner, to whom I referred in some detail when writing about Iran. I will follow the same method of differentiating between these two gentlemen by referring to the former as Bernhard Lt and the latter as Bernhard Lp. Due to the good relationship, also because the salesman Harry Montgomery, normally responsible for Nigeria was very busy in other West African countries, Bryan Hall asked me to work along with Altrom.

My first visit took place on 14th November, 1973. It was primarily an exploratory visit and was confined to the city of Lagos, which was then the capital of Nigeria. I was joined for a few days by Bernhard Lt and his wife Dagmar. I cannot recall anything of significance taking place apart from the fact that I was introduced to officials in appropriate government departments for future reference. I, on my own, visited an existing jute mill located at a town called Badagri, about 25 Km. (16 miles) west of Lagos. That factory was equipped with Cardella (an Italian manufacturer) machinery and had been, like all Cardella plants, a fiasco!! I went to that mill in the forlorn hope of persuading the management to install some Mackie machinery for comparison purposes, as I was convinced had they done so, they would have observed the immense contrast between the two types of machinery and would have been keen to replace at least the Drawing Frames and Spinning Frames. As I've hinted already, it was wishful thinking on my part as the Badagri mill from the outset had been grossly inefficient, consequently unprofitable, so not surprisingly the central government was not willing to provide the requisite foreign exchange. Therefore, on my first visit to Nigeria, I simply dipped my toe in the water.

In May 1974, I again visited Nigeria this time accompanied by Bernhard Lp with the express purpose of travelling north from Lagos to Sokoto in an all out effort to persuade the government of the north west province to invest in a jute mill primarily for the production of sacks for the packaging of agricultural products. We were well equipped with brochures, references, costs, and 16mm coloured film of a Mackie jute processing plant in Belfast. We decided to go by air on the outward journey, so booked an internal flight on Nigerian Airlines from Lagos to Sokoto, which touched down at Kaduna and Kano en route. It was an afternoon flight and it's departure from Lagos was somewhat delayed.

At the two intermediate stops the pilot hardly gave sufficient time for disembarking passengers to get off the plane and for joining passengers to embark!! Bernhard and I thought he was in a hurry to get back to Lagos for his dinner or for a date!! We later learned that flights were not permitted to land or take off at Sokoto airport after sunset, obviously for safety reasons there not being suitable equipment at the Sokoto airport to enable them to do so. However, our good captain "speed" managed to "hit the deck" and get airborne again in good time!! The flight was exhilarating or excruciating depending on each passenger's temperament. It didn't particularly bother Bernhard Lp nor me as during our extensive travels we had had numerous hair-raising experiences.

The meetings with the government officials of the northwest province were certainly not exciting and rather ineffective. It was very hot and during the meetings, particularly the one at which we showed the film, some of our guests fell asleep and proceeded to snore. It was therefore not surprising that our visit did not result in any business, indeed the officials responsible for industrialisation in the north west province were very non-committal. We did however leave sufficient literature and information to enable them to consider the proposition further, but the unstable political situation over the following decade prevented any project of this nature being implemented. When the military again assumed power in 1983, their priority was to try to stabilise the economy, so the establishment of a new jute mill was of no interest to the leaders.

To get back to Sokoto. I decided to return to Lagos by road as it was my desire to visit some areas where the cultivation of jute or kenaf was being attempted. As it was quite a long distance 800 Km. (500 miles) as the crow flies, and many of the roads were simply dirt tracks, it was essential to find a suitable vehicle. As Altrom had good contacts in Nigeria Bernhard Lp was able to arrange a robust four wheel drive. I can't recall whether it was a jeep or landrover, certainly one of the two. He also ensured that the driver was reliable and arranged for a Nigerian friend to accompany us as a guide and intermediary. Furthermore, as parts of the journey would be through jungle, a drum of extra petrol was provided, which took some space behind the seats. Consequently, when the party of four and their luggage got in there was not much spare room, but it was not uncomfortable.

Inevitably we had to spend one night somewhere on the journey. It so

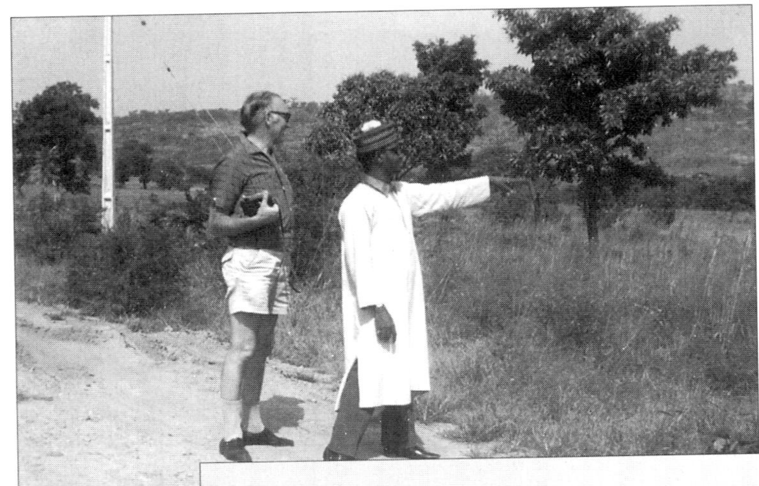

Author and Nigerian Government official look at jute plantation.

Author and Bernhard Lippuner (Altrom Ltd) standing on the type of 'road' we traversed on many sections of the journey.

Bernhard Lippuner with Nigerian driver.

Nigerian guide.

happened that at the end of the first day we were in the jungle, not near any town or city, but our Nigerian friend told us not to worry as there was a government guest house nearby. This did not really reassure us, as although we didn't expect a grass hut, we assumed the so called guest house would be very basic, but we were in for a pleasant surprise. It turned out to be a modern "chalet" in pristine condition. The person in charge was a middle-aged man dressed in a spotlessly clean white shirt and trousers. A further surprise awaited us as cold drinks including beer were available, and we were asked our preference for the evening meal, chicken or meat. After a very palatable meal we each retired to separate bedrooms, which were actually small houses built independently off the main guest house. I may be mistaken, but I seem to recall that there was no electric light in my room so I was glad of the torch that I carried with me on such journeys. The first thing I did was to have a good look around the room to ensure that there was no snake crawling around! In any event, we had a reasonable night's rest and after breakfast we set off on the second stage of our journey.

It was on this second day that we passed through areas where the farmers were cultivating kenaf (mesta in India) under the auspices of the Ministry of Agriculture. According to Joe McClelland, that government department had engaged an agronomist by the name of Tom Nasser as a consultant to advise the farmers on the best methods of sowing, fertilising

Government guest house.

and harvesting the kenaf plant. As his name would suggest, he was probably of Egyptian origin but was a naturalised German. In any case he was well qualified for the job. He in turn employed a Dutchman by the name of Fritz to do the hands-on work with the farmers. Joe McClelland formed a good relationship with both men, so was able to help them and be helped by them.

The most suitable areas were not near either of the jute mills at Jos and Badagri so to facilitate transportation plantations were established near railway junctions, two of which were Mokwa and Jamaari, the former in the centre of the country towards the west and the latter in the north east. One was very impressed by the quality of the plants and the resultant fibre. According to Joe McClelland who produced sacks from 100% locally grown fibre it processed very well. The government which had a shareholding in the Jos mill hoped that eventually there would be sufficient locally grown fibre to feed the factory but their partners, the Ethiopian family of industrialists, had other ideas for reasons of their own, which I will refrain from specifying.

The long journey from Sokoto to Lagos, over some very poor roads, also forest tracks, was navigated safely, thanks to the reliability of our driver and the local knowledge of our escort. Indeed it was very interesting and quite enjoyable. Nevertheless Bernhard Lp and I were pleased to get into

Jute growing and being harvested.

the hotel in Lagos, have a shower, and a nice dinner. I recall we indulged in the luxury of ordering a bottle of imported wine. I'm certainly not a connoisseur of wine and would not pretend to be, but for some reason the waiter asked me to perform the usual "ceremony" of tasting the wine before he poured it. I immediately detected a bitter flavour and from previous experience concluded the wine was "corked". This results from the bottles not being properly stacked, consequently tannin or tannic acid gets into the wine. Bernhard Lp, despite being Swiss, did not know what I was talking about, and was somewhat embarrassed when I called the head waiter. He, without hesitating, took the bottle away and after about ten minutes returned to thank me for drawing his attention to the matter. It transpired that the complete consignment was affected and would have to be dumped. Needless to say we got a replacement bottle of a different vintage and I felt rather clever.

During the time I was involved in Nigeria I visited the Jos factory only once, this to investigate a complaint about consignments of spare parts from Mackies. The management claimed that when packing cases were opened they frequently found that certain items were missing. In effect they were accusing Mackies of not shipping some components. A consignment had just arrived prior to my visit, so in response to my preceding instructions, all packing cases were kept intact until my arrival. They were opened in my presence and all parts on the shipping documents were found to be "present and correct". After that there were no further complaints, so I think someone had been playing tricks!

As a matter of interest I would mention that a Scot by the name of Jimmy Morrow had been employed by Mackies as a mill manager and had been seconded to the Jos factory. I think Jimmy had a heart condition. Unfortunately he had a fatal attack on the golf course (1977) in Jos and was buried there. That was most unfortunate as Jimmy was a very pleasant person and a most competent manager.

I've just learned that on the death of Jimmy the management contacted Mackies for help in the emergency. Bryan Hall had to think of someone who was familiar with the Jos mill and unfortunately Joe McClelland, who had already left Jos, was on another job. However, Mackies were seldom if ever stumped!! There was another equally competent erection engineer available, Alan Burgess. He had been in Jos in 1975 and 1976 installing additional machinery so was conversant with the factory. Alan was the obvious choice and when approached he was quite willing to undertake the assignment so in yet another instance Mackies rose to the occasion!!

That turned out to be my last visit to Nigeria as the political instability made the sale of a new jute mill plant almost impossible. This is a great pity as Nigeria could be a very prosperous country due to its large oil resources, but the output of that industry is only around forty percent mainly due to the activity of militant groups who attack the oil rigs and kidnap senior managers, particularly foreigners.

In subsequent years, that is after the mid 1970's, my efforts in Africa were concentrated in the Ivory Coast which will be the subject of the next section of this book.

CÔTE D'IVOIRE

(Note, this is the country's official name. It's name in English is frowned upon)

The Faded Miracle

Preface – History

Little is known about Côte d'Ivoire before the arrival of Portuguese ships in the 1460s. The major ethnic groups came relatively recently from neighbouring areas: the Kru people from Liberia around 1600; the Senoufo and Lobi moved southward from Burkina Faso and Mali. In the eighteenth and nineteenth centuries the Akan people, including the Baoulé, migrated from Ghana into the eastern area of the country, and the Malinké from Guinea into the north-west.

French colonial era

Compared to neighbouring Ghana, Côte d'Ivoire suffered little from the slave trade. European slaving and merchant ships preferred other areas along the coast, with better harbours. France took an interest in the 1840s, enticing local chiefs to grant French commercial traders a monopoly along the coast. Thereafter, the French built naval bases to keep out non-French traders and began a systematic conquest of the interior. They accomplished this only after a long war in the 1890s against Mandinka forces, mostly from Gambia. Guerrilla warfare by the Baoulé and other eastern groups continued until 1917.

France's main goal was to stimulate the production of exports. Coffee, cocoa and palm oil crops were soon planted along the coast. Côte d'Ivoire stood out as the only West African country with a sizeable population of "settlers"; elsewhere in West and Central Africa, the French and British were largely bureaucrats. As a result, a third of the cocoa, coffee and banana plantations were in the hands of French citizens and a forced-labour system became the backbone of the economy.

Independence

The son of a Baoulé chief, Félix Houphouët-Boigny, was to become Côte d'Ivoire's father of independence. In 1944 he formed the country's first agricultural trade union for African cocoa farmers like himself. Annoyed that colonial policy favoured French plantation owners, they united to recruit migrant workers for their own farms. Houphouët-Boigny soon rose to prominence and within a year was elected to the French Parliament in Paris. A year later the French abolished forced labour. Houphouët-Boigny established a strong relationship with the French government, expressing a belief that the country would benefit from it, which it did for many years. France made him the first African to become a minister in a European government.

In 1958, Côte d'Ivoire became an autonomous member of the French Community (which replaced the French Union).

At the time of Côte d'Ivoire's independence (1960), the country was easily French West Africa's most prosperous, contributing over 40% of the region's total exports. When Houphouët-Boigny became the first president, his government gave farmers good prices for their products to further stimulate production. Coffee production increased significantly, catapulting Côte d'Ivoire into third place in world output (behind Brazil and Colombia). By 1979 the country was the world's leading producer of cocoa. It also became Africa's leading exporter of pineapples and palm oil. French technicians contributed to the 'Ivoirian miracle'. In the rest of Africa, Europeans were driven out following independence; but in Côte d'Ivoire, they poured in. The French community grew from only 10,000 prior to independence to 50,000, most of them teachers and advisors. For 20 years, the economy maintained an annual growth rate of nearly 10% – the highest of Africa's non-oil-exporting countries.

Houphouët-Boigny administration

Politically, Houphouët-Boigny ruled with a firmness some called an "iron hand", others characterised his rule more mildly as "paternal." The press was not free and only one political party existed, although some accepted this as a consequence of Houphouët-Boigny's broad appeal to the population that continually elected him. He was also criticised for his emphasis on developing large scale projects. Many felt the millions of dollars spent transforming his home village, Yamoussoukro, into the new capital that it became, were wasted; others supported his vision to develop a centre for peace, education and religion in the heart of the country. But in the early 1980s, the world recession and a local drought sent shockwaves through the Ivoirian economy. Due to the overcutting of timber and collapsing sugar prices, the country's external debt increased threefold. Crime rose dramatically in Abidjan.

In 1990, hundreds of civil servants went on strike, joined by students protesting institutional corruption. The unrest forced the government to support multi-party democracy. Houphouët-Boigny became increasingly feeble and died in 1993. He favoured Henri Konan Bédié as his successor.

In accordance with Houphouët-Boigny's wishes, Henri Konan Bédié was chosen as his successor and the choice won the approval of the people, as in October 1995, Bédié overwhelmingly won re-election against a fragmented and disorganised opposition. However, he was not as shrewd a politician as his predecessor. Houphouët-Boigny had been very careful to avoid any ethnic conflict by selecting immigrants from neighbouring countries for administrative positions, while Bédié emphasised the concept of 'Ivority'. This policy caused strained relations between the various groups that made up the population.

There were serious repercussions to President Bédié's policy of discrimination. What had been a relatively stable political situation from Independence until 1995 became very volatile. In 1999 there was a military coup, which put General Robert Guéi in power. A presidential election was held in October 2000 when Laurent Gbagbo vied with General Guéi. The latter attempted to rig the elections, but, due to a public uprising, he had to yield to Gbagbo. In September 2002, while President Gbagbo was on a trip to Italy, a civil war broke out between rebels from the North, supported by mutinous soldiers and forces loyal to the government, causing the French to intervene.

President Gbagbo cut short his visit to Italy and negotiations between the two sides ensued, resulting in an accord being signed in January 2003, creating a 'Government of National Unity'. This proved to be very ineffective, so sporadic skirmishes still break out. The deployment of U.N. peacekeepers seemed to make little difference, so relations between Gbagbo and the opposition continued to deteriorate.

While in office, Houphouët built the world's largest basilica in the jungle near his home village – at a cost of approx. $300 million. He convinced Pope John Paul II to appear and bless the marble and glass cathedral with the gold dome.

Aftermath 2004 – 2007

Early in November 2004, after the peace agreement had effectively collapsed following the rebels' refusal to disarm, Gbagbo ordered airstrikes against the rebels. During one of these airstrikes in Bouaké, French soldiers were hit and nine of them were killed; the Ivorian government has said it was a mistake, but the French have claimed it was deliberate. They

Top: Large Basilica built by President Houphouet-Boigny in honour of Pope John II. L to R: Roy Watson (Mackie), Leon O'Haeyer (Filtisac) and John McCready (Mackie).

Bottom: The three people mentioned in the top photo, sit between two of the many pillars demonstrating how massive they are!

responded by destroying most Ivoirian military aircraft (2 Su-25 planes and 5 helicopters), and violent retaliatory riots against the French broke out in Abidjan.

Gbagbo's original mandate as president expired on October 30, 2005, but due to the lack of disarmament it was deemed impossible to hold an election, and therefore his term in office was extended for a maximum of one year, according to a plan worked out by the African Union; this plan was endorsed by the United Nations Security Council. With the late October deadline approaching in 2006, it was regarded as very unlikely that the election would be held by that point, and the opposition and the rebels rejected the possibility of another term extension for Gbagbo. The U.N. Security Council endorsed another one-year extension of Gbagbo's term on November 1, 2006, however, the resolution provided for the strengthening of Prime Minister Charles Konan Banny's powers. Gbagbo said the next day that elements of the resolution deemed to be constitutional violations would not be applied.

A peace deal between the government and the rebels, or New Forces, was signed on March 4, 2007, and subsequently Guillaume Soro, leader of the New Forces, became prime minister. These events have been seen by some observers as substantially strengthening Gbagbo's position.

Ismaili (relevant to Mackie business in Côte D'Ivoire)

The Ismaili branch of Islam is the second largest part of the Shia community, after the Twelvers. The Ismaili get their name from their acceptance of Ismail bin Jafar as the divinely appointed spiritual successor (Imam) to Jafar al-Sadiq, wherein they differ from the Twelvers, who accept Musa al-Kazim, younger brother of Ismail, as the true Imam. The Ismaili and the Twelvers both accept the same initial Imams from the descendants of Muhammad through his daughter Fatima Zahra and therefore share much of their early history.

Though there are several sub-groupings within the Ismailis, the term in today's vernacular generally refers to the Nizari community, who are followers of the Aga Khan and the largest group among the Ismailis. While many of the branches have extremely differing exterior practices, much of the spiritual theology has remained the same since the days of the faith's early Imams. In recent centuries Ismailis have largely been an Indo-Iranian community, but Ismaili are found in India, Pakistan, Syria, Lebanon, Palestine, Saudi Arabia, Yemen, China, Jordan, Uzbekistan, Tajikistan, Afghanistan, East Africa and South Africa, but have in recent years emigrated to Europe, Australia, New Zealand, and North America.

Incumbent

Prince Karim al-Hussaini became the present Aga Khan IV upon assuming the Imamat of the Nizari Ismailis on July 11, 1957 at the age of 20, succeeding his grandfather, Sir Sultan Muhammad Shah Aga Khan (Aga Khan III). In his will, his grandfather stated the conditions that led him to select his grandson as successor to the Ismaili Immat:

"In view of the fundamentally altered conditions in the world in very recent years due to the great changes that have taken place, including the discoveries of atomic science, I am convinced that it is in the best interests of the Shia Muslim Ismaili community that I should be succeeded by a young man who has been brought up and developed during recent years and in the midst of the new age, and who brings a new outlook on life to his office."

Prince Karim Aga Khan IV is the 49th Ismaili Imam, tracing their lineage to Ali, cousin of Muhammad, and his wife Fatima, Muhammad's daughter. The title His Highness was granted by Queen Elizabeth II of the United Kingdom in 1957, and his Royal Highness by the Shah of Iran in 1959. On July 11, 2007, Aga Khan was the Imam of Ismaili Muslims for 50 years.

The Aga Khan, heir to the family fortune and a society figure, is founder and chairman of the Aga Khan Development Network, one of the largest private development networks in the world. In Afghanistan, the AKDN has mobilised over $400 million in development projects, a large portion of which has come from the Network's own resources. AKDN continues to work with a variety of African and Asian countries to improve living conditions and promote education.

We in the United Kingdom know this country as the Ivory Coast but its government stipulates that the official name is the French version, which will be used by me throughout my recollections. The Côte d'Ivoire could be rightly be termed my "swan song" market, as for the five years prior to my retirement in 1990, my efforts abroad were concentrated almost exclusively on that country, which I visited annually and some years more than once. I should qualify that statement, as my concentration was not strictly on the country but rather on one company, namely Filtisac.

This company was unique in several ways, but mainly because it was part of a large industrial group, Industrial Promotion Services (IPS) established and controlled by His Highness the Aga Khan. The following résume gives pertinent details on both organisations.

Aerial view of Filtisac factory before expansion.

Industrial Promotion Services – Vehicle of third world industrial development

Industrial Promotion Services (IPS) was established in 1963 by His Highness the Aga Khan to promote the industrial development of Third World countries by private initiative within the framework of each country's Economic Development Plan.

IPS operates in several developing countries namely Kenya, Tanzania, Côte d'Ivoire, Zaïre, Bangladesh, and Pakistan. It is also established in Switzerland and Canada.

IPS seeks to achieve its goals through the combination of modern management techniques, advanced technology, local know-how and a sound knowledge of prevailing local conditions. With the participation of local and foreign private investors, local governments and international institutions, IPS has launched more than one hundred new projects in various fields, employing more than 10,000 individuals.

Investments in all IPS companies are channelled through the Aga Khan Fund for Economic Development (AKFED). The Fund plays a similar role in the economic sphere as the Aga Khan Foundation plays in the area of social development through its activities in health, education and rural development.

Filtisac S.A., Packaging Specialists

Filtisac – Jute was established in 1965 when a contract for its implementation (Convention d'Etablissement) was signed between the Government of Côte d'Ivoire and his Highness Prince Aga Khan.

Filtisac manufactures jute bags for packing, stocking and exporting coffee, cocoa and other agricultural products like rice and cotton. Its activity is directly linked to agricultural production of Côte d'Ivoire. Its purpose is to satisfy the country's needs for jute bags particularly for coffee and cocoa which are essential to the national economy.

In 1985, a new investment of about 3 billion Central African Francs (CFA) was undertaken to add to the initial investment of 2.6 million CFA in order to modernise completely the factory and increase its production capacity.

Under its diversification programme, in 1988 Filtisac had invested about 3 billion CFA in a new manufacturing unit for polypropylene and other synthetic products.

The construction was completed in June 1988 and production started in July of the same year. Manufactured products include bags (sugar, fertilisers), cloth (road stabilisation, cotton packing, plant shades), ropes

Finishing dept. where fabric is cut and formed into sacks.

in all sizes, polypropylene strapping, Leno bags and cloth for packing vegetables (onions, potatoes, egg plant), sewing thread, tapes, etc.

From Mackie's point of view Filtisac was also unique in that they were directly involved in that company to a greater extent than in any other jute mill throughout the world. Mackies not only supplied most of the processing machinery but for many years there were Mackie erection engineers on the management. I will identify these persons as I go along.

At this stage I consider it appropriate to refer to a close colleague, Harry Montgomery, as Côte d'Ivoire was actually his territory. Harry was a very pleasant person and a competent salesman, but as already mentioned, when he was inundated with work, I was requested by the Sales Director, Bryan Hall, to give Harry a helping hand. Harry never resented this or considered me to be an interloper, but gave me useful advice on the market. Unfortunately in the prime of life, Harry's health deteriorated and he died an untimely death in March 2001 while on a business trip to Kenya. Needless to say, all his colleagues where deeply shocked and saddened by Harry's death.

My first visit actually took place in October 1980 and was primarily introductory, so the discussions with the management of Filtisac were of a general nature. The mill manager at that time was Mr. S. V. Mitha, a Pakistan national. From the outset I got on well with this person and we forged a good relationship. During that visit Mr. Sidi Madatali, the Managing Director of Filtisac, gave a diner party which was held in the garden of his residence on a lovely balmy evening. It was a sit down affair, not a buffet, and it was most enjoyable sitting in the open air at a properly appointed table and having a four course dinner. This also afforded me the opportunity to meet the other Directors of Filtisac, particularly the President, Mr. A. P. Kassam. Most conversation was in French, but Mr. Sidi and many of the guests were fluent in English. I will elaborate on the question of languages later when I write about a visit to IPS Head Office in Paris.

In terms of the worldwide Jute Industry, in 1980 Filtisac was a small plant, its rated production being 10 million bags per annum on a treble shift basis. I doubt that it ever reached that figure as it was equipped mainly with the traditional type "Flat Loom" on which the weft yarn was laid by shuttle, restricting the speed at which it could be operated. There was a small number of "Circular Looms" which mechanically could be operated at a much higher speed, but demanded a better quality of yarn than the "Flat Loom" if the desired efficiency were to be achieved. The Circular type Loom, which was of French manufacture, was not accepted by the Jute Industry in general as it produced a tubular sack, which when filled with rice, or other agricultural products, retained its round shape so didn't lend itself to stacking which is essential for storage. In fact, it was hazardous to attempt to stack filled "circular" bags.

From 1980 onwards Filtisac embarked on a very comprehensive programme of expansion and diversification, consequently I had the privilege of negotiating several large orders for Mackies. Of course I was advised by our Contract's Manager, Jim Mawhinney. Unfortunately once more I have to digress and mention that Jim, despite being a diabetic, and travelling extensively, enjoyed good health up till the end of last year, 2007, when he became ill, which resulted in his death four months ago, so I lost another of my close colleagues.

The delivery of additional machinery was spread over a decade, consequently during that period there was always one, and at times two Mackie erection engineers engaged at Filtisac.

The name of Joe McClelland will have become familiar to the reader so it will be no surprise that it crops up again relative to Filtisac. Joe spent lengthy periods there in the mid 1980's supervising their modernisation and expansion programme. In early 1985 he informed the management of the company that it was his intention to return home to celebrate his 60th birthday with his family. However, as the auspicious date approached, Joe received a phone call from his wife, Iris, to inform him that she had received an invitation, accompanied by a return air ticket, to come to Abidjan for the special occasion. This had been sent by the Directors of IPS. This was motivated not only by the fact that they did not want any interruption to the programme at the factory, but also as a token of appreciation to Joe for his sterling work. In addition they also hosted quite a lavish party on Joe's birthday.

The Mackie erection engineer who initially assisted Joe was a Ronnie McBride who went to Abidjan in 1981. In November 1986, Ronnie resigned from Mackies, having been offered and accepted the position of maintenance engineer at Filtisac. He held this post until he returned to Belfast in 1993. However, the position was not left vacant as another Mackie engineer, Ronnie Martin, had been appointed in March 1993. This other Ronnie, like his predecessor, was very competent, having a good knowledge of Mackie machinery. Obviously the IPS Directors were cognizant of Ronnie Martin's ability as he held the post for 12 years until he decided to return to Belfast in 2005.

Up until the time of enlargement, IPS had found their factory manager from other sources, but at the end of 1986, they offered the job to Joe McClelland. When Joe declined they asked him if he could recommend a suitable replacement and he readily did so. He put forward the name of Alan Burgess who had wide experience as an erection engineer and had been head of the Spares Parts Department in Mackies for several years.

On the left – Ronnie Martin – senior maintenance engineer from 1993 – 2005.
On the right – Alan Burgess – general manager from 1987 – 1998.

Arrangements were made for Alan to meet Mr. Sidi Madatali, the President of Administration, in London. The interview must have gone well as Alan was invited to visit Filtisac to have a look at the plant and meet the other Directors. All meetings on that occasion must also have been satisfactory as Alan was offered the position of General Manager of Filtisac, which he readily accepted. He joined the company on 4th January 1987 and held the position for over 11 years until 4th July 1998.

During Alan's tenure the production of the jute processing plant more than doubled to twenty million bags plus per annum. This was attributable to several factors, one being very efficient management, another major factor was the replacement of the "Flat" and "Circular" Looms by modern MLS Weaving machines. The letters MLS stand for Mackie Looms for Sacking. This modern weaving machine laid the weft yarn by means of a flexible rapier which facilitated high speed operation. Development in the weaving field was largely attributable to a designer called Derrick Shimwell who lived in the Isle of Man. It is my intention to write a separate chapter on this gentleman who was a personal friend.

In addition to expansion there was also diversification. While Alan Burgess was Manager, a system of second-hand Mackie machinery was purchased from Spain. This unit was designed to produce high quality jute yarn is used by Filtisac for the manufacture of carpet yarn. Jute yarns are used in the back of Wilton and Axminster carpets, the lighter of the yarns

A section of the large installations of MLS weaving machines.

are woven in as weft and the heavier is termed "stuffer" yarn as it is used as a filler. The yarn was exported to carpet manufacturers in many parts of the world and Northern Ireland was one of their markets as Filtisac was the main supplier of jute yarns to Ulster Carpets over a number of years. Indeed, in order to ensure continuous and smooth delivery to their customer, Filtisac rented a warehouse near Portadown. To ensure that the yarn was delivered to Ulster carpets the product was packed in containers which helped to retain the requisite amount of moisture in the yarn.

The IPS head office was located in the former Rothchild mansion in Aiglemont on the outskirts of Paris. I was requested only once to visit Aiglemont, and was accompanied by our Contracts Manager, Jim Mawhinney. We did not see much of the office as the main discussion took place over dinner in a nearby restaurant. We did, however, meet several of the secretarial staff and learned that to get a responsible job in IPS a person had to be fluent in English. Consequently, the secretaries in the head office spoke lovely English. We also saw the Aga Khan's rather old BMW car sitting outside the front door. He apparently didn't have a chauffeur driven limousine to go to and from work.

Naturally there was continuous liaison between the IPS head office and Filtisac. During the time of my involvement the person responsible for this co-operation was a Belgian man named Guy Vandenbergue. He was a rather brusque character and not easily influenced so it took some time and effort to gain his confidence. Nevertheless Joe McClelland and I were successful in doing so. It was Guy who was sent to Belfast to assess the suitability of the Mackie MLS Weaving machine to replace the existing "Flat" and "Circular" Looms in the Filtisac Weaving Department. Although I was in Belfast at the time, the job of convincing Guy was delegated largely to a younger colleague, Gilbert Watt, ably assisted by the Foreman of the Weaving Development Division, Davey Mateer. The latter was probably the most experienced weaving technician in Mackies, while Gilbert had the know-how of weaving jute in mill conditions. Of course there was a very experienced weaver called Beryl in charge of the demonstration machine. The team obviously did a good job as Guy, on his return to his office in Paris, sent a very favourable report to Abidjan, resulting in a total of 74 MLS weaving machines being installed at Filtisac, the largest unit ever sold.

My last visit to the Filtisac Jute Mill took place in November 1989, the penultimate year of my career with Mackies. I was accompanied by the new Sales Director, Ashley Eves, and Joe McClelland. A word of explanation relative to Ashley is necessary. In the mid 1980s the situation in Mackies, financially and otherwise, had reached a critical stage, as the family had largely withdrawn its interest in the company in 1980, although there were still two Mackies, Mr. Leslie and Mr. Gordon on the Board of Directors.

The Industrial Development Board (IDB) of Northern Ireland had become involved in the company's affairs, something which would not have been tolerated when the Mackie family was in control. In any event, that organisation decided that a new Sales Director should be appointed and that he must be a person completely outside the company. Consequently, Ashley Eves, a New Zealander, was selected. Ashley was a qualified engineer who had spent all his working life in the U.K. and at the time of his appointment occupied a senior position in John Brown's of Clydebank in the manufacture of gas turbines.

The purpose of the trio's visit to Filtisac was to survey the MLS Weaving machines and to identify the parts that were showing abnormal wear so that steps could be taken to prolong the life of those components. Of course it was our desire not to disrupt production, so the survey was carried out on a Sunday as the plant operated for six days a week and the weekly maintenance took place on a Sunday. It was quite an undertaking to carefully examine each of the 75 MLS machines and to list the worn parts in less than eight hours. The task was made easier by the involvement of Joe McClelland who knew the MLS Weaving machine inside out.

Over the five years or so during which I liaised between Mackies and

Filtisac, I established very good relationships with Mr. Sidi Madatali and the other Directors of IPS / Filtisac, also with the mill management. At all times I found them to be very pleasant and reasonable clients and there was never any acrimony during the negotiating of several substantial contracts. Each time a contract was signed, Jim Mawhinney, our Contracts Manager, and I were presented with a genuine ivory ornament, and consequently I have quite a collection of valuable pieces.

Since the end of President Houphouet-Boigny's rule, the country's problems have been exacerbated by the two coup d'états (1999 and 2001) and a civil war commencing in 2002, which was triggered by socio-political tensions caused by the adoption of a new constitution and the election of Laurent Chagbo as President of the Republic. The crisis ended after a political agreement was signed by Chagbo and rebel leader, Cuillaume Goro, on 4th March 2007 in Duagabougou, Burkina Faso. According to Alan Burgess, who still keeps in touch with friends in Filtisac, the Jute Mill continues to operate reasonably well producing 15 million bags per year, which is about 75% of it's rated capacity. The bulk of the production is still on the MLS Weaving machines, and so I consider my efforts and those of my colleagues to have been well worthwhile.

INCIDENTAL COUNTRIES

Sri Lanka (Formerly Ceylon)

I REFER TO THIS as an incidental country, not to denigrate it in any way, but simply because it did not play a major part in my career, nor in Mackie's history. The same applies to the other two countries in this section. This was not due to lack of effort by the company's representatives. Indeed, Sammy McCoubrey from Calcutta visited the country several times when it was still Ceylon as its name was not changed until 1972. Sammy was a very positive salesman who didn't "suffer fools gladly", but when he formed a friendship he was very loyal and it took a lot to spoil that relationship.

The person who expressed interest in setting up a jute processing plant in Ceylon was a person named Pin Fernando, a professional golfer, who obviously desired some investment in industry after his golfing career ended. A jute mill seemed to fit the bill. A proposal was submitted for a suitable plant around 1960, and followed up by Sammy who visited Ceylon periodically over the following six years with no positive results. In 1967 Sharon, Sammy's oldest daughter, had reached the age of nine, and he, with his wife Sadie, felt it was time for Sharon to continue her education in the U.K. The couple, being strong family people, were not prepared to send Sharon to a boarding school, so they mutually decided to terminate their stay in India and return to the U.K., of course with the company's blessing.

During the subsequent three years, correspondence continued with Pin Fernando, but he seemed to be going round in circles so in 1970, I decided to visit Colombo to assess the situation. By that time the European staff in Calcutta had been largely replaced by Indians, this in accordance with the Indian government's policy. However, I still had the assistance of one Belfast man named Joe McMillen, note not Joe McClelland, whose name has appeared so frequently in preceding chapters. I decided that this Joe should accompany me so that if necessary, he could assume responsibility for Ceylon.

After several meetings in Colombo, it became evident that Pin Fernando could not raise the requisite capital for the setting-up of a jute mill, also that the Ceylonese government was not in the least interested. Consequently, Joe McMillen and I concluded that there was no possibility of a contract for a jute mill plant in the foreseeable future, so negotiations should be suspended for the time being. As far as I'm aware, there is still no jute mill in what is now Sri Lanka, so the country's requirements of sacks and other jute goods have to be imported.

We finished our business after lunchtime on the final day of our visit, and as there was no suitable flight until the following morning, we had time to spare. By the way, we had to travel via Bombay (now Mumbai) as there were no direct flights between Calcutta and Colombo. Joe, being married, wished to take a "wee" present home to his wife, Alice, so he suggested a look round the shops. Inevitably we landed in a jeweller's where I noticed two gold rings with an inset of a small blue sapphire, almost identical. I recall that the price tag was the equivalent of around USD 40. Of course, in that part of the world one seldom pays the asking price. As I had not a ring at that time and didn't wish to wear anything too flashy, I tried on one ring which fitted perfectly and looked well, so I decided to try to get a bargain. I can't recall if it was approaching closing time, as if so, I had a better chance of doing a deal, as the shop owner would consider it bad luck to lose a sale late in the day. After some bargaining I got the price down to USD 25 for one ring. On the spur of the moment I decided to make an offer of USD 40 for the two rings, not expecting it to be accepted, but after some hesitation with an appropriate abject look, the jeweller agreed. I turned to Joe and asked "have you a twenty dollar bill"? Thinking I was borrowing the money Joe handed it over like a lamb. I then handed over USD 40 and got the two rings and turned to Joe saying "you've just bought a ring". As Joe already had several he didn't need another, so he retorted "you so and so", but being a good sport, he saw the funny side.

After being recalled to Belfast, Joe McMillen was appointed head of the outside erection department, which allocated erection engineers for installations at home and abroad, but he never really settled in Northern Ireland. Through the good offices of Bryan Hall he procured a managerial post with a rope manufacturing company in Canada. That was over twenty years ago and after learning "the tricks of the trade", he set-up his own company called MCM Ropes and Riggings Ltd., which, as the name suggests, produced equipment for yachts. The venture was very successful, and having reached retirement age Joe has handed over the running of the company to his two sons Paul and Michael and his daughter Kate.

In November 2006, Joe, with his wife Alice, decided to stop off in Belfast en route to India to which he had been invited by a client. This gave Joe the opportunity of attending the annual dinner of the Mackie Old Boys Club. I reminded Joe of the purchase of the ring in Colombo, so many years previously. We each were still wearing our respective rings, so I reckon it was money well spent!!

Singapore

Around 1962, a group of Chinese businessmen decided to invest in a jute mill plant in Singapore for the manufacture of jute sacks. The company was initially called Singapore Jute Mills (Private) Ltd. This company, for various reasons, had a rather short and inauspicious history. The businessmen involved had "fled" Indonesia when President Soekarno wrongly blamed the ethnic Chinese for being unpatriotic because they would not join his "Parti National Indonesia (PNI)". The Mackie agent for Indonesia at the time, Dr. Oey Jam Hoey, also Chinese, took the precaution of making his permanent residence in Singapore and registered a company there, Sinitrada Co. Ltd., but at the same time retained his office in Jakarta.

Quite probably Dr. Oey was consulted regarding investment in Singapore, and being Mackie's agent, he naturally wanted to sell their machinery and a jute mill was the obvious choice. Admittedly the jute industry in Indonesia was an attractive investment but Singapore was a different proposition. Many more sophisticated industries were being established in the rapidly developing country, so given the choice, workers would not opt for a job in a relatively dusty jute mill. In my opinion, from the outset the odds were stacked against the jute mill being viable. There was also a major mistake in the design of the building chosen which added to the capital expenditure and to the operating costs.

In any event, the sacking plant never achieved profitability so the Chinese owners were greatly relieved when a western businessman by the name of A. Mercer, came along and offered to buy the company. My colleague, Sammy McCoubrey and I don't recall much about Mr. Mercer, apart from the fact that we questioned his business acumen. He renamed the company Mercer Mills Ltd., and brought in an Indian as finance director. He also decided to diversify into the manufacture of carpet backing. This did not mean further business for Mackie as Mr. Mercer chose to buy the requisite broad looms from our competitors F.L.T.M. of Leeds. To finance his plans he had to take a substantial loan from Chase Manhattan Bank.

As both Sammy McCoubrey and I shortly thereafter became based in Belfast, we lost contact with the Singapore company, but we gather that like the sacking unit, the carpet backing plant never took off.

Malaysia

When writing about Thailand and Pakistan I referred to the Adamjee family and in particular to Mr. Hanif Adamjee. In the mid 1960s, Hanif was still interested in investing in industry. He had two stipulations, the investment should not be in the subcontinent of India and Pakistan and it should be in the jute industry, which he knew best. After his project in Thailand had been finalised, Hanif asked me if I could suggest another country in the area, which would be attractive for investment. After giving the matter some thought, I suggested Malaysia as that country was industrialising and there was no existing jute mill.

It transpired that Hanif had a contact in Butterworth, a town on the mainland opposite the Island of Penang on the west coast of Malaysia. The person in question was not an industrialist nor a Malaysian, but a retired military officer from the Pakistan army, Brigadier General Gilani. These negatives didn't worry Hanif as he was interested only in having a front man with good contacts and the General filled the bill. Hanif and I flew to Penang to meet General Gilani and to assess other aspects of the potential for investment. At the outset of our visit we were introduced to a very competent lawyer, a lady of Chinese origin, but a Malaysian citizen who was conversant with all legal and political regulations.

Initially I proposed a plant comprising 76 sacking "Onemack" weaving machines, to give an annual production of 5 million sacks, the same as Hanif's Khon Kaen mill in Thailand. However, after taking all important factors into consideration, particularly the indigenous market, Hanif decided to go for a smaller unit of 46 "Onemack" weaving machines, the rated annual production of which was around 4.5 million sacks.

The new company was named Gilani Jute and Textile Mills (M) Ltd., and the Brigadier General was appointed Managing Director. Miss P. G. Lim was co-opted as advisor. The management was strengthened by the transfer of the very competent manager, Larry McVea, from Hanif's Thai plant.

The history of this company was rather similar to the Singapore set-up, perhaps for different reasons. Despite Hanif Adamjee's wide experience in the jute industry and Larry McVea's competence, the plant never really got off the ground. In my opinion, one of the negative factors was the prejudice in Malaysian government circles against companies which had no national shareholders. In any event, after a few years the company was wound-up. Thereafter, as mentioned in my article on Pakistan, Hanif Adamjee decided not to invest further in industry.

THE HOME FRONT

Generally speaking, the members of the sales staff were given most of the credit for business procured for the company, but they would not have got very far without the support of various "teams" based at the head office in Belfast. It is consequently appropriate to devote a section of this story to the people who were members of those departments. Time and space would not permit me to mention everybody involved, I will therefore confine my comments to those most directly associated with members of the sales staff, and in particular with myself.

The Travel Department

Undoubtedly this was the department on which the members of the sales staff were most directly dependent. It will be appreciated that an extensive trip abroad had to be meticulously planned, so that a sales person would not find himself in a compromising situation in a foreign country. I personally was most fortunate in that during the majority of my years of travel, Eric Slane, a very competent and experienced person, was in charge of all travel arrangements. The contribution that Eric made will be evident from the following outline of his responsibilities. He was responsible for obtaining passports and requisite visas, arranging vaccinations and inoculations. Eric had also to book airline flights, often with little known airlines in distant countries, and when required, rail and passenger ship bookings. To the list has to be added hotel reservations, as in many overseas countries, hotel accommodation was at a premium. Transportation was another facet of Eric Slane's job. The fleet of cars, including two Rolls Royce's and a Daimler, were kept in good running order by the mechanics in the garage, under the supervision of Sammy Baxter the foreman, and Billy McCartney the charge hand, but the co-ordination of the driver's duties was mostly channelled through Eric. There were normally four uniformed drivers for the limousines – Eric McCrorry, Val Young, John Lynas and Bob Greer. Allocation of drivers' duties may on the surface seem simple, but frequently it required a lot of juggling. For example, if a director required the use of a Rolls Royce, numerous important clients were arriving, and at the same time some staff members were to be taken to, or collected from the airport. The situation called for deft handling if no one was to be offended, but Eric Slane proved to be a good 'conjurer'!

Over the years Eric organised many tours for me, the majority of which were far from straight forward, but I cannot recall any mistake or omission made by Eric. He frequently went beyond the call of duty by assisting me and others in arranging private trips and holidays. On leaving Mackies, Eric became a partner in a successful travel agency but is now enjoying retirement.

Having been in the travel business for over 30 years, Eric has many tales to tell, lots amusing, but some rather sobering. One in the former category I think was concocted and embellished by a travel agent, not Eric I hasten to say! A British businessman, who frequently flew between London and New York, always did so by first class and insisted on having seat 6B, which incidentally was my favourite in the first class section of the Boeing 747 aircraft. On one occasion when the said businessman checked in at Heathrow, he was informed that the seat had been allocated to an earlier passenger. Instead of accepting an alternative seat, he more or less told the stewardess at the check-in desk that she had no business giving the seat to another passenger, no matter how important he was. The man, I won't put "gentle" in front of man, created such a furore that the stewardess called her supervisor, who went to considerable trouble to recall the other passenger, who willingly changed to another seat.

During the altercation, a queue had formed behind the irate man. When the next passenger came to check-in he said to the stewardess; "how do you remain calm and polite to such a rude man"? The young lady replied, "we have ways and means of dealing with such characters" and added, "he is flying to New York but his luggage is labelled for Sydney". The moral is, always be polite to airline staff. Let's hope this is only an amusing story and not factual!

Recently I heard two other stories, true and somewhat sobering. Mr. Stewart Mackie, the production director, periodically visited Scotland, sometimes on business and on other occasions for fishing or shooting. In January 1953, he requested the lady in the travel office to make some bookings for him. It was his desire to travel to Glasgow by air, but to return on the Stranraer to Larne ferry with some friends. The ferry was then operated by British Rail, and for some reason, which I cannot recall, it was necessary to have what was termed a "sailing ticket" in addition to a passenger ticket. If a passenger turned up without the former, he or she would not be permitted to board the ferry. The girl in the Mackie travel department pulled all the strings she could but was unsuccessful in obtaining a "sailing ticket" for Mr. Stewart, who rather reluctantly decided to return to Belfast by air.

Some would say that was due to lady luck, I personally would maintain it was providential. In any event, the day on which Mr. Stewart Mackie intended to travel, the 31st January 1953, there was a very severe northerly gale with 50 foot waves in the North Channel and the M.V. Princess Victoria sank with the loss of 133 lives, including some of Mr. Stewart's friends. When Eric Slane took over the travel department, Mr. Stewart cited this story and told Eric that when a problem arose with a booking for him not to force the issue.

The second story I learned from Margot Wills (nee McKee) who was then secretary to Mr. Lavens Mackie, sales director. She told me that Mr. Hanns Lowe of the Mackie London Office had planned one of his periodic visits to Belfast in January 1953. He intended to drive up from London to Stranraer and catch the ferry on that fateful day. When Hanns informed Mr. Lavens of his plans, he was advised not to make the long journey to Stranraer by car but rather to wait and fly to Belfast the following day. Hanns took the advice of Mr. Lavens and naturally was badly shaken when he heard the news of the disaster. Needless to say, Hanns was glad that he had taken Mr. Lavens advice. He rightly considered that Mr. Lavens had saved his life, and as a token of appreciation, he later presented Mr. Lavens with a pair of pistols with pearl handles, an expensive gift but well worth the money!!

Correspondence Department (Typing Pool)

In Mackie, departments were named differently from similar sections in other companies. We liked to be different.

When I joined the sales staff in April 1954, the head of this department was an Englishman known as "Papa" Sharp. He was a bachelor who at home was cared for by a housekeeper, consequently he was a bit of a fusspot, nevertheless he ran a "tight ship". When Mr. Sharp retired in 1960, following some provisional arrangements, one of the senior secretaries, a Miss Chris Kell, was appointed head of the department. Subsequently she married and became Mrs. Weatherup.

When I returned from India in 1972 on a permanent basis, Chris assigned a girl named Ruby Railton to be my secretary. Ruby was very pleasant and efficient so I was entirely satisfied with her work, but after a year or so, a situation arose which caused Chris to make a change. Mackie's man in Dacca (now Dhaka), Bangladesh, Colin Metcalfe, was recalled to Belfast. As Colin had a rather brusque manner, Chris had to be careful in her choice of a secretary for him, and decided that Ruby would fill the bill. Ruby's place as my secretary was taken by a Mrs. Peggy Turbitt, a pleasant and reliable person. Some situations in Mackies went on for years, while others changed frequently. When a director, Bertie Hunt, required a secretary, Peggy was an obvious choice, so a young lady, Marion Dornan, was assigned to me.

A secretary to a sales consultant in Mackie did not simply have to take shorthand and type letters, but was also involved in the preparation of highly technical and lengthy documents. For example, a proposal for a complete jute mill contained a quotation of prices, technical details, feasibility study, a labour loading table, power requirements, terms and conditions, etc., and ran into hundreds of pages. Up until the mid 1980's, these comprehensive proposals were prepared on standard electric typewriters, as P.C.'s were introduced only a few years before my retirement in 1990. Marion Dornan and I compiled many of these proposals, sometimes working all day on Saturday to meet a deadline. I got on well with all my secretaries but perhaps formed a special relationship with Marion; she is now secretary to a leading eye consultant. We still keep in contact 13 years later; indeed she typed the draft of the first two sections of this book.

The author's personal secretary – Marion Dornan.

Foreign Correspondence (Translation Department)

As Mackie's business was international, it was frequently necessary to have letters and other documents translated into one of the world's major languages. As many of the documents were highly technical, it was important for the translator to be conversant with the correct terminology. This could be acquired only by experience. The company was fortunate in having several linguists who worked in this department for almost their entire careers. This department was also most interesting because people of several nationalities worked there and some had fascinating stories to tell.

During my time with the company, two different people headed up the translation team. Initially the supervisor was a Miss Amy den Hoed, who was very fastidious about the spelling of her name. The first name had to start with a small 'd' and the second part with a capital 'H'. This lady's father was Dutch and her mother Irish, from Northern Ireland. She joined the company in 1946 and retired in 1975, having given 29 years unbroken service. Up until a few years ago she was often seen on the Lisburn Road, Belfast doing her shopping. She is now in a retirement residence but still very alert mentally. As Dutch was not widely used in international business, Miss den Hoed mostly translated into German.

When Miss den Hoed retired in 1975, she was succeeded by a German gentleman, Herbert Weiman, who had also an interesting background. He was born and spent his early years in Augsburg, southern Germany. Like most young Germans, he learned English and with the object of improving their fluency, he and a fellow student spent some time in England in 1959/60. Having completed their course, the two young men returned by ferry from Harwich to the Hook of Holland, then by the Rheine Express to Augsburg. During the train journey, they encountered two attractive young ladies in the corridor who were conversing in English with a somewhat strange accent. Boys being boys, they engaged the two girls in conversation and discovered they were from Northern Ireland. Herbert took a fancy to one of the girls, a Miss Anne Boland from Bangor, County Down.

The upshot was that Herbert and Anne's friendship quickly blossomed and led to marriage. Initially Herbert wished to reside in Germany but Anne could not settle down, so Herbert gallantly agreed to come to Northern Ireland. They arrived in Belfast on the 28th December 1962, obviously having enjoyed Christmas (Weihnachten) with Herbert's family in Augsburg. What a time to arrive in a new country without a job! To his credit, Herbert didn't let the grass grow under his feet. On someone's suggestion, he contacted Mackie and was granted an interview on the 7th January 1963, ten days after his arrival! Another pleasant surprise awaited Herbert. On arriving at Mackie on the Springfield Road, he was shown into the office of Mr. Bob Elliott, one of the company's sales directors, and was interviewed in German. Herbert must have made a good impression as at the end of the interview Mr. Elliott asked him when he could start, to which he replied tomorrow morning. Mr. Elliott told him to go easy. In any event Herbert commenced work a few days later and remained with the company until 1991, a period of 29 years.

Another interesting person was a young French lady, Françoise Segalat.

At university in France, her main subjects were English and philosophy. In 1970, the professor of English recommended that Françoise should spend a suitable period in the United Kingdom to get a good working knowledge of English. As "the troubles" in Northern Ireland were then at their height, Françoise told her professor that she would not consider Belfast as an option. To her surprise, the professor's response was that he would highly recommend Northern Ireland. He went on to say that the political unrest was confined to certain areas and that by taking reasonable precautions, she could avoid being affected. The professor added that having visited various parts of the United Kingdom, he considered the people of Northern Ireland to be the friendliest of all.

Having confidence in her professor, Françoise took his advice and came to Belfast in 1970, and now considers this to be her home. Initially she taught French in the Belfast Academy and in 1972, moved to Mackie as a translator where, as Françoise herself would say, she spent 20 very happy years. This was ironic as Mackie's factories and offices were in the heart of what was considered to be a "trouble zone" and Françoise, along with her colleagues, had her fair share of bomb scares and actual bomb blasts! Although French was Françoise's main language, she also had a good working knowledge of Spanish and Italian.

Recently I've been in contact with a local lady, Mrs. Hilary Harrison (nee Neill) to ascertain certain facts. Hilary, having worked in this department for nine years, was well qualified to answer my queries. Her languages were German and French, the two foreign languages which were predominantly used in Mackie business. Spanish and Italian came a close second. I was surprised to learn from Hilary that in the 1970's and early 80's, there were twelve translators plus the head of the department. Opposite are photographs showing the team at that time. Hilary consulted a former colleague, Marion Blass (nee Currie), who is married to a German and lives in Russelsheim. Together they were able to recall the names of most of the people in the photograph. Only two surnames are missing.

The company did considerable business in South America, particularly in Brazil. That market was initially the responsibility of a sales consultant, Jack McCluskey, and latterly Walter McNeill. In Jack's day the Portuguese translator was a Mrs. Jones, a local lady, and when she retired a competent replacement came along in the person of Helen McCann. Helen's parents were from Armagh, who went to Brazil as Christian Brethren missionaries. Consequently, Helen spent her early life in Brazil, so she was fluent in Portuguese. I understand that Lucia Browne, who appears in the photograph, was of Italian extraction. It will therefore be appreciated that there was quite a cross section of nationalities in the Mackie translation department.

There were various other sections of the Mackie set-up, which made a

The translation team –

Back row – Alison, Vivienne Whitley, Lucia Browne, Stella Young, Hilary Harrison, Marion Blass, Eileen, Helen McCann, Herbert Weimann.

Front row - Janet Heyburn, Francoise Segalat, Ethne Mitchell, Janet McCormick.

Visiting customer with technical and translation staff.

Herbert Weimann, Lyle Lavery, Harry McConnell, Stella Young, Francoise Segalat, Italian visitor and Jack Bunting.

very important contribution to the success of the sales staff, but I won't bore the reader with superfluous details. However, one considers it important to include a section on the major part played by illustrative brochures and technical catalogues.

Advertising Brochures, Technical Catalogues and Exhibitions

The Mackie family avoided publicity and the company was averse to advertising. The directors considered that the personal approach was much more effective. They did, however, attach a lot of importance to illustrative brochures and technical catalogues. When I returned from India in 1972, Bryan Hall, the sales director, asked me to assume responsibility for co-ordinating the preparation and printing of those publications, also to organise display stands for exhibitions. In the latter capacity, my ability was quickly put to the test by the meticulous planning which was essential for the British Industrial Technology Exhibition, held in Peking in March/April 1973, about which I've already written.

The considerable responsibility allotted to me in this capacity, was made much less onerous by the excellent team that was already in existence. This team was spearheaded by a very imaginative and innovative graphic designer, Barry Pitman. Barry was a Welshman married to a local girl. When I took over the job, Barry had formed a good relationship with a very skilful photographer, Jimmy Taylor. Together they produced a series of brochures, which were not only colourful, but also most informative and portrayed Mackie machinery in an excellent manner. Sadly, while still relatively young, Jimmy Taylor suffered from a fatal illness, but his assistant, William Johnstone, had been given a good training so stepped into the breach with little or no disruption. This was another unique characteristic of the Mackie set-up. Although the staff was not regimented, when a gap occurred in the ranks, there was always a suitable person to step forward.

Barry Pitman - Head of Advertising and Exhibitions

In those days, before modern methods came along, the production of spares catalogues was a painstaking job as all components of each type of machine had to be drawn by hand. Consequently, there were three technical illustrators continuously engaged in this work, the most senior being a reliable person called Stanley Gifford. The immensity of the task will be appreciated when it is understood that Mackie manufactured several hundred types of machines and there were hundreds of components on each machine. Furthermore, the design of many machines was constantly being altered, not basically, but in minor respects to suit the requirements of certain customers and, if necessary, to improve the performance of the machine.

In preparation for an exhibition we generally made a mock-up of the stand in Belfast to ensure that the machinery we intended to display, and other exhibits, fitted in and projected the right image of the company. The hands-on work was the responsibility of a senior draughtsman, Ken Magee, who was fastidious to a fault so that no detail was overlooked. At certain exhibitions there was a small kitchen and a bar on the Mackie stand, mainly to provide refreshments for existing and potential customers. As mentioned previously, these facilities were arranged by Mrs. Margot Wills, the customer relations secretary.

With reference to the bar, I must emphasise that the firm of Mackie was very much against drinking on the job. Indeed, in the directors' dining room at lunchtime, only water, milk and orange juice were served.

Entertainment

In this connection there is an amusing story. During the Second World War, there was a committee of senior military officers called the "defence college". Their function was to visit establishments throughout the United Kingdom where arms and other military equipment were manufactured, to ascertain if production was going in accordance with government plans. When coming to Belfast, the officers travelled by the Liverpool ferry, which arrived early in the morning. It was logical that their first visit would be to Harland & Wolff's Shipyard, where naval vessels were being built. After a relatively cursory tour the officers were served liquid refreshments in the M.D.'s office.

The next port of call was Short Brothers & Harland's Aircraft Factory, where Stirling bombers and Sunderland flying boats were being built. Here there was a repeat performance; a tour of the factory followed by cocktails. The story goes that the visitors arrived at Mackie's Albert Foundry, as it was called, around noon. On arrival they were met by a couple of directors and taken into the original board room, shown where to hang their hats and great coats, and handed white coats. Without further ado, the officers were escorted into the machine shops where shells were being produced. They were kept on the move till lunchtime, around 1 p.m., when they were taken to the directors' dining room, adjoining the workers' canteen.

The most senior officer of the delegation tells the rest of the story; "we, with relief, took our seats at the dining table, and anticipated with relish some refreshing drinks. When we had settled, an Irish colleen spoke over my shoulder and asked 'what would you like to drink'? I was about so say a gin and tonic with a little ice would be jolly good, but before I could do so, the waitress continued 'water, milk or orange juice' – that was the only factory we really inspected that day". Mackie was always different!!

Outside Erection and Student Training

During most of my tenure with Mackie, the two men who were in charge of what was known as the outside erection department were Bob Burton (senior) and Davey Rea. They had served their apprenticeship in the firm and had been outside erectors for a number of years, before being promoted to the staff and appointed to this position. Incidentally, a fitter who was engaged in the installation of machinery in a mill or factory outside the company was generally called an "outside erector". In some instances they were referred to as "continental fitters", but I personally, when talking to a customer, preferred the term "installation engineers" as it portrayed a better image.

The first responsibility of Bob and Davey was to select fitters from the various workshops who they considered to be sufficiently experienced and had the capacity to install and commission machinery. This obviously had to be done in consultation with the foreman of the workshop from which the fitter was being chosen. Not only was the foreman's opinion valuable but it was important not to disrupt the output of his workshop.

When choosing an erection engineer for a job, Bob and Davey had to ensure that not only was he capable, but also that he had the right temperament so that he would establish a good relationship with the management and workers in the client's factory. This was even more important in the case of large installations where a team of Mackie erectors was required. It would have reflected badly on the Mackie Company if there was friction between its representatives. Such a situation would also have rebounded on the salesman responsible for the complete contract, consequently the outside erection made its own contribution to the sales staff.

When Bob Burton and Davey Rea retired, they were succeeded by (two equally experienced men) Wesley Kell and Joe McMillen, both of whom had worked abroad, particularly in India.

Several foreign students with Harry McConnell – students' counsellor – second from right, and other technical staff.

I have said several times that when there was a job to do, Mackie always seemed to have a person ideally suited to the task. That was very evident when it came to student training. In almost every instance when a complete factory was being supplied, Mackie was requested to train, at its works in Belfast, the requisite number of students. On occasions there were in Belfast as many as twenty students, sometimes more, of several nationalities who had to be virtually wet-nursed, therefore, the person who undertook this task required great patience and diplomacy. There was already an ideal man for the job in the person of Harry McConnell.

Harry had served his apprenticeship, had travelled widely as an erection engineer, consequently he had a good practical knowledge of Mackie machinery. Added to his experience, Harry had in every way the right personality. He was a pleasant person, jovial with a sense of humour, was a great mimic, and could quickly pick up languages. Indeed, he had an evening job as a teacher of Spanish and Portuguese. In his years as a students' counsellor, Harry coached hundreds of students to the complete satisfaction of the students and their employers.

The London Office

The London office played an important role in the Mackie business activities, as will be evident from the following description of its functions. In its heyday there was a staff of four in the office, two executives and two lady secretaries. The person in charge of the set-up was a Mr. Hanns Lowe, about whom I will write in some detail as he was a fascinating character. His colleague was a Mr. Arno Grohmann, a German and in every sense of the word a "gentle" man. The two secretaries whom I knew were Miss Ingrid Doliéf, also German, and Miss Susan Magowan, who hailed from Northern Ireland.

I was never able to ascertain Hanns Lowe's background, but always assumed that he came from one of the Eastern European countries. If that was true, he had obviously anglicised his name, indeed in many ways he projected himself as the perfect English gentleman. He drove a Rolls Royce, smoked the best brand of cigars, had a house in the Highgate district of London, and an "estate" (a farm) in Kent. Don't get the wrong impression Hanns was a very pleasant and kind hearted person, also a very good host.

Practically all Mackie customers from abroad when visiting Belfast passed through London. In many instances the London office staff was requested to book hotel accommodation and to provide transport to and from the airport. Hanns had an arrangement with a car hire company, which provided Rolls Royce limousines. Nothing but the best for Mackie customers!! When on Mackie business the drivers of this company were given a small Mackie nameplate, which fitted in behind the band on their peaked caps, so that they could be easily identified by the arriving visitors. On some occasions, customers did not wish to come to Belfast, possibly because of "the troubles", and expressed the desire that meetings be held in London. There was a large room in the London office furnished for that purpose and if a meeting was prolonged, refreshments and even lunch could be served. Hanns and his staff always had things nicely appointed for such meetings. The appropriate sales consultant, and if considered necessary the sales director, would fly to London for such meetings.

When very important clients were involved, Hanns or his colleague would entertain them in the evening. The office was located in Mount Street in London W.1., which was convenient to the Grosvenor House Hotel. Consequently that hotel was often used for accommodation and entertainment. The lady secretaries had established good relationships with such establishments so had no difficulty in booking a table, or in obtaining theatre tickets.

Hanns and his colleague Arno Grohmann were also members of the sales staff and in that capacity worked closely with Bob Rodgers, the sales consultant for Germany, Eastern Europe, also Russia. Of course they had the advantage of speaking some of the languages spoken in that part of the world. Bob Rodgers also had a good working knowledge of German. In those days Mackie did good business in that area.

Hanns was particularly kind to me. When I was in London he would request Ingrid Dolíef to obtain two theatre tickets for a good show and to accompany me. Following the show, I would entertain Ingrid to dinner, which was most enjoyable as she was not only very attractive, but also highly intelligent. On one occasion Hanns also arranged for Ingrid to hire a car and take me down to his farm, where we had a most enjoyable Sunday the weather being favourable. Ingrid eventually married a Swiss businessman and went to live in Zurich. I had the pleasure once, when passing through Switzerland, to visit her new home and meet her husband and I regret having lost contact with her.

While I was still resident in India, Bryan Hall, the then Mackie sales director, arranged for Hanns to visit that country and I had the pleasure of showing him around. In addition to introducing him to important industrialists in Calcutta (now Kolkata), I arranged a fairly extensive tour. We visited Bombay (now Mumbai), New Delhi, and Agra to see the Taj Mahal, While in Calcutta, Hanns purchased a rickshaw, the type usually pulled by a man, and had it shipped to London and then transported to his farm in Kent. I understand that Hanns and his wife had a little pet donkey and he had a special harness made so that the donkey could be attached to the shafts of the rickshaw. Thereafter the "squire" could be seen riding around in his "chariot" pulled by "Neddy"!!

Hanns was a member of the Mackie team at the British Industrial Technology Exhibition held in Peking, China in 1973. Unfortunately, he and I did not see eye to eye on that occasion. Hanns considered that he could deal with the Chinese in the same manner as he dealt with the communist regimes in Russia and Eastern Europe, which I thought was a misconception. In my opinion, despite being communist, the Chinese were still Asian; consequently they were more sensitive than their European counterparts. I think that normally being the organiser, Hanns also didn't find it easy to accept me in that role. The situation was not helped by the visit of Jim Rodgers, the Mackie chairman at that time, who did not particularly like Hanns Lowe. Sammy McCoubrey, who shared a room with Hanns in the "hotel" in Peking saw the funny side of the "wrangle", made up a wee rhyme about "Hansie and Stansie in Peking". I hasten to add that neither Hanns nor I held any grudge and when he retired, he made a point of reminding me of our continued friendship.

THE MACKIE FAMILY

IT IS NOT MY intention to write in great detail about the Mackie family but to simply jot down my recollections of the members of the third and fourth generations with whom I was personally associated in business and otherwise.

The Third Generation

After being promoted to the sales staff, early in 1954, I naturally was responsible to Mr. Lavens Mackie who was then sales director and joint managing director with his brother Mr. Jack. It was Mr. Lavens who interviewed me for the job in India. The "audience" was short and to the point as Mr. Lavens didn't waste words. It went something like this; "Jebb, do you know about our Calcutta office?" "Well sir, I understand there are two staff members attached to it, a Bryan Hall and Pat Gailey." I didn't tell Mr. Lavens that the latter, who was in Belfast on leave, had tipped me off about the forthcoming interview a few days earlier. Mr. Lavens went on "that's right, but another man with practical experience is required to supervise the large team of erectors who will be engaged in installing machinery in Calcutta jute mills over the coming years, so would you be interested in the job? Give the matter some thought".

My immediate reply was; "I don't need to think about it I'm very interested". I refrained from telling Mr. Lavens that I was bored to tears in the office in Belfast. Mr. Lavens response was; "good, make arrangements to travel to Calcutta (now Kolkata) as soon as possible". He did not go into detail about the necessary arrangements but left me to use my own initiative. He bumped into me a few days later and said; "well Jebb when are you going?" Fortunately all arrangements had been finalised so I was able to reply; "I'm leaving on Friday 13th August".

As indicated in the section on India, Mr. Lavens visited India annually. Until 1959 he stayed with Pat Gailey and thereafter with Bryan Hall, but through business and socially I got to know him very well. Although his visits took place during the cool season, Mr. Lavens found the climate and the general environment rather trying and occasionally took his displeasure out on me, however, if he later considered his annoyance to have been unjustified, he was a big enough man to apologise. Of course I also experienced the other side of his temperament. When I was home on vacation he would instruct Sammy Baxter, the garage foreman, to put a good car at my disposal. He would also invite me to have dinner with him and Mrs. Lavens, either at his home in Parkgate, or in his local "The Pig and Chicken", which was then a very good restaurant.

If I have one criticism of Mr. Lavens, it is that he had a tendency to compare me with Bryan Hall. It is said that comparisons are spurious and that certainly was true in this instance, as I could never have been a suave and dynamic person like Bryan. I would describe myself as a reliable plodder and a good organiser. Nevertheless, I remember Mr. Lavens as one who gave me a great chance to make good in life.

I recall Mr. Jim Mackie (the third) as the typical chairman. He was always immaculately dressed and projected the right image. He was the one Mackie brother who took an interest in all aspects of the Mackie business: research and development, machinery design, sales, after sales service, and customer relationship. He visited the sub-continent of India in the latter part of the 1940's and the early years of the 1950's, which was before I went to India, otherwise I would have got to know him better. In any event, when I was home on leave he would occasionally call me into his office for a chat. He would discuss business in friendly terms and tell me to be open and frank with him about the performance of Mackie machinery in India.

Very early in my sales career I learned an important lesson from Mr. Jim. One day a salesman, Austin O'Donnell, with whom I shared an office, and a colleague were discussing a problem that had arisen on Mackie machinery in a French mill, and I was listening in. Mr. Jim came into the office and for a few minutes also listened to the discussion. He then interjected and said; "boys, you can stand there indefinitely discussing the problem and not find a solution. There are regular flights to that part of France. Decide which of you will go and get on your way." The moral being action is better than words. My first lesson on the spirit of Mackie!!

Some years later I heard a story involving Mr. Jim. I can't vouch for its veracity, but it is worth telling and it makes an important point. When Mr. Aleksey Kosygin was Minister of Light Industry in the USSR, he led a delegation to the Mackie factory in Belfast. I have not been able to ascertain the date of the visit, but it was certainly while Mr. Jim was Mackie chairman (he retired in 1968) and before Kosygin became Premier of the

Soviet Union in 1964. The story goes that the Russian delegation was in the board room with Mr. Jim having a general conversation, the business discussions having concluded. Mr. Kosygin was extolling the virtues of communism by saying that his children were not granted any favours, and had to work alongside ordinary people. Mr. Jim didn't comment but simply lifted the phone receiver and said; "Gloria, please come into the board room, no, don't remove your headphones". When the young lady in question entered the room, Mr. Jim signalled towards her and said "gentlemen, my youngest daughter, and she does not go home with me in the Rolls Royce but on her Vespa scooter". The spirit of Mackie once again demonstrated, on this occasion to the Kremlin!

Mr. Jack Mackie, when joint M.D. with Mr. Lavens, did not become involved in sales, but concentrated on the design and manufacture of all types of Mackie machinery. He was also intensely interested in the performance of machinery in customers' mills, consequently he attached great importance to reports from erection engineers engaged in installations throughout the world. If an erector failed to send in a written report regularly he was in trouble with Mr. Jack.

When there were over twenty erectors engaged in installing new machinery in jute mills around Calcutta, I decided that a consolidated report would be preferable to individual ones from each erector. To facilitate this, a monthly meeting of erectors, chaired by me, was held in the Calcutta office. The erectors were very keen on this arrangement for various reasons. Firstly, they didn't have to hand write reports, secondly, they could claim expenses incurred in coming to Calcutta, and most importantly, it provided an opportunity to meet their fellow erectors. Furthermore, as the meeting was held on a Saturday morning, they would make a weekend of it.

The report, prepared by me, was addressed to Mr. Jack, and every reported fault or problem on the machinery was thoroughly investigated by him, and remedial action taken in Belfast, or suggestions made as to how the problem could be solved on the spot in the client's mill. Due to Mr. Jack's personal attention, this arrangement worked very effectively.

Mr. Grenville Mackie was the "weaving man", having trained as a weaver in the Whitehouse Mill on the outskirts of Belfast. I got to know Mr. Grenville personally when I was invited to join him and Derrick Shimwell, about whom I will be writing later, for dinner at the Midlands Hotel, Belfast. A closer relationship developed when I experienced a similar problem to that which had troubled one of his family. He felt he could empathise with me. Mr. Grenville was also delighted when he learned that I was getting married fairly late in life and he gave Helen, my wife, and me a very acceptable wedding present.

I was not closely involved with the other two members of the third generation, Mr. Frazer and his cousin Mr. Stewart.

The Fourth Generation

Surprisingly, the first person of this generation whom I got to know was Peter Mackie, the second son of Mr. Jack. He had just completed his education and joined the Company as a trainee. He was assigned to work under an erection engineer installing spinning frames in Falls Flax Mill in Belfast. At the same time, another erector, Joe Getty and I were building and commissioning a hackling machine in the same factory. I recall that Peter was fond of toffees and used to bring a bag of his favourite type into work and share them around. Unfortunately, shortly after that there was a tragedy which claimed Peter's life so our friendship was short lived.

My association with John Mackie, the eldest son of Mr. Jack, developed during his several visits to Calcutta, particularly when he and his wife, Margaret, stayed at my apartment in Tollygunje, Calcutta. Margaret was the daughter of Sir William Walker, chairman of Jute Industries, Dundee, which owned a large group of jute mills and were very good customers of the Mackie Company. Margaret preferred to stay at Tollygunje rather than in a hotel as friends from the Inchcape Group lived nearby.

On one occasion when Mr. John visited Calcutta on his own, the "Haxalites", a left wing group, were causing havoc in West Bengal, and particularly in the city of Calcutta. For a period Mrs. Indira Gandhi, who was then Prime Minister, tried to control the activities of the "Haxalites" without using strong-armed tactics, to no avail. During Mr. John's visit they called a "hartal", a general strike, when everything came to a standstill, and it would have been foolhardy to attempt to get to the office. However, on yet another occasion, the Mackie spirit prevailed. Other staff members lived in the same compound as I did, and arrangements were made for Billy Luney, the Lagan Factory manager, to stay with me, so Mr. John chaired meetings in my apartment.

After a fairly intensive meeting all morning, Mr. John and Billy Luney decided to venture out for a walk in the afternoon. They hadn't gone far when they saw truck loads of soldiers patrolling the streets. They got into conversation with a military officer who told them that Mrs. Gandhi had lost patience with the "Haxalites", and had ordered in the army. We later learned that hundreds of agitators had been arrested, loaded onto military trucks, and taken to detention camps. I lived in Calcutta for several years after that and never again heard of the "Haxalites"!

I spent several enjoyable evenings and indeed one Saturday with Mr. John and his wife Margaret at their home on Simmy Island, Strangford Lough.

The third and youngest son of Mr. Jack was Mr. Patrick, better know as Paddy. He married Julie, the second daughter of Mr. Lance Turtle, a partner in the well know Belfast stockbrokers W. F. Coates. In the section about India, I have already written about Paddy and Julie's visit to that part of the world, but I was also involved with Mr. Patrick when on vacation in Belfast. Like his father, Paddy was primarily interested in machinery design and development. He and his brother, Mr. John, were responsible for the development of the 'M' series cards, which were designed to compete with the 'JF' cards, manufactured by Frasers of Arbroath, Scotland. Ironically, Pat Gailey, who was my first boss in Calcutta, was by this time president of Fraser's parent company, Giddings Lewis International, so indirectly was promoting the sale of Fraser Cards.

On my return to reside in Belfast in May 1972, my friendship with Paddy and Julie continued – indeed it became closer, and I got to know their daughters Tracy and Tara, also eventually their son-in-law, Tracy's husband, Martin Hamilton. As mentioned in the acknowledgements it was Tracy who gave me the idea of writing this book.

Paddy Mackie had many interests outside the Company the paramount one being conservation issues on Strangford Lough and the most important subject being water fowl. After many years of dedication to the issues Paddy was deservedly awarded the MBE. The award was presented to him on St. Patrick's Day 2004.

Paddy Mackie with his wife Julie and daughters Tracy and Tara, after decoration of MBE at Buckingham Palace.

Mr. Denis Mackie followed in the footsteps of his father Mr. Grenville, being primarily interested in loom design and development. Their efforts, in association with Derrick Shimwell, led to the production of the "Onemack" weaving machine. I purposely do not use the term "loom", as the "Onemack", which laid the weft yarn by means of a rapier, was revolutionary in the jute industry. As mentioned in the section on India, Mr. Denis also visited Calcutta to assess the huge potential market for modern weaving. Unfortunately his visit had to be curtailed due to a severe bout of dengue fever.

Although I was not directly involved in weaving research and design, I was kept fully informed of developments, initially by Mr. Grenville and latterly by Mr. Denis. I also got to know the latter very well during pleasant evenings at his home, when I also got to know his wife, Susan, a pleasant English lady.

I have already written in preceding chapters about the three sons of Mr. Lavens: Sven, Gordon and Derek, so my observations in this section will be brief. Like his father, Mr. Sven Mackie's business interests were concentrated on sales, and confined mainly to machinery for the production of semi-worsted and synthetic yarns. Europe was his sphere of activity as he spoke several continental languages fluently. Despite this fact, Mr. Sven did visit India and I had the responsibility of introducing him to leading industrialists in both Calcutta (Kolkata) and Bombay (Mumbai).

Sven Mackie

Apart from two spells together, one in the early days in Italy and the other years later in India, our paths diverged so I really did not get to know Mr. Sven socially. He married Simone Corry, the daughter of one of the Corry's, the well know Belfast timber merchants J. P. Corry.

After leaving the Company around 1969, Mr. Sven devoted his time to his farm near Downpatrick.

Like his older brother, Mr. Gordon went into sales. He also had his father's flair for languages and was especially fluent in Spanish, which enabled him to successfully negotiate one of the largest contracts in the Company's history, which I understand involved several hundreds of Onemack weaving machines. The contract was with the Cuban government of Fidel Castro, which most interestingly was represented by the world renowned revolutionary Che Guevara. In the early 1960's Che Guevara still had the confidence of Castro. He was firstly appointed president of the National Bank of Cuba, then the Minister of Industry. It was in the latter capacity that he negotiated the jute mill contract with Gordon.

Apparently Guevara was very impressed, not only by Gordon's negotiating skill, but also by his command of the Spanish language, and said he spoke like a native Cuban. I recently heard of an amusing incident that occurred during one of the meetings. At that time Gordon smoked so always had to hand a Ronson lighter. Guevara was also a smoker who, understandably, had a preference for Havana cigars, smoking them down to the last half inch. When they were in discussion he often picked up Gordon's lighter to get his cigar going. Apparently on one occasion when his cigar was just projecting beyond his beard and had gone out, Guevara, out of habit, picked up Gordon's lighter to rekindle the cigar end. Accidently or otherwise, Gordon had adjusted the flame, and when Che pressed the small lever, a flame of over one inch long sprang up. As a result there was a distinct smell of burning hair. Needless to say, Guevara was not amused, although not a word was spoken, but if looks could kill, Gordon would have been a dead man! Fortunately the incident did not cause a "diplomatic" row!!

While I was still travelling my contacts with Mr. Gordon were occasional. Inevitably when he became Company chairman in the early 1980's, our meetings were more frequent. My relationship with him was always cordial and we had a good working understanding. Naturally after he left the company in September 1989 and subsequently went to live in County Meath, Eire, our paths have crossed much less frequently. However, we do meet annually at the Mackie get-together, about which I will write later.

It was traditional in Mackies when a staff member had completed forty years service to present him or her with a wrist watch. I completed my forty years in May 1985 when Gordon was chairman, so he presented me with my watch.

During his very extensive travels Mr. Gordon took a great interest in people whom he met, and has written very interesting articles about the most fascinating, not only the rich and famous, but also ordinary folk.

The third son of Mr. Lavens, Derek, left the company in 1967 to pursue other interests. In recent years Derek has lived with his mother,

Gordon Mackie presenting watch to author when latter had completed 40 years service.

a most fascinating person, who celebrated her 100th birthday in March 2009. Until about two years ago, she used to send a pot of homemade jam to my wife Helen, with Derek when he called at our home. She is affectionately known in the Mackie family circle as "Mucki".

The other member of the fourth generation, Mr. Leslie Mackie, like his father Mr. Stewart, did not take a specific interest in sales, but was director for personnel and training. In the 1980's there was a dearth of school leavers who were interested in serving an apprenticeship in fitting or machining. With this problem in mind Mr. Leslie visited several apprentice training schools in Germany, and after assessing these he set-up a similar facility in the West Factory (a separate unit from Albert Foundry on the upper Springfield Road). This venture proved to be very successful as the intake of apprentice fitters and machinists was 100 per year.

Apart from my association within the Mackie Company, I had probably more links with Mr. Leslie than with any of his contemporaries. His wife was Ann Clokey of a family which owned a paint and glass company. Apparently there were two brothers in the business. Mr. Tom Clokey was responsible for a factory in Divis Street, Belfast, where a special type of glass "thermolux", was manufactured, while Anne's father Mr. Harold owned a separate company located in King Street, Belfast, which specialised in the manufacture of stained glass. Many of Mr. Harold's designs can still be seen in many churches and chapels in Belfast and elsewhere. My younger sister worked for several years as a secretary in the Divis Street branch of the company. I was also familiar with the Larchfield Estate, having spent many holidays as a boy on a farm at Legacurry, owned by an uncle. Furthermore, after Mr. Leslie purchased Larchfield Estate, my uncle, Jim McKibben, was one of his land stewards for several years, while my cousin, Bertie Rush, looked after his pheasants.

During my frequent visits to the Isle of Man I also got to know Leslie's sister Louis and enjoyed Sunday lunches on her private beach. Indeed, at one time her husband Herbert Bibby and I considered going into business together on the island, but freight costs made the project envisaged unattractive financially.

Mr. Leslie left around 1988 and Mr. Gordon around 1990. They were the last of the Mackies to leave the Company, which hastened its demise as it was already in decline.

Despite the demise of the Company, I am still in touch with most of the surviving members of the Mackie family. While Paddy, Julie and Tara lives on Mahee Island, Strangford Lough, Tracy and her husband

Leslie Mackie with his wife Anne, at their son Gavin's wedding.

Martin Hamilton have moved into Ringdufferin – also on the shores of the Lough. (This was formerly Mr. Jack's estate), from which they carry on commercial farming. Tracy undoubtedly has the entrepreneurial spirit and skill of Mackies.

I consider it incumbent on me to refer to David Chamberlain in this section despite the fact that he is not a Mackie. David was married to the eldest daughter, Sheila, of Mr. Jim the third, and played several important roles during my tenure with the Company.

When I was promoted to the sales staff in May 1954, David was making preparations to go to Japan for a spell. During his time in that country he was successful in selling several jute processing plants. He was eventually appointed a director and subsequently company chairman in 1979 – a position that he held until 1981 when he voluntarily left the Company.

During the 27 years of association our relationship was always very cordial and I found him a very fair-minded boss. He frequently gave me very valuable advice particularly when I was experiencing a serious personal problem, which affected my efficiency at work.

David Chamberlain

THE SECRET OF MACKIE SUCCESS

Research and Development

THE MACKIE COMPANY MANUFACTURED a wide range of textile machinery for the processing of all types of fibres, natural synthetic and manmade, with the exception of cotton. It will be appreciated that to keep ahead of other machinery manufacturers and developments in the textile industry in general, a high priority had to be given to research and development. It will also be apparent from the preceding chapter that several members of the Mackie family, in each generation, were exclusively involved in this field. The company was successful in all aspects of the textile industry in which it engaged but its major success was in the jute industry. My colleagues would probably react to this assertion by commenting; "you would say that as you were a jute man"! Nevertheless, statistics would prove my claim to be valid.

For the non technical reader I will endeavour to clarify technical terms when used. At the same time, I will not go into a lot of technicalities, but simply outline the ideas which contributed to the huge success of the Mackie Company.

It is surprising how many people ask me; "what is jute?" The average person knows about cotton, wool, flax for linen, and indeed synthetic fibres, but there is not a common knowledge about jute in the western world, consequently some information about jute fibre and its uses is appropriate at this stage.

Jute is a fibre obtained from the bark of a tropical herbaceous plant. The two cultivated species are known by the botanical names of C. Capsularis and C. Olitorius. The plant has a long history as it is mentioned in one of the oldest books in the Bible namely Job, Chapter 30, Verse 4, which was written around B.C. 1520. In that text the Hebrew word "Malluach" is translated into English as "Mallows". The tender shoots of both species of jute, but particularly C. Olitorius, are known to have been used as a vegetable or pot-herb in India, Syria, Egypt, and other Middle East countries. It was known as "the food of the wretched."

As to when the fibre yielding properties of the jute were put to use in the Indian Sub-continent is rather uncertain. There is, however, evidence of trade in jute cloth in Bengal in the sixteenth century. In some Bengali poetical works of that era, sackcloth made out of jute was referred to as an article of trade.

Dependent on a variety of factors, the height to which the jute plant normally grows can vary from 5 feet (1.5 metres) to 12 feet (5.6 metres). The diameter of the stem varies from 1/4 inch (6mm) to 1.1/2 inches (38mm). The thickness of the stem is highly correlated with fibre yield. The two species differ in the quality of the fibre they yield. The fibre of Olitorius is frequently finer, softer, stronger and more lustrous than that of Capsularis. The Olitorius fibre, if retted in clean water, has a pronounced colour; some grades are reddish and others yellowish. In fact, a good quality "tossa" is more brilliant and is rightly called the "golden fibre". The Capsularis fibre is ordinarily light in colour, consequently it is called "white jute" in the trade. "True" jute is cultivated mainly, but not exclusively in India, Bangladesh, and Pakistan. A substitute fibre is grown in many other countries in Asia, Africa, and South America.

The term "tossa" generally refers to fibre coming from Corchorus Olitorius, desi (literally "local") jute grown in the neighbourhood of Calcutta (Kolkata).

The utility of the jute plant is amazing; the only part that cannot be put to a useful purpose is the root below the ground level. Even the stick or stem around which the fibre grows can be used in the manufacture of low quality paper, and poor families often "plait" it to make walls or screens for their "bustees" (shacks). Furthermore, the fibre waste that accrues during processing can be "needled" into felt for insulation or underlay for carpets, not only in houses but also in automobiles.

Of course the fibre is the important element of the plant. The most common use of the fibre is for the production of sacks for packaging rice, grain and other agricultural products and for twine to sew the sacks, also for domestic use. Middle and low quality fibre is used for those applications. The best qualities of jute are used for backing for broadloom carpets and linoleum, hessian cloth, wall covering, and what are termed "stuffer" yarns for Wilton and Axminster carpets and rugs. More recently jute shopping bags have been introduced to replace plastic bags as jute is bio-degradable. Large superstores are now offering the new type of bags, which can be used repeatedly. I understand that Tesco has recently ordered one million jute shopping bags from a mill company in India.

Until around 1945, the jute fibre was presented to the Spinning frame in a "rove", which could be described as a thick cord. The formation of this involved a Roving frame, a rather cumbersome machine, costly to make,

Jute/Kenaf Cultivation

The scenes shown below illustrate the basic stages in the cultivation of jute and kenaf. Both are grown near water for irrigation, retting and transportation.

a: A typical plot of jute, the plants have nearly reached maturity. The growth period can vary from three to five months.

b: Retting of the fibre is normally carried out in canals or ponds. The cut plants are arranged side by side in bundles to form platforms, and are covered with reeds or rushes weighed down with logs. It is important at this stage that the bundles are completely immersed to allow effective retting. The average retting time varies according to the type of fibre and can take from one week to one month.

c: After retting, the fibre is stripped from the stalks and allowed to dry. It is now ready for transportation to a selection and baling centre or, if for local use direct to the jute mill.

d: Residue stalks being bundled, these are sometimes used in the production of hardboard or low quality paper.

Jute and kenaf cultivation

to maintain and to operate. Mr. Jim Mackie, the third, with his brother, Mr. Jack, designed and developed the Sliver Spinning frame, which meant that the fibre could be fed to the Spinning frame in the form of a “sliver”, a narrow ribbon varying from approximately 10mm to 15mm in width, depending on the yarn to be produced. Even a layman can appreciate how revolutionary this was. It eliminated the costly Roving frame, reduced the labour force, and produced a yarn of higher quality.

There was yet another major step in the field of jute spinning. On the old type Spinning frame when the bobbins, onto which the yarn was wound, were full, the machine had to be stopped and a squad of "doffers", normally girls, employed to remove the full bobbins and replace them with empty ones. This resulted in considerable "down-time" on the machine, plus the labour costs for the "doffers". Mr. Jim, in collaboration with a Swiss engineer, Dr. Heinreich Schneider, developed a semi-automatic doffing system. This involved two banks or rows of bobbins. When one bank was full the machine was stopped, a hand wheel engaged, the full bank was lowered and moved forward, and the bank of empty bobbins wound up to the operating position and the machine re-started. The "down-time" was only a couple of minutes, and no "doffers" were required, as the doffing procedure was carried out by the machine operator.

On modern high speed machines an effective stop motion is essential to bring the machine to an immediate halt, when a fault occurs in the material being processed. This is particularly so on Drawing frames, the machines on which the fibres are drawn out and "parallelised". Several designs were tried out in the late 1940's and early 1950's but none was completely satisfactory. Then Mr. Patrick Mackie came up with a very simple but effective motion. It was an oscillating shaft on which were mounted plastic "feelers", one for each sliver. When the sliver was intact, the feeler was carried forward on its axis, but if the flow of the sliver was interrupted, the feeler dropped and activated an electric switch bringing the machine to an instant stop. It was rightly called the P.M. (Paddy Mackie) Stop Motion. It is being used on Mackie Drawing frames to this date.

After the Second World War, there was also huge scope for improvements in the weaving section of a jute processing factory. The use of the word "factory" takes me back to the years 1945 until 1950 when I was involved in the installation of several new spinning plants in Dundee. Mackie staff used the word "mill" to refer to the complete jute processing plant, but not the Dundee weavers. They were the "aristocrats" of the jute industry and referred to the weaving section as the "factory". They were predominantly mature women who came to work well dressed in coats and hats and were inclined to look down on the workers in the "mill", which comprised the sections up to the Spinning.

As mentioned in the previous chapter, Mr. Grenville Mackie was the "weaving man" and was responsible for loom design and manufacture. In this field he had the collaboration of two gentlemen, a Mr. Oliver Shimwell and his son Derrick. Until after World War II standard flat looms were used to weave jute. On these the weft was laid by means of a shuttle containing yarn in the form of a "cop" or pirn. When the yarn was about to run out, the loom had to be stopped and a new cop inserted by the weaver. That resulted in considerable "down-time", which inevitably reduced the efficiency of the loom.

INFORMATION SHEET NO. 18

The 4¼" and 4¾" Pitch Apron Draft Sliver Spinning Frame

The MACKIE 'Apron Draft' Spinning Frame is complementary to the 'Slip Draft' type already described. It was designed primarily for the production of high quality yarns in the lighter range, namely Hessian, Carpet Backing and other yarns calling for similar quality.

The main contributory factor to the quality of the yarn produced is the unique Apron Drafting Zone, this being a plate and apron arrangement. (See photo No. 29.) One of the other attractive features on the Machine is the revolutionary tubular flyer which permits higher speeds than were possible with the conventional solid leg flyer. (See photo No. 29.) This new flyer also facilitates a large capacity bobbin resulting in fewer doffing stoppages. Precise details in this respect are given in table overleaf.

Apron Draft Spinning Frames are manufactured in two pitches i.e. 4¼" (107.95 mm) and 4¾" (120.65 mm). The Machine of smaller pitch is capable of producing yarn ranging from 5 lbs per spangle to 12 lbs per spangle: NM 5.76 to NM 2.40: 173 Tex to 416 Tex. A high quality blend or 'batch' of fibre must be used for the lighter yarns in this range to achieve good results. The larger pitch Machine has a basic yarn range of 8 lbs per spangle to 12 lbs per spangle: NM 3.60 to NM 2.40: 277 Tex to 416 Tex.

continued

No. 29

No. 30

Auto-doffing apron draft spinning frame for warp jute yarns

Until 1953, Mr. Oliver Shimwell and his son Derrick, lived in Perth, Scotland, which was very convenient as they were working with Jute Industries, the large Dundee Company, on the design of an arrangement, which could be attached to a traditional flat loom to automatically insert the cop. When this arrangement became marketable, Sir Willie Hutton, the Jute Industries director, with whom the Shimwells were working, suggested to them that the best company to implement the idea was Mackie

INFORMATION SHEET NO. 19

The 5½" Pitch 'V Roller Drafting' Sliver Spinning Frame

The MACKIE 'V Roller Drafting' Spinning Frame was designed specifically for the production of Sacking Weft and similar yarns from low quality blends containing a large percentage of short fibres.

The unique 'V' roller arrangement in the drafting zone ensures very positive control of the short fibres during the drafting process.

Pitch of spindles, as indicated is 5½" (139.7 mm) and the versatility of this Machine is evident from the range of yarn counts which can be produced, namely from 16 lbs per spangle to 50 lbs per spangle: NM 1.80 to NM 0.58: 555 to 1700 Tex.

This Spinning Frame can be equipped with either solid leg or 'Baxter' type flyers. The advantages of the latter are higher speed and a larger package. Precise details in this respect are given in table opposite.

For general view of Machine see photo No. 33.

SLIP DRAFT SPINNING FRAMES

	Mark I Solid Leg Flyer	Mark II "Baxter" Flyer
PITCH OF FRAME	5½" – 140 mm	5½" – 140 mm
MAX. FLYER SPEED	2800 R.P.M.	3100 R.P.M.
BOBBIN SIZE	7½" × 3½" 190.5 mm × 89 mm	7½" × 4⅜" 190.5 mm × 111 mm
BOBBIN CAPACITY	16–18 ozs 453–510 gms	30–32 ozs 850–907 gms
NUMBER OF SPINDLES	80	80
YARN RANGE	16–50 lbs/spangle NM 1.8–0.57 555–1736 Tex	16–50 lbs/spangle NM 1.8–0.57 555–1736 Tex

No. 33

Auto-doffing slip draft for weft jute yarns

of Belfast. Sir Willie's advice was taken resulting in a most satisfactory arrangement between the Shimwells and Mackie, which was to last for many years.

In parallel with the Shimwells development of the cop loader, Mr. Grenville Mackie had developed a "modern" flat loom called the "Mackswell", "Mackie and Mack" were registered trade names.

An agreement was reached between the two parties whereby the

Mackswell loom could be fitted with the Shimwell Auto Cop Loader, which thereafter was designated the M.S. (Mackie Shimwell) Cop Loader. Around 1952, the Shimwells decided that it was necessary to have more permanent facilities for their research and development. Also, now that royalties were being received, income tax was an important consideration. After careful research, Mr. Shimwell senior found an ideal residence on the Isle of Man, Ballamoar Castle. Although called a "castle", the house was not excessively large. There were outhouses, which could be used as workshops and stores, and it was ideal for commuting to Belfast. Initially the property was rented and the Shimwells moved there in 1953.

For the following six years, father and son worked together on weaving development with the object of designing a Shuttleless loom. During that period, a variety of systems for laying the weft yarn had been introduced by other loom manufacturers. Some of the alternatives were Flexible Rapiers, Air Jets, a small missile projected across the loom. Those were relatively successful on certain types of yarn but jute was a different proposition due to the dust generated. Mr. Grenville Mackie, in collaboration with the Shimwells, had a preference for a rigid Rapier system. Research and development went on simultaneously in Belfast and at Ballamoar. The requisite components for the Shimwells were supplied from Belfast and the services of a fitter were provided when required. Of course, there had to be close liaison between the two parties to avoid duplication.

A little romance always makes a story more interesting, so let's briefly forget about technical matters. Derrick, the son, did most of the commuting to Belfast. At that time there was only one domestic airline, British European Airways (BEA), which operated regular flights between Liverpool and Belfast via Douglas on the Isle of Man. One of the stewardesses on that sector was an attractive young lady, Pamela Jones, from Liverpool. During 1957, Derrick was a regular passenger, and being a tall handsome man, attracted the attention of Pamela Jones. Initially the friendship was cursory but soon blossomed into romance. Apparently in 1958 they were both in Belfast and staying at the Royal Avenue Hotel, when Derrick invited Pamela to accompany him on a drive and "popped the question" while driving through the countryside. They were married in 1959, which was an eventful year for Derrick as his father died in March that year. I will revert to the Shimwells later as they and I became close friends.

The first weaving machine which resulted from the joint effort was called the "Tumack". The machine was designed to weave two fabrics simultaneously one on top of the other, hence the name. The weft yarn was inserted by two rigid rapiers, one on either side. The "Tumack" never really took off mainly for two reasons: firstly the operators did not like

Ballamoar Castle – Shimwell residence where much research and development was undertaken.

the idea of two cloths as it was difficult to detect and repair faults on the underneath fabric. Furthermore, the mechanism was rather complicated, so the two parties had to rethink their ideas, Mr. Grenville in Belfast and Derrick in the Isle of Man, who had taken over after his father's death. The upshot was that a more simple machine was designed to weave a single fabric and for obvious reasons was called the "Onemack", which was a notable success. The most popular models were the SA30 for sacking, and SB48 for the production of hessian and similar jute fabrics. During subsequent years the "Onemack" was improved and modified and well over ten thousand were sold.

One major disadvantage of the rigid rapier system was the width of the machine, as extended tracks were required on each side to support the rapiers This was totally impractical when it came to weaving wide fabrics such as carpet backing up to 5.5 metres (6 yards), consequently the idea of Flexible Rapiers was seriously considered. The outcome was the design and development of the MLS Weaving machine for sacking, the MLH for hessian fabric, also the "Gripmack" weaving machines, J550 and J470, for the production of carpet backing and similar fabrics.

To give Derrick Shimwell a better understanding of the immensity and complexity of the market for modern weaving machines for jute fabrics, it was arranged for him to visit India in September 1961. Derrick decided that Pamela, his wife, should accompany him. It was then that I got to know them. Naturally over the following eleven years I met Derrick when home on vacation, but it was not until I was based in Belfast that I got to

Onemack weaving machine for production of sacking and hessian fibres.

Gripmack weaving machine for production of carpet backing and multi-width fabric.

know the Shimwell family really well.

In the autumn of 1972, Derrick invited me to visit the Isle of Man to see his mini-Mackie workshop at Ballamoar Castle. I found that Derrick had quite a set-up in one of the outhouses with weaving machines in various stages of development. Mr. Grenville ensured that the requisite jute yarn was supplied from Mackie, Belfast, to enable Derrick to thoroughly test his ideas. Despite the fact that his workshop was next to his home, Derrick was never tempted to shirk work. He spent many hours each day cutting, filing, welding and mocking-up arrangements to try out.

During the following fifteen years, I spent many happy holidays at Ballamoar, particularly at the New Year. In the early days when the Shimwell girls, Fiona and Tania were young, we had great fun together. Ballamoar has a large entrance hall with a full-sized billiard table. It was delightful in winter evenings with a log fire burning brightly to play billiards and other games with Derrick and the girls while Pamela prepared gourmet dinners.

Unfortunately in later years Derrick suffered from the debilitating illness Parkinson's, but refused for a long time to let it get him down. Eventually it took its toll and Derrick died in November 1992. I still keep in touch with Pamela, Fiona and Tania. As I have said previously, Mackie gave me the opportunity to meet so many lovely people and to make lasting friendships.

There was another factor which contributed to Mackies success. There were within the Mackie complex demonstration units of machinery for the processing of various types of fibre – primarily jute, sisal and fibres for semi-worsted yarns. These plants were operated on a production basis but had several other purposes. They were used to train students who were sent to Belfast by customers, also to carry out tests on sample fibres supplied by clients. Another important facet was experimenting with new types of manmade fibre coming into the market.

Pamela and Derrick Shimwell

THE NAME AND SPIRIT OF MACKIE LIVES ON

In its heyday, the Mackie complex covered 133 acres (54 hectares) and the total area of the buildings was approximately 1.4 million square feet. There were three manufacturing units – Albert Foundry, Woodvale Works, and the West Factory. In addition there were several ancillary buildings – the largest being what was termed the "Biscuit Factory" – so called because it had been previously occupied by a company named Kemps, which produced biscuits and which had gone out of business.

The vastness of the Mackie establishment is strikingly shown on the aerial photograph overleaf. The shooting of this picture was organised by Mr. Leslie. He hired a single-engine aircraft and removed the door to enable Jimmy Taylor, the Company photographer, to get a good panoramic view. To further facilitate the cameraman, Mr. Leslie flew well below legal altitude at around 400 feet (122 metres). I assume that Jimmy was secured by some sort of harness to prevent him from falling out of the aircraft even at that low altitude!!

The main unit, Albert Foundry, was so named having in mind the fact that the original works were located in Albert Street, Belfast, until December 1893 when the move to the Springfield Road was completed. As the name also suggests, the Iron Foundry was located at the new site, as were the main Machine Shops and registered Head Office. During my time with the Company, Woodvale Factory was an assembly plant for Carding Machines, Spinning Frames, Winding Frames and other ancillary equipment, predominantly for the processing of jute.

In 1964, when the demand for the 'Onemack' weaving increased, extra assembly space became essential. It so happened that the Government had built what was called an 'advance factory' on the upper Springfield Road, about a mile west of Albert Foundry. The prime purpose for such a factory was to attract an overseas company to invest in Northern Ireland,

The shaded area shows the vastness of the Mackie complex. 133 acres (54 hectares).

but Mackie managed to come to an arrangement, probably with the Industrial Development Board, to lease the premises, which were ideal for the Company's requirements. It was named the West Factory.

Later on when there were insufficient young folk completing the requisite apprenticeship course, a Training School was set-up in part of the West Factory, with facilities to teach around twenty teenagers the rudiments of fitting and machine operation. In the mid 1970's when there was a dearth of candidates for the Training School, I was authorised to purchase a second-hand single deck bus. With the assistance of Barry Pitman, our graphic designer, William Johnstone, who had succeeded Jimmy Taylor as Company photographer, and other qualified technicians, I had the interior of the bus attractively furnished with model machines, a model of the Company's Sports Complex, photographs, and colourful brochures. There was also a mini-cinema to show movies, depicting the prospects for a successful apprentice / trainee to graduate to the 'Outside Erection' or Sales Staff, with opportunities for extensive travel, indeed long term, to reach a managerial position. The bus toured grammar schools and colleges in both communities and proved to be very effective in attracting young people to seek employment with the Company.

In addition to storage, the "Biscuit Factory" was put to a variety of uses. For example, as there was copious space, Barry Pitman and his team found it ideal for building a "mock-up" stand for exhibitions. However, one of the floors was utilised by Mr. Leslie and his quality control team for a unique purpose. The Carding Machines were equipped with large cast iron cylinders of up to 5 feet (1.52 metres), which had to rotate at high speeds. These cylinders were covered with "clothing", i.e. wooden staves about 3/4 inch (15mm) thick, densely pinned with steel pins. The quality of these cylinders had to be rigorously tested, so the following procedure was implemented.

A fixture was rigged up, in a suitable area of the "Biscuit Factory" on which the cylinder, complete with staves, was mounted. A variable speed electric motor was attached, to which was connected a remote control switch. From behind a safety screen the quality control team set the motor and connected cylinder in motion. The speed was gradually built up to the point of destruction, when the staves and other components started flying off. The duration and speed of the test were carefully recorded. The velocity at which the disintegration took place had to be well beyond the required operating speed of the Carding Machine. This is only one example of how Mackie ensured the high quality of their equipment.

The statistics given in the first paragraph of this chapter will undoubtedly convey to the reader the immensity of the task of maintaining security, not only because of the huge area involved, but also due to its location. At the height of the troubles there were forty four security guards on duty. Furthermore, a night shift was operated, not simply to enhance production, but primarily to provide a presence in the hope of deterring terrorist attacks in the 'quiet hours' of the night.

As the troubles intensified the problems of employees getting to and from work became more difficult. The traditional route for workers from the Shankill Road area was through Cupar Street and Kashmir Road on foot and these became dangerous passages. At times routes out of the Company were a matter of guesswork and it became a regular pattern for work to stop early and employees to be sent home early. Eventually, in the early 1970's, this led to a change in working hours to start twenty minutes earlier. The earlier stopping time was meant to allow employees to exit the area before the traditional riots and blocking of roads at peak traffic times commenced.

Some major incidents of disruption caused by rioting and terrorist activity are recorded opposite.

1970 Rioting at the junction of Kashmir Road and Springfield Road following house searches by the security forces resulting in all the windows of the Company building fronting Springfield Road being smashed.

1971 In August the riots following the introduction of internment resulted in the smashing of all windows, the attempted forcing of doors to the factory and the death of one security employee.

1976 An explosion and consequent fire in the Machine Shops caused the rupture of oil tanks and required many days to clear up and put right.

1978 A car bomb left outside the gate in Forfar Street exploded while being examined by police and caused the death of several policemen.

1986 Terrorists gained entry to the front hall during working hours and placed several explosive devices, which caused severe damage to the front offices. This damage was so severe that a decision was taken to seal off that section of the building and move all the offices to the building adjoining Springfield Drive.

1987 The Company's West Factory, which had been vacated and was being used for storage of parts and completed machines, was badly damaged by terrorist action.

As well as these major incidents, there were several hundred other incidents involving terrorists' acts, vandalism and theft, related to the troubles. The monetary damage to the Company was incalculable, as security measures alone cost £500,000 annually. Nevertheless, the Company managed to survive during the 1980's under the Chairmanship of Mr. Gordon Mackie and the production management of Mr. Leslie Mackie. The situation was substantially helped by the receipt of orders in March 1983 for two jute processing plants. Sales potential during that decade was further enhanced by a resurgence of linen as a high-fashion fabric. This fortuitously coincided with the coming on stream of a revolutionary new flax Spinning Frame called the "Linmack", which had been under development for some years, and ensured the Company's trading position for the remainder of the 1980's.

The year 1989 proved to be very strategic for the Company. A major decision was taken by the shareholders, the Mackie Foundation, to sever its connections with the Mackie family, ending an association of approximately 150 years (1840 – 1989). Mr. Gordon was replaced as Chairman in August 1989, by a person who had not been closely associated with either the family or the Company. It was therefore not surprising that Mr. Gordon

Shows damage to front of main office building as result of rioting

Shows damage to main gate as rioters tried to force entry.

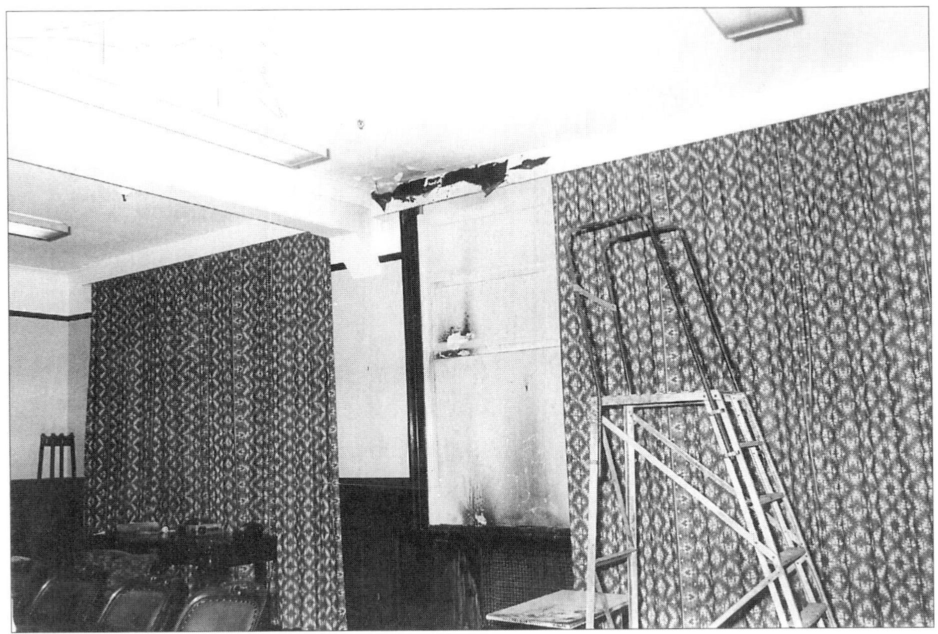

Shows damage caused to front offices when rioters did gain entrance

immediately left the Company, thus severing the connection with the Mackie family, as Mr. Leslie had previously left the Company in 1988. Furthermore, in 1989/90 the financial situation was so precarious that the Industrial Development Board recommended that the directors should endeavour to find a partner willing to inject capital into the Company to keep it afloat, or alternatively to sell the Company as a going concern. The directors decided in favour of the former option.

In early 1990 it was thought that a suitable partner had been found, this being an American Company, Lummus Industries Inc., of Columbus, Georgia. A textile machinery manufacturer in the non-competing field of cotton ginning. The Company was renamed Lummus Mackie Ltd. Initially this seemed to be a successful partnership, but it quickly proved to be a "bad marriage"! Indeed, in less than two years, the American partner had to file for administration so it became necessary in early 1992 to disentangle the Belfast operation.

During the following seven years, the Company went through various upheavals, which would not make interesting reading. Sufficient it is to say that no change in financing and management could again make the Mackie set-up competitive with Chinese and Indian manufacturers who were producing machinery of Mackie design in substantial quantities. The final saga came in 1999 when Mackie International Ltd. went bankrupt and an Irish company, Bridge Textile, with the encouragement and assistance of an ex-Mackie employee, Harry Montgomery, acquired the rights to manufacture the full range of Mackie machinery. Bridge Textile very quickly entered into a joint venture with a Chinese company, Zhejiang Golden Eagle Co., Ltd. to manufacture the Mackie range of machinery in China. That Company was well equipped for the undertaking as the management had wide experience in the textile field. Originally they were engaged in the processing of silk in it's entirety from the cocoon to the finished article. Furthermore, in 1994 they had embarked on the manufacture of flax processing machinery. The Flax Line Drawing Frames they produced were mainly based on the Mackie design, but for the Spinning they opted for a Russian Ring Spinning Frame in preference to the "Linmack" as the former was more basic in design, consequently cheaper to make, and it suited the market in China. The Chairman of the Chinese Company, Mr. Fu Guo Ding, was obviously a very shrewd businessman as he set up a separate company for the new venture and named it Jinying Mackie International Machinery Co., Ltd. He undoubtedly appreciated the reputation of the name "Mackie"! Indeed, some years later when it was suggested to him that the name should be deleted from a certain contract to solve a problem that had arisen in the documentation, Mr. Fu nearly had a heart attack!! His response to the person who put forward the idea was that the name "Mackie" was worth millions in the textile machinery world!!

Mr. Fu's business acumen was also demonstrated in his realisation that potential customers in the subcontinents of India, also in other markets outside Asia, preferred to deal with Europeans, and if possible, with salesmen and technicians who had worked for Mackie.

With this in mind, at a very opportune time, in 2005 when all other shareholders had been eliminated, Mr. Fu registered a trading company in the United Kingdom under the name Golden Eagle Mackie (UK) Ltd. I understand that Golden Eagle is a literal translation of Jinying. The office of this U.K. Company is located at Mallusk in a business park on the outskirts of North Belfast. The office is staffed by four former Mackie employees, two who were originally installation engineers and then became sales consultants, Gilbert Watt and Tommy Allen. The third person, Joe Cummings, had been a senior draughtsman and machine designer. The trio make a formidable technical and sales team. However, the office could not function effectively without the fourth member, a lady named Cathy King, who had been secretary to two technicians who headed the Spares Department in the Mackie organisations. Consequently Cathy is very conversant with the current technical terminology and with Mackie methods. All three men would acknowledge that Cathy is a valuable member of the Belfast team.

Staff of Golden Eagle Mackie UK Ltd. L to R Joe Cummings, Tommy Allen, Cathy King and Gilbert Watt.

The Chinese Company management demonstrated their confidence in Mackie experience in two other aspects. Firstly, at the outset of their new venture, they enlisted as consultants two men who had previously been managers on the Mackie production staff, persons of wide experience, a Billy Hamilton and his assistant Charlie Lindsay. These two consultants no doubt gave valuable advice to their Chinese counterparts on the best techniques of manufacturing components and complete machines. There was yet another sphere in which Mr. Fu and his management showed their appreciation of Mackie experience. Whenever possible they, through their Belfast Office, employ former Mackie installation engineers to supervise the erection and commissioning of new machinery in their customers' mills. The foregoing facts validate my claim that the name "Mackie" lives on!!

The spirit instilled by Mackie in its employees has proved to be very enduring. It is over eighteen years since my retirement, but I still have some form of contact with the majority of my former colleagues, if not in person, then by phone or email, even with those who now live abroad. For many years these contacts were cursory, but then a more permanent arrangement was initiated. At the beginning of 2004, two younger colleagues, Gilbert Watt and Ronnie Martin, put to me the idea of setting up a club for former males who had worked for the Company. The idea appealed to me so we initially formed a small committee. I agreed to act as honorary president, while Gilbert was prepared to assume the responsibility of secretary, and Ronnie that of treasurer. It was decided to call it the "Mackie Old Boys Club". The word "Club" had to be included otherwise we could have been referred to as the MOB, which might have been appropriate but rather unpropitious. Considerable work was involved in the initial organisation as postal addresses and phone numbers had to be ascertained. Gilbert won't mind me saying that although as secretary he undertook this task, the burden was shared by Cathy King, the secretary at Golden Eagle Mackie (UK) Ltd.

The club had a small start there being only eighteen persons at the first reunion dinner. However, the response increased rapidly to the extent that there are now one hundred and forty three members and the average attendance at the annual dinner is seventy two. We have an excellent rendezvous at the Villa Italia restaurant on the University Road, Belfast where the food is excellent and we are well looked after by Jackie, the manageress and her staff.

It is most gratifying that there are always several members of the Mackie family present at the annual reunion dinner. If possible, Paddy, Leslie, Gordon and Derek, all male survivors of the fourth generation, will attend. At most dinners there are overseas members. Pat Gailey, the first M.D. of the Lagan Company, who now lives in Dundee, and Arthur Larkin, who was the senior representative in France, who now lives in London, always travel over to Belfast for the event. On one occasion there were two guests from further afield, Sengupta from Calcutta (now Kolkata) and Joe McMillen from Vancouver, both of whom were on the Calcutta staff. What is even more noteworthy is that seventy plus persons who occupied vastly different positions in the Company, varying from the shop floor to the boardroom, can spend an evening together without any acrimony or friction. The "spirit" of Mackie definitely lives on!!

As mentioned previously I never got into the habit of keeping a diary, so I have had to depend on my memory and information from other reliable sources. At the same time I have endeavoured to check the accuracy of the facts recorded in my memoirs. Despite the care taken there will inevitably be omissions and mistakes. I therefore ask the indulgence of the reader.

The title of this book "One Among Many" has a significance, as at one time the Company had well over 200 Erection Engineers who all played their part.

APPENDIX

The Mackie Brothers 1914 to 1973

At the turn of the twentieth century there was an imposing list of textile machinery builders in the UK – Fairbairn, Lawson, Coombe, Barbour, Horner, Urquart, Lindsay, Robinson, Orchar, Low, Keay, Parker, Leslie, Ferguson, McDonald, Smalley, Rice, and Evans. One by one between 1900 and 1968 they dropped out of the race. One of the last to go was Fairbairn Lawson Coombe Barbour, called 'the combine' which finally gave up the struggle in the 1960's. Year after year individual competitors were forced to merge, to combine or get squeezed out of business. Despite these pressures the Mackie textile engineering business prospered and remained exclusively in family hands until given to trustee ownership in 1976. Even after that several family members stayed with the Company for a further 12 years to provide their expertise and help keep the Company afloat.

The Mackie brothers, Jim, Jack, Fraser, Grenville and Lavens, as well as their cousin Stewart, joined the family business during or after the Great War of 1914 – 1918. They were the third generation in the business all grandchildren of the original founder. In 1915 much of the Company's foundry and engineering output had been switched from textile machinery to armaments, as it did again during the Second World War of 1939 – 1945.

James Mackie senior's brother Tom Mackie was in charge of production in 1916. He with Victor Sinton, and Peter Paisley were to the fore in training girls up to do engineering work in the shell shop. Their task was to turn out the Swedish designed Bofors cannon shot, mostly four and ten pounders. They also made hollow exploding shrapnel shells of ten and fifteen pounds. It was during the First World War that a shortage of skilled machinists led to the employment in the Mackie works of some of the first female lathe operators to work anywhere in Britain. Ellie Grey, daughter of John Grey, the manager of Ewart's mountain mill was first to join. She was immortalised by the Belfast artist Willie Conor, in a painting he called 'Doing her Bit'.

Willie Conor, a local treasure, painted many a testimonial to the men of iron like those who had built the Titanic in 1911. James Mackie invited him up to Albert Foundry in 1917. He recorded the female employees in the shell shop and made a splendid drawing of Ellie Grey operating a lathe and wearing a long skirt with an apron. Willie had an eye for the real Belfast, and this is what he said of the city, "I suppose to some Belfast is ugly and sordid. I never found it so, I never run short of subjects with which to illustrate its industry and the beauty that it holds for me".

How could this small family owned business become an institution, beating all the competition out of sight, and then vanish, leaving scarcely a ripple? There seems to have been four major reasons – firstly family unity – blood as nature intended proved thicker than water. Secondly, the family ethic, summed up in a slogan sent by Tommy Lipton the tea baron and a personal friend of James. It was a simple one liner – 'There is no fun like work'. The third was an absolute commitment to the non-stop design, development and manufacture of new products. Finally, of course, luck played its part, since the Company was in the right place at the right time.

The conventional outsider's view of a family business is that it is a haven for nepotism and the incompetent. The reality was that the Mackie family led from the front. Whoever worked hard and had the leadership qualities that it took to run an organisation with several thousand people went to the top and was given the job. It was certainly never a question of shareholding. Each brother was given a chance to make his mark and each specialised in one or other aspect of textile machinery design and engineering.

The family was there to run a profitable business but the customer was always right. There was no protected home market and the Company's machinery trade had been based on the export market from before the Great War. Years later during World War II, the works was almost entirely occupied with the production of armaments. Apart that is, from building a few hundred flax pulling machines which were authorised versions of an original Belgian design by Soens. The Company also continued to make spare parts for the local textile industry. Armament production was undertaken as a matter of direction from the British government rather than by family choice. The Mackie family sentiment was that the production of weapons of war was a desperate shame but if it had to be done then they would do it bigger, better and more efficiently than anyone else. During World War II the Mackie works on the Springfield Road was a hive of activity turning out armour piercing shot by the million. At any one time you could see Sterling bomber fuselages, Sunderland flying boat tail fins, gun barrels and a vast array of other wartime bits and pieces.

The Mackie armour piercing anti-tank shells, tungsten carbide tipped and stamped JMB were a special success. They were encased in an aluminium outer 'sabot' or shoe which was cast and machined to fit the inner shot. The shot itself had a tungsten carbide nose which cracked open the enemy armour. Tungsten carbide is an extremely hard metal and very few companies knew how to work it but since it was used in the wear resistant parts of jute spinning machines the Mackie Company knew what to do to shape it. In the North African campaign against General Erwin Rommel, the arrival of the JMB shells shortly after the British defeat at Tobruk, helped turn the tide from defeat into victory. The British tank crews threw out the old fifteen pounder shells they had been using onto the sand and stocked up with the JMB armour piercing shot before roaring into battle at El Alamein. Afterwards Winston Churchill sent the company a telegram of congratulations and thanks for that particular war effort. In some particular sizes of armour piercing shells the Mackie Company made ninety out of every hundred of the British war requirement. These top secret shells were deadly killers. They matched anything the Germans could make and they were still on the 'secret' list long after the Second World War was won.

The five Mackie brothers and their cousin Stewart Mackie (Tom's son) pulled out all the stops in their industrial war effort. They split the JM&S management responsibilities between the four brothers and a few senior colleagues, among them Peter Paisley, John Gailey, Moore Hill and Sam Annesley. The fifth brother Fraser ran the Strand Spinning Company. Their father James Mackie senior had lost his mental faculties due to atherosclerosis in 1930 and his son Jim took his place.

During the Second World War the workforce, both direct and in outside units, built to a peak of 10,000 people in 1943. 2,000 of them were subcontract workers in the engineering shops of local flax spinning and weaving mills.

The administration and control of the Springfield Road workforce was the responsibility of Stewart Mackie. His attention to building the skills of the workforce played a major part in the Company's success. It was a tough and thankless job as during and after the War more than 20,000 engineering workers served their apprenticeships or had their training at Mackie's. To quote from Jonathan Bardon's History of Ulster – "The Mackie Company overcame traditional male trade union opposition to female labour with more success than any other firm in Northern Ireland". Bardon does not appear to have understood that the Company's success with female workers in the Second World War stemmed from its pioneering use of female engineering workers in Mackie's during the Great War of 1914 – 1918.

When the Second World War ended in 1945, Tom retired and Jim became chairman. He worked very closely with his brothers Jack and Lavens as his joint managing directors. Jim was offered a knighthood for wartime services. This may have been an indirect way of acknowledging the wartime contribution of Jim's wife Marsha. She was an American citizen who had run the American Red Cross in Britain. When asked would he accept? Jim said certainly, he would be delighted, but on condition that his four brothers were knighted as well since all of them had worked just as hard and achieved as much as he had.

The English establishment was not impressed, what a nerve to suggest such a thing – they were not to know that in the Mackie family standing together was a golden rule; a quality emphasised by James Mackie when instructing his five boys, and central to the Company's success. James's words to his five boys had been simple, "You may fight like tinkers amongst yourselves, but against the competition you must fight together like a pack of wolves".

In 1970 Jackie Mackie was asked to take over the government owned Harland & Wolff shipbuilders as chairman, but he declined the offer with a polite and pointed reply, "Government has done little or nothing to assist Mackie works since the end of the war and done much to jeopardise it. I have 4,000 employees of my own to look after". Bang went the prospect of another knighthood, but Jack, an unassuming man in the family tradition, did not give a damn. He hated the fuss which surrounded the award of a CBE which he was given in recognition of his many years of effort on behalf of sheltered employment in the Lord Robert's workshops.

Jim the eldest Mackie of the five brothers was a keen development engineer. He led the Company's textile machinery design and sales effort in the 1920's and 30's with the help of John Gailey. Jim, whose wife Marsha was American, developed a close friendship with Malcolm Stone of the Ludlow Corporation of Massachusetts. The Ludlow Corporation was then the biggest jute spinners in the US and later owned a mill in Calcutta. Using Henry Schneider's auto-doffing patent, which the Mackie Company had acquired in 1924, Jim worked with Ludlow to perfect the auto-doffing sliver spinning machine for jute and flax fibres. By the time of the Second World War it was almost perfected but as war work intervened it only went into mass production in the 1950's. By 1960 the works was making a hundred frames a month, about 800 tons a month, by weight to this one design. At the same time the Company was churning out 40 drawing frames and 30 cards per month for the world's jute industry. A wide range of machinery for other fibres such as sisal and flax and man-made fibres to completely different designs was also being produced simultaneously.

Jim's brother Jackie Mackie concentrated on textile machinery design and manufacturing rather than on sales. He was helped out on the engineering side by two brothers Moore and Norman Hill. Jack had a personal interest in aviation and when the company was asked during the war by the Ministry of Supply in Whitehall to build Short Stirling bomber fuselages and Sunderland tail assemblies it was Jack and the Hill brothers who ran the Woodvale aircraft production line. This purpose built factory turned out more than 70 complete Stirling fuselages. The contract was on a fixed price basis and a completed fuselage and tail assembly was delivered to Long Kesh for assembly at a cost of £32,000. Short Brothers who had designed the Stirling were only ever willing to build the aircraft on cost plus basis and their costs were far higher than the Mackie version.

After the war Jack Mackie and Bob Matier developed, designed, and built the world's first ring spinning machinery for the linen industry. Between 1950 and 1970 over half a million spindles were built. The use of nylon instead of brass for the ring traveller was the crucial breakthrough. It was patented by Jack and hundreds of millions of travellers were made in a special plastics moulding shop set up for the job. Jack had earlier pioneered the use of moulded Bakelite for artillery shell caps.

Fraser Mackie ran the Strand Spinning Company from 1922 onwards. The factory had originally been built as a flax mill but when World War II broke out the supply of flax tow from Europe stopped so Fraser redesigned the flax process machinery to spin yarns from viscose fibre made in Carrickfergus by Courtaulds. This long staple viscose yarn was a great success and made an important contribution to the war effort. After the war the machinery Fraser had pioneered for viscose spinning was further developed and modified to become the Mackie semi-worsted system for carpet yarn spinning. Between 1958 and 1970 about seven hundred systems were built and sold around the world. Each system made about 600 tons of yarn a year so the total output of synthetic fibre yarns on the Mackie system around the world reached half a million tons a year.

Mr Lavens Mackie, Sales Director.

Grenville Mackie originally trained as

a weaver in Whitehouse Mill in the 1920's. During the 30's he joined his brothers in the Mackie works. He was given the job of making flax pulling machines during the war. This was achieved by adapting the Belgian Soens design and several hundred machines were made and used in Northern Ireland and England. After the war Grenville took over the engineering and management responsibility for loom design and manufacturing. This led to the introduction in 1958 of the first shuttleless loom to be designed and made in Britain. The Mackie 'Onemack' loom was improved and modified over time and eleven thousand machines were eventually built.

Lavens the youngest brother joined the Company in 1925. He had trained in textile engineering in client textile mills in Europe and became a fluent German and French speaker. He worked in the sales section of the company with Jim and John Gailey in the 20's and 30's and took over as sales director after the war ended. Both before and after the war he travelled the world to meet textile machinery clients and to advise them on how to improve their products. Just before the war started, Lavens obtained a licence from Oerlikon in Zurich to make their design of anti-aircraft 'Pom Pom' shells. During the war he had the job of managing shell production backed up by Sam Annesley. This was easily the Company's largest wartime activity. The war demanded anti-tank shells with ever greater armour piercing capability. Lavens led the shell shops to success by designing and making the famous JMB (James Mackie Belfast) AP (armour piercing) shells which were decisive in the North African campaign. An acknowledged expert in textile processing Lavens was to follow Jim briefly as Chairman of the Company before his sudden death in 1966.

After getting back into textile machinery production at the end of the Second World War, the Company had twenty immensely successful and profitable years, despite the UK treasury's best attempts to tax it out of existence as a private company. The Company had a perpetual fight on its hands to retain enough of its earnings from the export market for expansion, diversification, and research and product development. Innovation, for Mackie's was defined as the design and production of new and more productive textile machines. It was a mandatory life-or-death strategy for the Company, but one which had to take a back seat when the family decided to exit the business in the 1970's.

The first fifty years of the company's business was a battle for survival, the middle fifty years were a struggle against the competition and the Second World War became a herculean effort. The post war period however reaped the reward of the pre war years of intensive product development with fifteen gold years of world market leadership and profitable trading.

In the 1950's along came cheap synthetic fibres. In particular during the mid 1960's, cheap polypropylene resin became available. The arrival of low cost plastic film which could be cheaply woven into lightweight textile bags and packaging spelt big trouble for the international jute industry. By that time the flax/linen industry in Europe also had its back to the wall, and the collapse of textile manufacturing in Western Europe was under way. The decisive blow to the business came in 1968 when west Belfast became the cockpit of thirty years of civil war and political unrest. By the early 1970's all the brothers except Jack were dead or had retired. The end of family ownership was meticulously planned in the strictest secrecy in 1973. By 1976 it was all over bar the shouting.

The Company continued a precarious existence in the west Belfast war zone under the sworn enmity of the provisional IRA. This is what the Amalgamated Engineering Union said about the Company in April 1988. "Mackie, a continuing success story of a Belfast company, this title may seem strange to people who worked for Mackie's in its heyday, but the fact of bare survival in textile machinery manufacturing is an achievement under current circumstances".

A Brief Chronology

Some dates of interest:

1911 Start of the Strand Spinning Company, in Jaffe's mill on the Newtownards Road in Belfast. Peter Paisley erected most of the flax machinery there and went on to become a director of the James Mackie & Sons Company.

1914 First shell shop set up to make wartime munitions. Female workers started making light shot in 1916. Victor Sinton set up the shell shop so well that the Ministry of Supply put him in charge of all war material production in Belfast. Peter Paisley took over the running of the JM&S shell shop but left soon afterwards to join the army. Jim and Jack Mackie joined the engineering staff as trainees.

1924 First experiments to design spinning machinery based on Dr. Henry Schneider's patent with strong encouragement from the Ludlow Corporation of Boston.

1930 Tough times during the world recession. A fitter's basic wage without bonus was three pounds and twelve shillings for a 46 hour week. The Company managed to avoid any layoffs during these difficult years.

1936 Textile machinery deliveries extend beyond Europe to all round the world.

1937 Start of a jute mill for in-house Research & Development.

1940 Armament production again gets under way, especially armour piercing shells and later followed by aircraft fuselages and components. 75 Million heat treated armour piercing shells were made during the period 1940-1944. Millions more were made post war.

1943 Death of James Mackie, J.P., D.L., 'The Boss' after twelve years of ill health.

1950 Wet Ring Spinning introduced for flax.

1954 Start up of Lagan Jute Machinery Company in the Angus works, Calcutta.

1956 Death of Thomas F. Mackie, C.B.E., J.P., on the 16th August.

1957 Centenary of the Mackie machinery business.

1966 Death of Lavens Mackie (Chairman) on 29th June.

1969 The world's first simple synthetic fibre extrusion machinery delivered to make polypropylene fibres.
Death of James A. Mackie, C.B.E., 13th September.

1975 Jack Mackie, C.B.E., J.P., retired as chairman. He died in 1987.

1976 Sale of Lagan Jute Machinery Ltd., of Calcutta to the Indian Government.
All of the shares of James Mackie & Sons Ltd. are donated to a Trust to be used for the benefit of employees, specifically excluding any Mackie family member from future ownership in the Company.

The author in his 'Heyday'

A PERSONAL TESTIMONY

During the forty-five years about which I have written, I travelled many thousands of miles by air – sometimes on very unreliable airlines. Also covered hundreds of miles by car on dangerous roads, and on occasions lived in very primitive conditions. Despite these facts, apart from a bout of dengue fever during my first year in Calcutta, I didn't have any serious illnesses, and was not involved in any major accident or mishap. Many people say - "You have been very lucky or fortunate" … I prefer to use the term – providential protection.

As a boy of twelve I committed my life to God through placing my faith in Jesus Christ as Lord and Saviour. During the seventy-plus years since then, I have frequently failed to live up to my commitment – but God has remained faithful …as is evident from my story. While I am grateful to the Mackie Company and family for giving me the opportunity to live a very interesting life … I give God the credit for His preservation and guidance.

Stanley Jebb

Professor Sir Bernard Crossland

AFTERWORD

In the nineteenth and twentieth centuries Belfast was recognised as one of the major centres of manufacture, and particularly engineering manufacture, in the UK. James Mackie & Sons Ltd. was one of the major engineering manufacturing companies in Belfast during this period. It originated when James Mackie Snr (1823-1887) in 1846 purchased the assets of Scrimegour and continued its business of manufacture of textile machinery for the rapidly developing textile industry in Northern Ireland. James Mackie Jnr (1864-1943), known as 'The Boss', took over the business on the death of his father, and he was personally responsible for establishing a substantial export business while maintaining a home market. The six members of the third generation of the Mackie family continued to expand the business particularly their overseas market.

An important contribution to the success of James Mackie & Sons Ltd. was their share of the world market for textile machinery, which depended on the support of their Export Department in Belfast and their overseas sales team including Stanley Jebb, the author of this book. The overseas sale of jute textile machinery in particular made a very major contribution to the success of James Mackie & Sons Ltd. after the Second World War. The importance of overseas sales and its supporting organisations is an aspect which is not widely recognised or written about. This book remedies the neglect of this most important aspect of developing an overseas market and providing support for customers in what were mainly third world countries.

Stanley Jebb's book is based on a lifetime's experience largely in the Far East selling mainly jute processing mills for transforming jute fibre into cloth and bags, used extensively in third world countries for bagging agricultural products. This not only involved the supply of the textile machines but complete turnkey factories and the provision of training of shop floor operatives, maintenance staff and management to operate and maintain what was highly sophisticated machinery. It also involved the organisation for staff from Belfast to erect and commission the machinery.

To support their considerable business in the Far East, James Mackie & Sons Ltd. set up a 100% owned Lagan Jute Machinery Co. (P) Ltd. in Calcutta. This company was sold in 1977 when the Mackie family withdrew from their family business and created the Mackie Trust to operate the Belfast factory on behalf of the workers. However, a member of the family remained a director of the Indian owned company until its closure in 2008.

It was necessary for the sales team to satisfy the technical requirements of the proposed plants, while being fully conversant with what the competition had on offer. The financing of such projects frequently involved the overseas sales staff in negotiations with the Government Departments and officials and seeking overseas sources of funding, before the final agreement could be signed and sealed. It demanded that the overseas sales staff were on friendly relations with the decision takers, which included hospitality and the organisation of visits to Belfast to the factory and meet senior members of the staff.

Stanley Jebb gives a most interesting account of his long period abroad and the many countries he visited and the people he got to know. He gives interesting pen sketches of the origins of the countries he visited and their political set-up. He also notes his many social and business contacts on which the success of overseas sales representatives depend.

I recommend this book as a very good read for young people in general, and in particular those who are seeking an interesting, challenging and rewarding career. It should be compulsory reading for those in the manufacturing industry interested in gaining overseas business, on which the success of the UK depends. For myself I wish that the book had been available and that I had the opportunity to meet the author, when I was appointed as one of the four trustees of the Mackie Trust after it was formed in 1977. It would have helped me to better appreciate the importance of overseas sales and the problems of achieving them.

Professor Sir Bernard Crossland